M000209072

Taking Their Word

Taking Their Word

Literature and the Signs of Central America

Arturo Arias

UNIVERSITY OF MINNESOTA PRESS

MINNEAPOLIS • LONDON

Chapter 2 originally appeared in Spanish in *Mulata de tal de Miguel Angel Asturias: Edición crítica* (Madrid: Colección Archivos, 2001). Chapter 4 was originally published in *PMLA* 116, no. 1 (January 2001). Chapter 5 was first published in *MLN* 117, no. 2 (March 2002). Chapter 6 was first published in *Nuevo texto crítico* 15–16, nos. 29/32 (2002–2003). Chapter 9 was previously published in *Explicación de textos literarios* 28, nos. 1–2 (1999–2000). Chapter 10 was originally published in *Latino Studies* 1, no. 1 (March 2003).

Copyright 2007 by the Regents of the University of Minnesota

All rights reserved. No part of this publication may be reproduced, stored in a retrieval system, or transmitted, in any form or by any means, electronic, mechanical, photocopying, recording, or otherwise, without the prior written permission of the publisher.

Published by the University of Minnesota Press
111 Third Avenue South, Suite 290
Minneapolis, MN 55401-2520
http://www.upress.umn.edu

Library of Congress Cataloging-in-Publication Data

Arias, Arturo.
  Taking their word : literature and the signs of Central America / Arturo Arias.
    p. cm.
  Includes bibliographical references and index.
  ISBN 978-0-8166-4848-1 (hc : alk. paper)
  ISBN 978-0-8166-4849-8 (pb : alk. paper)
  ISBN-10 0-8166-4848-4 (hc : alk. paper)
  ISBN-10 0-8166-4849-2 (pb : alk. paper)
    1. Central American literature—20th century—History and criticism.
  2. Central American literature—Mayan influences. 3. National characteristics, Central American, in literature. I. Title.
  PQ7471.A75 2007
  860.9'972'0904—dc22

                                                      2007004495

Printed in the United States of America on acid-free paper

The University of Minnesota is an equal-opportunity educator and employer.

12 11 10 09 08 07   10 9 8 7 6 5 4 3 2 1

Contents

Acknowledgments

Most of this book was written in Spanish over the course of the past ten years. Its point of departure was signaled by my receipt of the Martha Weeks Fellowship at the Stanford Humanities Center in 1994–95. I want to recognize the center's belief in my work and the warmth with which it has continued to receive me throughout the years. My first thanks go there.

During my "crossing of the desert," my friends Néstor García Canclini and Antonio Cornejo Polar never stopped believing both in my capacity and in the importance of Central American cultural production. They also pushed me to make my work better. Antonio is no longer with us, but his presence remains through his endless inspiration. I want to thank them both.

I thank several colleagues for their insightful comments about the manuscript. Cynthia Steele and Marc Zimmerman read the first draft of this book meticulously and made significant suggestions about substance and structure. Their carefully thought-out recommendations made it possible for me to conceive of the larger theoretical arguments expressed in the first section of this book, which I entirely rewrote as a result. John Beverley, Arturo Escobar, and George Yúdice offered judicious comments on the final draft, and I thank them most sincerely. I especially thank Claudia Milian Arias, who read a good part of the manuscript and made all kinds of sound grammatical suggestions.

Finally, I owe more than I can acknowledge to Jill Robbins, more than my wife and my dearest of friends, a scholar who moves gracefully in and out of many fields of knowledge and is always willing to raise new questions, problematize theorizations, and edit my English. It is to her that I am the most indebted, will remain forever indebted, and dedicate this effort of many years, this book, and all my love.

INTRODUCTION

Is There a Central American Literature?

In an academic discussion a few years ago regarding the programmatic changes needed to accurately reflect the local Latino population at a Southern California university, a Southern Cone professor asked ironically, "But is there even such a thing as Central American literature?" At the time, the question seemed laughable, because every Latin Americanist recognized the quality of canonical Central American writers—Rubén Darío, Pablo Antonio Cuadra, Miguel Angel Asturias, Augusto Monterroso, Claribel Alegría, Roque Dalton, Ernesto Cardenal, Sergio Ramírez—from a traditional literary perspective. After thinking carefully about the matter, I began to wonder whether the question might be implicitly, even unconsciously, racist, given that the bulk of Central American literature cannot escape the representational problems of indigenous subjectivity. The region is heavily marked by its indigenous, mostly Maya, origins and by the continuous presence of a significant Maya population engaged in nation-building.

The question also seemed to signal the final collapse of the romantic notion of "Latin Americanism," that sense that we Latin Americans were all citizens of a larger *patria*, or motherland,[1] a *patria grande* (big motherland) that extends from the Río Grande on the U.S. border all the way to the Tierra del Fuego at the southernmost tip of the continent. This nineteenth-century notion, very much in vogue during the 1960s in the wake of Guevarist enthusiasm for a continental revolution, had already been on the wane, but parochial prejudice had not been spelled out so clearly for me since the end of the "guerrilla period" as on that day.[2]

The notion of a *patria grande* had populist roots as well. It was espoused by nonintellectuals like my father, who told me about Latin Americanism when I was a child. In 1958, when I was eight years old, we listened to the soccer World Cup transmitted from Sweden to Guatemala on the radio. It was six months before the triumph of Castro. When Argentina lost in the quarterfinals, my father told me: "Now we root for Brazil." I asked him why, and he responded, "Because they are the only Latin American team left in contention." That lesson shaped my identity not just as a Guatemalan or a Central American, but as a Latin American. As a writer, I locate myself more in those affective spaces where my personal story of Latin Americanism begins than in any type of theoretical ideology.

Of course, my current insertion into the U.S. academy has led me to reframe the issue to address the question implicit in a colleague's question: "Is there a need to study Central American literature in the United States?" It might seem at first glance that the basic premise of this book represents a clear "Yes." Nevertheless, it is a question that has to be asked, along with a much broader one: Why should we bother studying literature at all in this day and age?

Indeed, why should "we"? Some theorists of *testimonio* argued in the mid-1990s that we no longer needed to study "highbrow" Latin American literature and tried to make a valid point for its dismissal.[3] A more wide-ranging issue, raised since the late 1980s, was that, with the end of nation-formation in the world and the subsequent weakening of nation-states in general as a result of the emergence of globalization, the study of literature was no longer needed to frame national identities, the raison d'être for the formation of literary canons in the first place. Therefore, replacing literary studies with cultural studies—with the understanding that the latter addressed the specific practices of powerless people, subalterns—seemed to make perfect sense. Another of the repercussions of postmodernity was the understanding that critics did not occupy an objective position from which a work's meaning could be determined (indeed, objectivity was no longer a credible claim for any field of study). All knowledge producers had only a fragmentary understanding of everydayness, dependent on time, location, and chance.[4] Michel de Certeau's *Practice of Everyday Life*, for example, outlined the basic conditions within which cultural activity can be produced by those considered nonproducers by traditional analysts. Later John Beverley's *Subalternity and Representation* called into question the role of the academy in reading and representing the subaltern. For Beverley, the importance of academic work consisted of making subaltern voices heard in academia; he considered writers of literature as belonging to national elites exercising hegemonic power.

The careful attention paid to specific literary texts seemed to get lost amid the broad categories and heterogeneous objects of "cultural studies." However, if we understand literature not just as a fetishized elite product, but as a tool for understanding cultural and cross-cultural practices, as Gayatri Spivak argues in *Death of a Discipline,* we can appreciate its importance in elaborating understanding and solidarity across linguistic, national, ethnic, and cultural borders, not to mention even differences of social class.[5] When the object of literary studies becomes not so much the analysis of the formal aspects of given genres but the portrayal of everyday cultural detail, nontraditional cultural producers, and the conditions and effects of sedimented linguistic turns, literature allows for the exploration of imaginary, eccentric representations of otherness in contrast to the weighty centrality of U.S. culture in a globalized world.

The idea that an abysmal sociocultural distance separates literary authors from subaltern subjects—taken from models in the "cosmopolitan centers"—is even less true on the margins, where writers have often been political activists or militants themselves, fighting for and alongside those very subaltern subjects.[6] In a different sense, these authors could themselves be seen metaphorically as "subalterns" vis-à-vis the cultural producers from cosmopolitan centers. For example, although many Central American novels compare quite favorably to the best in the world (witness the comparison of Asturias to Joyce or the tendency to regard Monterroso as Borges's successor), the writings of both Asturias and Monterroso occupy a lower rank than texts emerging from subhegemonic nations, such as Mexico or Argentina, in terms of circulation and consumption. This ethos has validated the social relevance of their work in more meaningful ways than the subalternist perspective allows. More careful attention to literary detail in those works is not an elite activity. As Spivak points out, scholars in cultural studies often confuse "representation" with "plot summary masquerading as analysis of representation."[7] The result is that the richly woven tapestries of language and culture are lost or literary study itself is trivialized because the literary enterprises do not lead simplistically to political action.

A dismissive attitude toward literature is especially problematic for the study of areas of the world that have been doubly marginalized, as is the case of Central America, which is marginalized both by the cosmopolitan center and by countries exercising hegemony in Latin America. It is also a problem for areas where very little documentation exists about everyday life and where discarding an entire category of documents from the overall archive in favor of others is a wasteful luxury. The substitution of *testimonios* alone for literary texts also risked essentializing the former, simplifying complex social processes and relations and fetishizing their subaltern subjects. At worst, this tactic produced results that were the polar opposites of the changes desired by defenders of the *testimonio*. Thus, David Stoll launched a campaign against the cultural representations in Rigoberta Menchú's *testimonio* that was successful largely because American critics, not Menchú, claimed that her text sought to represent all the poor people of Guatemala and all indigenous peoples on the continent.

The importance of literature for representing peripheral societies has not significantly declined in many marginal areas of the world, despite the fact that cinema and other visual media have now displaced the centrality that the novel occupied in the nineteenth century in cosmopolitan centers. In Central America, cinema and other visual media productions are in their infancy. The images that people in the region see on television, in the movie theater, or on the Internet very rarely represent their reality. These people are also unable to project their personal vision onto the worldwide screen. For this reason, the novel's ability to give heteroglossic representations of its people and to assert their identity and history remains of primary importance. This is true as well for a significant portion of the Central American population living in the United States, who need a representation to become visible and "crawl into the place of the 'human.'"[8] The interactions between the United States and the Central American nations and societies it has dominated (and invaded, aiding in the slaughter of their best and brightest) since the early twentieth century can best be examined through a study of literature, which can frame and contextualize those "neocolonial" forms of subjugation that result from expanding capitalism and globalization. A truly interdisciplinary study (without forgetting or ignoring, of course, other cultural forms and the works generated by nontraditional cultural producers) enables us to come to terms with a problematic relationship that defines itself as being neither in the North nor in the South.[9] Rather, it is a relationship that exists fleetingly in the tension created in the space between two polar sites where a multiplicity of peoples and cultures flow dramatically in our time.[10] Whereas Latin American novels might have originally been conceived in the nineteenth century, imitating those of Europe, as "foundational fictions" for the construction of emerging national identities,[11] in the present they have become, de facto, vehicles for portable identities migrating from South to North, and then back to the South, in what Juan Flores presently labels "cultural remittances."[12] These are identities that are detached from conventional national anchorings, and they represent a border-crossing experience that identifies—and helps frame the identities of—new transnational social subjects.

One could still ask, however, why we should study the literature of such a small area. Why Central America and not some other tiny, marginalized place equally capable of producing substantive works? Are we just imposing on overburdened, underfunded academic departments some sort of democratic representation, akin to that of the United Nations Assembly?

My answer encompasses practical and ethical issues. One could argue that U.S. foreign policy in Central America throughout the twentieth century was largely responsible for the economic and political instability in the region, which prompted the large flow of Central American immigrants to the United States, particularly from 1980 to the present. Central Americans are now the largest Latino population in Southern California after Mexicans, and they constitute a substantial percentage of the population in most U.S. urban centers, as well as in rural areas such as the Deep South or the northern Midwest. Indeed, the first soldier to die in Iraq shortly after the 2003 invasion was a Guatemalan residing in Orange County. The number of Central Americans, and Central American–Americans, is growing rapidly. They are attending schools, inserting themselves into the U.S. economy in significant ways, and supporting their home countries with remittances of foreign exchange. But more than this, they are searching for their roots and identities after the devastation of civil wars in the 1980s, followed by migration and semirefugee status in their new country, as they simultaneously struggle to differentiate themselves from Mexican migrants. Thus, when we consider Central American discursivity, we are not simply dealing with a minor form of expression within a larger foreign, or exotic, field. There is now a pragmatic need to study it if we are interested in creating or maintaining a dynamic understanding of a culture that is contributing to the ever-changing landscapes of culture and identity in the United States itself.

When we study Central American literature, we also engage in a fascinating exercise of cultural translation, because this literature resists appropriation by South American literature and by the literatures of foreign countries of the diaspora (there is Central American production in Mexico, the United States, and Europe, in addition to the region itself). Only by understanding these factors can we come to terms with a people that is significant inside U.S. borders. The Central American nations are intimately tied to U.S. society as well. They will continue to be significant on the U.S. horizon, especially because the Central American Free Trade Agreement was implemented in July 2005. The region's literature (discursivity, textuality) constitutes a bridge between what we could label "traditional literature" and subaltern expression (*testimonio*) as nowhere else in the hemisphere, with the possible exception of the Andean region with its emerging indigenous literature. This bridge is linked to the representational parameters on this side of the continent given the politics of location, the recent civil war experience, and the emergence of indigenous movements.

We could analyze all of these texts as forms of "narrative textuality," an approach that encompasses all genres (the novel, short story, *testimonio*, essay, and even some variants of epic poetry such as Ernesto Cardenal's *El estrecho dudoso* (The doubtful strait). One could examine, as well, the semantical and graphical signifying parts of the text, the inscription of some form or another of encoded meaning within the general field of writing qua text (even if it escapes visible determination in Derridean fashion). But we can also shift to the nature of this literature as a narrative, that is, a communicative occurrence presented in a temporal, sequential order, stressing the potential eventfulness of duration. The narrative process either displays a transformation taking place or else represents objects persisting in time; it describes an event that becomes an entity and is retold as an event. This is a reduced expression of the traditional definition of narrative, one that usually includes discrete, specific, and positive situations and events, as well as conflict, and is meaningful in terms of a given human(ized) project and world. By adopting "narrative textuality," we can avoid the false conflicts between a supposedly elitist literary creation and the allegedly more political, popular, and subaltern *testimonio*. Instead, we can focus on the varied textual discursive production of the region, the tapestry of languages, characters, conflicts, and cultural locations of Central America.

The title I have chosen for this book, *Taking Their Word: Literature and the Signs of Central America,* reflects this logic. I propose that we pay closer attention to Central American words themselves, mostly written, but some spoken and then transcribed by others. These Central American words are all cultural signs coming out of an eccentric location, marginalized even within the Latin American continent. They carry, in themselves, a singular sedimentation of cultural meaning that is slowly becoming a part of mainstream America. To understand these signs, we have to engage them in a cultural dialogue that forces us to position "ourselves"[13] critically (not just to try to understand "otherness" from a mainstream American perspective favoring stereotyping tropes). This gesture is not just a rhetorical, or "feel-good," indulgence. The meaning of a particular culture—its identity, its symbolic comprehension of itself—becomes more explicit to the degree that it is contrasted with a different one, as long as we do not reduce this comparison to a simplistic binarism. It helps us to better understand not just the other, but ourselves as well. If we do this, a dialogue evolves (or, in a worst-case scenario, a *différend* in a Lyotardian sense), one that overcomes the closedness and one-sidedness harbored in an insular identity or symbolic understanding of the self. Allowing the possibility of being engaged in conversation by the other leads to a crucial relationship between ethics and politics.[14] This process implies a breakdown of provincialness that is evidently conditioned to "our" ability to "hear" the other subjects and value their word as word. "Taking their word" thus implies accepting the word of "the other" at face value, rooted in a particular discursive site (in relation to its translocality), accepting their word both as their property (in the process of naming themselves, allowing these "othered" subjects to be the rightful "owners" of their subjectivity) and as an enunciative strategy for the sake of gaining agency (as a linkage of subjectivity). The latter implies an utterance that is partly performative, partly a "truth effect" (in the Barthesian sense), partly the codification of a singular affection, partly the suture of contradictory worlds (the West and another originating, or native, *cosmovisión* or "worldview," a concept explained in chapter 3), partly the muddled source of a given truth (however incomplete) and of a certain authenticity (however cloaked). It implies a critical trust on the part of the scholar in relation to the wording or wordling[15] of the peripheral or subaltern subject that is being engaged.

In the latter sense, I can think of no literature more in need of embedding itself within American critical discourse than Central American literature.

Embedding operates like invisible expressive devices residing within the readership's horizon of expectation. Readers or critics can "read" a text only to the degree that their horizon of expectation is met, a process that enables the illusion of meaning to take place or gives sense to the text being read. The readers' critical reflections about the text being read become, in turn, embedded within the original text, as happened with Diamela Eltit's narrative textualities and Nelly Richards's critical reading of them. However, critical understanding of narrative textuality can insulate readers or critics from writers who disturb this embedding process as bearers of other, exotic, eccentric discourses that do not fit into the original design, much as a different type of shingle alters the pattern in the roof of a house. In this sense, the creation of a more representative space for noncanonical, nonrepresented literatures or cultures can begin only by breaking down the original embedding process and by creating new patterns, kaleidoscope-like, with the loose shingles at hand, to continue my metaphor. In other words, by breaking down "old readings" that claim to have established an order of meaning for what "Latin American literature" is supposed to be, homogenizing and reducing simplistically what is in fact a heterogeneous production, a liminal experience of the West with significant tension at its point of suture with numerous heterogeneous others, by bringing in alternative voices coming from different directions, we can truly question globalizing processes as the continuous, linear Americanization of the world.

When we look at Central American literature in this light, we can see a new, eccentric design emerging from the movement of a heterogeneous group through old patterns of representation. As Beverley stated in *Subalternity and Representation,* by privileging one position, be it subaltern, hybrid, or otherwise, a critic (or a reader) necessarily negates the claims of others, an inevitable, risky gamble whenever an epistemic change takes place. My intent is to explore the alternative knowledges generated by exploring this eccentricity; but, at the same time, to understand why it is necessary to generate positions in order to compete in the cultural market.

My study of Central American discursivity in this book also follows Walter Mignolo's reasoning concerning how in imperial centers the colonization of knowledge constructs certain representations of "Latin America," which are then reproduced by Latin American intellectuals. In both these instances, "Central America" has been the invisible hinge between North and South, with the brief exception of the 1980s, when political scientists paid attention to its revolutionary struggles before moving on to world systems theories. Pursuing a subjective approach to Central American discursivity thus permits me to elaborate a sketch about where "we" (Central American natives transplanted to a U.S. site and recodified as U.S. Latinos with a pining for our as-yet-undefined cultural roots) are coming from, both epistemologically and politically.

I now turn to the specific problems and preoccupations addressing the Central American region, this conglomerate of small, poor, disparate nation-states struggling to remain at least nominally independent over the past few decades. There is no escaping the fact that, like it or not, Central America is a region, a group of nations, whose colonial experiences and languages closely resemble each other even if they are not actually the same, so that we can assume that they share a significant number of common traits. Moreover, they have an unquestionably common history and a geographical delimitation that brings them together rather than separating them, such as chains of mountains that may mark who is inside or outside of a given valley, oceans that territorially define the land they touch or surround, common rivers, and so forth. What makes Central America a region, then, could be synthesized though a common history, a common language, a similar colonial experience, and a geographical setting that compacts these nations and brings together their peoples.

Unlike what Benítez Rojo has argued about the Caribbean, the designation of "Central America" as a region was neither foreign nor recent.[16] Archaeologists were the first ones to know this, of course, and their ideas are summarized in the following quote from Schele and Freidel:

> Now we call this world Mesoamerica, a term which refers not only to geography, but to a Precolumbian cultural tradition that shared a 260-day calendar, religious beliefs including definitions of gods and bloodletting as their central act of piety, the cultivation of maize, the use of cacao as a drink and as money, a ballgame played with a rubber ball, screen-fold books, pyramids and plazas, and a sense of common cultural identity. The worldview that was forged by the ancient peoples of that land is still a living and vibrant heritage for the millions of their descendants.[17]

The term *Mesoamerica* was invented by Paul Krickhoff in 1943 as both a geographical and a cultural term. The area, however, was first conceptualized as a region by Mayas over two thousand years ago, until their abandoned city-states withered into oblivion around the seventh century A.D. It was re-created anew as a region through military conquest in the twelfth century (by the Toltecs) and again in the fourteenth century (by the Aztecs), and then was integrated into the world capitalist system in the sixteenth century through another military conquest (by the Spaniards, who named it the Kingdom of Goathemala). In the nineteenth century, the region reinvented itself without lasting consequence as a federal republic (the United Provinces of Central America) at the moment of its independence from Spain (an action implemented by conservative sectors in 1821). It ratified this status in a second independence declared by liberals (this time from Mexico, in 1823). The designation was meant as self-referential—indeed, it was aimed at fixing on the horizon a sense of collective being—and as an identitary differentiation from Mexico, Central America's "other" in the early nineteenth century. The five Central American nations reunited briefly in the mid-1850s to expel William Walker, a Tennesseean who threatened to colonize the region in the name of the Confederate States of America and proclaimed himself president of Nicaragua. They symbolically reunited again in 1921 to mark, as a united region, the centennial of independence from Spain. Ultimately, the region dreamed of itself as a future socialist utopia from the 1960s to the 1980s before being disarticulated by rising transnational factions identified with diverse globalizing forces. Ever since the early nineteenth century, local academics, intellectuals, and social scientists have struggled to systematize the economic, political, social, and cultural dynamics of the region. Since the early twentieth century, in the wake of the construction of the Panama Canal, the United States has exercised continual pressure to refragment it (and American social scientists seconded this effort with a design to study its countries on a case-by-case basis and not as a unified region whose processes of neocolonization parallel one another).

Central America is positioned, through this rationale and history of foreign interventions, as a region—a region that is placed just south of the Republic of Mexico. The area might actually begin at the latter country's Isthmus of Tehuantepec (where Maya cultures have existed for more than two thousand years), and ends where the Darién rainforest begins, roughly halfway from Panama City to Panama's Colombian border (an inhospitable strait that truly separates Central America from South America; not even the Pan American Highway could be built through this rough terrain).

Central America is marked by its indigenousness, an indigenousness that has yet to be fully theorized and critically grasped in terms of how, in its marginality, it relates to such other unrecognizable margins as the Garífunas. Nonetheless, in Guatemala alone there still are twenty-two different Maya groups, and their own rivalries can be fierce. El Salvador has Lencas and Pipiles, who are Nahuatl speakers. Nicaragua has Miskitos, Sumus, and Ramas. Costa Rica had the Chiriquí, Chorotega, and Chibcha, who were culturally closer to the Incas and related to the Rama of Nicaragua. Panama has the Kuna of San Blas. It is clear, then, that to this day the Central American region has outgrown neither its origins nor its heavy indigenous cultural imprint.[18]

Central America is also, in all its space (small as it is), a source of "our" collective affection. It engages our affective needs when it is located as our place of origin. "Central Americanness" is also a sentiment or subjectivity, and, because it relies on a contingent perspective suggesting an ethos or telos, it carries essentializing risks. Whereas many critics regard emotions with suspicion because they may lack the reliability of conceptual thinking, I prefer them precisely because of their ability to theorize the rhetoric of caring, affection, and justice. As a novelist and as a literary scholar, I am all too aware of the statements made nearly a century ago by thinkers such as Bakhtin and Wittgenstein, that conceptual thinking fails to grasp the feelinglike quality of literature. As Culler said so elegantly, "Theoretical treatments of identity can therefore seem reductive in comparison with the subtle explorations in novels."[19] Grief, fear, hope, nostalgia, and compassion are among many affections that inform Central American subjectivity, whether an individual is located on the isthmus itself or outside of it. In this sense, I want to explore emotions that shape our understanding of a place and a culture, because they are, as Martha Nussbaum argues, highly discriminating and intelligent responses to what is of value and importance for our respective lives.[20] Like her, I would argue that there can be no ethical theory without an adequate theory of the emotions, of our affective spaces. Unlike her, I am in no position to propose one. Yet I do plan to take into account the spaces of affection from which we theorize our particular situations and the ethical implications of so doing. In this sense, the need to speak from a Central American perspective is a means to construct a subjectivity that can carry with it the risk of inventing a Central American identity. Nevertheless, more than the latter, I am interested in the need to articulate a discourse as a mechanism for constructing a subject. Our affection leads to an "emotional memory" that can be seen as a social imagination, a reconstitution of memory and desire, and a multidirectional way to articulate a reflexive response concerning the events of the present that construct an alternative ethos. In this sense, it is also an attempt to reimagine who "we" are, a step we take before reformulating the directions of our work.

The book is divided into three parts. The first, "The Outcasts of Global Citizenship," problematizes the representation of Central American narrative textuality from its pre–civil war period (Asturias, Alegría) and its civil war or guerrilla period (Belli, Guardia) to the transitional stage (Armijo) and the postwar era.

In the first chapter of this section, "Revolutionary Endgame: Globalization and the Trajectory of Narrative," I argue that the end of the thirty-year-long guerrilla cycle and the utopian dreams of revolution that came with it changed the symbolic framework of most Central American subjects. It transformed those imagined spaces into a symbolic horizon constituting a matrix, a culturally fluid space where a vast array of discursive mechanisms construct and deconstruct representational issues that define and redefine priorities, identities, and cultural projects. The chapter provides an overview of the literature produced during the 1960–90 "guerrilla period" before proceeding to explain how—and indeed why—the narrative textuality of the postwar period differs from the previous one. This section problematizes some of the implications of this change.

The subsequent chapter, "Erotic Transgression and Recodification of Values in Asturias's *Mulata*," analyzes the most innovative novel of the 1960s, Asturias's *Mulata de tal* (1963, translated as *Mulata*, 1967). It places the text's symbology within an expansive contextual political framework. This chapter contends that the masochism present in the text is associated with the sociopolitical situation of post-1954 Guatemala. For Asturias, his country's CIA-led invasion in 1954 was devastating. Intuitively, he saw his nation as the victim of two competing social systems and attempted to frame this conflict textually by employing a masochist symbolic code.

The last chapter of the first part, "Identity or Literariness: The Emergence of a New Maya Literature," traces the lineage of much of the Central American narrative to the Maya-K'iché text, the *Popol Vuh*. It explores how this singular genealogy works in two contemporary texts, Roberto Armijo's *El asma de Leviatán* (Leviathan's asthma, 1990) and Gloria Guardia's *El último juego* (The last game, 1977), before moving on to contemporary Maya literature and analyzing three novels, Luis de Lión's *El tiempo principia en Xibalbá* (Time begins in Xibalba, 1985), Gaspar Pedro González's *La otra cara* (1992, translated as *A Mayan Life*, 1995), and Víctor Montejo's *Las aventuras de Mr. Puttison entre los mayas* (The adventures of Mr. Puttison among the Mayas, 1998). It concludes by discussing the importance of emerging Maya literature as a vital counterstatement to Ladino discursivity, one that enables subaltern actors to acquire an actualized dominion of their world from within the confines of literature.

The second part of the book is titled "Forever Menchú." This part has a series of chapters dealing with the controversy surrounding Rigoberta Menchú's *testimonio*. They are titled "Authoring Ethnicized Subjects: The Performative Production of the Subaltern Self," "After the Controversy: Lessons Learned about Subalternity and the Indigenous Subject," "Reading Truthfully: An American Reading of a Subaltern Text," and "The Burning of the Spanish Embassy: Máximo Cajal versus David Stoll."

The first of these chapters questions some of the premises of David Stoll's book. It explores the problematics of "truth" and the relationship between political solidarity and subaltern narrative. The follow-up chapter addresses the specific ways in which Stoll continues to read Menchú out of context in his chapter "The Battle of Rigoberta," which was published in *The Rigoberta Menchú Controversy* (2001). There he portrays her discourse as "propaganda" for a guerrilla organization. By making her ethnicity redundant, he conveniently forces her into the stereotype of the devious, conniving person of color. Stoll's account masks the underlying threat and subterranean tension that subjects of color bring to the surface of American white society. The third chapter analyzes the different protocols of reading in the United States and Latin America that have contributed to misunderstandings regarding "truth," "morality," and "ethics." The fourth chapter engages with a close reading of Stoll's *Rigoberta Menchú and the Story of All Poor Guatemalans* (1998). More specifically, I am concerned with Stoll's sixth chapter, titled "The Massacre at the Spanish Embassy," a highly biased account of the tragic events that took place in Guatemala City on 31 January 1980. At that time, security forces burned down the Spanish embassy, killing everyone inside with the exception of the ambassador. My analysis calls into question not only the veracity of Stoll's arguments, but also the ulterior motives that may have guided the author to make them.

The first three chapters of this part were originally published as articles in various academic journals. Aside from correcting minor typographical errors, eliminating sentences that seemed redundant, and updating the notes, I have not revised them; they have been left largely as they originally appeared, as a record of a singular pre-9/11 chapter in U.S. academia. The fourth chapter, originally delivered at the Twenty-third Latin American Studies Association (LASA) International Congress in Washington, D.C., just three days prior to 9/11, has not been previously published.

The third part of this book deals with cultural consequences emerging from two different large-scale movements of people (diasporas?) that define the past twenty-five years of Central American history. The first of these was internal displacement, and I use as an example the movement of Maya peoples within Guatemala as a consequence of a civil war that peaked between 1979 and 1984. The overtly racist nature of this war not only reconfigured the ethnic picture of the nation, but also allowed for an opening of Mayas' conceptions of themselves, for they were displaced from their lands of origin toward exile, immigration to the United States, or internal migration to Guatemala City. The other diaspora linked to the first large-scale immigration was that of Central Americans as a whole, who fled the regional civil wars of the 1980s by moving north, primarily to the United States, in a quest for peace and stability.[21] For the most part, they entered the U.S. domestic realm through narratives of political defeat or economic disillusionment while bearing the stigma of being "leftist supporters" in the eyes of American authorities (with the exception of anti-Sandinista Nicaraguans).

In both cases, new identitary issues emerged as the "neoliberal" economic model consolidated itself in Central America, combined with the defeat of insurgent revolutionary movements and the emergence of democratization processes in the wake of the fall of the Berlin wall. The new set of parameters explains the cultural traits of the postguerrilla period, all of which fall under what has emerged in the context of globalization. The term *globalization* has often been used to mark the tendency toward the homogenization of culture all over the world, replacing local specificity with U.S.-produced mass culture. In the economic realm, it means the integration of markets and the increasing flows of capital, information, commodities, and people across national boundaries and between continents. In politics it has often been invoked to explain the decreasing power of nation-states because national decisions are made in response to transnational flows of capital rather than the will or needs of the national population. Current globalizing tendencies have had an impact on race, gender, nationality, and class on a variety of levels. The chapters in this section of the book outline how they have affected Mayas and Central American populations residing in the United States.

The first chapter, "The Maya Movement," deals with the ways in which concrete daily racist actions and events challenge the authenticity not only of the ethnic subject in postwar Guatemala, but also of theorists attempting to place an ensemble of heterogeneous issues within the unifying context of globalization. It also highlights the ways in which globalization affects the unfolding of the ethnic subject's identity when cultural power is reorganized within new parameters that push analyses in the direction of decentralized, multidetermined sociopolitical relations.

The second chapter, "Central American–Americans? Latino and Latin American Subjectivities," interrogates while contextualizing the invisibility of Central American culture to the great majority of U.S. citizens (Latino and non-Latino) despite its overwhelming presence in the United States. For "Central American–Americans," life exists on the margins of those others (Cuban-Americans, Mexican-Americans), whose identity often is constructed through the abjection and erasure of the subject denominated Central American–American. Thus, Central American–Americans are a group doubly marginalized in "our" overall understanding, if not imagined space, of what Latinos and Latinoness constitute in the United States.

Finally, "American Central Americans: Invisibility and Representation in the Latino United States" examines the specificity of Central Americans in the United States in relation to issues of identity, history, and politics. It also considers the contrasting relationship between Central Americans and Mexican immigrants in the United States, historicizing the dynamics of power between the two regions since colonial times, with the idea of advancing our understanding of inter-Latino relations in the United States. The chapter also seeks to address the invisibility of Central American refugees in the United States, arguing that the historical memory of rape and violence has led Central Americans in the United States to keep themselves on the margins of social visibility and presentability. This strategic nonidentity contrasts the identity politics of reaffirmation that constituted the Chicano and Nuyorican movements with the present-day situation of Central American–Americans.

PART I

The Outcasts of Global Citizenship

1

Revolutionary Endgame: Globalization and the Trajectory of Narrative

International headlines during the 1980s demonstrated a large-scale concern for Central America's revolutionary struggles. From a metropolitan point of view, however, the region "faded from view" in the ensuing decade, once its political instability appeared to have settled. Indeed, the 1990s pointed to the beginning of a new period in Central American history, one dating from the electoral defeat of the Sandinistas in February 1990. Since then, globalization has exercised a structural determinacy over the entire region.[1] The end of the thirty-year-long guerrilla cycle, and of the utopian dreams of revolution, changed the symbolic framework of most Central American subjects.[2] It transformed those imagined spaces, or the symbolic horizon, that constitute a matrix, a culturally fluid space, inside of which a vast array of discursive mechanisms operate, constructing and deconstructing representational issues that define and redefine priorities, identities, and cultural projects in any given community.

Unlike in metropolitan areas of the world, however, narrative textuality has continued to be the major representational form for framing subjective notions between place and self, between self and meaning in Central America.[3] Narrative texts are vehicles that, however porous, multilayered, or uneven, articulate those symbolic traits that mark the subjects' cultural imaginings, or what Rossana Reguillo has called the "emotional memory" of a region.[4] Indeed, as a tenuous postwar peace settled on Central America, novel production, circulation, and consumption rose to unheard-of levels.[5] In this context, by winning the 1998 Alfaguara Literary Award with *Margarita, está linda la mar* (1998, translated as *Margarita, How Beautiful*

the Sea, 2005), Nicaraguan novelist Sergio Ramírez became the best-known
Central American novelist in the Spanish-speaking world since 1967 Nobel
Prize winner Miguel Angel Asturias.[6] His emerging international notoriety
ensured a smooth transition from Sandinista vice president in the 1980s to
full-time novelist and internationally recognized man of letters at the end
of the century.[7] This, combined with the overall blooming of new publishing houses, however small, and an abundance of new fictional works, became
tangible proof that literary production continued to matter in postwar Central America.

Before discussing the production of narrative textuality during the 1990s,
however, I want to consider the general tendencies that prevailed during the
guerrilla period. Consequently, although this chapter will first explain the
nature of the postwar period, I will primarily reflect on the historical emergence of the "guerrilla" or "revolutionary" novel of period from 1960 to
1990. This will ultimately lead to brief considerations of the new forms of
cultural production emerging in the 1990s, when a new generation of writers began to tell the stories of a postwar culture that was, once again, in flux.

Contextualizing the Central American Transition to the 1990s and Beyond

The guerrilla period, though marked by political upheaval, was also one of
empowerment, of positive belief in the transformative capacity of people,
whereby passivity became activity. There was a generalized sense that the
region had finally come into its own and could join the ranks of nations
experiencing modernity upon the triumph of its revolutionary movements.
The 1980s therefore represent not only the specter of a collective tragedy,
but also the apparition of utopian hope. They were a decade of great expectations, when changing the world still seemed possible and when being an
actor on the world stage provided a shot of adrenalin. New tropes to define
the effervescence of the period were invented from within the region to
substitute for the worn-out phrase "banana republics": the terms *Sandinistas, Farabundistas, Mayas,* and *Garífunas,* among others, entered the international vocabulary in the 1980s. Salvadoran poet Roque Dalton labeled
this period "el turno del ofendido," a phrase that can be loosely translated
"the invisible peoples' turn to gain visibility."[8]

As late as 1976, it still was said that the Central American drama concerned absolutely no one. "Repression in Guatemala is worse than others,"

wrote Nobel Prize winner Gabriel García Márquez, "not so much because of its unquenchable intensity, nor because of its heartless ferociousness nor because of its prehistoric duration, but rather because there is almost nobody left in the world who still remembers it."[9] The Colombian's words, stated just prior to the acceleration of the civil war's dynamics (the Sandinista urban offensive in 1978 and its triumph in 1979; El Salvador's coup in 1979, unleashing civil forces that organized political masses; the Maya insurrection in the Guatemalan highlands in 1980, leading to a genocidal campaign against them beginning in 1982), are an excellent example of Central Americans' perception of themselves as located in the marginality of marginality. This is what Ileana Rodríguez calls the layering of meaning that constitutes "a symbolic universe that determines the conditions of the future production of discursive practices."[10] Between 1978 and 1990, Central America managed indeed to remind the world of its existence, to capture its attention, and it enjoyed doing so. But in the 1990s the region returned to its previous invisibility. Central Americans went back to feeling as if they lived in a marginal outpost in the tropics.[11] Once the cold war ended and local conflicts were more or less settled, the U.S. government moved on to other concerns, such as Iraq. Central Americans, of course, could not "move on." They were still coming to terms with hundreds of thousands of "disappeared" citizens and were healing their psychic wounds. They could not move on unless they migrated illegally to the United States, as massive numbers have done since the early 1980s.

I have already mentioned in the introduction to this book how the region has been reimagined time and again throughout history. In the most recent period, nevertheless, it has actually been pushed to questioning its viability as a collection of nations in search of a broader unity. Certainly the Central American Free Trade Agreement, imposed by the second Bush administration in 2005, will not solve this problem. As a consequence, Central Americans now doubt both their regional and national identities in more unsettling ways than in previous epochs.

There is now a minimalist democracy, but it has come at a steep price and with a shaky peace burdened by deep governmental corruption, unparalleled poverty, violent crime, and citizen insecurity. Ironies abound in the sociopolitical reality of this world. The current political stability is grounded in the political accords between the guerrillas and the military, allied with the traditional elite sectors of society, and they reflect a globalized neoliberal model that has not led to economic prosperity and has increased the disparity between the rich and the poor. State-sponsored political repression has mostly disappeared, at least enough to permit cultural expressions such as the mural painted on the cemetery walls of San Juan Comalapa, in Guatemala, sketching the guerrillas' history as a testament of Maya resistance.[12] Still, justice has not been served to those responsible for massive human rights abuses in the civil war period, and there is no room, or hope, for a better, more egalitarian life. Subsistence conditions have spread, and with them violent crime, so that the citizens' financial and physical insecurity is nearly intolerable. Cultural production is up—Central America has added to its ranks a Nobel Prize winner (Rigoberta Menchú, who won the Nobel Peace Prize),[13] empowered an indigenous population, and produced excellent films and prize-winning novels—but Central American cultural products still circulate almost exclusively within the region, so they really do not count for much in the globalized arena.

The cultural production of Central America, however, is rich and varied. It deserves critical attention, and not only because it is interesting and important to explore the creative articulation of memory presently taking place in the wake of a social conflict described by Carey as "unmatched by any other region in the world."[14] It also illustrates the diversity of discourses and rhetorical forms that, under globalized conditions, are seeking to represent both continuity and fragmentation. Those echoes can be heard, however, only if we listen first to what was said between 1960 and 1990, the period of guerrilla struggle, revolutionary illusions, and greatest political instability.

The 1960s: The Emergence of Revolutionary Literature

The 1960s witnessed a new wave of Central American fiction that signaled a fundamental break with the previous literature of the region. Without question, the most innovative novel to come out during this decade was Miguel Angel Asturias's *Mulata de tal*, published in Argentina in 1963. However, because Asturias (1899–1974) was by then an older, well-established writer living in Europe and seldom interacting with younger writers residing in Central America, I will not include him in this chapter; I will provide a separate analysis of *Mulata* in the second chapter.

Another important writer linking the older generation with a younger one was Guatemalan short story writer Augusto Monterroso (1921–2003). Two of his most important works, *La oveja negra y demás fábulas* (1969, translated as *The Black Sheep and Other Fables*, 1971) and *Movimiento perpetuo* (Perpetual movement, 1972), appeared in installments in Mexican cultural magazines throughout the 1960s before making their appearance in book form. In a way analogous to that of Borges, Monterroso broke with traditional notions of the short story by means of parody and reinvented postmodern forms of the fable, the essay, and other marginal journalistic genres that he imbued with splendidly original and humorous propositions by turning their signs around and reconstituting them as if they were just devices to be deconstructed and reconstructed. Monterroso was a strong influence on Sergio Ramírez, who befriended him in the 1970s. He would also be an influence on younger Guatemalan writers who began publishing in the mid-1970s, especially Dante Liano.

Claribel Alegría and Darwin Flakoll's *Cenizas de Izalco* (1966, translated as *Ashes of Izalco*, 1989) was the first in a series of narratives from the younger generation to express the cultural transformation of the 1960s in literary form.[15] Among the outstanding initiators of Central America's new wave were Roque Dalton,[16] Alfonso Chase, Lizandro Chávez Alfaro, and Carmen Naranjo.[17] These narrators experimented with innovative discursive practices, informed by literary developments taking place elsewhere on the continent.[18] Given the political crisis of the decade, however, they did not confuse formal experimentation with lack of social content. Being a writer in Central America meant being a public figure, a moral barometer, and a spokesperson for the opposition to the region's military regimes. Most of these writers, therefore, belonged to or sympathized with leftist political parties, and they were engaged on a daily basis not only with political leaders, but also with worker, peasant, and student activists. Given the cultural climate of the times, when sympathy for the Cuban revolution was rampant and violent methods for toppling military regimes were the order of the day, writers had little choice but to represent politicized social issues, however innovative they might be in terms of style. The only major writer who did not participate in leftist politics was the Salvadoran Alvaro Menén Desleal. However, he made a point of befriending his more leftists comrades Dalton, Roberto Armijo, Manlio Argueta, Italo López Vallecillos, and José Roberto Cea, and he did not lose contact with them when he began working for the Christian Democratic government in the 1980s, at the peak of the Salvadoran civil war. Nevertheless, despite his highly innovative work, he was parodied and criticized by Dalton in *Pobrecito poeta que era yo . . .* (1976) and ignored by most Central American cultural critics because of his "tainted" political past, though a few admitted that he might be one of the best short story writers ever.[19]

The singularity of post-1954 Central America—traumatized by the invasion of Guatemala in June of that year, sponsored by the U.S. Central Intelligence Agency (CIA), which removed democratically elected President Jacobo Arbenz, who was anathema to U.S. interests because of his forward-looking nationalism—dictated that literary content after that crucial event had to be of a political nature if the "writer" was to fit into the region's games of truth. Given the ferment of the times, this was partly a coercive practice of Central American civil societies, particularly of their intellectual sector. But it was also an ethical response to the Guatemalan invasion and its consequences, which led to regional chaos.[20] Those conditions—the dizzying series of political events and hidden agendas—could be framed only by literary language, in part because the social sciences in Central America were dominated by Europeans and Americans. Central Americans had not yet developed their own body of scientific work, though they would begin to do so in the course of the decade.[21]

Because the voice of nationalism has primarily been the voice of the middle classes in Central America, a sector to which intellectuals and artists usually belong, it is not surprising that the writers and artists who appeared after 1954 were influenced by this voice as they attempted to symbolically represent those events through literature in the midst of rampant social strife. As Dalton stated, El Salvador's *generación comprometida* (politically engaged generation)—which organized itself in 1956, after Guatemalan poet Otto René Castillo joined young Salvadoran writers in his post-1954 exile, and included outstanding young poets and narrators such as Dalton, Argueta, Vallecillos, Menén Desleal, Armijo, and Cea, among a singularly notable group of writers—adopted Asturias's adage "To be a writer is to be the moral consciousness of his people" as its guiding principle.[22]

Paradoxically, Central American writers did not have to worry about average readers. Despite the fact that the illiteracy rate was higher than it is at present, regional agencies such as the Consejo Superior Universitario Centroamericano (Central American Universities' Superior Council, CSUCA) subsidized national university publishing houses and created a regional one, EDUCA (Central American Universities' Press; the acronym is the Spanish word "Educate!") in 1968, aimed at progressive intellectual elites at home and abroad. Often writers themselves were named to head universities' presses, as happened with Armijo and Ramírez. In consequence, writers knew at the time that their readers were only a tiny fraction of the middle classes and enlightened individuals from the upper crust. But, given the heritage of "the lettered city," they enjoyed enormous political respect.[23] They benefited from what Idelber Avelar calls "the traditional aura of the *letrado*";[24] intellectuals were not competing with ideologues because they were the ideologues themselves. This independence enabled the new literature emerging in the early 1960s to make a significant break with the traditional narrative discourse of the 1950s. The latter had been heavily marked by social realism in a style imported from the Soviet Union and imposed by writers and artists belonging to the Communist Youth during the late 1940s and early 1950s. It was a form embedded in cold war issues.[25] The new tendencies resulted from a rebellion against social realism, but they were also signs of a rejection of the communist political line that had originally sponsored it as emerging radical organizations of the early 1960s broke with Soviet-sponsored communist parties and created guerrilla structures imitating the Cuba model that attempted to implement Guevara's teachings and theories. At a literary and cultural level, this political schism manifested itself as a transition in linguistic consciousness that produced new artistic and literary forms arising out of what García Canclini calls "an alliance between artistic innovation and the internationalization of culture" that "made the populations' tastes more sophisticated."[26]

Alegría and Flakoll's *Cenizas de Izalco* experimented formally with creating new symbolic codes and broke away from old historical paradigms to redefine Salvadoran society from the perspective and viewpoint of the *"matanza."*[27] What is more, the novel displaced the centrality of a masculine gaze in favor of a feminine one, which was unheard of in Central American fiction, particularly in narratives with a political focus.[28] *Cenizas de Izalco* became, de facto, a parting of the waters, signaling the end of social realism. Since its appearance, the style and form in which any major Central American novel is written has figured just as strongly as its content. In other words, after *Cenizas de Izalco*, it was no longer enough to write about "political themes." The work had to exceed the boundaries of the ordinary; it had to be politically transgressive and linguistically innovative as well. An

example from the beginning of *Cenizas* will suffice to show how different it
is from a traditional "realistic" novel:

> The luncheon dishes clash and rattle in the kitchen. María grumbles to herself
> in a steady monotone, and Dad, strangely shrunken now, defenselessly old,
> lies asleep in the darkened bedroom. I've taken off my sandals, and the choco-
> late brown tiles are cool against my feet. The whitewashed arches march
> around the patio: circus elephants linked tail to trunk, enclosing the blaring
> bougainvillea, the file of rosebushes, the central fountain where Alfredo and
> I used to splash and scream, the shaded jasmine, the papaya tree, the star pine
> with its ivy-choked trunk.[29]

Thereafter, we hear that Frank Wolff (whose last name we discover only
at the end of chapter 2) mentioned in his diary the rumblings of the Izalco
volcano when Carmen was seven years old (these descriptions will indeed
appear in the diary at the end of the novel). But we still do not know who
Frank is, nor are we aware that the narrator is Carmen, the daughter of
Frank's lover, Isabel. We find that out in the first chapter, but not immediately.
First, Carmen will visit the market in Santa Ana and mix her childhood
memories with her reflections during the narrative present in which she is
"telling" the story. As curious readers, we have to gradually build the story of
Frank and Isabel in our minds. We are not spoon-fed facts about the main
characters, their circumstances, and the setting. Rather, they reveal themselves
to us, gradually and from within, through an introspective mode that reveals
them as thinking and feeling people charged with subjectivity. They open
up to each other in a continuing dialogue, in an exploration of one another's
consciousness, which is revealed to the reader, in turn, through Carmen.
This textual process was utterly new and revolutionary in Central America.

Chase, Dalton, and Argueta plunged into new narrative techniques as a
result of the great success both of boom novelists and of *Cenizas de Izalco*.
They thus generated a novelistic "miniboom" within Central America in
the 1970s.

The 1970s: Prefiguring Insurrections

In the context of the literary transformations that took place in the 1960s,
writers appropriated oral voices in their narrative during the next decade.

Between 1969 and 1983, at least a dozen writers from the six Central American Spanish-speaking countries published some eighteen major novels, testimonials, and collections of short stories.[30] In that work, the narrative process became more important than plot, incarnating the spoken language as it regulated information and resisted traditional representations. Through these strategies, language became a form of representation in itself. The "new" Central American novel became a playing field for verbal exchanges that could imagine new models of reality, of space and time. Roque Dalton's *Pobrecito poeta que era yo . . .* begins like this:

> Young man, panting (so to speak) slightly because of the street's heat (this country is an old fire, etc.). Has found in this bar of such a European name . . . appropriate companionship to drown his sorrows . . . precisely because of this blasting heat and has not been able to lose yet a certain air that betrays his holy need to reach once and for all a certain final destiny (of his journey? Of his life?) Passionately his, ungiving.

In a similar way, Marcos Carías's *Función con móbiles y tentetiesos* (1980) opens as follows:

> Come to David's: It's halfway down and today is his birthday. Half a body under the door, a foot forward, a smile directed to the gallery and the drink chest-high. The one in the corner right in front is Amapola. Amapola is not precisely a girl; the ample sleeves and the shining earrings belong to the seduction of that night. The telephone wasn't heard. Personal statistics reveal that 63 percent of the time he felt the telephone before it rang. Said the doctor: "People like you."

Both texts consist of superimposed voices that string themselves together to give shape to the narration. A singular social group is constructed from dialogues, monologues, and fragments of writing or speech that form a sort of chorus of dissimilar voices and discourses that gradually come to constitute a representation of a certain sector of society at a given point in time.

Writers of the 1970s reinvented a need to instrumentalize language as an intellectual weapon for emancipatory projects, given their belief that literature was another instrument of—if not an instrument for—the revolution to come. This forging of a new social imaginary by means of assembling a bricolage of polysemic discourses was an intuitive process. The achievements of these texts were not the result of a priori reflection or of artistic or political manifestos, nor were they simply imitations of what was taking place on the rest of the continent at the time or a full conceptualization of the problems at hand. The path, if found at all, was discovered only along the way.

This should not surprise us. Cultural works do not emerge on a rational plane, but rather arrive flexibly, immersed in "spontaneous" (despite the obvious Romantic connotation of this qualifier) enunciations that correspond to alternative forms of knowledge. These intuitive heuristics—the creative emotions behind the emergence of words—become "internal to themselves, a thought of the object's value of importance," as Martha Nussbaum would say.[31] With a few scattered elements at hand, the most marginal of writers is capable of inventing an entirely ("brave") new world.

Nonetheless, Central American writers chose to imitate some of the stylistic variations inherited from boom writers (especially from Cortázar and Fuentes, close friends of Alegría, Dalton, and Ramírez) while displacing the subject represented, unaware both of the risk of what Avelar calls an "aestheticization of politics"[32] and of the usurping subalterns' voices. It was an emotional estimation that led to this, an operative tactic in the context of polarizing political forces of the day combined with a blind faith in the liberating forces of literature. It mostly led to what Nussbaum calls an "evaluative and eudaimonistic" process,[33] that is, to using emotions as judgments of value.

This conundrum explains why contemporary Central American writers mimicked discourses and sought to engage with and interpellate not only those hegemonic centers of cultural decision making, but also nonhegemonic subcenters that, in their eyes, had monopolized the "subaltern power" of the marginals validated from the center (Mexico, Argentina, Brazil). These contradictory attitudes were the price most of them paid for their will to be part of something larger, different, more modern or "developed." In this sense, the modernization of national economies can be understood through what María Josefina Saldaña-Portillo has labeled "national development as a promise of the postcolonial era,"[34] which could somehow be forced into visibility through the boundaries of both the writers' own bodies and their bodies of work (because the only alternative that they could visualize was the helplessness of their national identitary shame, a realization of inadequacy).[35] It was a contradictory attitude. If it was an aesthetic rhetorical operation, not unlike Avelar's assessment of boom writers, this literature was separated from the region's abject backwardness. But it was also different in that it did not pretend to be an effective surrogate for it. It did not so much try to integrate Central America into modernity through literature as it used the modernity of literature to justify the revolutionary need for social and political transformations, thus creating an illusion of avant-garde writers as the equivalent of avant-garde revolutionaries.

Indeed, as Ileana Rodríguez and Saldaña-Portillo have pointed out, the narrative of the revolution was the narrative of the construction of the self as well.[36] Rodríguez had in mind the revolutionary speech acts of leaders such as Che Guevara or the Guatemalan writer Mario Payeras, who saw himself as a revolutionary who also happened to write. However, this was also true of literary writers of this period, who regarded themselves as writers who also happened to be revolutionaries. Their narratives attempted to constitute an ideological basis for revolution as an implicit justification for the constitution of their own selves as revolutionary leaders. If this was primarily true of Dalton, it was also the case for Ramírez, Argueta, and Armijo, among major figures of this period, and even for minor ones such as Guatemalans Marco Antonio Flores and Mario Roberto Morales. In this light, Central American writers—particularly male heterosexuals—reexamined themselves continuously to verify that they had not gone astray from established routes delineated by "the cause." They needed to constantly reconfirm that they had not "lost the way"; hence their constantly claiming the right to speak in the name of "the people," not as writers, but as revolutionary leaders. Their attitude underlined the contradiction of both their desire to lead their communities—an action perceived by both writer and polis as an ethical duty—and their temptation to seek recognition as modern masters in metropolitan centers.[37] The implicit ambiguity generated a lot of infighting among them. In Guatemala, the public rupture—public because it took place in a series of personal attacks published in the editorial opinion columns of the local press—between Marco Antonio Flores and Mario Roberto Morales in the late 1970s acquired epic dimensions. In the same vein, José Roberto Cea claimed the mantle of moral leadership over fellow Salvadoran poets Armijo and Argueta in the early 1980s because he was then residing in the country, while the other two were exiled, in France and Costa Rica, respectively. In Nicaragua, writers participating in public readings fought about details concerning who would serve as the opening reader and who would close the act. These fights about literary leadership were veiled political debates about the "correct" path that writers allegedly had to take in those dire circumstances. In all cases, writers of this period wrote as if history belonged to them.

Perhaps no text of the 1970s exemplifies this attitude better than Dalton's *Pobrecito poeta que era yo . . .* The story, set in San Salvador in the early 1960s, is about how certain young writers become social climbers and opportunists, while others become militant revolutionaries. One character, Alvaro (using the first name of Menén Desleal and modeled to a certain extent on him), slides from creator of *Teleperiódico,* his country's first television news program, to a plagiarist, usurping the subaltern voice of a peasant named Tata Higinio for his short stories. Another character, Arturo, is a law student. The fashion of the times dictates that if one wants to be a poet, one studies law. Roberto criticizes Asturias, the Guatemalan Nobel laureate, but has difficulty rising out of his own mediocrity in a futile attempt to redirect his revolutionary energy to sexual liberation and poetic lyricism. Ultimately, he is arrested. From the diary of another character, Mario, we notice that this character begins as a progressive lawyer but, incapable of taking the necessary steps to become a militant, slides into alcoholism and despair, trapped in existential conformism. He obsessively asks himself, "What do I write for?" As Jorge Chem Sham has pointed out, Mario's diary problematizes the conflict between bourgeois individualist selfishness and revolutionary consciousness, a crisis that leads to the disintegration of the subject.[38] Despite Mario's eventual suicide, it is through his rambling meditations that the harshest questions about the nature and function of the writer are verbalized, questions of an ontological, existential, and political nature that vindicate a *letrado* tradition, thus overprivileging literature as a means for framing national identity. The text's final section represents the confessional attempt of José, the main character of the novel and Dalton's alter ego, to bring about the "revolutionary politicization of aesthetics," in Avelar's terms, more through his body than through his body of work.[39] As a member of the Communist Party who has recently returned from Cuba, his hallucinatory narration is that of being captured by the army, tortured, and interrogated by a CIA agent who accuses him of being Castro's man in El Salvador. His subsequent escape from prison is told in the first person. And yet this is not a happy, triumphalist ending. Despite his escape to Cuba and then Czechoslovakia, José questions his own alleged

heroism and survival: "Prácticamente todos mis amigos están desapareci-
dos: presos, perseguidos, o . . . ¿Y yo? ¿Por qué . . . ?" (Practically all my
friends have been disappeared; jailed, persecuted, or . . . And me? Why . . . ?
translated from p. 349). But José even questions his continuity in the party.
By the text's end, he is drinking beer in Prague, fatter and alone, still wondering what the right path ought to be, in a typical romantic ending that
reaffirms Schlegel's notion of art as unfinished, as noted by Lara-Martínez.[40]
Pobrecito poeta que era yo . . . is a narrative of the revolutionary writer's
attempt to construct a revolutionary literary self and to anchor modernity,
as Lara-Martínez claims, in an "age of poets."[41] Despite its serious attempt
to bring about what the same critic labels an "Augustinian conversion" to
revolution on the part of the poets,[42] the novel represents their collective
failure to combine aesthetics and politics. José's obsessive desire to evoke
and reinvent his arrest and torture is part of his desire to be heard by others as a revolutionary. He has conjured up a confessional narrative to represent himself as a hero and revolutionary leader. Even though he has already
failed to recognize this configuration within himself, he cannot admit it or
acknowledge it to others. Technically still alive at the novel's end, the revolutionary poet, as symbolic subjectivity, is already dead.

The 1980s: New Subjects, New Genres

In much the same way that the narrative of the 1970s preceded the political
crisis of the end of that decade (Sandinista triumph, Salvadoran coup d'état,
Guatemalan indigenous insurrection, all in 1979), the narrative that began
to emerge in the mid-1980s preceded, to a certain extent, the new postwar
period, which began after 1990 with the electoral defeat of the Sandinistas.
By this time, it was clear that both the Salvadoran and Guatemalan civil
wars would end in peace negotiations.

Just as the narrative of the 1970s did not pretend to start from scratch but
evolved from the premises first developed by Asturias in his best efforts—
Hombres de maíz (1949, translated as *Men of Maize,* 1995) and *Muluta de tal*
(1963; translated as *Mulata,* 1967)—the narrative movement of the mid-1980s
did not signal a rupture with their predecessors, either. Instead, it meant to
continue building on the body that preceded it, that corpus of singular works
that went from Alegría and Flakoll's *Cenizas de Izalco* (1966) to Ramírez's
¿Te dio miedo la sangre? (1977, translated as *To Bury Our Fathers,* 1985). In

some curious way, the writers of the 1980s were a generation that felt they no longer had to "prove" their revolutionary credentials through literary experimentation. That had been a problem for Asturias, as well as for El Salvador's *"generación comprometida"* of the mid-1950s. The writers of the 1980s simply assumed the experimental legacy as their own, together with the extreme limit-establishing experiences of the end of the 1970s. Taking for granted this political and aesthetic condition as definitive of their region, they attempted to then renarrate forgotten elements of previous epochs that had lost prestige in the face of the urgent political crisis: magic, illusion, fantasy, and desire. Nevertheless, these writers, still young in the 1980s, needed to close the chapter on the political militancy that had shattered their lives.

The fundamental contradiction they found at the peak of the social crises of the 1980s was this: how could a person who comes from the margins of the periphery, the so-called marginality of marginality, participate in relationships of power linked to cultural production and, at the same time, manufacture resistance weapons without yielding to hegemonic metropolitan power (the one that buys or rejects manuscripts and guarantees the production, circulation, and consumption of cultural products)?

By the war years (1979 and the early 1980s), the "manufacturing of resistance weapons" was a role performed more and more by the testimonial genre, even when testimonial compilers were themselves writers (Dalton, Ramírez, Alegría).[43] By then, "formal" literature had gradually displaced itself to a more libidinal representation, in the direction of those spaces of desire and emotion that articulated alternative, nontotalizing forms of subjectivity. This was partly the result of the appearance of women (Alegría, Naranjo, Guardia, Belli) on the narrative scene, because women's narrative textuality created an alternative revolutionary subjectivity to the masculinist model of personal development that Saldaña-Portillo criticizes in the writings of both Guevara and Payeras.[44] Women rewrote gender representations from within the emotional domain, the nonrational, nonconscious sphere. It was in those areas that the continuity with bourgeois morality had been preserved most markedly in the revolutionary ranks by professed revolutionary leaders who remained, at heart, self-sufficient *machistas* who, as Ileana Rodríguez wrote in *Women, Guerrillas, and Love*, "neglected, demeaned and marginalized women" (xv), a problematic that Rodríguez labeled "the constitution of the new individual/collective subject as masculine and feminine" (30). The best example of the counter-*machista* tendency in the 1980s is

Gioconda Belli. Her *La mujer habitada* (1988, translated as *The Inhabited Woman*, 1994) and *Sofía de los presagios* (1990) are considered emblematic of emerging postmodern traits in Central American narrative, as well as to represent a turning point in the affirmation of feminist literature in the region. Needless to say, they also prefigure those issues that would most concern Central Americans in the ensuing postwar period.

La mujer habitada begins with an indigenous woman named Itzá, a reconstruction of the trope of the woman combatant, in what constitutes an attempt to destroy the master narrative of the "white" nation-state that had emerged a century and a half earlier. A game is then established: an orange grove grows between two axiological spaces, that of Itzá and that of Lavinia, a member of her country's elite, with "features resembling those of the invaders' women." Her connection with Itzá is through her gender identification as a "warrior woman." Lavinia makes a big show of being rebellious even before she joins a political revolutionary organization. The following describes Lavinia's feelings on being introduced to a man named Felipe in the firm that hires her as the first woman architect: "The two men [Felipe and his friend and colleague] appeared to enjoy their attitude of labor paternalism. Lavinia felt at a disadvantage. She took an internal bow to masculine complicity, and wished that the introductions would be over. She didn't like feeling like she was on display. . . . And she hated it. She didn't want that anymore. She was there to escape it" (16).

When Lavinia drinks the juice of the oranges from her tree, the spirit of Itzá enters her veins. This symbolic fusion prefigures the process of being cut up, of having violence done to one's body, of being dismembered by one's Western other. It also seems to address an implicit, unspoken, lesbian desire: "I want her to take me to her lips." It is a troubling image of female empowerment, however. Only if both women are "like men" can they be combatants. On the other hand, it could also signal the erasure of women, or at least of femininity, within the revolutionary process. The superior hierarchical role played by Itzá, however, causes Lavinia's Westernness to lose its universal transparency, and her character thereby becomes visible as a performative gender construct.

In this mixture of voices (Itzá-Lavinia) there is a deliberate contamination of two dissimilar historical and subjective environments.[45] This places into question the transparency of the representation, without a doubt. Yet, simultaneously, it also challenges the code through which the Nicaraguan indigenous past has traditionally been interpreted. The text does run the risk of reifying and essentializing indigenous subjectivity in Lavinia's yearning for a completeness that goes beyond the text, beyond what Brian Massumi calls "the dual structuring of specular identity in which one compensates for a lack in the other," a perspective that can be "crossed but not bridged" without becoming the other.[46] *La mujer habitada* also reminds us that indigenous peoples' presence as subjects of subaltern representation is not normative; rather, it is a recurrent slippage in Central Americans' own gaze of their singular identitary horizon, a slippage informed by a national, yet regionwide, fear of being "non-Western." Still, we know Itzá's past not only from the discourse that expresses it, but also from the scent of her presence in the present of the text and from her promise to continue to be in the future. This reiteration, a metonymic chain meant to inform the text's significance, is performative of the text's regulatory will to sustain the indigenous trace as the power of truth in the Central American identitary process. The entire text poses a dialogical relationship between Lavinia's discourse and Itzá's that, beyond the parallel struggles leading to their respective deaths, aims to examine the terms in which womanhood has emerged historically in Central America, and thereby to redefine the female subject.

I stated previously that by the 1980s, nationalist issues were being represented more and more through the testimonial genre. This transition also had to do with subaltern interests'—especially indigenous ones in the Guatemalan case—becoming more protagonistic in the battle of words. I will not go more deeply into the issue of the testimonial in this chapter, because that subject is largely examined in part II of this book. Nevertheless, we can superficially verify this tendency when we observe that in the 1980s, nationalist discourse was mainly found in testimonial texts such as those by Rigoberta Menchú, Mario Payeras, Nidia Díaz, Elvia Alvarado, Ana María Castillo Rivas, Omar Cabezas, or Víctor Montejo, while other writers, such as Ramírez, Cardenal, Chávez Alfaro, and Argueta, either shifted to less political genres such as crime stories, baseball, cosmic mysticism, eroticism, historical adventurism, and children's stories or stopped writing narrative altogether (as did Carías, Chase, and Guardia, who remained silent until the late 1990s).

When the subject is presented in this way, the emphasis unjustly falls on the contents of the texts. After all, the transformations taking place were fundamentally linguistic ones. While a change of tone took place in "formal" literature, revolutionary discourse was gradually displaced from the realm of literature to the realm of *testimonio.* These changes enabled narrative textuality to drift away from a revolutionary rhetoric that was fast becoming a cliché in the late 1980s and yet continue to operate more at an affective, emotional level of perception through other means without retreating altogether to a poetics of "pure beauty."

The 1990s: Globalization Trends, New Literary Markets

After 1990, globalizing forces were introduced thorough transformations that ushered in a new transnational model of economy and society, as William I. Robinson has pointed out. As a result, Central American subjects helped create regional literary markets that no longer conformed to old, national models.[47] The emergence of these markets changed the author's romantic disdain of readers, who were now essential to the author's success. They also curbed utopian or messianic revolutionary inclinations and transformed the writers' self-perception as prophetic voices speaking in the name of the masses.

Amid the region's vast transformations, and embedded in broader issues such as the end of cold war and the triumph of neoliberal globalization, narrative textuality changed as well, registering these subtle alterations as might a finely tuned seismograph. The study of narratives from this period should enable critics to explore the aftermath of the region's cataclysmic wars, as well as those transitions taking place in the symbolic, unconscious sediment of their cultures, much as Jean Franco narrates regarding the rise and fall of the lettered city.[48]

Possibly the best place to explore this phenomenon is in the narrative production of Sergio Ramírez. As I stated at the beginning of this chapter, by winning the 1998 Alfaguara Literary Award with *Margarita, está linda la mar,* Ramírez became the best-known Central American novelist in the Spanish-speaking world. A quick glimpse at the novel does indeed give an indication of what has changed. It narrates a broad period of Nicaraguan history, from 1907, when celebrated poet Rubén Darío returned to his home country and wrote a poem on Margarita Debayle's fan, to 1956, the year of the assassination of dictator Anastasio Somoza García (who was married to Margarita's sister Salvadora) and its immediate aftermath. Though the novel sticks close to the historical events, politics have been reduced to a mere plot device, unlike Ramírez's own *¿Te dio miedo la sangre?* (1977), which also covered a broad historical span—from 1930, when Colonel Catalino Lopez was ambushed in a cinema by a column of one of Sandino's ruthless generals, Pedrón Altamirano, to 1961, when Bolívar brought back to Nicaragua the body of his father, Indio Larios. Nevertheless, in the earlier novel it was the political doings of the cast of characters that provided the narrative momentum, and the political dimension of language was brought home in the slippery meaning of its ending, where the son scatters his father's papers on the highway, leaving open the question of whether he will ever make it back to his home country or will later join the struggle against Somoza.

In *Margarita*, on the other hand, it is the thrillerlike preparations for Somoza's assassination that provide the momentum for the story, and the narrative emphasis falls on the conspirators' conversations about Darío while they prepare the assassination attempt. Despite the fact that what is about to take place is a political assassination, politics itself serves only as a backdrop to the evocative flow of history, where the story of Darío's legendary life and the events of Dr. Debayle's scientific career are portrayed. Together with the thrilling escape attempt of the perpetrators and the tragic, bloody ending, these elements overshadow specifics of the assassination itself, which serve as a means of plot advancement but fail to transmit the frisson of an epochal experience.

In *Mil y una muertes* (A thousand and one deaths, 2004), Ramírez's latest novel, both the evocative historical flow and the author's presence remain, even though the object of representation has now been displaced to France in the second half of the nineteenth century. The political acts plotted are those of Louis Bonaparte, friend and protector of Nicaraguan photographer Castellón, who also drank with Darío in Majorca before finishing his days in Poland during World War II. The text traces Ramírez's desire to discover who this enigmatic photographer was and to capture the abject, feverish imagination of marginalized genius. This novel is even one step further removed from *Margarita* in terms of conveying a meaningful sense of politics beyond the thrill of the act of storytelling itself. There is no longer even the pretension that a worthwhile political experience can be transmitted: the narration, conventionally nontransgressive, is that of a literature meant exclusively to entertain.

Traditionally, period changes in Central America—as, perhaps, everywhere else—have been marked culturally by stylistic changes, not just thematic ones. After all, it is not just a matter of what is represented; how it is represented also matters. The space itself is perceived differently because rhetorical tropes are used, as Ileana Rodríguez argues, for understanding the continuities and mutations of topographies.[49] In these processes, the relationship between writer and reader is redefined, as we can witness in the transition undertaken by Ramírez in two of his most emblematic narratives. Whereas in *Margarita* and *Mil y una muertes* the Nicaraguan author retains traditional representations of his country's reality (the legacy of Darío, Somoza's dictatorship and its corrupt implications for all social sectors, Ramírez's own travels as vice president of Nicaragua), it is when we focus on style (narrative point of view, usage of time and voice) that we notice that, topic notwithstanding, *Margarita* and *Mil y una muertes* are constituted by new verbal signs that allude to a different imaginary concept of "the social" than was seen in his previous work.[50] Ramírez's most recent work does evoke memories of the epic of insurgency. Yet it is narrated in a tragicomic way, instrumentalizing "the will to elude the defeat," in Avelar's words.[51] Ultimately we have the posturing of the writer as a codified body image to defend the inviolability of the ontological field of the past revolutionary hero, reconfigured now as a wise *letrado*. Whether it is in *Sombras nada más* (Only shadows remain, 2002) or *Mil y una muertes*, the character now occupying center stage is the writer himself. In *Sombras*, a woman presently residing in Miami reproaches him over how she was represented in ¿*Te dio miedo la sangre?* In *Mil y una muertes*, the writer retraces his travels as vice president and then reconstructs Castellón's life after his exit from political power. In both cases, he occupies center stage, conveying the sense that he has chosen to memorialize himself and he has earned his spot as a subject of memorialization. The stories around which his last novels are woven—that, for example, of Alirio Martinica, a close aide of Somoza who, failing to flee, was arrested and ultimately executed by Sandinistas in *Sombras*, or that of Castellón arriving in France in 1870 thanks to Napoleon III's gratitude to his Nicaraguan father for helping him escape from prison in 1846 and becoming a well-known photographer in Europe—are but background material. They serve to evidence the writer's skills at storytelling, which indeed are first rate. But good as they are, his postwar novels are primarily parables of the exemplary hero making a self-reference so as to convert the narrated event into the regularization of a revolutionary *letrado*. The writer as reified iconic celebrity travels throughout the world—Miami,

Poland, Majorca—to evidence his status and recapture the sensation of power he lost with the end of the revolutionary cycle.

In a similar vein, Gioconda Belli's latest novel, *El pergamino de la seducción* (The parchment of seduction, 2005), is a historical novel about Juana la Loca (Juana the Mad), daughter of Isabel and Ferdinand and herself Queen of Castille following their deaths. Belli's novel chronicles Juana's romance with Felipe el Hermoso (Philip the Beautiful), heir to the Hapsburg crown. Belli claims that, contrary to the legend of her hopeless love for a philandering husband, Juana was driven mad by palace intrigue and political conspiracies. Though she pretends to represent "the psychological tragedy that some women live" in an "erotic novel" of historical dimensions, what we have in fact is a sentimental romance with a dash of kinkiness to snare morbid readers. It is globalized entertainment à la Isabel Allende for mass consumption, despite Belli's disclaimers that Juana "writes from within a feminine vision" to understand women's "domination."[52] Here we are far from *La mujer habitada*.

In this light, when we rethink contemporary Central American narrative, we can see in its most recent examples how a certain past intoxication with revolutionary utopias has given way to a heavy hangover. With the exception of Ramírez, no writer has returned to civil war topics, and certainly none of the young ones earning new kudos in the 1990s has touched them. I could say that a good part of this reaction is due to "war fatigue," a temporary chiasmus, but it goes beyond that simple explanation. Up until the 1950s, more or less, "formal" literature (poetry, novels, literature with a capital L[53]) tried to create a national cultural identity as a way of problematizing flawed nation-states that privileged a tiny segment of the elites while keeping the great majority of their populations in abject poverty. Whether from a radicalized Catholic social perspective (Asturias), a social democratic one (Mario Monteforte Toledo), or a nascent Marxist one (Dalton), they all attempted to create nationalist discourses that sought to achieve moral hegemony among broad sectors of society, to use Gramscian terms, so as to rally the masses around new, modernizing projects that required a radical transformation of the nation-state itself. In the 1990s, however, Central American writers could no longer believe that literature was instrumental in the formation of class consciousness or was a privileged space in which to formulate projects for social transformation with a nationalist bent. Caught between a past that they could not forget and a future of apocalyptic prophecies, many writers no longer knew what the role of literature was. Marc Zimmerman has written a brilliant chronicle of this process in a section of his book *Literature and Resistance in Guatemala* titled "Cultural Politics, Literature, and Postmodern Currents under Serrano Elías." I will simply add here that, influenced directly or indirectly by globalizing tendencies and hybridizing them in their own tropical way, younger writers articulated a pastiche of myth and ritual either to convey satires of cultural memory or to evidence its lack. We can see this in the works of Horacio Castellanos Moya, Jacinta Escudos, Rafael Menjívar Ochoa, Carlos Cortés, Rodrigo Rey Rosa, Maurice Echeverría, Ronald Flores, Eduardo Halfon, and Erick Blandón, as well as those of older writers, such as Anacristina Rossi, Franz Galich, and Magda Zavala, who are now producing fascinating new postwar novels. A new addition to the latter group is Guatemalan Carol Zardetto, whose novel *Con pasión absoluta* (With absolute passion) won the 2004 Mario Monteforte Toledo Prize for the Central American Novel.

The work of all these writers has produced a fundamental transformation in the process of reconfiguring national memories, as well as in the construction of postwar subjectivities and citizenship. It also reopened the question of Central American identity. In this sense, there was no greater questioning than that in Castellanos Moya's 1997 novel *El asco,* a title that could be translated as "Repugnance," which refers to the disgust the narrator feels about being Salvadoran.[54] The novel questions the validity of any positive outlook on national identity (and earned the author a collection of abusive death threats). Indeed, given the disaffection of the 1990s, the concept of identity itself was in peril of disappearing altogether as a frame of reference. This was the case even among writers such as Castellanos Moya who still employed remnants of a rhetoric borrowed from the guerrilla period, even while pointing those signifiers in new directions. Reality began to be codified with full knowledge of language's inability to shape national identities. As we can see in texts such as the ones cited or those of Rey Rosa, the central problem of textuality became that of representing language without any intention of conveying extratextual meanings.

Perhaps, in this sense, Jacinta Escudos's *A-B-sudario* (A-B-shroud, 2003) is already pointing in a new direction. In this text, there is no recognizable nation at work. The cities are denominated "Sanzívar" or "Karma Town." The narrative has multilocal elements that push the book to a wider literary geography and the characters, as a result, to a postnational self. The text activates surprising verbal patterns and anecdotal interactions in unruly language generated by an unruly self. It constitutes a denunciation against the disorder of society on the part of a shamefully (and not so shamefully) acting subject, and this abjection renders the book a raw, dark, often sad (and biting) study of life.

Despite these exciting new trends, the narrative of the 1990s has, so far, been largely ignored by serious criticism, though some writers have been promoted by their Spanish editorial houses. Unfortunately, without a critical response, literary discourses do not project themselves far beyond their existing boundaries and those permitted by the Spanish-language publishing business—that is, their own countries of origin and, occasionally, Spain.[55] The authors of such discourses are writers in search of transnational readers and critics. And yet they continue to write, even if book sales increase only minutely, and young aspirants still consider the profession worthwhile, undaunted by the postwar torpor that clouds their horizon and the inevitability that, someday, in Central America as in the rest of the Western world, writers—at least those who write literature with a capital *L*—will have become an endangered species.

The End of Political Literature

Throughout most of the twentieth century, Central American literature was conscripted to the service of nationalism because of its capacity to promote popular identifications with a given territory and history and its ability to place national symbols in everyday practices. Central American narrative textualities of the 1960s and 1970s were conceived as a type of refoundational discourses for those "new nations" to be built by revolutionary struggles. It was at this juncture that testimonial discourse operated briefly in an analogous fashion, as a sort of phantasm of a new type, or variation, of foundational discourse, presenting subaltern subjects in a progression toward a qualitatively more satisfactory self-realization.

However, the ruptures that initiated the present historical period have changed the nature of the region's literary discourse. Given that it can no longer fulfill its previous functions, if it ever truly did, it is now moving in new rhetorical and representational directions as it attempts to name an as-yet-undefined postwar present.

Undoubtedly, Central American literary discourse has been disempowered politically while, paradoxically, being empowered as a commodity by globalizing trends. We can safely assume that it now aspires more to a different illusory power, that of an exoticized commodity validated in the transnational or postnational space, even though, often enough, it is no more than a copy of its old self, a pastiche, a defanged placebo, ideal for consumption in metropolitan centers for its representation of a certain tropical frisson without the risk of genuine transgression. I will address this issue further in other chapters of this book.

2

Erotic Transgression and Recodification
of Values in Asturias's *Mulata*

In one of the many provocative scenes of Asturias's novel *Mulata de Tal* (1963, translated as *Mulata*, 1967), the aged Nana Hollín covers her naked body with leftovers so that dogs can lick her.[1] Even though in this orgiastically bestial act she ends up covered with dog urine and is so badly bitten on her genitals that she cannot cure herself afterward, Hollín enjoys herself as a child would because she believes that, at this stage of her life, only dogs dare to caress her given how old, ugly, and wrinkled she is.[2] Other visceral scenes from this novel highlight sex, bodily excretions, and personal suffering. Consider, for instance, the moment when the ugly dwarf Huasanga goes to the land of the giants to plead that her husband, Chiltic, be handed over to her. Jealous, the giantess Giroma (Chiltic's first wife, when he was still known as Celestino) throws her to the bottom of a latrine. She is rescued from a horrible death by the church sexton. He, a hunchback like all inhabitants of Tierrapaulita, tries in turn to possess her, thinking that she embodies the mushroom that straightens backbones. Huasanga is saved from this second ignominy by flies that are attracted by the excrement covering her entire body. This grotesque description is not at all atypical in this singular novel. If readers were to notice only the contents without perceiving the underlying rhythm, tone, and what Gerald Martin calls "the to-and-fro organization of the syntax," they might presume that they were simply reading a sadistic text.[3]

As I suggested in chapter 1, Asturias's *Mulata* was the most innovative novel to come out of Central America during the 1960s. The importance and complexity of this forgotten masterpiece by the 1967 Nobel laureate, one that is still practically ignored by critics to this day, warrants a special chapter.[4] My comments here are concerned with the sexual and fecal codes operating within it. This undertaking might appear odd at first, but I argue that the sexual symbology of *Mulata* articulates a reading that will allow us to understand the protagonists as masochist subjects, and their symbolic powerlessness in turn makes a political reading possible.[5] The politics might be unusual, but they represent the legacy of transgressive surrealist experience that Asturias learned from Robert Desnos in the 1920s.[6]

It may seem bizarre that at the peak of his politicization Asturias would have written what appears to be simply a sexually transgressive novel. However, we have to understand that, for Asturias, the body is always a political body as well. Following this line of thought, I will argue that, to exacerbate Guatemala's post-1954 defeat and make it visible, the masculine representation is rhetorically expelled in the text in favor of the feminine or maternal element.[7] In this lettered symbolization, the Mulata can be seen as evidence of the fantasy of the "phallic woman" in a Freudian sense, representing, among other things (because a symbol is not an allegory and embodies a multiplicity of meanings), the oppressed individual's capacity for resistance in the populist tradition that all avant-garde writers of the 1920s attempted to embrace. This fantasy is associated with a subconscious desire to represent a castration complex that one can easily trace throughout the novel, thus complicating the apparent simplicity of the Mulata as emblematic of the oppressed. This unexpected complication is typical of Asturias, who always shies away from linear simplicity. In this case, he alludes to the inner demons of the masses: contrary, irrational, ambiguous, and untrustworthy, yet seductive, dynamic, sexy, and irresistible at the same time. These symbolisms signal the paradox of populism typical in the author's work, one that celebrates the popular aspect of the masses while simultaneously yearning for an aristocratic, cosmopolitan aestheticism.

I also propose that the masochism present in the text is part of Asturias's framework to represent the sociopolitical situation of Guatemala. For him, the events of 1954—an invasion sponsored by the CIA that overthrew a democratically elected government and unleashed thirty-seven years of civil war—were devastating. Intuitively, he not only understood them as epitomizing a loss of autonomy (both personal and social), but also grasped that his nation had been the victim of the clash of two competing social systems, capitalism and communism, that could lead, from the perspective of the 1950s, to the destruction of humanity.

Earlier I stated that in certain circumstances readers might presume that they are just reading a sadistic novel. Regardless, I doubt that this is literally the case, but I do think that it is difficult for many readers to explore without fear the abundant presence of openly sexual and fecal symbolic codes and to understand their implications. It requires even more fortitude to look beyond a reading of the sexual symbology in the novel to consider a political contextualization that explains much of its meaning.[8]

We could then speak of the contextual presence of at least two broad issues at the time of the novel's conception that would lead to two different types of reading. On the one hand, Asturias was marked by the political trauma of 1954, as I have already mentioned, and by his subsequent exile, with its concomitant loss of family, country, and political ideals. On the other hand, and possibly as a psychological consequence of these traumatic events, Asturias experienced an array of deep personal conflicts that led him to study psychoanalysis. One result was the development of a very close relationship with his therapist, Dr. Simeón Falicoff.[9] It was also at this time that Asturias's creativity began to move in new directions. He went back to Robert Desnos and, through him, either discovered or rediscovered the works of Bataille, whose name he minimally knew from his Parisian years.[10] It is even possible that he questioned his sexual orientation within a broader analysis of his difficult matrimonial relations.[11] It is almost certain that he experimented with drugs and with their hallucinogenic effects.

Initial Points of Departure

If we construe masochism as framed by French critic Gilles Deleuze, there is a vast difference between the sadist subject, who enjoys control of a situation or scene, and the masochist subject.[12] The sadistic relationship enables the sadist to exercise power over an involuntary victim. The masochist, on the other hand, voluntarily establishes a relationship with a partner chosen to play the dominant role. Deleuze suggests that masochism has its roots in the symbiotic relationship that originates at the pregenital stage between a son and an orally inclined mother.[13] Linda Williams insinuates that Deleuze's vision defines masochism as a plot organized jointly by a mother and a son attempting to supplant his father and to place her as the main figure of power.[14]

I will not argue that there are no sadistic elements in *Mulata*, but I believe that they are marginal in the face of the other type of relations established by the main character, Celestino Yumí. His point of view is adopted by the narrative voice, which, as a result, codifies our reading.[15] That is, given that the bulk of the narration is, overall, presented from Yumí's perspective, it is reasonable to conceive of him as the main subject of the writing. When we do so, we verify that in all of his bilateral relations, whether with Tazol in the first part, with the Mulata later, with Catalina after that, and with his putative son Tazolito even later, there is a strong masochist component. This is reinforced by a series of metaphoric and symbolic chains that seem to constitute a rhetoric of masochism. These include the presence of urine, the theft or loss of sexual parts, the processes of transformation into giants and dwarfs, and the moon imagery that is always associated with the backside of the Mulata.

Celestino submits himself to all the other characters after he has established a "pact" with them, analogous to the masochist contracts studied by Deleuze. In fact, it is the latter who, when speaking about Sacher-Masoch, reminds us that "the middle ages distinguished with considerable insight between two types of commerce with the devil: the first resulted from possession, the second from a pact of alliance."[16] This is significant given Celestino Yumí's pacts with the devil in the novel. Paraphrasing Deleuze, the goal that a masochist sets for himself is that of escaping from transgression against the paternal figure. The masochist subject identifies with the mother while offering himself to the father as a sexual object. Because this latter action would renew the castration threat that he tries to avoid, he chooses instead to be punished by the mother as an exorcism of this potential castration. The role of the active participant is thus assumed by the mother as a result of the subject's repression of the homosexual choice. At the same time, the subject shifts the blame to her, whether by identifying her as the projection of the "bad mother" that enables him to obtain possession of his father's penis or by making this type of identification impossible by preserving the projection and substituting himself as the victim.

In the first part of the novel, Celestino establishes a "contract" with Tazol, who begins at that point to play the symbolic role of father. In this scenario, the Mulata represents the bad mother. In that capacity, she enjoys the pain and humiliation of the dwarfed Catalina, while Celestino participates meekly at her side, without being the agent of any sadist action. In the second part, the same scheme is repeated, although the characters are changed. Celestino, now transformed into the dwarf Chiltic, reproduces his previous role. But it is the demon Cashtoc who now embodies the symbolic role of the father. The giantess Giroma—Celestino's first wife, Catalina, transformed—plays the role of the bad mother. Catalina-Giroma will become dominant not only over her husband, but also over the Mulata. Both will be humiliated and will have to submit to her power. The repetition of analogous situations in different scenarios underlines the recurring compulsion of the masochist. The textual production constructs a rhetorical imaginary that disseminates signifiers in a different direction from that of their traditional signifieds. This diffusion of signifiers signals a displacement of meaning in the text, thereby pointing out the subject's need to perpetually renew his search, given that his achievements are always unsatisfactory. The Mulata acts in a first moment as the "cruel mother" with whom the masculine subject has "written" a contract (a wedding, resulting from Celestino's pact with the devil). In the second moment this role is played with the giantess Giroma, with whom Chiltic has written another contract (his first wedding, prior to the pact with the devil). The triangular nature of this relationship (besides linking the married state to possession by the devil) adds to Kossofsky-Sedwick's contention that all ménage à trois relationships imply a subliminal homosexual desire between the males; in this case, the other male is personified as the devil, a trope for how gay desire is perceived in the text. In the first part, Catalina's humiliation seals the pact between Celestino and the Mulata.[17] Celestino, however, feels sorry for his wife. He projects his own masochism in his empathy for her. Evidence of Celestino's remorse is given through his pact with Tazol:

> Yumí bit his lip. Living together, not being able to talk to her, his real wife, changed into a toy, a diversion, a doll in the hands of his other wife. Hearing his Niniloj being called Lilli Puti. . . .
>
> But if he was suffering in his self-esteem, greater yet was the redoubled affliction of his fears. Fear that the Mulata, a vandal by nature, and with no law except her own whim, would tire of the little dwarf and her clothes and would smash her somewhere, beat her, or punish her, as she did. (49)[18]

Because of this remorse, Celestino conspires with Catalina–Lilli Puti to get rid of the Mulata. In so doing, they offend Tazol, because Celestino has broken his pact with him. Tazol punishes the couple by taking away their wealth in a cataclysm unleashed by the Mulata. If the Mulata represents the homosexual self of Celestino—as I will argue later—the reading presented here is one in which the inability to confront sexual phantasms is the equivalent of a loss of power.

In the second part of the novel, the same situation repeats itself but with variants. It is the humiliation of Celestino—symbolically, the castrated father in this scenario, and also the fetishized dwarf, who is exhibited, admired, and caged, all at the same time—that seals the pact between Catalina-Giroma and her putative son Tazolito. Here it is over Celestino's body that the masochist scenario takes place, in a way analogous to that of the first part, but with a Freudian twist: Tazolito kills Chiltic-Celestino with a stone's throw.

When Cashtoc abandons Tierrapaulita, Giroma returns, followed by Celestino, who miraculously reappears after having "died" as the giant Chiltic. This detail breaks the logic of cause and effect within the fantasy ambience of the imagined geography of the text. It denotes not only Giroma's obsession with Celestino's and Giroma's not losing their power to bewitch, but also the text's obsession with not losing its bewitching power to remodel realities in the act of naming them. Within the textual sequence, this decision will generate Celestino's possession by Candanga, the Christian devil, followed by Cashtoc's fight against him. The latter is now inside the Mulata's body (and she, in turn, is inside the body of the sexton, Jerónimo de la Degollación). The fight will bring about the final destruction of Tierrapaulita.

Outside of the initial romancing of the Mulata—which, in the second part of the novel, Celestino associates more with the power of wealth than with libidinal desire—Celestino illustrates no sexual initiative. He contents himself with following and fearing the Mulata's desire in the first part, Giroma's in the second. Out-of-proportion desire is always manifested by females. The character who collects all the stolen sexual parts (I will explain this later) is also female: Huasanga. These factors suggest and push for a new way of reading this novel.

From Transgression to Masochism

In Masoch, language is persuasion and education. We have a victim in search of a torturer with whom he or she wishes to form an alliance to make his or her designs become a reality. The masochist wishes to persuade the torturer to cooperate with the victim. The masochist's submission is one more step in his or her ascension toward a certain form of ideal society. This description fits a character like Celestino Yumí much better than a sadist one would.

According to Deleuze, masochism produces a singular type of transformative truth that leads to a transcendental experience. This is the type that Yumí experiences, dying twice in the text: first as Chiltic, and then in the destruction of Tierrapaulita. Masochism, taken to its extremes, is a singularly creative form with which to fight against unconscious or unthinkable aspects of the negative experience. Yumí is unconscious of this process, of course, but he nevertheless behaves according to such premises.

In "Preface to Transgression," Foucault develops the linguistic implications of Bataille's argument. Transgression desecrates, but it is affirmative as well. Beginning with Sade, a sexuality emerged that crosses and recrosses the line with death as the only possible site from which one can organize a discourse about life. That is why transgression supplants dialectics and also supplants the type of self-reflection in which the subject is outside of the object of his thought.[19]

Through Desnos, Asturias perceived Bataille in a way uncannily close to Foucault's. For both, transgression was a linguistic phenomenon. It was to be found in the process of transgressive writing, manifesting itself at the limits of language, where rationality disappears, where the subject breaks apart. In that limit, both visualize a language that turns against the subject. This turn is not the illuminating gesture of self-reflection. Language becomes illogical, violent, denaturalizing all subjectivity, desecrating it as an act of dissipation. This process may be linked to Judith Butler's argument that we credit language with the power to cause injury because we attribute agency to it.[20] But, in its power to interpellate, language is not only capable of producing injury. It also offers us the possibility of a social existence.

Libidinous Language and a Codified Sexuality

At the *feria,* the country fair, of San Martín Chile Verde, Celestino parades himself with his fly open. This action is the consequence of his "pact" with Tazol, although it is not Celestino's agency that we see here. Rather, it is his submission. This first scene in the text, the first one to invoke a sexual display, reads: "Cheat! Tramp! Pig! Having fun among the simple people down from the hills and villages to have a good time at the fair, which was less of

a fair than a lair of wild delights" (3).[21] From the very beginning, we have
an exhibition of exuberant and free-floating signifiers naming one guilty of
an act of misbehavior. These signifiers escalate as follows: from an epithet
for one who has committed a social transgression (cheating) to one for a
person in a condition that leads to misbehavior (that of tramp) to one that
names the one guilty of this particular misbehavior (pig). It is a formula-
tion of descriptive, colloquial utterances (more evident in the original Spanish than in its English translation) that concurrently evoke an erotic delight.
We have an excess of onomatopoetic playfulness that evokes smells and colors, a parody encrypted in the very subversive nature of the enunciation.
Asturias "metaphorizes" the erotic body in the act of writing. The erotic
and the novelistic imaginary become one and the same through his linguistic inventions. In the first few lines of his discourse, he is in fact sending a
warning to the reader not to take his signifieds seriously. These meanings
are not a firm foundation on which a coherent sense of plot, in a traditional
sense, can be built, although a "plot," in the sense of a conspiracy, does
indeed take shape.[22] Asturias wants his readers to respond to literary representations that must be symbolically restaged as fantasy. He creates a hal-
lucination based on the images we perceive and not an attempt to create a
mimetic illusion of the real: "Slicker! Licker! Tricker! Cheat! Son-of-sixty-
thousand-whores! Married and, judging by his fly that fluttered like a tav-
ern curtain, in search of one of those women who go around bearing and
say they are maidens, or, in more respectable terms, go around pairing and
say they are laden!" (3).[23] The density of the linguistic wordplay subverts the
possibility of a "naturalized," simplistic comprehension of the words' social
meaning without entirely erasing their implication. The meaning is that
the character may or may not be a trickster or a cheat, that the character
may appear to be so, or that the character may be only slightly so. The text
sends the reader in two directions at once. On the one hand, it wants to see
itself as a staging of a grotesquely carnivalesque discourse, with words that
overlap more in sound than in sense, as in Foucault's articulation of an
illogical language. On the other hand, it invites the reader to a moralistic
reading by the very ubiquity of its signifiers. These ironic representations
suggest at the same time freedom, laughter, and a transgressive verbiage
charged with a dose of morality that does not become heavy only because
of the unequaled, suggestively resonant, enunciative energy:

And every new moon the dwarf took care to carry fresh plants to the Mulata. Sometimes she heard the laughter of the happy mad-woman. Grass for the Mulata and golden grains of corn for the Grumpy Bird who had converted into the guardian of that cave walled up like the cheek of a mountain. Only a pigmy could have slipped in where she did, just like a horse spider, completely without shape in his movements. Inside she would climb from rock to rock without the Mulata's noticing. Marijuana smoke, the laugh of a happy woman, and the eternal speechlessness of the moon filled the cavity. (62)[24]

The rhythm is established by this energetic enunciation of words, phrases that circle around the chains of signifiers establishing the themes of violence, eroticism, and perversity. This rhythm maneuvers the reader in between or through the "grotesque" or "unpleasant" transgressive elements, constituted primarily by scatological references. The text affirms an interest in improving human beings by exposing their violent nature. And yet, to improve human beings, it has to celebrate their virtues at the same time. Thus it is language, an abundant irruption of unstable signs, that allows the text to solve this apparent contradiction: "Lots of people, and among them this fellow with his prodigious fly that would stay open a little when it was being closed and would stay closed a little when it was being opened, as if it had been put together with buttons made from dying-with-laughter bone and buttonholes of open-close Sesame . . . now it's open, now it's closed!" (3).[25] The sequence of symbolic codes that conforms this network of signifiers begins to constitute a chain. For instance, in Spanish the "buttonholes" *(ojales)* connote a sense of yearning *(ojalá)* that points to the eye *(ojo)* that the Mulata wants to pull out (establishing one more intertextual relationship with Bataille in the process). The eye sees the bear *(oso)* that the Mulata buys, and so forth (this chain, modeled on surrealist associations, is explained in more detail by Jill Robbins in "The Abject Poetics of Asturias and Buñuel"). Obviously this wordplay is lost in the English translation, which prioritizes word meanings over wordplay. Transgressiveness is present in these codes, but in a carnivalized form. We have a situation in which performative subversion takes place not only in the subjects' bodies, but also in the linguistic signs. It would seem as if Asturias had answered, thirty years before it was posed, Butler's question about how one inscribes on the body the figure of the invisibility of the subject's internal life, its hidden dimension.[26] Asturias responded in much the same way as Butler. We have a fantasy of a fantasy, a world that does not pretend to be anything but a simulacrum. It is the transfiguration of a subject that is already a linguistic sign, given that there is no such thing as an original myth. What the text builds, then, is the illusion of a primeval myth.

At another San Martín Chile Verde *feria,* Celestino—already wealthy and free of Catalina—meets the Mulata. He sees her from the vantage point of the "macho," with a male-dominant gaze, and he names her with enunciations that represent his only sexualized agency in the entire text. The narrative description underlines a masculine subjectivity that will be questioned in the second part of the novel. The Mulata, he tells us, has a "coltish body looking for someone to tame her" (37). She is represented, on the one hand, as a sensual mulatta à la Carmen Miranda, a Brazilianized configuration (she is depicted as "rubbing against him with everything there was in her of a flexible root, a root that had been buried for centuries under ebony wood," 38). And yet, at the same time, the signs themselves are indicative of suspicious elements in such a designation. Instead of yielding to Celestino's desire, an act in accordance with the stereotype of the trope of the mulatta, this Mulata insists that he first sign a "pact" with her (she agrees to yield "only as long as you marry me," 38). Then "the Mulata's whim of receiving him from behind embittered him" (41). We thus have a masochist fantasy of a Sadean Mulata that, truthfully, is a symbolic play of signifiers. The Mulata, the text assures us, is the moon. As readers, we respect the text's authority and give credence to this designation. The moon, affirming the narrative voice, can receive men only from her backside, because this is how the "original" legend is constituted. Nevertheless, this begs the question: to what legend does the text refer? The Asturian fictionalization of a nonexistent Maya legend is built into the first part of the novel as a performative strategy that establishes the political terms in which identity is articulated. This same foundational framework is subsequently criticized and deconstructed in the second part. The premises of such legend are, indeed, false on two grounds: there is no known Guatemalan legend that articulates those Asturian imaginary terms, nor does Maya mythology conceive of a sadistic moon. In the text, however, we inherit this preconceived notion of a sadistic and animal-like Mulata:

The Mulata was terrible. When she was in a bad mood she would throw herself at him, just because he was he, trying to scratch out his eyes. And at night,

stretched out at his side, she would weep and bite him so hard that many
times her great mouth of a proud beast was smeared with blood, blood that
it savored and swallowed, while she scratched him over and over as she touched
him, and her white eyes would show no pupils, her breasts would be teary
with sweat. (42–43)[27]

From this description, another sequence of symbolic codes is threaded to
the previous network of signifiers. The "eye" *(ojo)* that unifies the two is
associated with biting, smearing, blood, scratching *(arañar* in Spanish). The
eye anticipates the Spider *(Araña* in Spanish), the transformed identity of
Father Chimalpín in the second part (thus the Spider is dressed in a cassock).[28] This chain is tied to sweating or crying, which conforms to part of
the urination chain as well. The white eyes without any pupils are another
allusion to Bataille's *Histoire de l'oeil* (1928, translated as *Story of the Eye,*
1987),[29] explicitly adding another dimension of reading (Bataille's novel is
also a masochistic novel, as John Phillips has argued).[30]

We learn something else. The Mulata never has a proper name, embodying instead the trope of a fetishized mulatta. In the first part of the novel,
the discourse is insistent that she must always be associated with the moon.
But though in the alleged mythical conception of this reading her role would
be that of a goddess, a sacred being by implication, the text oxymoronically
refers to her as a "mulata de tal."[31] The Asturian expression alludes to
the Spanish phrase *de tal por cual,* which is Central American slang for a
vulgar, ordinary woman. It is a composite denoting its own chain of pejorative meaning through an implied downward descent: ordinary-bastard-
prostitute. A public woman, likely lacking a "decent" birth, is by implication
a bastard, in the traditional sense of the children of the Malinche. Why
would a rich man, in search of social status (in an alleged mimetic plot)
marry an abject figure the same day he meets her? Besides, the moon, other
than being represented as a feminine figure in a Maya context, is also represented as a Freudian one. In this particular case, we have a sadistic and
hermaphroditic moon that, according to the text, believes the myth that
Celestino has golden bones, another tall tale deconstructed in the very last
chapter: "I don't know what she is, but she isn't a man and she isn't a woman
either. She doesn't have enough inky-dinky for a man and she has too much
dinky-inky for a woman. Since you've never seen her from the front . . ."
(53).[32] The Mulata plays the emblematic role—in a Freudian reading of

sadomasochism, analogous to Deleuze's own—of a "phallic woman." She threatens Celestino with symbolic castration. Because she also represents the moon, the Law of the Mother, this implies a fear of castration from the mother as well. To this mix we have to add the fact that the dwarf Catalina becomes a toy or fetish object. According to Freud, all fetish objects are substitutes for the phallus a woman has lost. They are a mechanism for assuaging the fear of castration of masculine subjects.[33] If the simulacrum of the phallus is at the base of Sadean representation, the fear of losing it is at the base of Asturian representation.[34]

When Catalina convinces the Mulata to go to the cave where the moon sleeps, we confirm that, in this illusory simulation, only women deceive others. Only women lie, and only women exercise power. Fear of women becomes symptomatic of fear of the mother figure. In this way the masculine subject of this narration establishes another chain of symbolic castrations that lead to the battles with the two cassocked priests in the second part: "The priest let it be known that he was coming. The noise of the clapper of his legs and feet beneath the bell of his cassock" (194).[35] Feminized by their clothing, these priests are echoes of victims or martyrs. They fear, above all, to be "possessed" (by devils, of course, which, in a Freudian fashion, can be interpreted as representing the paternal phallus).

When Celestino and Catalina head for Tierrapaulita to learn black magic, they are no longer interested in money. Now they want power. Both configurations are tropes of systems that tempt the couple. Because of these temptations, they will later be possessed by both "Earth-born" and Christian demons. Indeed, in the original Spanish, "Earth-born demons" are explicitly Maya, while Christian demons are Spanish, a nuance lost in the English translation. This representation alludes to a simulacrum of political systems in conflict with each other, a clash of differing views of the world.[36] In this reading, the masculine subject is always the object of temptation. In the story, Catalina becomes a sorcerer and accumulates power, but only in exchange for another pact with Tazol. A sterile woman unable to bear children, Catalina becomes the mother of the Earth-born demon's son, Tazolito: "Catalina squatted down, big-bellied, legless, as if she had to pass water, and she did, the water of a woman pregnant by Tazol" (108).[37] And later: "Catalina felt gas on her stomach, but although the parcel she was carrying was using her womb as a drum, he was beating it with the palm of his hand. It was not gas. The heir of Tazol, whom she was carrying in her belly, was talking to her from between her buttocks, with a compressed voice, as if he could not express himself well between those enormous cheeks that were inseparable because they were so fat" (111–12).[38] Tazolito establishes a new pact with Catalina. If she frees his father, he will protect the couple. Tazol then intercedes with Cashtoc, a more powerful Earth-born demon who rules Tierrapaulita, on the couple's behalf. At this point, Catalina substitutes for the Mulata as the "phallic," or castrating, woman. She becomes the "red" (i.e., communist) wife in the political interpretation, the one who leads her husband to perdition, much like María Vilanova, the wife of Guatemala's president Jacobo Arbenz (1950–54), who allegedly influenced her husband to favor communists, leading to the U.S. invasion in 1954. As a masochist subject, Celestino will become excited by Giroma's power, but he will also feel threatened by her newly gained power to castrate. Indeed, as Giroma, Catalina becomes a giantess and turns Celestino into a dwarf renamed Chiltic. We can easily decode this inverse repetition of the previous situation. That Catalina now cries and urinates in intimate situations, much as had the Mulata when she threatened Celestino in the first part of the book, relieves his anxiety. The liquids (urine, tears) make the vulva visible, easing the fear of castration. At this moment in the text, the dwarf Chiltic acquires stilts, and his ability to walk on them earns him recognition among the townspeople. The masculine fear of castration is quelled by the stilts, fetish objects of symbolic phalluses.

The narration then shifts to the cycle of excrement. Tazolito is born from Catalina's anus, while she squats on the ground to urinate. Nana Hollín covers her naked body with food so that dogs can lick her, the scene described at the beginning of this chapter. Again, filth is associated with the mother figure. Indeed, Phillips has already pointed out how in *Histoire de l'oeil* Bataille had established a correlation between the moon, filth, blood from the vagina, and bad smells: "I cared only for what is classified as dirty. . . . I associate the moon with the vaginal blood of mothers, sisters, that is, their menstrua with their sickening stench."[39]

In a midnight mass at Christmastime, Tierrapaulita's priest decides to marry Chiltic to Huasanga, because both are dwarfs.[40] Jealous, Giroma throws her to the bottom of a latrine, as I described earlier. Thinking that she is a clay or mud doll because she is covered with excrement, the sexton tries to possess the doll. He is prevented from doing so by thousands of flies that cover her body. Afterward, Huasanga goes to the dance of the giants nearly naked, wearing a fluorescent breech clout, accompanied by a monkey-shaped figure made of flies. This image is an illusion of how abjection has been transformed, becoming an aesthetic representation.[41] In the ensuing fight between Huasanga and Giroma, the former pulls off Catalina's genitals, symbolically reactivating the fear of castration. This act demonstrates the need to punish the "phallic woman" (the monkey made out of flies prevents Tazolito from rescuing his mother's sexual organs, linking abjection with sexual loss). This initiates the sequence of vulva thefts that will continue to the very end of the novel. Female genitalia acquire the value of a fetish object from a semiotic as well as a psychoanalytical point of view. In a contradictory way, the emphasis on the feminine sex proclaims its illusory superiority. The theft of the female sex organs implies the impossibility of orgasm, a negation of feminine pleasure. But it also makes it impossible for the masculine subject to negate with his phallus the difference between the sexes. Thus, the stealing of female genitalia has repercussions for the masculine subject as well: it signals his impotence.

In Deleuze's scenario, when a woman acquires power, the masculine subject makes a contract with this "ideal woman," the phallic woman, so as to be reborn in her arms. This situation corresponds to Celestino's life in the text. His transformation from a dwarf to a giant is a simulacrum of his recuperation of masculine prowess, but it is an illusion generated by Giroma to distance him from Huasanga. Having succeeded, Giroma then incites Tazolito to kill him with a stone's throw, making it clear that she controls Chiltic's destiny. Thereafter, Celestino is reborn a great sorcerer, but he is only an instrument of Giroma and Candanga. Indeed, the only action he initiates after seducing the Mulata is his fight with Father Chimalpín, the (cassocked) Spider. Even in this deed, he is possessed by Candanga. Besides, the priest is an emblematic figure of the Mulata, who had previously entered the body of Jerónimo de la Degollación, thereby underlining the eminently homosexual nature of the sexton, of the Mulata herself, and of Celestino's desire.

This climactic scene—in every sense of the term—is conditioned by the sequence of urine and excrement imagery in the text. The sexton tells Celestino the story of the chamber-potters, "under whose ample black capes ladies of quality could urinate silently and maidens, too, could make a flutey sound as they produced their lakes of beer" (207).[42] But the chamber-potter could read the true nature of subjects by interpreting their excretions. Therefore, he exercised power over the person urinating.[43]

Abruptly the sexton interrupts his tale. He unfurls his cape, "using the pretext of presenting [Celestino] with the basin (he tried) to despoil him of his male attributes" (210).[44] In actuality, Jerónimo de la Degollación makes an effort to possess Celestino. This is clearly a homosexual gesture. But Jerónimo is also the Mulata, the first phallic woman. This action complicates the sexual symbology for the reader. Celestino has never stopped desiring the Mulata, a sign implying a minimal recognition of his homosexual desire. Upon being openly confronted by Jerónimo, however, Celestino reacts as any Latin American *macho* would: he is incapable of recognizing his desire. The problem for the reader is that these events are not presented in a realistic-mimetic type of representation. They appear as an illusion. Celestino suddenly produces thousands of erections, as long thorns grow from the many smallpox scars covering his entire body and transform him into a gigantic porcupine. He then attacks Jerónimo—who has made his desire evident—and leaves him nearly dead. This action can be seen as an attempt to destroy the "perversion" that he feels inside himself. Soon thereafter, he goes after the Spider, Father Chimalpín, an emblem of homosexuality. We have, then, a situation in which Celestino's (the giant porcupine's) response is both fantastic and phantasmatic. He attempts to penetrate or perforate the bodies of Jerónimo, the Mulata, and the priest in imaginary ways with his barbs or penises. Because the priest can be seen as his father (*priest* in Spanish is *padre,* the same word as that used for *father,* and that is how he is addressed in the original Spanish), this turns the confrontational battle into a reproduction of his psychological struggle with the paternal image. The subject's hatred of the paternal image can be read in this instance as a recognition of the homosexual tendencies of the father and as a deconstruction of the virile subject.

As Deleuze points out, what the masochist subject cannot stand is not so much a transgression against the father; rather, it is that of having the questionably virile personality of the father residing inside himself, reflecting in this manner the "machista" (male chauvinist) performative behavior of the father.[45] Celestino has to "pay" for transforming himself into a porcupine or father. With the active intervention of the mother (Giroma) and her fetish object (Huasanga), Celestino is definitively stripped of his father's power. He ends up paralyzed, and the Mulata is reduced to half of what she was: one arm, one leg, one eye, and so forth. The exorcism of the father figure implies the loss of the sexual organ and an ensuing impotence.

From that point on, sexual excesses are attributed to Catalina, the new phallic woman. A skeletal woman is summoned by one of the great wizards to complete the body of the Mulata by merging both bodies into one. The skeletal woman tells the Mulata that, when night falls, Catalina restores movement to her paralyzed husband to give free rein to her sexual furor, but she gets jealous when she discovers that Celestino is fantasizing about the Mulata while having sex with her, in her incarnation as Giroma. Even reduced virtually to the status of a dildo, a machine of *jouissance,* Celestino cannot get rid of his homosexual desire. This takes us to the end of the novel, where Celestino's second death and the destruction of Tierrapaulita imply the final expulsion of the paternal figure.

Transgressive Power as a Phantasmatic Political Representation

If we see the text as a symbolic recodification of Guatemala's political experience, a masochist reading acquires a new meaning. The subject's incapacity to live with his mother and father figures implies the impossibility of finding common spaces in which to forge social, communal, or national ties. The only elements left floating in the text's vast sea of discursivity are the titanic clashes between demons with hybrid indigenous traits and Christian demons within geographical confines that resemble those of Guatemala. Then the text concludes with the apocalyptic destruction of Tierrapaulita. Why?

The invasion in 1954, sponsored by the CIA, brought to an abrupt end the modernizing process that had enfranchised diverse sectors of the Guatemalan community. The country went from a phase of democratic, populist Ladino governments during the period from 1944 to 1954 to one of national disintegration. The latter implied the call for an armed uprising as the only possible way to reconstitute the state, mythified in the memory of a happier time, a quieter time, a more peaceful time obliterated in a violent, desperate present. Due to this catastrophic situation, Asturias could no longer conceive of anything but the fragmentation of a cultural landscape dominated by self-destruction and irrational anger, in which President Arévalo's dream of forging a new, modern nation (1945–50) had been reduced to the status of one more false hope. This political dystopia explains why Asturias could no longer visualize any social coherence and could articulate only a semblance of a community through linguistic artifices expressing images whose spatial and temporal substance have lost all historical texture and density.

In the desolate landscape left after the battle of Guatemala had been lost, he could only gather heterogeneous signs and a multiplicity of voices clamoring for meaning without ever finding it. That is why Prieto argues that Celestino Yumí and Catarina Zabala represent the antithesis of Goyo Yic and María Tecún, hero and heroine of Asturias's earlier novel *Hombres de maíz* (1949, translated as *Men of Maize,* 1995).[46] The metafictitious value of the text can be appreciated only when the reader understands that this narrative's simulacrum is the codified chronicle of the destruction of a nation.

The initial "Faustian pact" of the text has, in this political reading, a different signification. It represents an interest on the part of Celestino to sell himself to "capitalism," understanding the latter as a trope. In this scheme, acquiring capital becomes synonymous with "sinning," that is, opening one's soul to the devil. Its true objective consists of signaling both metaphorically and ironically that when someone sells out to a superior force, it is the equivalent of being possessed by the devil. When this subject (be it an individual, as in the text, or a nation, as in the political reading of the text) becomes the junior partner of a greater power (be it Tazol or the United States), it will be humiliated; this is the price to be paid for despoiling one's neighbors and rising above them in the pecking order. As this process of selling out is set in motion, it initiates a loss of identity that ends in the disintegration of the subject. This is evident in the novel when, in exchange for all the wealth that Tazol offers Celestino, the latter is forced to walk with his fly open at the *feria* of San Martín Chile Verde. Celestino still has agency, but he has also become the "plaything" of a greater force, capitalism, which is understood here no longer just as a trope but also as an agent that enables the injurious actions of the subject to take place. This is the basis of the moral of the story, one that enables the reader to demand accountability from the text's characters. At the end of the first part of the novel, Cashtoc paradoxically plays the role of a moralist. He says:

> Real men, the ones made out of corn, have stopped existing in reality and have become fictitious creatures, since they did not live for the community, and that is why they should have been suppressed. That is why I annihilated them with my Major Giants, and just as long as they do not reform, I will annihilate all of those who forget, deny or reject their condition as kernels of corn, part of an ear, and become self-centered, egotistical, individualists . . . until they finally change into solitary beings, into puppets lacking any senses! (173)[47]

In a brilliant essay, Susan Rubin Suleiman reminds us of the argument that Derrida makes in his 1967 analysis of Bataille's work.[48] We could apply the same argument to *Mulata* that Derrida makes, namely, that the transgression of discursive rules implies a transgression of the law in general: "Discourse only exists in terms of positing the norm and value of meaning" (316), and this is the foundational element of legality.[49] Indeed, for Asturias, legality was transgressed by the U.S. invasion of 1954. The nation, alongside Asturian literary production, was marked by a tenebrous sense of living on the borderline of an unnamable present that felt to him like a living hell. Consequently, the strategies of representation that had constituted *Hombres de maíz* had become obsolete. Reading the new signs of an uncertain banishment, of an unwelcome uprootedness, in his post-1954 discursivity Asturias tried to gather metonymically the transgression of Guatemalan law that had fragmented his world. He accomplished this by destroying the value of discursive sense, as represented by the modernizing rationality that articulated the logic of 1944–54. Metaphorically speaking, and in colloquial Guatemalan terms, the country was a victim of the "evil eye," and the eye is a predominant trope in *Mulata* as in Bataille's *Histoire de l'oeil*. The Guatemalan progressive dream was transformed into a chaotic nightmare. Asturias captured this national dread through erotic transgression. In so doing, he anticipated Sollers's argument that the body has become the fundamental referent of discursive violations in modern literature.[50]

Let us return now to the beginning of *Mulata*. Tazol, who incites Celestino to take the road to perdition, is described as the demon of the dry leaves of maize. It is the same maize that generates life in *Hombres de maíz*. In this case, the maize has become the bedeviled shadow of itself, and its dry leaves have been transformed into a demon. Transgression slides here from experience to representation. Asturias lives his country's invasion as a "perversion" that opposes the reproductive role of society. *Mulata* thus employs sexuality, in opposition to reproductive sexual activity, as the text's axis. Eroticism is undoubtedly revealing of Asturias's libidinal phantasms. But it can also be read as a convenient backdrop against which the linguistic transgression of the written production is staged as a discursive practice that exceeds the traditional limitations of sense, textual unity, and representation, factors analogous to the political grounds of the 1954 invasion. The experience of transgression articulated by Asturias is inseparable from his consciousness of the frontiers, the borders, that have been violated. Here the enunciation "violated border"—especially in its Spanish sense, where "violation" and "rape" are one and the same—can be understood in the double entendre of both its textual representation and its extratextual context. The representation of the Catholic tradition as emblematic of ethics, morality, and communal principles was transgressed by the hierarchical support given, either tacitly or actively and aggressively, to the country's invasion and to the "deconstruction" of its political system. The invasion destroyed all possibility of reaffirming a new model of a hybrid national state that could preserve a Mestizo community surrounded by Maya symbology.[51] Asturian language, then, expresses all this destruction by way of another transgression, this time a linguistic one, accentuated by carnivalesque excesses. The body of the nation was dismembered by crooked people, and in *Mulata* the characters' bodies are dismembered as well, or else represented as crooked, in a very literal way. But language is twisted as well, and it points toward fragmentation, a lack of completion, and an absence of logical rationality. These absences and incompletions are emblematic of a body (both an individual *and* a social body) that has lost all integrity.[52] To paraphrase Suleiman, the meaning of *Mulata*—its "sense," if one may—resides, in a Derridean way, in the novel's own commentary about its lack of sense, its senselessness. It is a text that tries to displace the rationalism that justified Guatemala's invasion as a kind of death. The text accordingly places itself beyond a facile, rational comprehension and in a space that opposes eroticism with death. Its aim is to break the limits of consciousness so as then to be able to call for its reappearance, now constituted as a new form of political consciousness. The text stages a total lack of modesty with the goal of calling for a return to it.

Circulating freely on the symbolic horizon of the text—in this nightmarish landscape—are both demons, Cashtoc and Candanga, who deny agency to all other subjects. They manipulate them as puppet masters in their effort to impose their respective system. The subjects' representation enters into a crisis because both demons play the metonymic or metaphoric role of masters, sources of power/knowledge, and the only subjects exercising a panoptic vision of their own domination. The human characters are all "crazy" (the same analysis made of all the priests represented in the text by Tiopagrito, a minor character himself) in a Foucauldian sense: they are incapable of communicating rationally because they lack a common language. They are capable of uttering only fragmented dialogues that denote an absence of sense, a lack that points to the final destruction generated by the clash between opposing systems. The camouflaged representation of the political unconscious metonymically stages the consequences of the invasion and the defeat of the nationalist project. The Guatemalan invasion happened as a result of a larger conflict between superpowers, a struggle between two contending demons, the United States and the Soviet Union. Therefore, the subjects' identity was dissolved beyond its ethnic specificity because the possibilities of bringing their symbolic horizon to fruition were denied by the 1954 invasion and because the possibilities of survival would be forever denied while both superpowers remained on an apocalyptic collision course that denied true agency to all subjects. We are left, then, only with the traces made by both demons and with those of the systems for which they stood, which are camouflaged by the actions of their respective victims. Both demons are the true actors of the perverse final destruction where, synechdochically, the text finally confronts its own fears. Of human beings there remains only a symbolic echo of a remote past: "It was dawning on the mountain of the wild boars. A sun soaked in indigo, a land soaked in blue. Crags covered with blue-greenish lichens on which the tusks of the Sauvages had drawn capricious signs. Could that be their way of writing? Did they keep their annals in those drawings made with the tips of their tusks?" (74).[53]

In this passage we clearly see the contrast between Celestino and Catalina's abject world and the apparently childish simplicity enjoyed by the "Sauvages." We are also told that the Sauvages were once good people, but were transformed into wild boars by the devils because they refused to be dehumanized. They are equivocally designated Sauvages by the very signification of that word, a deliberate misspelling of *savage* (*salvajo* instead of *salvaje* in the original Spanish) that implies an opposite meaning. Something similar happened to many of Guatemala's citizens in 1954, including Asturias himself: they were labeled "communists" when they were, in fact, democrats. They were punished for their stand and transformed into an animal-like condition. In reality, the Sauvages are the only truly civilized subjects in the entire text.

The Sauvages also represent the Mayas and their lost culture. The description of them is accompanied by a meditation about the nature of writing, framed as undecipherable hieroglyphics that secretly articulate the collective memory of a lost splendor. The reference to hieroglyphic writing, of

course, immediately evokes classical Maya culture. Since the nineteenth century, Maya civilization has been a trope for "lost" civilizations, a fantasylike
conception—in the eyes of many Westerners and Guatemalans as well—of
a better world that has been annihilated. Instead we are left with the bedeviled, perverse world of the text's imaginary present, which has converted
the "noble savages" into their polar opposite. It is a world with competing
systems on a collision course, a path that will lead to the ultimate destruction narrated in the novel's last chapter. Tierrapaulita is destroyed by "white
phosphorus," that is, the "whitening" of the Americas, but the image of its
destruction is also linked to the historical present by an atomic bomb.

The Originality of the Text

Prieto affirms that *Mulata* is "a delirious fable that breaks with all canonical definitions of taste, reason, and order." He emphasizes its carnivalesque
nature while pointing out the grotesque in its irrational laughter, disguises,
festivities, and popular-festive merriment. This leads him to make another
assertion: "I don't necessarily assume that Asturias was familiar with the
work of Bakhtin, although this is by no means impossible."[54]

Prieto also claims that Asturias was influenced by Callois, Mauss, and
Bataille.[55] It is certainly credible that he would have read some Callois or
Mauss in the 1920s. And yet it is also doubtful that he would have based his
most mature creative project on old notes of his youthful readings, dating
back thirty years. In addition, it is rather reductionist to assert that Asturias
turned to Callois, Mauss, and Bataille for "theoretical guidance." It is equally
impossible that Asturias would have been familiar with Bakhtin's work on
carnival, which did not even circulate in the Soviet Union until it was re-
edited in 1963 (in Russian) and was not known in the West until a French
translation came out at the end of the 1960s. What is more, Asturias was
not a scholar in the traditional sense of the term. He did not keep tabs on
cutting-edge theoretical material, nor did he speak or read Russian, although
he did speak French.

There are two flaws in Prieto's otherwise brilliant work. On the one hand,
he assumes that a Latin American writer would need to follow a path previously opened by European theorists, and on the other, he presupposes that
a writer needs a theoretical orientation in order to generate a creative act.
In the realm of ideas, there is no such thing as a linear, progressive history

that moves from the "center" to its periphery. In fact, ideas can be rediscovered, reconceptualized, or reprocessed by just about anyone, which is why
artists on the periphery can appear to prefigure theoretical writings from
the center.[56] *Mulata*'s grotesque eroticism is not an imitation or a mechanical reproduction of theoretical propositions. Asturias did not read Bataille
and then restage his work with Maya characters, as a peculiar sort of a
Hollywood-type remake. He was possibly aware of Bataille's work from very
early on, and he was even more familiar with Desnos, but not so much
because he reread them constantly. Instead, I suggest that the coincidence
of the similarities in their work is due to their similar genealogical backgrounds in Catholicism. The latter negates carnality and sexual gratifica-
tion, as Pope Benedict XVI has reminded us recently. It negates all forms of
sexuality except the one leading to procreation. Asturias and Bataille had
other parallel features. They both underwent a psychological crisis in the
process of unmasking the power of their respective fathers, whom they had
both previously perceived as all-powerful forces. Both were traumatized
sons who finally confronted their fathers, symbolically staging this conflict
over their mothers' bodies.[57]

Following this line of thinking, we should also not forget that French
critics did not associate the violation of sexual taboos with the violation of
discursive norms until the middle of the 1960s. Barthes, Kristeva, Sollers,
Blanchot, and Foucault "rediscovered" Bataille for the first time, transforming him posthumously into a cultural hero.[58] Asturias, however, performed
this transgression in his *Leyendas de Guatemala* (1930, translated as *The
Mirror of Lida Sal: Tales Based on Mayan Myths and Guatemalan Legends,*
1997), reaffirmed it with *Hombres de maíz* (1949), and raised it to its highest expression in *Mulata*, published in 1963, the same year that Bataille died.
In *Mulata* Asturias was a precursor, not a follower, of an erotic-transgressive
fashion that took off after the end of the 1960s. He was also a precursor to
postmodern literature, which in Latin America is associated with what has
been labeled "postboom" narrative to indicate the production emerging after
the "literary boom" of the 1960s (e.g., that of García Márquez, Fuentes, Vargas Llosa, and Cortázar, among others).[59]

To creatively conceive his apocalyptic vision, Asturias did not need theoretical guidance from anyone. All he needed to conceive a new creation, to
invent something new, were a few scattered elements at hand. He had studied psychoanalysis, and he possibly recycled ideas he had previously read

in old books that he vaguely remembered in the mid-1950s, or else he borrowed a few traits from Vasconcelos, conceivably from his own notes from
the late 1920s or early 1930s,[60] but he did not do this in a mechanical way.
With an abundance of roguery or mischief, as well as a vital creative strength
that was his life's only anchor, he dug deep into his unconscious—the personal as well as the social—to imagine a way of resituating himself in the
world. Perhaps he reinvented Mauss. But he did not use him for theoretical
guidance. He certainly had a promiscuous relationship with vaguely remembered texts or else with those he simply thought he had dreamt. They were
useful as points of departure from which to creatively wrestle with his
phantasms and to reconstitute them in a text that orders itself arbitrarily in
discursive elements, not thematic ones. The novel does not try to legitimize
itself on a rational plane that would consciously recognize an intertextual
relationship with Mauss or Callois. On the contrary, it is a decentered text
whose plurality of voices and rhythms emerge in enunciations that correspond to alternative forms of knowledge, that is to say, apparitional traces
of postmodern bricolage. With a few scattered elements at hand, the writer
can reinvent a whole world.

3

Identity or Literariness: The Emergence of a New Maya Literature

entral American narrative textuality has been labeled an "invisible literature," one that few people read outside of its area of origin due to techniques of market domination.[1] This invisibility has a great deal to do with the circulation of cultural products from and in the peripheries, which I label the "marginality of marginality" to evoke the ways that critical disciplines and practices constitute the relevant subjects of literary production and reproduce the invisibility of certain works within hegemonic centers of cultural decision making. This form of "written invisibility" is also related to the contradictions generated by a literature encoded within an indigenous source, such as the Maya-K'iché text *Popol Vuh* (1540s).[2] Even contemporary symbolic figurations in Central American literature differ in significant ways from traditional Western parameters, rendering many of its signs "illegible." This is a problematic issue for critics who either are unfamiliar with this Mesoamerican cultural matrix or favor urban or metropolitan topics as distinctive signs of Latin American literature's modernity.

In chapter 1 I considered the general literary tendencies that prevailed in Ladino or mestizo cultural-symbolic zones during the guerrilla period so as to better reflect on the new forms emerging in the 1990s. I proceeded to present, in chapter 2, an analysis of Asturias's *Mulata de tal*, contending that the novel's importance and complexity warrant a particular reconsideration of this work, for it signals a phantasmatic delineation of a Maya cosmogony. In this chapter I will trace a short genealogy of the *Popol Vuh*, working my way up to Gloria Guardia's *El último juego* (The last game, 1977) and Roberto Armijo's *El asma de Leviatán* (Leviathan's asthma, 1990) while incorporating some reflections on Augusto Monterroso's work and on Asturias's *Hombres de maíz* (1949, translated as *Men of Maize*, 1995). I examine both the indigenous "Mongolian spot" that exists at the heart of mestizo literariness and the perverse role that racism has played in Central America's referential symbolic horizon.[3] I conclude by contrasting contemporary Maya literature to mestizo production, not only to make evident that their parallel lives inevitably lead to fissures in our understanding of what Central American literature might be, but also to propose a different conception of the present-day meaning of "literature." I argue that certain subaltern forms of textual knowledge can, and do, become functional for contemporary social movements claiming political agency.

A Traditional Vision Prefabricated in the 1960s

Augusto Monterroso, winner of Spain's Prince of Asturias literary award in 2000, recounts in *Los buscadores de oro* (The gold diggers, 1994) that on 23 April 1986, at sixty-five years of age, he was invited to Siena, Italy, shortly after his work had been acclaimed in Spain. After being introduced with lavish praise, he began by saying, "Despite what Professor Melis has said, it is quite probable that you don't know who is about to speak to you. I will start by recognizing that I am an unknown author or, perhaps more accurately, an ignored one." He went on to poignantly describe the way he had felt thirty years earlier, weeping at the humiliation of his exile. He realized that he had arrived at "the highest point to which I could aspire as an author from the fourth world of Central America, which was almost like coming from the very first world, from the primal innocence alluded to by Don Luis de Góngora."[4]

Monterroso had not yet arrived at the highest point of his career. That happened when he was awarded the Prince of Asturias literary award, which, alongside the Premio Cervantes, is one of the most important literary awards in the Spanish language. Upon receiving the award, Monterroso commented:

> Central America, as Eduardo Torres could have said it, has always been de-feated, both by nature and by enemy ships. . . . But it is my duty to point out, once more, that, as the centuries have gone by, it has not only been bananas that we have produced. I will remind you that our Maya ancestors, refined astronomers and mathematicians who invented zero as a mathematical concept

before any other civilization, had their own cosmogony in what we know today as the *Popol Vuh,* the national book of the K'ichés, mythological, poetic, and mysterious.[5]

This is a curious way for Mayas to emerge into public recognition. Monterroso had written about Maya motifs only once, in his first collection of stories dating from the mid-1950s. Yet he acknowledges a literary genealogy traced from the *Popol Vuh* (without ever reneging on Cervantes). Indeed, Central America is the locus of a regional literature that bears the mark of its origin—the Mongolian spot of its Maya *Popol Vuh* origins. When we speak of the invisibility of this literature, its "ethnic roots" cannot be discounted as a possible explanation for its exclusion from cosmopolitan literary society. At the same time, the Mongolian spot stands as a trope for ethnic identity.

Dr. Erwin Bälz (1849–1913) was a German internist, anthropologist, and personal physician of the Japanese imperial family. He traveled to Japan to teach Western medicine at Todai (Tokyo) University. While in this position Dr. Bälz became personal physician to Crown Prince Yoshihito, subsequently Emperor Taisho, and was a cofounder of modern medicine in Japan. As a matter of curiosity, Dr. Bälz is also the father of the modern martial arts. He found the martial arts of the past to be of value to promote physical fitness, and he proposed that the students at Tokyo University begin to study *kenjutsu,* the art of Japanese sword fighting, as an excellent method of physical fitness training. Up to that time, martial arts had been considered signs of feudal barbarism by a country yearning for modernity, indeed an appropriate analogy to the role of the Mongolian spot in Guatemala. Regarding the topic of this chapter, in 1885 Bälz published a paper in a German anthropological journal calling attention to an unrecorded feature among Japanese babies: very often infants were born with a dark blue stain low on the back that gradually faded and disappeared after about a year. He called the stain "Mongolische Flecken" (Mongolian spots). During the early years of the twentieth century, such stains were described in many other peoples; they even came to be associated with Jewish origin and were renamed Semitic spots or stains. Certainly these blue-black stains are not exclusive to Mongolian people, and the name is unsuitable because it has no relationship to mongolism (Down syndrome).

According to this nineteenth-century anthropological myth of the Mongolian spot, then, descendants of indigenous peoples were born with a purplish spot in the small of the back, a physical signature of sorts of the Mongolian lineage of the indigenous peoples of the Americas. In Guatemala, this led to a widespread fear of being born with a Mongolian spot and thus harboring physical evidence of mestizos' mongrel origin though attempting to pass for "white." It was a principal factor in preventing the development of American-style gyms in the earlier part of the twentieth century. Men and women refused to allow anybody else to see them naked, allegedly because of Catholic modesty. In reality, it was because of their fear of having a Mongolian spot detected on their bodies, despite the well-known "fact" that this spot disappeared a few months after birth. Nevertheless, it remained an invisible scar, a phantasm of an inferiority complex, forever.

As a postscript to this craze, in the 1960s and 1970s it became radical chic for middle-class leftists to claim to harbor a Mongolian spot, and some went so far as to paint false ones on their bodies to justify their indigenous ancestry and make claims within the Central American left. Indeed, as Melissa Biggs indicates, in Mexico's National Museum of Anthropology a wall map illustrates the prevalence of the Mongolian spot to this day. The text says that the spot is hereditary and considered original to Asiatic populations. According to the text, its appearance in other human groups reveals the *mestizaje* (mixing) that exists on all continents. As further proof of intercontinental mixing, the text offers the "Mongolian eye." A helpful map compares the parts of the world in which the "Mongolian" and the "European" eye prevail.[6]

In pointing out the earliest ("Adamic") stage of the Latin American literary boom, Idelber Avelar notes that

> Emir Rodríguez Monegal curiously recasts the age-old Latin American polarity between the urban and the rural by arguing that boom novels are the proof that the conflict, now transcended for good, had been false from the beginning: . . . Monegal's strategy . . . systematically associates the rural with simplism and preartistic primitivism: "The classic opposition between urban and rural novels has been dissolved at its base. . . . Those narratives of peasants and jungles, with two-dimensional characters and mechanical, documentary expositions are now long gone."[7]

He goes on to observe that, for the Uruguayan critic, "the 'overcoming' of the dichotomy was conceived as the elimination of one of its terms." After stressing the fact that some of the boom novels that Monegal defended were indeed rural or semirural, such as *Cien años de soledad* (1967, translated as *One Hundred Years of Solitude,* 1970), by Gabriel García Márquez; *Pedro Páramo* (1955, translated as *Pedro Paramo,* 1994), by Juan Rulfo; *La casa verde* (1965, translated as *The Green House,* 1968), by Mario Vargas Llosa; and *Grande Sertão: Veredas* (1955, translated as *The Devil to Pay in the Backlands,* 1963), by João Guimarães Rosa. Avelar concludes that the real issue was that for the boom's discursive imaginary, the urban became synonymous with the universal.[8] To Avelar's conclusion I would add that the urban was conceived of as a metropolitan or modern space precisely because it was a trope for European modernity. It was a secure identitary space for hybrid Latin Americans fearing a slide toward mongrelization, in opposition to the trope for rural Latin America essentialized as primarily an indigenous or African space. Implicit in that oppositional binary, of course, was a racialized recycling of Sarmiento's "civilization or barbarism" dictum.[9] In this logic, to be a metropolitan or modern subject, one had to be "white." Because race was an unacknowledged issue in Latin America during the 1960s, the dominant urban, cosmopolitan "liberal" (signifying a leftist, middle-class chic) thinking was fundamentally racist, although its appearance was disguised as "modern." A cultural renaissance of indigenous peoples or Afrolatinos within modern parameters was inconceivable at the time, confirming the unacknowledged racism prevalent among most Latin American literate people.

Gerald Martin has written that Monegal criticized Asturias's reception of the 1967 Nobel Prize for literature for *Mulata de tal* because he saw his novel as the embodiment of the rural novel.[10] He adds that Angel Rama was equally blind to Asturias's merits. Martin concludes that these critics deliberately suppressed knowledge of Asturias. Instead, I would argue that there is a racist bias in their arguments. That is, literature written by writers originating in the marginality of marginality was automatically dismissed as "premodern" on the grounds that such writers merely "copied" their readily available indigenous sources. By contrast, those emphasizing urban or metropolitan topics were celebrated primarily for accentuating their European roots in the process of elaborating stylistic experimentations. According to this bias, urban or cosmopolitan writers were read (and celebrated) for innovative styles, whereas writers such as Asturias were read (and panned) for content, while their equally innovative styles went ignored. Once their work had been found guilty of essentialized primitivism, it was simply assumed

by those with metropolitan "taste" that no possible notion of style or textual strategy could be submerged there. Embedded in this prejudice (besides
ignorance of the complexity of texts such as the *Popol Vuh*) was the traditional conceptualization of *mestizaje* by Mexican anthropology attributed to
Gonzalo Aguirre Beltrán in the early 1940s. His work was responsible for that
country's Instituto Nacional Indigenista (Indigenist National Institute), a
paternalist institution in charge of gradually assimilating indigenous cultures
into a Western perspective. In Beltrán's understanding, *mestizaje* represented
the "harmonious image of what is obviously disjointed and confrontational":[11] the fusion of indigenous and Western cultural patterns. Those
smooth visions were deliberately designed to emphasize the modern, urban
aspects of Latin America strictly derived from European roots. At the same
time, they made its "shameful" indigenous or African component invisible.
Greatly overlooked was the fact that representations of *mestizaje* production portrayed an asymmetrical fusion. Implicitly, the Western face was
expected to prevail, because it was believed to be the only one capable of
signaling a "civilized state" for, and hence a civilized public face of, the
Americas. Indigenous aspects were to be present only as a sort of embell-
ished adornment on a cosmic body with a rational, Western head.

Cornejo Polar has written astutely on the pitfalls and virtues of *indigenismo*. I will not repeat his arguments here. However, I wish to emphasize his
statements that *indigenista* works assume the Westernized sign that domi-
nates in its productive process and that the best *indigenismo* also assimilates
literary forms that organically pertain to the referent. It is in this contention
that Cornejo Polar sees the sociohistorical importance of *indigenismo* as
materializing "in heterogeneity, its best ideological and literary possibilities."[12]

Asturias was categorized as a neo-*indigenista* by Prieto to denote a qualitative leap over the more traditional, romantic authors who wrote "*literatura mestiza*," according to Stephen Henighan.[13] Asturias went further than
others in the 1960s in soaking his style and diction in that of the *Popol Vuh*
while making a staunch defense of indigenous values. Other than the absur-
dity of continuing to categorize writers according to thematic inclinations
at this late date, the paradox is that Asturias created the illusion of speaking
from an indigenous perspective, one that was welcomed primarily in Europe,
especially in Paris, as Henighan argues, where in the 1960s the reception of
Latin American literature was still full of preconceived notions according

to Sylvia Molloy, who chronicles this process.[14] Moreover, Asturias also myth-ified the allegedly hybrid quality of *mestizaje* as a harmonious synthesis of Western and Maya values, in line with Mexican anthropological thinking. Offering himself as a representative of a "Central American experience" that encompassed Mayas, he thus homogenized Guatemalan experience and con-flated it with Maya experience as "Central American," which was, of course, a profound misrecognition. The net result was that, stylistic efforts notwith-standing, he was also guilty of relegating Mayaness to a subaltern role. Maya culture provides symbolic icons for his conception of nationality. Neverthe-less, the subaltern voice was expressed exclusively by the mestizo *letrado*. Given that the acquisition of agency implies control of one's enunciations, his attitude wrestled agency away from the Mayas, keeping them from pro-ducing their own identity. Asturias named the Maya community, spoke for it, and also spoke in its defense. But he did not speak *with* it. And the com-munity did not speak. Thus his discursivity not only stripped identity away from the Mayas but also attacked them symbolically, representing them as passive, suffering victims. In this sense, his *Hombres de maíz* (1949, trans-lated as *Men of Maize,* 1995) illustrates the limits of the representation of subalternity when the latter's enunciation is suppressed. The resentment present-day Maya intellectuals feel toward Asturias illustrates the emotions at play in the construction of community politics.

If we consider *Hombres de maíz* emblematically as representing the utmost possible consciousness to which a mestizo *letrado* can aspire in his immer-sion in the modernizing parameters within which the subliminal and dis-continuous emergence of the subaltern subject is traced, we can clearly see the difficulty of representing contradictory expressions of a complex het-erogeneity that have escaped the literary discursivity of the continent. Indeed, *Hombres de maíz* becomes a conceptual, theoretical, and political problem. And yet it was Asturias who defended "indigenism" against Vargas Llosa in their 1960s debate and who turned that experience into a means of affirming his commitment to Maya culture. It is tragic that after his death he has been found so wanting. He has been accused both of coming up short and of improperly stepping into the indigenous realm. If nothing else, these positional oscillations evince the way that this localized phenomenon lies at the base of the constitution of specific subjectivities within a heteroge-neous region where even its most distinguished *letrados* come up short.

A Brief Reflection on the *Popol Vuh*

Up to the present, a debate continues over the authority or authorship of the *Popol Vuh*, which was originally written around the 1540s in K'iché Maya, but employing a Latin alphabet. Only one thing remains clear: after the holocaust of the Spanish Conquest, surviving Maya-K'iché leaders or priests of the Kavek lineage sensed their imminent extermination. The need to write a record of their experience on Earth became urgent. Much as their classic ancestors had done by carving glyphs on stelae to record their deeds and history with astronomical associations, they chose to leave a testimony to explain their origins and their culture. In doing so they produced the *Popol Vuh*, which Gordon Brotherston has called "an unrivaled point of reference for cosmogonical texts from cultures to west and east."[15] The text offers an account of the origin of the world up to the victory of the hero twins Hunahpu and Xbalanque over the lords of the underworld. In the dominant tale of the *Popol Vuh* that antedates the creation of the world, the twins are summoned to Xibalbá by its lords because they have made too much noise playing ball. The lords think that they can easily destroy the twins, as they destroyed their parents, by requiring them to pass a series of impossible tests. However, the twins use their cunning and ingenuity and transform themselves into different beings to pass all the tests to which they are submitted and ultimately to defeat the lords of the underworld and expel them from the world that will be inhabited by humans. The *Popol Vuh* then continues with the creation of the first humans from maize, signaling the emergence of the K'iché people, followed by the history of their rulers up to the arrival of the Spaniards. The *Popol Vuh* empowered those rulers to make claims even under Spanish rule. Brotherston adds: "Far from diminishing the text, having the practical function of the *título* [composed to defend under Spanish colonial rule an interest or privilege dating from before the invasion] sooner enhances it and alerts us to how different levels of time and purpose are conjoined in the narrative overall."[16]

In the *Popol Vuh* K'iché leaders declare that they have received the insignia and gifts of Quetzalcoatl or Kukulkán, the feathered serpent, the highest deity in the cosmos, god of arts and culture. In other words, they declare that they, too, were civilized peoples. Or, rather, that they were *the* civilized peoples. To them, the Spaniards were simply the barbarians who won the war.

The writing of the *Popol Vuh* is a paradigmatic example of Central

American discourse up to our times. Most salient Central American texts recognize it as the codifier of the set of principles that anchors a regional identity and constitutes the Mesoamerican cultural matrix. Its legacy is that of a web of significations by which a broad community assumes organic connections to a commonly imagined pre-Hispanic past. That might be why its legacy crosses the boundaries of the region's literary genres, blurring distinctions and configuring a variation of spatial models over time. It might also explain why Central America's discursive methods are as confusing as the twisted layout of the Guatemalan highlands that Rodríguez labels a "massive narrative confusion."[17] The region has "national" narratives that are also regional in many instances. Sometimes they represent the isthmus, others just the "historical federation,"[18] and, occasionally, only Mesoamerica.[19] There are times, though, when the space stretches all the way to Tula, located to the north of the central valley of Mexico, as in the *Popol Vuh* itself.[20] These discursive topographies articulate imagined communities that may be national or subnational but that are also regional. They can also be stateless, as is the case of the Maya, a majority in Guatemala, or of the Garífuna, scattered across the Caribbean coasts of Belize, Guatemala, and Honduras. Yet they all have meaning for Central Americans past and present. The distinctiveness of this singular situation has no place in the conception of Latin American literature articulated in the U.S. academy, which prefers adhering to the simplistic topography of its own invention to unraveling the thick texture of these complex symbolic layouts. Furthermore, I am also quite convinced that, without knowledge of the *Popol Vuh*, the literary distinction of this region cannot truly be read. In the United States, Gordon Brotherston is, without question, the best interpreter both of the *Popol Vuh* and of indigenous literatures in general. Yet, due to the artificially compartmentalized divisions of the academy, Brotherston's work might be better known in Native American and anthropology departments than in Spanish, romance language, or modern literature ones. It is thus important to restate his words here: "In proposing a way of life defended today by the Quiché (for example, in the lucid words of Rigoberta Menchú), the *Popol Vuh* serves as a charter for that nation and human society more generally. Even more . . . it does this thinking not out of narrow human advantages but by invoking and honoring the species and life forces that have filled its cosmogony."[21] Implied in his understanding is the notion that the *Popol Vuh* expresses an ecological worldview in which animals have a place alongside humans in the world. The *Popol Vuh*'s recurring metaphors lead to the reader's illumination of the subject's charming yet mystical union with the cosmos.

In the first chapter I mentioned that Belli's *La mujer habitada* (1988, translated as *The Inhabited Woman,* 1994) posits indigenous peoples' representation as emblematic of a recurrent slippage in Central Americans' gaze on their identitary horizon, informed by their fear of being "non-Western." I also problematized Asturias's work in chapter 2, as well as in the first section of this chapter. But let us now take a look at this question in two less well-known cases. They are exemplary of tendencies observed in contemporary discursive methods and show how these particular labyrinths rediscover their *Popol Vuh* roots in the most unexpected places.

Voices in Time, Dialogues in Space: *El Asma de Leviatán*

In 1990, the year of the Sandinista electoral defeat, Salvadoran author Roberto Armijo's *El asma de Leviatán* (Leviathan's asthma) appeared in print.[22] The novel is emblematic of the end of an era and of the tentative beginning of a new period. While the text remains inscribed within the framework of the guerrilla period, by its very form it manages to "outrun" mimetic realism and articulate a new imagined community within postmodern parameters.

El asma de Leviatán calls into question the centrality of the writer or intellectual as protagonist of a political vanguard, in the militaristic sense of front-line rather than in the artistic sense of avant-garde. In this it signals a determining shift from Roque Dalton's *Pobrecito poeta que era yo . . . ,* published fifteen years before. Armijo's novel does not renounce the central position of the literary. Instead, it renounces the centrality of the *"pueta"* (poet, in Salvadoran slang, the figure of a *letrado*) as a universal intellectual in the Foucauldian sense.

The text is constructed from fragments of discourses of "otherness," speeches within speeches, utterances within utterances, that embed the voice of a second speaker inside the utterance of a first one. The diegesis here is the protagonist Roberto's process of writing, during his exile in Paris, a novel titled *El asma de Leviatán.* As he writes it, he discusses its contents and premises with his Chilean friend Lucho and suffers asthma attacks brought on by the inclement Parisian weather, as well as by the Salvadoran political crisis. These meteorological and political conditions make him feel like a prisoner of his body. Nevertheless, Roberto succeeds in a romance with a woman nicknamed the Cartesian Maiden.[23] In the midst of his writing, his father, a country doctor by the name of Terencio Pineda, dies in El Salvador. Roberto evokes the things his father told him about his home country (which include, in an analogous embedding process, what his father was told by his own father, his father-in-law Francisco Navarrete, his brother Alfonso, and his friend and neighbor Jacinto Pichinta, a peasant of indigenous origin). These multiple voices enable Roberto to reconfigure his subjectivity. He fantasizes a return to El Salvador as the war comes to an end.[24]

By displacing the narrative through time and space, *El asma de Leviatán* addresses the question of the peripheral subject, allowing for a play of difference between those with hegemonic roles within regions of subnations (Dr. Pineda) and those with subaltern ones (Pichinta). The novel fuses art and life into an ethical quest for the transformation of the self. As Roberto reconstructs and reimagines his identity, he displays an illusion of control. Nevertheless, the embedding process makes it evident that this is the contingent nature of his imaginary process. For Roberto to find the authority to speak and illuminate the nature of his identity, he needs first to identify with the iterative and enunciatory aspects of the stories told by others. In this way he substantially negotiates his articulation in two important ways: between those others and with them. The authority of the various voices is validated by their ethnic or national origin, by the aesthetics of their existence, and by their roots in the collective imagination that shapes subaltern styles of being. Thus Roberto, who is nicknamed "the poet," must gather within his own voice the voices of his father and of Pichinta. They give meaning to a story that sometimes seems to verge, deliberately, on a foundational myth, a teleological design, foregrounding nostalgic memories that bind the present to national sources as a complex rhetorical strategy of social belonging. It is the only way in which Roberto can reconcile his self-image with his being. He can speak only insofar as he is conscious that his voice is not just an individual, solipsistic voice. He needs his voice to be a heteroglotic voice, gathering all other voices that constitute the ambivalent discourse of "what El Salvador is," of "what it is to be Salvadoran."

The poet does not try to set himself up as "the voice for those who have no voice," subsuming the notion of "people" under his own ethos. Rather, he limits himself to retelling the stories his father told him and the ones he heard from Pichinta. Roberto contextualizes elements of tradition, popular rites, and communal lifestyles. This play of voices apparently authorizes the poet to speak without turning his speech into an appropriation of the other's discourse. However, the embedding process itself makes it evident that Roberto wants to justify his existence and his identity, because he feels comfortable in Paris. He talks about tradition, but as a cosmopolitan man.

As is fitting within the reconstruction of a romanticized tradition, a distinct longing for the lost pre-Hispanic past is verbalized through Pichinta. His voice not only articulates episodes from the *Popol Vuh* but also constitutes itself as a founding discourse in a manner analogous to that of the classical K'iché text. Political emotions become virtually synonymous with indigenous agency. They are the only elements that provide social solidarity capable of constituting a community. The racialized body is linked to political identification vis-à-vis emotions.

Anchored in the heterotopical space denominated as "El Salvador," *El asma de Leviatán* represents textual indigeneity or indigenousness as the founding discourse of an imagined Maya-Toltec nation after a tabula rasa of the present has been made. But what actually surfaces is the fragmented, schizophrenic voice of the mestizo subject willing into existence a transcultural identity. The colonially silenced subaltern subject speaks from within mestizo discourses that reinstall indigenous culture at the center of Salvadoran subjectivity while paradoxically being questioned by mestizo wisdom. Textually, subaltern discourse does not mimic and parody colonizing discourse to emerge in its own light. Mestizo discourse mimics and parodies hegemonic rationalist discourse. Then, with a deft parry, it yields the floor to subaltern discourse before putting in the last word. Consider this:

> Jacinto Pichinta, when speaking of corn, said it was a gift from heaven to the Indian, and told about the miracle of the little ant—which, he said, was sent by an earlier God. This tiny animal went deep down into the earth to get the seed. Jacinto would say that we had been made out of corn, which I would always deny, because for me, the Holy Bible says we were made from a puff of dust; but to get back to our corn, it's a plant that sustains us and gives us strength. (238)

The quoted passage implies the paradox of intuiting "Indianness" while validating Western heritage.

El asma de Leviatán tries to resolve this contradiction by recounting its construction as a literary artifice. Armijo, in a Proustian gesture, creates a writer named Roberto, who should not be confused with the Roberto, né Armijo, who wrote the novel. This separation of the authorial function enables Armijo to differentiate between the biographical subject and a creative consciousness that produces a precarious and imprecise discourse. The evidence that literariness is not "reality" in a positivist sense, but a "discursive reality," obtrudes upon the reader:

> "How's your novel coming?" "Oh, *Leviatán*. You know, I'm having problems with the ending." "What do you have so far?" "Well, I've been thinking, see how you like this, maybe with a journey." "What? I don't get it!" "I mean, it'll follow my route. I walk from Xibalbá to *Sèvres-Babylone*, walk around Paris all night, then I go back, pick up my bags and leave." . . . "Ah, Netza,[25] not bad!" (224)

The problem of returning home consists of boarding a boat that may be in Le Havre or perhaps "sleeps in Xibalbá." The boat is named *Leviatán*. The Bible, Hobbes's social contract and concerns about governmental abuse of power, and the *Popol Vuh* are meshed discursively to symbolize the oxymoronic nature of both rationalism and identity as order and chaos. Roberto's return, though, is not a "real" return to a homeland; it is only a condition of possibility at the limits of consciousness. The poet goes to a dreamed, imagined El Salvador placed on a level with Xibalbá, the underworld of the *Popol Vuh*. His house is metaphorically the Maya hell, but his true hell lies in the crisis of his own subjectivity. Given the unresolvable tension of his being, he can escape from this contradiction only via the creative act. He can constitute his subjectivity only through aesthetics.

This phenomenon goes beyond the intratextual limits of *El asma de Leviatán*. Other texts with similar traits from the same time period include Alegría's *Cenizas de Izalco* (translated as *Ashes of Izalco*), Dalton's *Pobrecito poeta que era yo . . .*, and Belli's *La mujer habitada*. These works are in addition, of course, to the work of Guatemalan authors, where such traits appear almost without exclusion. In nearly every novel from the 1960–90 guerrilla period, the desire to ground a collective identity in the *Popol Vuh* is present.

Obviously there are dangers in this desire, similar to those addressed in my previous critique of Asturias in this same chapter. An authenticity-inauthenticity duality immediately appears: everything Maya is "authentic," and Western traits become a "false consciousness" that undermines the very identity of the mestizo intellectuals who propound it. We could claim, in their defense, that their own subjectivities were a site of contestation and struggle when the texts of 1960–90 were being written. Recall that at this singular historical moment old paradigms were being questioned and new subjectivities configured, partly as a result of these writers' inscriptions, contingently enmeshed in the heated political strategies of the period. Still, the drawbacks are evident. Maya legitimacy is usurped to validate mestizo power. After all, thematization and conceptualization are also forms of possessing the other. They also create the delusion that in order to be able to interpret experience as a subaltern intellectual in a metropolitan center, one first needs the validation of indigenous origins to authenticate oneself.

Gloria Guardia: The Parodic Undermining of the Panamanian Elite

Panama has the most forgotten narrative written in Spanish in all of Central America.[26] It is the country geographically and culturally furthest removed from the Mayab,[27] even if it has an indigenous population of its own. The Kunas are rain forest inhabitants with little presence in urban or modern Panama. An examination of Gloria Guardia's *El último juego* (The last game, 1977)[28] proves fruitful because, through its subtle use of parody, it reveals the constructed marginality of women and the absence of vitality inscribed in criollo men, that is, the criollo men who exercised power in the country up to the time of General Omar Torrijos (1968–81).[29] *El último juego* presents this period as a consequence of Panamanians' negation of their indigenous roots, a sort of identitary displacement resulting from their desire to be different from the rest of Central Americans.

The discursive voice in *El último juego* is that of Roberto "Tito" Garrido, a lawyer, career diplomat, and member of one of the most powerful families in the country. Garrido is Panama's chief negotiator of a new Canal treaty. Mariana is his lover. The voice, whether as a train of thought or a stream of consciousness, belongs to a man. However, it is a voice appropriated by a woman, the writer Gloria Guardia. That being said, when Roberto gazes on Mariana, we do not simply have the objectification of a woman by a man. We have the staging of this tableau—woman as object of a male gaze, as imagined by another woman, and with the express intent of unmasking the process by which gender-specific disciplinary practices are carried out. The writing itself deconstructs Garrido's logic of appropriation, leading to an emotional and identitary displacement. It is a subtle process, one in which masculine subjectivity is gradually dismantled to subvert the monological world of the aristocratic patriarchy that Garrido and his cohorts represent. This process premediates a subtle transgression: to articulate Garrido's utterances so that the patriarchal discourse itself—via the guile of ironic discourse—subverts its own claim to power. Metonymically, Garrido is Panama, itself a synecdoche of Garrido.

In a telling moment, Garrido recalls his body entwined with Mariana's and savors the naturalness of their "dark skin" mingling together. We have here an invocation of an indigenous component perceived as a lack in Garrido. This self-image is that of a criollo and not that of a mestizo, one that filters in later on when he has a run-in with a Japanese businessman. Garrido speaks back to him haughtily, and the man takes offense:

> "That's the way we are, what of it?" I retorted, hoping to have done with the topic once and for all. "You know me, you know Panamanians, you should be used to it." . . .
>
> "But that doesn't change the fact that it's a rash, harmful attitude," he said again arrogantly, with an undisguised tinge of I'm-better-than-you-are Indio." (84)

The Japanese man never accuses Garrido of being an *Indio* (Indian).[30] The pejorative term is never uttered. But the latter gets angry because he claims to "read" the accusation in the former's eyes. This strong reaction (and emotion) reaffirms the contradiction of the absent ethnic element and enables readers to understand Garrido better. Until this moment, he has appeared as the emblem of a universalist modern narrative. He was educated at Choate, "where Joe and Jack Kennedy went to school" (87), followed by Johns Hopkins University. His paradox is that, although his wealth was vast and his schooling privileged, he felt his body was read by the metropolitan center as that of an *Indio*. As a subject who conceives himself as a criollo, that is, as "white," his fury is due to discovering that his body is a signifier of the "dark-skinned" inhabiting the modern metropolis. The implied ethnic makeup normalizes and stereotypes him, preventing him from "passing" as a modern, cosmopolitan individual, as someone who "naturally" belongs to a global caste of white rulers. It undermines his self-mastery. His body has the sociosymbolic inscription of being "Indian/dark," as this is read by hegemonic culture (albeit Japanese in this case). Because power operates through cultural and social norms, Garrido's authority, through discourse, is clearly invalidated before his interlocutors.

The fear of the "dark" side is a central aspect of Garrido's memory of his mother. She once told him that no son of hers could be lazy, because that trait belonged "only to Indians.... Those idiots spend their lives flopped in their hammocks waiting for a coconut to fall off the palm tree for them, and they'll probably still be waiting when all their teeth have fallen out!" (124). This maternal racism was embodied in a woman who "whenever she showed me affection, did it so furtively that even I didn't notice" (125). Racism is also a failure of affection and tenderness, besides an incapacity to recognize the other. Thus the duality of Garrido's identity—divided between a Western-ized image and its "Indian" shadow—is symbolically resolved in a space dominated by jingoist rhetoric. He is the son of one of the "fathers of the fatherland." He symbolizes *"panameñidad"* (Panamanian-ness) as it was un-derstood until the late 1960s. But once "the Colonel" comes to power, this concept is displaced by radical-populist discourse. Its extreme is manifested in a militant communiqué from the Urraca Commando, a guerrilla squad-ron that occupies Garrido's house in a push to eliminate U.S. military bases.[31] Garrido no longer recognizes himself in this new nationalist discourse.

During this transition Garrido finds himself narcissistically attached to a picture of his grandfather, one of the fathers of the nation. The other *pana-meñidad,* however—the one grounded on indigenous peoples—remains veiled from him. He recoils from it when he sees it starkly defined in the commando unit's name and orders: Urraca is the name of the indigenous Panamanian chieftain (d. 1531) who led the resistance against Spanish con-quistadors in the region of Veraguas and Natá.[32] What Garrido does not understand is that he cannot decode the meaning of the Urraca Commando's behavior because he no longer has power to grant meaning. His preexisting sense of possessing an essentialized power that predetermines all meanings localized in his country now obscures his being. This is to say that he can no longer be "where it's at" in order to be. Through the invasion of his home, Garrido has, in a single blow, lost his ability to be a figure of desire. This loss can be traced in the following events: Garrido loses Mariana's respect at first (then loses her altogether); then he is replaced as a figure of power/ ideology (Zero, the commander in charge, occupies this space now) and as a figure who articulates the relationship between the subject and truth (again, displaced by Zero in that role).

Garrido tries to repress his anxiety, but it crops up in his internal mono-logue. At a crucial moment, he recalls with horror the time Panama broke off diplomatic relations with the United States. He realizes that he cannot be "U.S." And yet he does not know what it is to be Panamanian because he has always occupied an interstitial space as the negotiator. He cannot name ethnicity as a determining identitary factor, for he takes offense when Zero accuses him of being a "fucking *rabiblanco*" (161). For him, the insult expresses class resentment; he does not associate it with a racialized skin color. The need to affirm himself as white, Western, and rational prevents him from recognizing those cultural signifiers.

The occupation of Garrido's house by the Urraca Commando plays a central role in the brutal emergence of guerrilla warfare. This gives rise to a textual opposition between a discourse questioned by other discourses in the text and an emblematic action central to questioning Garrido and the world he represents. In this reaccentuation, his discourse attempts to exclude the Urraca Commando from the realm of meaning. But the representation of the latter's action politicizes the internal oppression of the subaltern subject, producing new meanings in the text's reading. We have a new disjuncture, one in which Garrido still exercises the power of the word. He has lost control, however, over the actions taking place around him in his own house. The commando's action inverts the relations of power. Thus, Garrido is represented as perceiving his belief system through the commando's belief system, even though the reader perceives the guerrillas' belief system through Garrido's language. We have a dual process of translation that pretends to conceal the positive valorization of guerrilla action.

In this setup, Garrido restages the drama of the discontinuity of the Central American mestizo, the elision of such a problematic identity placed at the center of twentieth-century Central American nationalism and the anguish generated by its lack of ethnic consciousness. As an integral member of the country's elite, the mestizo subject does not recognize him or herself as belonging to or constituting an ethnic group. The book presents, through a psychological process of disavowal, a pushing of the ethnic memory out of a consciousness that moves to neurotically holding onto the fantasy of being a "Western, white, Christian" criollo subject while being "displaced" from equally imagined European roots.

The overall premises set forth here are shared by many Central American texts of this period. Suffice it to mention Dante Liano's *El misterio de San*

Andrés (1996) or Mario Payeras's as yet unpublished "Al este de la flora apaci-
ble," written in the late 1980s.[33] Where *El último juego* differs from most is
that Guardia succeeds better than others in avoiding the pitfalls of appro-
priating indigenous subjectivity for nonindigenous characters. Understanding sensibly the vulnerability of otherness, her nonreductive representation
of subjectivity is more ethical. *El último juego* never truly represents an
indigenous character within the text; it only evokes one through the name
of the guerrilla unit. By displacing discourse from Garrido's subjectivity to
Mariana's (and carnivalizing the former) and by translating meanings within
the multiplicity of discourses present in the text, Guardia manages to avoid
usurpation, essentialization, or false identitary claims that could legitimate
the illusion or empowerment of an "ontological profiling" of the "other."
We are to understand the use of translation here as a "concept-metaphor,"
in Gayatri Spivak's sense of the term, whereby translation functions as the
very precondition of all forms of intelligibility. Garrido names the specter
of indigenousness as the missing link in fully understanding Central American modern subjectivity. Needless to add, the only truly convincing literary representation of the indigenous subject could be provided solely by a
literature written by indigenous peoples themselves.

The Emergence of a New Maya Literature

At the risk of oversimplifying a complex situation, we could say that the most
important response to the postwar period changes in Central America, to
the exhaustion of *testimonio,* and to the hybrid contradictions of representation of the subaltern subject by the mestizo *letrado* is given by Maya literature. Maya literature is a notable effort because of both its bilingualism
and its representation of a uniquely different gaze on the Americas as a
whole. By introducing into the literary or symbolic process new linguistic
and representational challenges, Maya works manage to provincialize Spanish (in the Dipesh Chakrabarty sense) as an organic vehicle in the constitution of symbolic imaginaries, and they especially succeed in problematizing
the nature of the nation-state itself.

Regardless of the genres in which Maya works appear—there is poetry,
fiction, *testimonio,* and theater written in various Maya languages, translated
into Spanish most of the time by the authors themselves—Maya literature

reflects the changing role that "literature" plays in subaltern societies. While their cultural practices include many other expressions, from traditional weaving to painting, theater, and representational ceremonial forms such as the celebration of the Maya New Year in nontraditional sites such as the Central Park of Guatemala City, literature has gained in importance as literate practices and education have also increased in Maya society, without necessarily becoming a new *doxa*. Figures for consideration include Gaspar Pedro González, head of the Literature Division for the Ministry of Culture in the early 2000s, and Victor Montejo, appointed to the cabinet as Secretary of Peace in 2004 (he resigned in mid-2005). I now shift to analyze some of these writers.

El tiempo principia en Xibalbá (Time begins in Xibalbá, 1985), by Kaqchikel writer Luis de Lión, is the pioneer novel.[34] Written in Spanish, this experimental text destroys all possible attempts at linear chronology. It is built exclusively through prolepses and analepses with iterative phrases and images to the point that the prologue is the last part of the book and its last line connects with the first to complete a *Finnegan's Wake*–type circularity. This is clearly one of the most complex novels ever written in Central America. In it, Kaqchikel or Castillian linguistic fusion is indicated either by words that function much like tropes in the text itself, such as *patojos* (kids), *naguas* (skirts), *canillas* (legs), *aire más baboso* (air of stupidity), and *la trompa* (the mouth, but literally "snout"), or popular sayings associated with village-style life, as in *hacer una mi necesidá* (literally, "fulfill a need," but the implication is that of bowel movements, with a grammatically incorrect possessive pronoun, and *necesidá* spelled as pronounced in rural Guatemala, not as the Castillian *necesidad*). These expressions are but a small sample. The *Popol Vuh* is explicitly mentioned in the title, and on page 16 it is addressed as "that strange book," a coded *mise en abyme* of temporal elements appearing in the larger context of the work itself. The text also borrows the duality of the twins who overcome the lords of Xibalbá, which is manifested here in a nonindividualized voice that switches from one point of view to the other in homodiegetic fashion. It can certainly confound the reader and upset all discursive equilibrium, until the "Epitaph." After a surreal psychic turn evocative of Asturias's metonymical chains of signification in *Mulata de tal*, the reader discovers that the two main characters, Pascual Baeza and Juan Caca, are in reality two sides of the same being:[35]

And he was alone.

Then, to console himself, he looked for his other.... He looked in the mirror that was one of the few things that Concha had left him. He desired that
at least the other one would accompany him. He stood in front of the pillar,
afraid, without looking at himself yet, only leaning his face out little by little.
When he thought that all of him was already on the other side, then he crossed
his eyes to greet him, to be greeted, to be told not to worry, that He was with
Him, keeping him company. (98)[36]

This split personality signals the split Maya-Ladino identity traversing
both text and society, which destroys the individual(s) in question as well
as the village. The protagonists Pascual Baeza and Juan Caca represent two
faces of the excruciating difficulties confronted by Westernized indigenous
subjects after becoming Ladinoized. Pascual is an army deserter returning
to his village to die. He tries to kill himself with alcohol:

When Pascual returned to the village he brought, besides the years that had
taken him from childhood to manhood, a face as if he already belonged elsewhere . . . he brought in his mouth strange words, unknown, as those of a
man who has learned other languages; he brought on his feet shoes, instead
of sandals; he brought on his head a *vicuña* hat instead of the charming palm
hat, and on his body different clothing than that used in the village. He was
no longer from here. (45)[37]

Disappointed by the submissive attitude of his fellow villagers in the face
of rampant Westernization, Pascual decides to leave again. But before doing
so he visits the church and, recognizing the wooden image of the Virgin of
Concepción as a symbol of colonial power, he steals it and rapes it "in the
same way a Ladino would possess his wife on the wedding night" (60).[38]
This is a gesture brimming with ethnic hatred. The Virgin is referred to
elsewhere as "la ladina" and "the only Ladina in the village" (la única ladina
del pueblo, 64, 65). Despite the evident *machista* attitude implied in this
abject gesture, it has to be understood as well in both literary and social
terms. Regarding the first point, this rape echoes the rape of the sister of
the Maya protagonist, Tol Matzar, by the hacienda owner in Mario Monteforte Toledo's *Entre la piedra y la cruz* (Between the stone and the cross,
1949). Here de Lión reverses its ethnic signification. The rape of indigenous

women by Spanish, criollo, or Ladino men has been common since the Conquest. To this day, the rape and murder of women by men continues to be one of Guatemala's most heinous crimes. The second point alludes to Pascual's formation as a subject by the Guatemalan army. In Foucauldian terms, the state makes bodies what they are and who they are. The Guatemalan army was thus instrumental in fashioning rapists as it penetrated all realms of everyday social life. There is ample evidence of how the army made rape conceivable on the Guatemalan social horizon, employing it as a punitive counterinsurgency measure throughout the late 1970s and 1980s, along with murdering Maya children. In a place and a time where the politics of identity collapse under the weight of multiple identifications, racial resentment becomes confounded with machismo. Through this literary gesture we have a problematic masculinist expression of agency represented in the text. Through Pascual-Juan's split experience, known to the reader only at the end of the text, the entire (male) community acquires consciousness of Ladino racism in an unresolved misogynist gesture. The implied "deconstruction" of the image's power functions in the text in a way akin to sacrifice. De León invites the reader to imagine a rite that violates received notions of colonialist acceptance. However, given that Pascual-Juan's gesture results from a false consciousness, the act becomes a destructive sign. This act destroys the possibilities for the emergence of true consciousness. There is no rebirth after Xibalbá in the novel. The protagonists' case is more like that of the twins' fathers, who were defeated and mutilated by the lords of the underworld, than that of the twins themselves, who emerge victorious in the *Popol Vuh*.

Juan Caca, operating more as a symbol of indigenous impotence in the face of Ladino power, is portrayed as a self-hating homosexual, echoing again de León's *machista* attitude. Caca is the trope of the cowardly, untrustworthy gay man. In a nightmare, his mother berates him for his sexual preference. To end those fears, he abruptly marries Concha. But they sleep in separate beds, driving her to sexual desperation. As a result, she begins to entertain other men, then escapes and makes love to Pascual-Juan's aggressive, heterosexual, alcoholic, army deserter self, in the main altar of the church. When the authorities find them, she dresses as the Virgin to avoid reprisals, becoming the new virgin-whore.

Setting a destructive reverberation in motion, the community destroys the wooden image of the Virgin in a collective transgressive gesture, placing

Concha, desired by all the men, in her place. The gesture ends with the destruction of the village. This new sign (Concha, the desired whore) is not permitted to dominate the previous one (the Virgin). When the villagers take Concha out in a ritual procession, the women realize that their men have never loved them but only used them to procreate, and they try to stop them from loving Concha. Blind with desire, the men torture and kill the women and children in a sadistic rampage. At the end of the procession, Concha asks for a drink of water. Taken to a fountain, she strips and plunges into the water. The men start fighting among themselves "like beasts" to see her naked, and they kill each other.

At the end of the text, Juan possesses in a dream a woman who could be the Virgin of Concepción, Concha, or even his mother. These variations of womanhood conflate those images in a slippage of the community's incapacity to differentiate between identities and understand their separate codes. When Juan wakes up, he discovers that his penis and testicles are rotting and falling to pieces.

The sacrificial destruction of the symbol of colonialism does not profit those performing sacrifice in this instance (as it would in classical precepts of Maya sacrifice) given their inability to preserve the meaning of Mayaness. The force of their collective energy leads only to dissipation and loss. In this respect, the text imposes a new code of reading. Both the transgressive factors of the rape of the Virgin and her substitution by Concha demand to be read from anticolonial, antiracist perspectives. The text is also the bearer of homophobic and misogynous elements that problematize the nature of subaltern manhood itself. Attempting to reconstitute a Maya cosmogony from within the *Popol Vuh*, de Lión elaborates the epistemology of a decolonizing project that signals the end of Ladinization as an alternative for Maya agency.

More traditional in form is Gaspar Pedro González's *La otra cara* (1992, translated as *A Mayan Life*, 1995),[39] which was originally written in Maya Q'anjob'al. It is the first novel to become a best seller among its people, and the year of its appearance can be read as emblematic. Seemingly a pastiche of naive realisms, *La otra cara* traces the life of Lwin (Lwin in the original Q'anjob'al, Luín in the Spanish translation) from birth to death, as well as the lives of his father, Mekel, and mother, Lotax. Lwin is a resident of the hamlet of Jolomk'u in the municipality of San Pedro Soloma, in the Cuchumatán Mountains of Guatemala. His life is emblematic of the racist violence connected to never-ending governmental abuses and everyday discrimination by Ladinos in all walks of life. Similar to José María Arguedas's *Todas las sangres*, as Maureen E. Shea has pointed out, *La otra cara* is a bildungsroman.[40] Lwin, just like Rendón Wilka in Arguedas's text, grows up immersed in his community's traditions. But then he leaves his village to be educated in a Ladino school, where he suffers brutal discrimination from the teacher and Ladino students. Lwin ends up being seen as a suspicious character in his own community. For this reason, Ana Yolanda Contreras points out that for Lwin, Ladino education constitutes a decentering contradiction, for he rejects his indigenous culture while simultaneously failing to Ladinize himself.[41] In the end, he develops an ethical conscience based on a reimmersion in his ancestral roots, and he becomes a political organizer. In this role there is a similarity to Menchú's acquisition of consciousness in her renowned *testimonio, Crossing Borders* (1998), and there is a dramatic moment of revelation similar to those criticized by Saldaña-Portillo. Menchú's moment follows a trait in guerrilla commander Mario Payeras's *testimonio, Los días de la selva* (1980, translated as *The Days of the Jungle*, 1982), that is, what Saldaña-Portillo calls a "racial residue of colonialist desire" that underwrites the protagonist's self-representation.[42] *La otra cara* presents this contrast through a retroactively constructed moment of innocence:

> One morning [Lwin] left the house unexpectedly without his machete and without telling anyone where he was going. He wandered about, with no destination.
>
> He had climbed to the top of that mountain where he had gone with his grandfather when he was a child. There he sat and analyzed the options he could choose for the remainder of his life. Lwin was not a man who had been born to lose. He would move ahead despite these problems. He wanted to fight on for his family and his community and was looking for the most appropriate way.
>
> Various possibilities rose to consciousness, and he analyzed them one by one. Thus passed hours in meditation. As evening fell he came down from the mountain, finding comfort in the warmth of his people. (212)

Saldaña-Portillo argues that in Payeras's *testimonio* this attitude "primitivized the peasant or indigenous subaltern in their representation of the requirements for transformation, consciousness, and agency."[43] But what are we to make of Lwin, then? What González stages as the emergence of his indigenous consciousness is precisely what Saldaña-Portillo lambastes in Payeras's Ladino attitude. Yet this process of regaining local knowledge from within his originary responsibility is what allows Lwin to emerge as the condition of possibility for a new form of agency: "Lwin had finally discovered something very important" (213). Should we not suppose that what Saldaña-Portillo takes as ethnic differences might instead be gender differences and that some masculinist behavioral patterns are less ethnically marked than others? After all, as David Theo Goldberg has pointed out, ethnically embedded presumptions about social subjectivity and ethnicity reinforce one another.[44] Thus it is not surprising that an ethnicized subject could conceivably adopt hegemonic behavioral patterns, enabling the discriminated against to be almost but not quite the same as the dominant subjects, at least in this regard. Homi Bhabha reveals these patterns through the concept of mimicry, a process that also naturalizes masculinist domination on both sides of the ethnic divide.

In this case, without explicitly naming his guerrilla affiliation, Lwin ends up as a successful grassroots organizer, similar to many CUC (Committee for Peasant Unity) activists of the late 1970s. However, it is notable that in the text, the entire initiative is Lwin's. He does not follow the leadership of radicalized priests, veteran Ladino organizers, or members of the EGP (Guerrilla Army of the Poor), as many CUC members did. Agency in the text is attributed exclusively to Lwin: "'Let's go, Lwin! Guide us in this struggle,' shouted everyone" (217). His representational change is a gesture similar to what Martin Lienhard has described as "losing its mythic quality and taking on a remarkable degree of subtlety and clarity. . . . It is their self-representation which now seems to be the order of the day."[45]

Despite the apparent simplicity of the realist narrative, there is a combination of subjects and languages at discontinuous times that surface from the beginning. This approach creates a separation between a first narrative, Lwin's life as such, and a second, in which the contextual elements of the *Popol Vuh*, embedded in the descriptive prose, generate a complex heterodiegetic layer of symbolism that solidifies the diegesis. Identity is in the domain of signs. The text of *La otra cara* begins like this: "It all began when the gods inscribed their great signs on the stelae of time. It was on the day Thirteen Ajaw" (5). The repetitive mention of classical Maya motifs gives rise to a textual interplay between past and present; there is a desire represented by the vast space given to the symbolism of ancestral images that have under-lined the uninterrupted continuity of culture and community for more than fifteen hundred years. This not only erases traditional Ladino period-icity, marking a temporal rupture with the advent of the Spanish Conquest and colonization that separates the classical Maya period from contempo-rary Mayas, but it also creates within the text a foundational act to nurture that imaginary continuity of Maya history. The narrative voice organizes these symbolic objects, serving as an actualizer of the foundational princi-ple. At first, there is a narrative distance from Lwin's actions. But as we move through the novel, the symbolic embodiment of the narrative voice becomes more confused with the subject of representation, underlining Lwin's role as the present bearer of the classical heritage.

The novelistic subject is estranged between contemporary and Maya time and between "the shadow of the wings of Ajaw" (5), the times of the great Tiox (Great Spirit), and the temporal mimesis of Lwin's life, from birth to death:

> Soon the dark contours of the high mountains appeared like giants in the night. It was a night of a thousand centuries of history. It didn't seem to be the same wind, the same night, the same contours. It seemed that Ajaw was aging among the pines and that his hands had lost the ability to sculpt life on inde-cipherable stelae.
>
> The moon, like a great eye in the night, came sailing over dark waves of sleepy clouds. It shone its great gaze at Jolomk'u. (5)

The first temporal segment works as a symbolic referent articulated within Lwin's temporality. This is the point through which social claims on behalf of the Maya people as a collectivity are to be formulated. From this same position, a preoriginary-ethical reasoning is gradually constructed to open up the space-possibility of communicative action with the hegemonic Ladino world. In contrast to Lwin's own voice when addressing the racism suffered at school or, for that matter, his father Mekel's voice addressing racism at work, the prophetic words of the eldest man of the family are linked in a diachronic relationship with later events:

> "I've seen that your little head has two whorls," continued the godfather. "The strength of Mother Nature and of the ancestors is with you. You are predes-tined for service," he concluded. (29–30)

These declarations acquire the discursive nuances of an analeptical affirmation charged with the epistemological responsibility for subverting the structures of domination.[46] The writer transfers this responsibility to the reader, who discovers "the other face" of the novel's original Spanish title (which is lost in its English translation). Ladino readers are forced to recognize Lwin as a dignified, ethical subject, as a validated other. They must acknowledge that underlying their preconceptions are various problems with names and naming. Names and naming mean power: "The secretary read in a Spanish that limped into Mekel's ears, the paper with the name of Lwin Mekel, changed to Pedro Miguel for the Ladinos, planted like his umbilical cord. It was one more link in the line of Lwins and Mekels from Jolomk'u" (16). The reader is conscripted into valuing Lwin as an equal participant in the new community, real, possible, future, as Enrique Dussel would say.[47] At the end of the text, closure between the first and second narrative is brought by the last words Lwin speaks as he dies a natural death in old age. After a successful run as a political organizer, his parting words are these: "Let . . . there . . . not . . . be . . . any . . . group . . . that gets . . . left . . . behind" (226). These words are a direct quote from the *Popol Vuh*. They were also one of the slogans employed by the CUC (the major peasant mass organization at the peak of the civil war) during the early 1980s. A fusion of past and present, classical and present-day Maya, finally takes place at the close of the novel.

In the first book of Maya literary criticism, *Kotz'ib': Nuestra literatura maya* (1997), Gaspar Pedro González writes:

> *Kotz'ib'* covers the different ways of expressing knowledge through signs, symbols, colors, weavings, and lines. Maya literature, as a cultural product of a society, and with a particular philosophical point of view about the world and about life, should not always be subjected to analysis according to the norms of Western culture. This is because the eyes and the feelings of their authors are framed within the worldview of their own culture. (7)

We cannot ignore some of the conceptual problems in this argument. It responds to the critic's positionality and to his privileged relation with his object of study. By deploying this strategy, González restates the problematics of interpretation in relation to Maya languages as well as their philosophical worldview. With the goal of inventing their literary history, he adds: "Methodologically, the present work is organized in three historical moments: the Prehispanic period, the Colonial period, and the Contemporary period."[48] To put it differently, by articulating dissimilar historical periods between the Ladino and Western worlds in relation to a struggle over historical meaning, he generates a foundational resignification for Maya symbolic codifications of power with all the risks involved in such a meta-narrative process.

González has also theorized the concept of "worldview" *(cosmovisión)* as a will to become constituted as subjects through an agency process permeated by the community's cultural values, regardless of whether these are liminal to Western values or a hybrid of both Western and Ladino values.[49] This concept is different from the notions of both transculturation and heterogeneity, because what matters is neither the transposition of cultural values from one culture to the other nor the emergence of an alternative *mestizaje* that creates new heterogeneous cultural traits. What matters is who exercises the power/knowledge relations in this course and what emerges organically from their own initiative and agency process—a process that takes into account a revaluation of their own culture and languages.

The third text I will analyze in this section is *Las aventuras de Mr. Puttison entre los mayas*[50] (The adventures of Mr. Puttison among the Mayas, 1998), by Jak'alteko writer Víctor Montejo.[51] This novel is an acerbic satire à la Swift of the presence of American anthropologist Oliver La Farge in the Jak'alteko community during the 1930s.[52] In the text, when the anthropologist arrives for the first time, the village takes him for a priest. This confusion reflects a symbolic allusion to a previous colonial oppression that will now be replaced with the anthropological American order, demarcating two different forms of power/knowledge: "I say he's a priest, because of his tremendous height. His hair is blond, his eyes are green or blue; and now that he's walking under the sun it looks like his blood is about to explode under his baby mouse skin" (2).[53] Mr. Puttison appears as a jovial gringo who easily wins the trust of the young men in the village of Yulwitz, which is, like González's village, located in the Cuchumatán Mountains. From the dialogues between Mr. Puttison and members of the community emerge a series of rhetorical movements that allow Montejo to play Western and Maya values against each other. For example, Mr. Puttison goes out hunting with Pel Echem and discovers that Echem is afraid because he believes that dwarfs haunt him. Mr. Puttison insists that he is confusing skunks with dwarfs and provokes Echem by saying that he has heard that his father was no coward and often hunted alone at night. Pleased by Mr. Puttison's words, Echem tells the story of how his father ran into the guardian of the forests, who forbade him to hunt any more deer. Mr. Puttison finds the story "wonderful" as folklore (139; the word used in Spanish is *maravilloso,* emphasizing the incorrect usage of adjective gender to signal Mr. Puttison's foreignness and mark a separation between him and knowledge). But he does not draw from it any lessons about ethical behavior. On the contrary, for Echem the objective of the narrative is to corroborate the transfiguration of the guardian as symbolizing the normative principle that collective well-being stands above that of an individual.

A similar example of this opposition emerges when Mr. Puttison and the character Xuxh Antil are discussing names, an action noted in *La otra cara* that has always implied empowerment in Maya culture. After Mr. Puttison insists that he be called Dudley instead of "Mister," the following exchange takes place:

> "Okay, Mister," said Xuxh Antil. "You must also learn to say the names of your friends in Popb'al Ti' language. Always call me 'Antil' instead of 'Andrés.' I like that name a lot, but it is the name of a type of toad that during the rainy season climbs into the trees to sing." (66)[54]

Mr. Puttison misses the irony and limits himself to replying "interesting." Although for Antil his Spanish name is a form of verbal aggression, it is the verdict that there is a fundamental asymmetry in their relation of power that operates as an injurious, perlocutionary performative utterance that is instantiated by the particular linguistic act of naming. Mr. Puttison is oblivious to it because, having the power to mark Antil's consciousness with that hurt, he is himself unaware of his "naturalized" imperial stand. Curious about the semiotics of identity, he asks how his own name would be pronounced in their language:

> "Don Lamun says that your name would be pronounced *T'ut'* in our language.
> Mr. Puttison stood up angrily and screamed:
> "Oh, please, don't give me another name. My name's Dud."
> "Yes, mister, but the letter D doesn't exist in our language. The closest is *T'ut',* but it is also something else." Everybody laughed.

"What is *T'ut'* then?"

Xhuxh Antil came forward to explain with a picaresque smile.

"*T'ut'* is the noise made by air when you fart. (66)[55]

In the second set of exchanges, Mr. Puttison becomes offended because he finally detects a stigmatization in the act of being named that, for the first time, generates in him an awareness of being othered in a reductionist way, of losing his privileged insularity. He then insists on being called Mr. Puttison, a name that implies a recognition of (cultural imperialist) authority, instead of *T'ut'*, a designation he perceives as an insult instead of an invitation to laughter. Such joviality completes the villager's ethical stance of making room for his subjective existence within their boundaries. Mr. Puttison remains fully unaware that insult is constitutive of subaltern identity, and he is unwilling to dehegemonize his position to learn how to occupy the subject position of the other, as Spivak conceptualizes this notion.

As the reader of the novel can see from this quoted passage, subject position is assigned in both instances of translation, but the exchange is not really about translation. Rather, it is about respect for otherness. The configuration of Maya ethics is expressed not through conceptualization, but through sudden flashes of knowledge bursting through conventional dialogue as a radical heterogeneity. The stories dismantle the possibilities of Western reason.

Ultimately, Mr. Puttison's alleged quest for subaltern knowledge is reduced to a simple economy of desire: the acquisition of wealth. In a gesture parallel to that of the original conquistadors, Mr. Puttison steals the treasures that he finds at the cave of Smuxuk Witz. Antil has told him, "Our ancestors chose the cave to hide their treasure from the ambitious conquistadors" (148).[56] Enforcing a new form of colonization, Mr. Puttison carries away "the sacred objects of his ancestors" (185).[57] The monetary model conveys the textual understanding of a process of destructuring of the anthropological or American order of things. The episode of the theft is a symbolic compromise between the obsession for the social control of others and the rupture of those same fantasies by a manifestation of an instinctual drive for wealth.

For Mayas caught in this conundrum, opening up to the world—emblematized by the signifiers depicting Mr. Puttison—generates the kind of dissidence that threatens to destroy the village. It deepens its contradictions,

delegitimizes diversity, and preserves an obsolete model of ethnic homogeneity that threatens to generate a potential implosion. Montejo configures
Antil as the representation of the modernizing, decentered subject. In the
text he is marginalized by his primary condition as an innocent being who
lacks the malice necessary to decode the foreigner's falseness. Victimized by
both sides, an innocent Judas, he represents the aporia of premodern Maya
subjects, who were not able to open themselves up to the world and not
able to step out of marginalization. It is not insignificant that the novel is
set in 1930, when the Maya subject still lacked rights. At that moment, Mayas
had no citizenship legitimation; they were conceived of by Ladinos exclusively as available bodies at the service of exploitation. This implies the
constitution of the subject simply as a biopolitical subject, a notion a priori rejected by Maya thought, which cannot separate natural and human
space because it articulates both in a holistic fashion.

The Importance of Maya Literature

This brief review of Maya literary representations risks an unwelcome reductionism, but it already demonstrates a strong, vital counterstatement to
Ladino discursivity. Maya textuality enables subaltern actors to reacquire
an actualized sense of their world from within the confines of literature.
Textuality becomes a vehicle for remembering inescapably traumatic events
and redressing them in imaginary spaces, enabling a reworking of historical trauma. Metaphorically speaking, it functions much as does a critical
excavation of clandestine cemeteries where the bodies of the massacred have
been secretly hidden. These excavations enable closure for the families of
the disappeared and provide material evidence of the perpetration of heinous
crimes. In analogous fashion, these writings trigger an awareness of the
eminently violent, racist nature of interethnic relations. They highlight the
need to redress these wrongs while also providing a continuous understanding of an alternative code of ethics provided by the *cosmovisión* of the
Popol Vuh.

Starting in 1985, Demetrio Cojtí Cuxil began to publish articles on the
need to expand the use of Maya languages.[58] His efforts led to the creation of
the Círculo Lingüístico Francisco Marroquín, an independent nongovernmental organization, the model for the governmental Academy of Maya Languages created in the 1990s. Both the *círculo* and the academy systematized

the writing of all surviving Maya languages and published dictionaries of each. This was radically new, given that Maya languages had belonged to the oral tradition since the Spanish Conquest and virtually nothing had been written in them since the *Popol Vuh* in the middle of the sixteenth century. Nora England, who collaborated in all of these efforts, explains: "Maya are concerned with language maintenance in the face of increasing signs of language shift, they are concerned with expanding the domains of usage of Maya languages, especially written language, and they are concerned with achieving a balance between language as a marker of local identity."[59]

Considering the previous section of this chapter, the artificiality of separating the Maya novel from the *testimonio* becomes clear when labels are assigned in this slippery category known as "literature." Both narrative genres explore the construction of identity through the representation of the political in a transformed aesthetic space. There are other Maya writers not analyzed in this chapter, such as Francisco Morales Santos and Humberto Ak'abal, whose poetry, while nonnarrative, is also rich, complex, baroque, and politically weighty. Their best works illustrate the rich cross-pollination of the classical Spanish heritage with the Mayas' millennial poetic tradition in an unstable but extremely fortunate confluence. Originating from the same town as de Lión, Morales Santos writes in Spanish, whereas Ak'abal writes in K'iché.

The examples selected allow us to note salient issues of what could be labeled "subaltern representation" in a form different from the more commonly studied genre of *testimonio*. Like the latter, the emerging Maya novel disrupts the myth of a homogeneous nation-state. Maya fiction raises issues such as the confluence of nation, class, ethnicity, and subjectivity, new ways of producing national identities, and the tense negotiation of multiculturalism in Central American countries.

Fiction, poetry, and *testimonio*, as distinct genres, imply different forms of thinking and different ways of communicating with what also may be a differentiated audience. But they all constitute a continuous textuality conforming a Maya cultural politics, operating in an unprivileged peripheral space. They aspire to reterritorialize Mayas' displaced identities through a belated embrace of the "lettered city," one in which Maya languages are spoken and written before being translated to Spanish and English. What are we to do when we reconsider the role that textuality is playing in the emergence of Mayaness? Is it an illustration of the power of the margins?

Or does it signal a class division among Mayas "lumped together" by the Western gaze under the "subaltern" rubric popularized by left-leaning Western academics who nonetheless suggest an undifferentiated "non-Western" mass? If it is a class division, does it imply the ascendancy of a Maya *letrado* elite privileging Western forms over other indigenous forms of expression? If so, what does it mean to be that oxymoronic construct, a Maya *letrado*, stigmatized by one's hegemonic other, located outside of the literary marketplace, not writing primarily in Spanish? We are witnessing, regardless, a process that contributes knowledge, experience, and authority to new writers or leaders employing rhetorical devices to serve non-Western interests, interests that are indicative of Latin America's local grassroots movements providing Deleuzian "lines of flight."

Unlike a good part of the 1990s mestizo literature analyzed in chapter 1 of this book, Mayas' emerging literature conveys a meaningful sense of politics. It is transgressive. At times, this is at the expense of the act of storytelling itself, which implies that it is not a literature meant to entertain. Challenging Western parameters through mimicry of form, it represents an epochal disruption to the Central American mestizo canon. It inverts knowledge/power relations. Alternative knowledge producers become the purveyors of self-generated cognizance, one that originates from nontraditional and nonconventional sites even if it is expressed in a traditional, even anachronistic, form: that of the novel. The attitude of Maya writers destroys the myth that information and learning are produced exclusively by cosmopolitan academics or through the disciplining of academic institutions. In so doing, it provincializes cosmopolitan critics, writers, and academic institutions and challenges the knowledge-producing machine. As Joanne Rappaport has argued, the recent growth of ethnic movements has created scenarios in which grassroots intellectuals can find their voice, identify their audiences, and participate in open political action.[60] This overall process also evidences that a new geopolitics of knowledge is emerging, one that blends grassroots knowledge with political activism. And a newly energized literary production is part of it. This also implies that these forms of knowledge can—and, in effect, do—become operative for contemporary social movements. It also illustrates a community's ability to multiply the points of entry through which they can insert themselves within globalized textures, building self-controlled parallel spaces within foreign bodies. At the same time, we cannot ignore problems already evident in this emerging corpus, notably the pervasive machismo that goes hand in hand with the weak representation of female subjects. So far, these female subjects have only an emblematic presence as decorative beings, good wives, or loving sisters, but are clearly imagined as secondary to the male protagonists of their respective narratives. They also lack all forms of agency. The day when a Maya woman novelist will emerge still seems distant at this point.

Finally, I cannot but recognize that I speak as a mestizo. I pay attention to Maya signs while being fully aware that my critique could easily become an intervention that evaluates narrative production in translation and in the language deployed to colonize Maya culture. My critique is offered in the spirit of generating discursive space for a dialogical relationship. I am aware of the Ladino-mestizo responsibility in "othering" Mayas. I recognize this as one of the contemporary predicaments of Central American mestizo intellectuals. Maya knowledge producers will in time employ different formulations as they create a critique of their own discursivity through their intellectual practices.

PART II

Forever Menchú

4

Authoring Ethnicized Subjects: The Performative Production of the Subaltern Self

"Can the subaltern speak?" The question certainly was not mine.[1] However, the case of Rigoberta Menchú and the attacks on the "factuality" of her mediated discourse in the *testimonio I, Rigoberta Menchú* (1984)[2] forced me to reconsider it. Gayatri Spivak's seminal question presupposes that once the voice of a subaltern subject has been recorded in print, he or she is no longer a subaltern subject, because the "speaking subject" must enunciate the language of reason in order to be "heard" by Western interlocutors. That is, "authentic" discourse is a suppressed or hidden "truth" precisely because of the Westerner's inability to comprehend it in its own terms; thus the subaltern subject is forced to use the discourse of the colonizer to express his or her subjectivity.

In the first part of this book I was concerned with the representation of Central American narrative textuality, from its pre–civil war period through the civil war or guerrilla period to the postwar period. Nevertheless, emphasis fell on the novel. In the second part of this book I group a series of chapters dealing with the controversy surrounding Rigoberta Menchú's *testimonio* as a way of problematizing both the nature of *testimonio* and its relation to subaltern subjects. In this first chapter of the second section I will attempt to extract from the debate surrounding Menchú's text some meaningful contribution to current thinking about issues regarding the status of the ethnicized subject and of *testimonio* as subaltern textuality in the academic circles of the United States.

The contradictions that derive from the subaltern's positionality created the conundrum in which Menchú was trapped. In his book *Rigoberta Menchú and the Story of All Poor Guatemalans* (1998), David Stoll found her, on the one hand, not Western enough when it came to the rigor of her logic and her use of facts, and he thus accused her of invention, fibbing. On the other hand, he found her too Western in her politics, and he therefore claimed that her ideas were not representative of what he judged to be authentic "native" Maya thought. Central to this contradiction is the very nature of discourse itself. Authenticity and "truth"—if they exist at all—resist comprehension, expression, and definition. What is more, even the most strategically planned elocution may elude the speaker's intentions because of the polysemic nature of language. When someone tries to reduce the multiple meanings of any given discourse and ignores the slippages inherent in translation (in this case from K'iché to Spanish to English), the polemics generated seem inevitable.

The testimony of Rigoberta Menchú,[3] a Maya woman from Guatemala, was an important instrument in a discursive war tied to cold war politics.[4] The debate centered on whether Menchú told the "truth" in her book. This issue opened up the problematics of "truth," the nature of the *testimonio* as a genre, and the relationship between political solidarity and subaltern narrative. We can expect absolute truth only if we believe in perfectly verifiable truths or if we still see or insist on seeing the "authentic" indigenous subject as a "noble savage" whose alleged primitiveness maintains him or her closer to some imagined "natural" truth. According to these criteria, any indigenous person who uses discourse strategically is either losing authenticity or being manipulated by external forces outside of his or her control. Therefore, that person must be seen de facto as a pawn of either the Western colonizers or their revolutionary opponents, whose strategies he or she mimics.

This is the argument that Stoll made in the book that sparked the controversy surrounding the 1992 Nobel Peace Prize recipient. In constructing an argument about Menchú's inauthenticity, Stoll found discrepancies from Menchú's original account in interviews he conducted with other Mayas. He claimed that Menchú's inaccuracies suggested that she was a spokesperson not for the Maya people but rather for the radical, revolutionary left in the form of the Guerrilla Army of the Poor (EGP), for whose ends she distorted "Maya truth." Thus, although Stoll began with a seemingly neutral and objective concern ("A recurring question is, Whom to believe? How do we weigh the reliability of Rigoberta's account against the versions I collected and documentary sources?"), he quickly demonstrated an ideological bias ("I hope to convince readers that the EGP never developed the strong social base in Uspantán that Rigoberta would have us believe").[5] This sentence rhetorically linked Menchú to the EGP, implying that she was a propagandist for the organization. Ironically, this maneuver also revealed the strategic manipulation of information in Stoll's own account. It even led us to question whether we can define *fact* in the Guatemalan context, where information often led to torture and death. This also begs the question about the role of "truth" in *testimonio*.

The Function of *Testimonio*

The concept of *testimonio* became popular from a theoretical point of view at the end of the 1980s. Georg Gugelberger refers to it as a "desire called Third World literature,"[6] adding that the genre became the center of the polemic around the canon debates. John Beverley claims that what is of interest is a text's "truth effect." Testimony does not produce or reflect exact historical data, he explains; rather, it places in question the privileged nature of literature as an institution at the same time that it becomes a new literary genre of the subaltern sector of society. Thus, *testimonio* does not produce or reproduce reality, but rather, in a Lacanian sense of that which resists absolute symbolization, it produces a sensation of experiencing reality.[7]

Testimonio was never meant to be autobiography or a sworn testimony in the juridical sense, but rather a collective, communal account of a person's life. This is what Menchú implies when she says, "This is my testimony. I didn't learn it from a book and I didn't learn it alone. . . . My personal experience is the reality of a whole people" (1). The *testimonio* of the 1980s also implied the logic of collective political action. A *testimonio* was assumed to exercise a formative influence and thus play a pedagogical role analogous to that of slave narratives in the United States prior to and during the Civil War. This role was necessarily contingent, for it exceeded the symbolic dimensions from which it originated, marked by violence and a conflictive space. Inasmuch as the genre was developed as a means of empowering subaltern subjects and "hearing" their voices, one can hardly be surprised that it was a tool for political agency.

Whereas the notion of "truth" figured in *testimonio,* as Elzbieta Sklodowska explains in "The Poetics of Remembering," the end-of-the-century debate surrounding the "truthfulness" of Menchú's testimony is oddly out of place in an era that has redirected its critical energy from investigating "the truth" to the study "of inventing, making, creating or . . . constructing" (251). After all, she claims, recent studies across a broad range of disciplines in the humanities and social sciences focus on the "constructed" or "invented" nature of such notions as ethnicity, sexuality, nationality, and gender. If these concepts fit the category of "created objects," it is logical to assume that Menchú's testimonial narrative, too, should be approached with "a self-conscious acknowledgment of [its] artifactual nature" (252). Though no one has denied that Menchú's text is an appeal for international support to stop the genocide of her people, very few critics have actually paid attention to the way in which the *testimonio* is understood by its reading publics. The real issue in the present debate revolves more around these problematics than around the notion of *testimonio* itself as a genre or that of the potential inability of Westerners to grasp a subaltern *testimonio*. By virtue of its hybridity, the *testimonio* has invited different and conflicting readings from literary critics, anthropologists, oral historians, philosophers, and political scientists. This interdisciplinarity makes it clear that the interpretation of *testimonio* is contingent on the reader's ideological purpose and disciplinary focus. As Sklodowska indicates, the lesson drawn from the current whirlwind of declarations surrounding Menchú's book may be that it is an open text that can be read according to different parameters. Thus, where Stoll sees lies and fabrications, Sklodowska sees allegories and metaphors.

Rigoberta Menchú's *Testimonio* as Political Discourse on Ethnicity

A significant percentage of indigenous Mayas, including the Menchú family and their community, fought in the late 1970s against the oppressive rightist military dictatorship in Guatemala as allies of the left, albeit with their own agenda for ethnic empowerment and cultural signification. It is estimated that approximately 150,000 Mayas out of a total population of 5 million were massacred or disappeared during the peak of the conflict (1978–84), and the Guatemalan army acknowledges razing at least 450 villages. The international invisibility of this massacre before the publication of Menchú's *testimonio* prevented the opposition to the government from garnering public support abroad. Arturo Taracena, a noted Guatemalan scholar and the representative of the Guatemalan Opposition in Exile in

France during the early 1980s, helped organize the visit that first took Menchú to that country in an effort to raise awareness of the oppression in Guatemala. After Menchú arrived in Paris, Taracena conceived the idea of recording Menchú's life story as a way of furthering solidarity work on the European continent. It was he who introduced Menchú to Elisabeth Burgos-Debray and arranged for a week of interviews. These interviews resulted in the book *I, Rigoberta Menchú.*

In her *testimonio* Menchú speaks of the pain of her people and their modes of resistance to Ladino oppression. She mixes this account with their struggle for land; Maya rituals of birth, marriage, and death; the exploitative nature of plantation work; the death of siblings as a result of malnutrition; her migration to the city; her experience of racism while working as a maid; the radicalization of many Mayas as a result of experiences similar to hers; the creation of self-defense organizations; their destruction by the army; the subsequent death by torture of most of their members, including Menchú's parents and brothers; and her own survival by fleeing the country.

In the case of *I, Rigoberta Menchú,* one must acknowledge the force of the writing, its metaphoricity, and its rhetorical devices as a "productive matrix."[8] That circumscribes the social engagement of the Maya subject and makes this particular struggle available to others as an objective of and for action. Menchú's visibility at the end of 1981 was limited to circles close to the Guatemalan opposition and its solidarity groups in Mexico. They saw her as the daughter of a Maya grassroots activist and martyr of the burning of the Spanish embassy,[9] whose name had become emblematic of that misadventure. She was a member of the Committee for Peasant Unity (CUC) and worked on its behalf in Mexico City.[10] However, the nature of exile implied that "political work" done outside of the country had to focus on international solidarity or diplomatic work. This was particularly true of disempowered peoples who continued to be framed by a cold war mentality according to which any "leftism" represented a potential threat to the United States.

Menchú's background was Maya and Catholic, and her text therefore represents an interstitial space in which she often talked about traditional Maya religion to underline her ethnic roots while also painting a social scene of communalist unity among the Mayas along Catholic lines, as Duncan Earle points out in "Menchú Tales and Maya Social Landscapes: The Silencing of Words and Worlds,"[11] thus flirting with an essentialist attitude. She does not nuance the complexity of Maya society in her text, limiting herself to using the Mayas' traditions and experiences of racism and oppression as a way to justify their claim to human rights protection.

Even from within this singular displacement, we can see the absence of a simplistic binarism in *Menchú*'s enunciations. Let us look at an example:

> I remember that, when we grew up our parents talked to us about having children. That's the time parents dedicate themselves to the child. In my case, because I was a girl, my parents told me: "You're a young woman and a woman has to be a mother." They said I was beginning my life as a woman and I would want many things that I couldn't have. They tried to tell me that, whatever my ambitions, I'd no way of achieving them. That's how life is. They explained what life is like among our people for a young person, and then they said I shouldn't wait too long before getting married. I had to think for myself, learn to be independent, not rely on my parents, and learn many things which would be useful to me in my life. They gave me the freedom to do what I wanted with my life as long as, first and foremost, I obeyed the laws of our ancestors. (59)

In this paragraph we can immediately discern at least four contradictory attitudes: (1) Menchú's seeming obligation as a young woman to have children; (2) a certain fatalist attitude on the part of her parents about a Maya young woman's possibilities to fulfill her dreams; (3) a personal need on her part, the two previous attitudes notwithstanding, to be independent and learn to exercise her freedom; and (4) a paradoxical subordination of all of the previous attitudes to the laws of Menchú's Maya ancestors. These concerns represent the symbolic array of concepts by which this particular group attempts to define itself through its culture and to differentiate itself from other, primarily Western, groups. We have here what Alberto Moreiras has defined as largely unconscious "work on a culture"[12] to create ethnic borders through difference rather than through the representation of a revolutionary dogma.

The style and content of the entire narrative reinforces the hybridity of Menchú's discourse. The interpellation of competing discourses undermines the rigidity of Western ideologies, weaving a new rhetoric of the self, building a site for the performance of sly transgressive practices that push away from tutelary powers (in this case, the Guatemalan non-Maya revolutionary left). What Marxist revolutionary would say the following?

It was about that time that [my mother] said she was going to learn from a *chimán*. That's what we call a man who tells the Indians' fortunes. He's like a doctor for the Indians, or like a priest. My mother said: "I'm going to be a *chimán* and I'll learn with one of these men." And she went to the *chimán* and he taught her many things out of his imagination connected with animals, with plants, with water, with the sun. My mamá learned a great deal, but who knows, perhaps that wasn't to be her role in life. Nevertheless, it helped her a lot to learn and dedicate herself to other things. My mother loved the natural world very much. (213)

The focus here on the audacity of Menchú's mother within a Maya religious context and worldview provides a stark contrast to the residual racism and masculinism of Western-looking revolutionaries whose anticapitalistic and anti-imperialistic stance often disregarded ethnicized subalterns and misconceived their premodern past. Even so, one cannot read Menchú's text as feminist in the Western sense, even when it seems to be so, as in the following passage:

My mother used to say that through her life, through her living testimony, she tried to tell women that they too had to participate, so that when the repression comes and with it a lot of suffering, it's not only the men who suffer. Women must join the struggle in their own way. My mother's words told them that any evolution, any change, in which women had not participated, would not be a change, and there would be no victory. She was as clear about this as if she were a woman with all sorts of theories and a lot of practice. My mother spoke almost no Spanish, but she spoke two languages— *Quiché,* and a bit of *Kekchí.* She took all that courage and all that knowledge she had, and went to organise her people. (196)

Menchú's mother does not construct a feminist theoretical discourse; rather, her life itself is a "living testimony" in Quiché (or K'iché, as it is presently spelled) and Kekchí (K'ekchí). What is more, the activism she proposes can be understood only within the context of Maya cultural practices, so that women "join the struggle in their own way." There may be an ingenuous certitude about the nature of her qualities, but there is no simplistic leftist) or feminist rhetoric.

One can also discern in Menchú's text a debt to liberation theology, a theology developed by some in the Roman Catholic Church who defended the poor and pushed for fundamental social change. Menchú's discourse borrows a great deal from the scriptures, as George Lovell, Christopher Lutz, and Víctor Montejo explain in a forthcoming book.[13] Menchú comments: "The Bible taught me [to struggle for justice]. I tried to explain this to a Marxist *compañera,* who asked me how could I pretend to fight for revolution being a Christian. I told her the whole truth is not found in the Bible, but neither is the whole truth in Marxism, and that she had to accept that . . . as Christians, we must also defend our faith within the revolutionary process" (246). The relationship between Catholicism and Maya culture is a complicated one. It is well known, for example, that despite their apparent conversion to Christianity, the conquered Maya people continued to worship their gods in the figures of Christ and Catholic saints. A visit to the church of Chichicastenango easily confirms that the Mayas' practice of Catholicism became a form of mimicry that only masked their cultural autonomy within a new, hybrid religious context. In purely anthropological terms, it should be more interesting to speculate about the forms of mimicry present in the passage from Menchú's text than it is to worry about her supposed Marxism, which itself would be no more than the mimicry of the simulacrum of the Soviet ghost that many U.S. policymakers saw in the Central American guerrilla movements.

Menchú understood herself to be a Maya subject. She did not visualize herself as just another member of the Guatemalan opposition, and she was perceived as a representative of the Maya peoples by non-Maya members of the opposition as well.[14] However unsystematic her approach might have been, she visualized a double task: on the one hand, to explain the nature of Maya culture and subjectivity to the outside world, and on the other, to argue for its rightful place within the Guatemalan opposition. These attitudes forced Menchú into an inevitable duality: she had to embrace elements of Western discourse to make herself heard by her target audiences, but she also had to guarantee the preservation and continuity of her Maya identity, which was the validating element of her discourse. This is why she performs her identity as she does, mediating Maya "secrets" and Western parameters of understanding, and it is why she says at the end: "Nevertheless, I'm still keeping my Indian identity a secret. I'm still keeping secret what I think no one should know. Not even anthropologists or intellectuals, no matter how many books they have, can find out all our secrets" (247). Doris Sommer has speculated on the meaning of the trope "secrets" here:

[We may well ask] whether we should not know them for ethical reasons, because our knowledge would lead to power over Menchú's community. . . . [But] even if her own explicit rationale is the nonempirical, ethical rationale . . . she suggests another reason. It is the degree of our foreignness, our cultural difference that would make her secrets incomprehensible to the outsider. We could never know them as she does, because we would inevitably force her secrets into our framework.[15]

Menchú might be an organic intellectual in the Gramscian sense and might have more education than she admitted publicly. But she is no "intellectual" in the Western academic sense of the term. Therefore, for her, "Maya identity" is a very fluid notion. It has more to do with a certain oral tradition inherited from her grandparents and parents, which corresponds more to the particular region in which she grew up and the singular economic insertion of her own family than to a truly "pan-Maya identity."

The concept of identity more often than not signifies a binary opposition stressing the tension between a "self" and an "other" as part of a rhetorical continuum. Thus, as Moreiras points out, this perception tended to underline "difference."[16] In the Maya case, difference arose between Mayas and non-Mayas, that is, Ladinos. However, it was an attitude that presupposed a homogeneity of Maya identity that in fact did not exist. All Mayas, heterogeneous among themselves, had in common their difference vis-à-vis Ladinos, who were not a homogeneous entity either. Maya identity cannot, as a result, be more than a symbolic expression to determine agency. Catholicism, Protestantism, and Maya religion might divide Maya communities, but Mayas silenced the fact that they did not get along among themselves until the end of the war for the sake of empowerment as an ethnic group and because they saw a common denominator in the 1980s massacres that went back to the times of the Spanish Conquest. Even for ordinary Mayas, this is no abstraction. The relationship between the events of the sixteenth century and those of the 1980s is clear: both are still an open, suppurating wound. Given the symbolic nature of identity, however, and the fact that Mayas are still searching for communitarian origins and a sense of collective identity—a trait among groups whose very survival is threatened—combined with the absence of an established protocol to frame what it "means" to be Maya in the first place, we have to read *testimonios* such as Menchú's as open-ended texts whose function is also exploratory and tentative: they are often a first attempt to frame a rhetoric of being and to name agency for a particular subaltern group. As a result, they are, by their very nature, allegorical or, as Moreiras says, an allegory of an allegory.[17] Their argument is framed within the boundaries of an ethical insistence on subalterns' right to be themselves, thus implicitly defending a cultural plurality or hybridity.

Ethnicity is a language- and power-driven self-awareness. The construction of ethnicity is an activity whose effects are never firmly fixed; it is never present. Always re-presented and reiterated, it is produced in the slippage. It is constantly and simultaneously both under erasure and reiterated, an irreducible dilemma of representation charged with ironic overtones, hyperbole, broken syntax. Ethnicity is constructed performatively and functions metonymically. Ethnic performativity is a function of the reiterative practice of regulatory discursive regimes that control the formation of personal and collective identity. There are lines of flight in it, because it is an assemblage of a multiplicity of perceptions without a center or verifiable data other than the actual process of its own reiteration as a "truth effect." Its repetition, a sort of never-ending dress rehearsal, produces and sustains the power of the truth effect and the discursive regime that has constructed it and operates in the production of racialized and ethnicized bodies.

The *testimonio* as a written means to begin exploring the contours of a collective identity is a concrete historical genre that evolved in Latin America during the *guerrillerista* period (1960–90) just as it had, in similar fashion, in other parts of the world during specific historical moments, such as the Spanish Civil War, the Algerian war, or the Palestinian struggle for a homeland. Homi Bhabha, among others, finds similar expressions in Southeast Asia, and, of course, African texts of a similar nature have appeared during that continent's numerous struggles for liberation from Western powers.

These imperfect, reaccented discourses carry within them a budding questioning of Western leftist thinking by virtue of their own bilingual, ethnicized nature, which challenges myths of interpretative transparency and mastery. Within this context, Menchú's writing is not only the product of temporal conditions in particular spatial locations, but also a transgressive way of re-placing, if not re-lacing, revolutionary discourse from within a crypto-feminist, subaltern perspective. It undermines naive meanings about the alleged simplicity of subaltern subjects, yet at the same time impairs doctrinaire meanings of traditional Marxist revolutionary rhetoric. For these reasons, although Menchú's discourse is a privileged place from which to subvert Guatemalan Ladino dominant discourse, the slippages within it mark issues that the official left has never cared to confront.

However, given that these discursive elements emerge within her zig-zagging narrative logic, it is also inevitable that they would create a certain degree of cultural misunderstanding. For this reason, the Guatemalan left does not realize that it is being criticized in the text because it chooses to emphasize and identify with those passages that support its ideological tenets. On the other hand, non-Guatemalan observers would naturally derive different conclusions from analogous passages because their readings are framed more by their singular ways of perceiving political issues.

The misunderstanding signaled earlier has led some to wonder how Menchú's voice was mediated by the collaboration of Elisabeth Burgos-Debray in the compilation of her testimony. In an interview with Stoll that is quoted in his book, Burgos-Debray claimed that she considerably edited the transcription of Menchú's oral testimony:

> Her Spanish was very basic. She translated from her own language [in her head]; this is what cost me a lot. Yes, I corrected verb tenses and noun genders, as otherwise it would not have made sense, but always trying to retain her own powerful form of expression. Rigoberta's narrative was anything but chronological. It had to be put in order. . . . I had to reorder a lot to give the text a thread, to give it the sense of a life, to make it a story, so that it could reach the general public, which I did via a card file, then cutting and pasting. It was hard to give it a sense of continuity in Rigoberta's own words. (185)

Stoll uses this quotation to argue that Menchú's words could not possibly have been her own. What is implicit in his observation, however inadvertently, is that to make the text "intelligible" to "the general public," Burgos-Debray attempted to subordinate the "subaltern" Maya component of the text (in the sense in which Spivak defines it), turning it into a hybrid Western or Maya document with clear Western legibility. It is as such that Menchú's story is now coming under attack.[18] However, Stoll himself contradicted his own argument when he stated in subsequent interviews that he had heard the bulk of the tapes of the Menchú interviews in Burgos-Debray's possession and that they pretty much flow in the same format as the book. Therefore, we must ask, did Burgos-Debray change the manuscript and disguise

Menchú's Maya voice, or is the book a relatively faithful transcription and translation of the recording? Why did Stoll contradict himself? What is at stake here?

The Anthropologist, the Subaltern Subject, and "Truth"

Demanding representational accuracy in the positivist sense, modern (used here in opposition to *postmodern*) normative conditions have framed, formed, commodified, reified, and reiterated that which has come to be called "ethnicity." In this context, the dominant power's "regime of truth" has always recognized the intellectual who interprets the subaltern subject in the name of Western accuracy. It has been less interested in deconstructing particular strategies deployed by the subaltern subject in metropolitan or foreign spaces, or even in its ways of attempting to frame historical data in non-Western parameters. It is for this reason that Menchú's discourse became stereotyped: it turned into that "otherness" that is at once the object of desire and derision that Bhabha discusses. Menchú opened up the indigenous or Native American fantasy that operates at the same time as the stereotype of phobia and fetish for neoconservative cultural inclinations.

Stoll's book evidences the problematics of a positivist assessment of *testimonio* in its shifts between a supposed scientific "objectivity" and a tendency to "take sides" in the complicated matter of "veracity" in Menchú's discourse. In his text there is no treatment of textual absences, just of closed monads, elements irredeemably separated from the trace of the signifier that names them. His only concern seems to be "a verifiable truth": the "tangential relationship to her life, family and village" (189). For this reason, Stoll ridicules the notion of "collective memory" (190) and criticizes the framework of the *testimonio* in general on the basis that it is not one conducive to finding a certified truth. He sees in the genre "a significant amount of reinvention" (192) and a lack of linear clarity. Indeed, as I explained earlier, the *testimonio* is not the equivalent of a sworn testimony in which every fact has been verified and can be classified as evidence of a crime.[19]

Stoll claims to maintain a "pure" view of Menchú's narrative while at the same time recognizing the myths that may lead the scientist and the public in general to misinterpret them. For example, he views the sympathy for Menchú outside of Guatemala as symptomatic of what he calls "romancing the revolution" (277):

> *I, Rigoberta Menchú* is one of many works to win a mass audience by appeal-
> ing to Western expectations about native people. . . . Since indígenas and
> peasants tend to be viewed as rustic innocents, they may have to charm their
> audience just to get a hearing. . . . Anthropologists are not completely inno-
> cent in this regard: although we refute the crudest expectations, our studies
> of culture and tradition have encouraged new forms of paternalism. (232)

Those romantics who idealize the claims of "native" peoples seem to be
Stoll's "others" here, although he suggests that anthropologists have operated under the same myths. He also admits Western anthropologists' role
in granting their subjects a special claim to truth even as they interpellate
that truth according to Western symbolic systems. Stoll himself contends
that he is "innocent"; however, he is uninfluenced by mythologies regarding the "indigenous" speaker. Yet his use of words such as "innocent," "hearing," and "win" reveal that his text has more in common with the protocol
of the U.S. judicial system than with a self-aware anthropological project
that values different discursive and cultural systems.

In fact, Stoll's book reveals an indifference to cultural difference—particularly in relation to Maya concepts of time, history, and community—
that is surprising in the work of an anthropologist. It also reflects a poor
understanding of the social and cultural realities of the Ladino Western elite
in Guatemala, where the government, the newspapers, and the judicial system have worked more like an obscure (and obscuring) Kafkaesque laby-
rinth than like the ideal "enlightened" image projected by its U.S. counterpart.

Stoll's principal rhetorical device is to repeatedly suggest the connection
between Menchú and Marxism without ever offering conclusive proof of it.
For example, he states:

> Cuban promotion of Rigoberta and Elisabeth's book suggested that it might
> be speaking for the guerrillas more than for peasants. The internecine disputes
> dividing Rigoberta's neighbors dropped out of the story, making armed strug-
> gle sound like an inevitable reaction to oppression, at a time when Mayas were
> desperate to escape the violence. *I, Rigoberta Menchú* became a way to mobi-
> lize foreign support for a wounded, retreating insurgency. (xiii)[20]

The mention of Cuba cannot be accidental: for U.S. readers, it is an emotionally charged trope of Soviet intervention in Latin America. By rhetorically

associating Menchú with Cuba here, Stoll insinuates that Menchú herself was an arms-wielding insurgent combatant, even though he is seemingly focusing on the uses of her text after its publication. One could claim that what Stoll's text does best is to expose the double bind of the colonizer's discourse regarding "truth," "ethnicity," "culture," "ideology," and politics. Indeed I believe that it has generated so much debate because it points to unresolved contradictions in the cultural logic of the West. This is so especially with regard to the predominance of left-right polemics over other types of political speech and rhetoric available to subaltern subjects in a non-Western framework. The nature of the controversy surrounding Stoll's book in the U.S. press and among the U.S. intellectual elite suggests that the Central American debate is about U.S. politics and paranoia more than about a Maya "truth."

This obsession with an imaginary cold war perspective denies Menchú any agency outside that dynamic because it ignores political, economic, and social issues within Guatemala. It negates the possibility that Menchú's text was a strategic discourse in defense not of leftist guerrillas per se, but of a certain sector of the Maya people that Menchú perceived as victims of a genocidal policy perpetrated by the government of Guatemala itself. Menchú was certainly not making up her story, nor does Stoll ever say she was. If Menchú crafted a strategic discourse to prevent the continued genocide of her people, how can we question the authenticity of that act?

Stoll uses the testimony of other "authentic natives" to contradict the "authenticity" of Menchú. This textual strategy implies that the subaltern subjects' claim to truth remains intact even as it silences the most prominent subaltern voice. Morever, by deciding himself which of these testimonies represents the "authentic" voice of the Maya people, Stoll implies that the subaltern's discourse can be validated only by a white anthropologist. Thus, although he uses new tactics, he still reverts to the classical attitude of his field, maintaining intact the hegemony of the white anthropologist while apparently giving credence to the subaltern's discourse. Stoll is right in arguing that Guatemalan history needs to be reconstructed with multiple voices, but he undercuts that project with his own text. After all, Western anthropologists have imposed their own views on indigenous people, not respecting their truth in their own terms. Guatemalans, Maya and non-Maya alike, need to reconstruct their history with multiple voices and not with a single voice or truth, but they do not need a self-chosen American arbitrator to do so.

Assuming that indigenous peoples are incapable of strategically realizing their own goals outside of Western paradigms, Stoll gives the following explanation of why peasants join a guerrilla organization or support insurgents: "Perhaps peasants are inspired by revolutionary ideology, that is, the idea of transforming society. Or perhaps . . . they think they have something more immediate to gain. Or perhaps they are pressured into cooperating with the guerrillas, after being swept up in a process of provocation, retaliation, and polarization that forces them to choose sides" (63). While ethnicity is central to Menchú, nowhere does Stoll offer the explanation of an ethnic reaction against racism as a possible reason for Mayas' joining the EGP. He also does not quote Guatemalan sources that document that even well-off Mayas gave this very explanation for joining the guerrilla movement (Arias, Porras, Payeras, and Colom, among others). In this sense, the situation is analogous to that of South Africa's African National Congress (ANC): even though some of the rhetoric of the ANC had a clear Marxist content, it attracted even upper-middle-class South Africans because its primary goal was to end racism. One of the issues not yet studied in depth to this day is precisely the abyss that exists between official revolutionary rhetoric and the actual subjective motivations of individuals joining an organization onto which they project their own phantasms or desires, which often contradict the organization's own rhetoric.

Why does Stoll avoid the issue of racism? In Menchú's book, it is very clear. She tells us: "My grandfather used to curse the Spaniards. The Spaniards were at the root of our plight. They began taking so many things out of our lands, they began stealing from us. Our ancestors' finest sons were those who were dishonoured. They even raped the queens elected by our community. That's how the *ladinos* came into being" (189). To ignore such an assertion implies that ethnicity is only a trope for muddled thinking rather than a political issue based on perceived differences between groups. In this sense Stoll's narrative seems a throwback to, on the one hand, a "disdain" for understanding modes of being different from those of the West and, on the other, a marked resistance to accepting or valuing that particular difference.

Cognizant of both the imprecision of language and the limits on cultural understanding, most Western academics recognize that they exercise less authority than in the past, though they experience greater dialogism when engaging "otherness." Writing in general is unable to "capture" otherness by virtue of the floating signifiers that perpetually defer meaning and resist rational interpretation in a sea of contradictions that trap any semblance of "truth" in semantic ambiguities or silent regions that hide the other's secrets. Those dark voids of reason become indefensible positions that, to paraphrase Derrida in *Writing and Difference,* cannot make our meaning coincide with their meaning.

Stoll does acknowledge the impossibility of "knowing the truth" when he says, "Still another reason these incidents are difficult to recover is that bystanders were confused about exactly who was doing what to whom" (33). He is also aware of the contradictions that his own discourse generates. As a result, he defends his version of things by arguing that the left wants to cover it up:

> In the case of the book you have in your hands, a white male anthropologist is accusing an indigenous woman of making up part of her story. The important issue is not whether she did or not. Instead, it is Western domination, which I am obviously perpetrating. Reasoning like this enables Rigoberta's story to be removed from the field of testable propositions, to instead use as a proof-text that foreigners can use to validate themselves. (277)

The subtle rhetorical shift in the last sentence to the xenophobic term "foreigners" cancels out Stoll's acknowledgment of his own "otherness" (that is, his own "foreignness" within Guatemala itself. The "foreigners" here are not anthropologists like him. They are Guatemala's own leftist intellectuals, who repudiate scientific methods by removing the story "from the field of testable propositions" and "use" Menchú's text for their own ends. The slippage of the term "foreigners" gives away his ideological fabric and undermines his allegation that what he intends to do is provide a constructive critique.

Stoll divides Mayas into two groups in his work: Menchú and "reliable witnesses." He complains that Menchú got the dates confused as to when the army first sent troops to the town of Uspantán, even though he knows that, when she recorded the material in January 1982, she was suffering from war trauma and had to rely on only her own memory of the events that took place in her community three years before. He never criticizes his own "reliable witnesses" about their inability to remember dates. In fact, it is amusing to point out that Stoll himself, armed with historical data, confuses dates as well. For example, he transposes the dates when activists were secretly

organizing the community (1977–78) with those when the army first initiated the repression in the area after the EGP occupied Uspantán in April
1979. Errors like this undermine his own claim to truth, whose declared
purpose is to root out and correct the errors in another text that does not
make the same type of claim to truth.

Stoll's apparent belief that the interviews with other Maya subjects are
untouched by envy, fear, or greed, as well as the conclusions that he derives
from them, suggests that he sees Mayas as "informants" in the conventional
sense of positivist anthropology. He never relinquishes his position that his
voice is the only one authorized to comment on and frame the meaning of
the raw material that they provide. Nonetheless, the contradictions of this
position become obvious immediately. Unable to offer any proof other than
the credibility of his informants and his own word that such discursivity is
more trustworthy than Menchú's because it is not tainted with political
partisanship, Stoll reinforces the weight of their authority with disruptive
justifications like the following: "Given the vagaries of memory and the
translation of eyewitness accounts into secondhand ones [Stoll does not
speak any Maya language], it is hardly surprising that there are conflicting
versions" (69). Despite these elliptical permutations, doubts about concrete
facts remain, and he is forced to admit it. Some of these involve the case of
San Pablo, where everyone agrees that the army attacked the village, yet no
one agrees on why or how it happened, how it started, or how many were
killed.

Another element that deflates the illusion of totality is that Maya subjects speak in the midst of a community occupied by the army, in a space
in which armed soldiers and intelligence agents roam freely. As a consequence, their discourses are even less "objective" or "truthful." They are always
more metamorphosed and metaphorized than in the standard context in
which communication takes place. Stoll is thus forced to admit, "Perhaps my
sources in Chajul were still too afraid of the Guatemalan army to acknowledge what they had witnessed" (69). Or, "Obviously the two widows could
be afraid to acknowledge what they remember" (87).

His recourse is to go back to the generic "witness" issue as a defense: "The
important point is that [Menchú's] story . . . is not the eyewitness account
that it purports to be" (70). He is thus able to "know" more than Menchú
on the grounds that he never claimed he was present when the events happened, whereas, according to him, she did. For Stoll, Menchú's eye has to

be the narrating "I," disregarding the fact that, as an ethnic *testimonio,* her book is a communal performance and reappropriation of the collective historical signs, and for Mayas there is no clear separation between an individual subject and a community, between "being" and "belonging." In this instance, Stoll's positioning appears to be the synecdoche of a desire for "authorization" in the face of cultural differentiation that makes it problematic to fix the "native's" will to power. The anthropologist's desire for panoptical control is set off balance, disquieted, by the subaltern subject who dares to speak for herself. When the invisible subject claims a right to be seen and heard in the language of its oppressor, the native's refusal to address the colonizer in his own terms is justified by the colonizer in the language of paranoia, as both Bhabha and Slavoj Žižek have pointed out. Could we explain Stoll's argument in these terms? That is, could we say that he refuses to admit he is playing the performative role of an oppressor, because he claims to make his gesture in the name of an alleged and undefined "truth" whose representativity he either confiscates or craves?

We know from Edward Said that the exercise of a certain type of cultural production by Western academics—themselves products of the liberal humanist tradition that presented their privilege as a "natural" superiority over subaltern subjects—was decisive not only in framing the historical context of colonialism, but more specifically in constructing the strategies for the marginalization of ethnic subjects. The subjectification of those individuals was in turn made possible and plausible, as Bhabha argues, through the stereotypical discourse the humanists themselves created.

What some scholars still do not realize is that when we identify with a certain political discourse, we relate to a fantasy that stages a scenario hidden behind the shifting meaning of the words. Encoded in this fantasy is a resistance to meanings by virtue of the impossibility of translating and transculturating subaltern languages into anything other than metaphorizations. These shifting meanings prevent any categorical assertion about established truths, an indeterminacy that provides the grounds for legitimizing "listening" to subaltern subjects, that is, recognizing the validity of given discourses that operate as symbolic expressions of agency, as tropes for the construction of given identities, even if they do not fit entirely within the Western conception of rationality, which we now recognize are ambiguous and indeterminate as well.

Tentative Conclusions

The controversy engendered around Menchú gives us a better understanding of the issues with which her uncanny centrality in U.S. cultural debates confronts us. These include the nature of testimonial literature, the need to rethink the concept of identity, and the desires and fantasies of subjective transformation, but also the identity politics that operate as a phantasm of the fears of disempowerment on the part of hegemonic subjects. It also brings us back to the question of whether a *testimonio* should be read only as a narration of "urgency" or else as an "unhomely fiction," that is, as "a fiction which would focus on those freak social and cultural displacements, as a fiction which relates the traumatic ambivalences of a personal psychic history to the wider disjunction of political existence."[21]

Perhaps the two salient issues of the debate are the performative nature of ethnicity as a creative assemblage of the self and the problematics of reading *testimonios*. If we accept the first notion as valid, we must recognize that only the *bricoleur* assembling his or her own particular sense of ethnicity can claim any "truth-effect" for his or her singular performativity, because no one else can "read" or decode the set of rules from which the subaltern subject might be operating in the process of exercising agency by reinventing his or her own self as a way of restructuring relations of power with hegemonic subjects. As for the second, we can ask ourselves whether reading a *testimonio* involves the reader in a continuous "act of faith" unlike that involved in literary reading. This is a broad issue that needs to be explored further, for it leads to the question of how the reader's solidarity or political identification with victims, dissidents, and opposition movements works in the case of a *testimonio*. Answering this question implies a new theory of reading given that, although Stoll argues that human rights is solely a legal discourse, it is in fact a kind of affective, empathetic reading in which individuals who enjoy guaranteed freedoms or hegemonic positions discover and sympathize with subaltern subjects. It is a reading, however, that may lead to concrete political action. Thus reading a *testimonio* is a radically different process not only from reading literature but also from reading legal documents, scientific data, and other such texts. For this reason, the question of how the reader of a *testimonio* "authenticates" its meaning is quite complex, and it remains an unexplored issue.

[In the Menchú-Stoll debate the indigenous subject is being held up to a standard of "truth" that those who flaunted other discourses have never had to meet. Menchú's efforts were aimed at ending the massacre of her people at a time when indigenous people did not enjoy any kind of international sympathy, much less privileged status. Her text and her subsequent political efforts forged the recognition of Maya subjectivity as well as the acceptance of the growing social, cultural, and political importance of Maya people. Menchú performed a role to achieve these aims, and fortunately she has been largely successful. If her text, which did not make any historical claims to truth, achieved the goal of ending the massacre and creating respect for Maya culture, does it really matter if it did not conform to the way Western science contextualizes documentary "facts"? The success of subaltern subjects in representing themselves destabilized the Western scientific structure of power. As a result, traditional academics now have a harder time preserving their privileges. The resilience of Menchú herself, her own political achievements after Stoll's book, and the overall emergence of the Maya community as a collective actor in Mesoamerican politics suggest that the hierarchical tower constructed by modern Western academics may indeed be built on the shifting sands of cultural displacement, indeterminacy, and mistranslation. Our recognition of the power/truth dynamic of all texts, regardless of their genre, razes that vertical structure originally construed by Western canonicity, placing on a horizontal plane the heterogeneous nature of all textuality.

5

After the Controversy: Lessons Learned about Subalternity and the Indigenous Subject

I n the United States, the debate over Rigoberta Menchú's *testimonio* generated by David Stoll's book centered on whether Menchú told the "truth" regarding details of her personal life. According to her critics, her "lies" discredited her testimony and reduced the moral authority of leftist intellectuals who taught testimonial texts. This focus on verifiable facts conveniently ignored a discursive war tied to cold war politics. For this reason, in the previous chapter I explored the problematics of "truth," the nature of the *testimonio* as a genre, and the relationship between political solidarity and subaltern narrative to question some of the premises on which Stoll's book is based.

In this chapter I would like to address the specific ways in which Stoll's new defense of his book in "The Battle of Rigoberta," a chapter published in *The Rigoberta Menchú Controversy* (2001), continues to read Menchú "out of context" for an uninformed U.S. audience. In that chapter Stoll portrays Menchú's discourse as "propaganda" for a guerrilla organization, the Guerrilla Army of the Poor (EGP). By eliminating Menchú's own articulation of power and how it is linked to the specific political contingency of a heterotopical space named "Guatemala," Stoll invests Menchú with a different reality.[1] In Stoll's new reading, she becomes the phantasm of a communist liar. By insinuating that Menchús' signifiers are brimming with ideologems that make her ethnicity redundant, he also conveniently forces her into the stereotype of the devious, conniving person of color. The result is this: although in the international political arena and in Guatemala Menchú has survived the controversy that sought to besmirch her image, she has gained a negative public perception in the United States, and her persona has been stripped of agency here. This iconic transmutation of Menchú facilitates a reversal of meanings in her text, thus creating a more generalized American *méconnaissance* of her reality.

When the connections with Guatemalan political history are reestablished, however, a different reading of Menchú comes forth. In this one, what we see is a singular Maya political actor speaking out in an embryonic pluricultural discourse that evokes the illusory potential for the political transformation of her country at a particular crossroads in its fortunes.[2] It is only when we reconnect a subaltern reading of her text with Guatemalan problematics and insert both into a historical continuum that we can grasp what her voice can mean for Latin American cultural studies. Indeed, we could claim that the Menchú controversy is not one about what she said, that part of it is an imaginary act. Rather, it is a symbolic lesion about the unwillingness of hegemonic intellectuals to listen to subaltern ones.

In "The Battle of Rigoberta," Stoll states that he remains adamantly convinced that Menchú's story is simply the EGP's version of events. An a priori assumption is thus inscribed within his rhetorical strategy: that as a subaltern, ethnicized woman, Menchú could be easily convinced to mimic the EGP's line with the same degree of innocence with which her father, Vicente Menchú, mimicked—in Stoll's understanding of this event—the students' slogans on the eve of his death amid the flames that engulfed the Spanish embassy in Guatemala City. In his chapter of *The Rigoberta Menchú Controversy,* Stoll says: "The story that [Menchú] told and Elisabeth Burgos turned into a book was instead an answer to the question: Why should *we* care? About another far-off conflict in which people *we* don't know are being killed for reasons *we* don't understand" (392, my emphasis). From this quote it is all too clear that if we are Guatemalans, or even nonwhite Americans, we cannot connect with Stoll's imperial "we." It is a noninclusive pronoun from which all those to whom this is not "another" conflict but a do-or-die home affair, and certainly not a "far-off" one, are excluded, a fair-enough assumption in a local newspaper or a supermarket tabloid, but unacceptable in an academic publication.[3]

Given that Stoll jumps from the previous quote to a rhetorical question in which he asks himself whether Menchú's version was the inevitable response of all Guatemala's poor to the symptoms of oppression, we can safely conclude that his stake lies in undermining what he perceives to be the EGP's narrative. He reads it as claiming that yes, violence was the only possible response to decades of military dictatorship, exploitation, oppression, and discrimination against the majority of that nation's citizens. Stoll worries that unless this story is questioned, the Guatemalan left will always remain on the moral high ground. It is from this perspective that we should read his critique. It reiterates the thesis he had previously presented in his second book, *Between Two Armies* (1993), that the Ixils (a Maya ethnic group) who supported Guatemalan revolutionaries in the early 1980s did so because they were caught in the cross fire between the guerrillas and the army, not because revolutionary violence expressed the community's outrage or aspirations.[4] When told of this thesis, César Montes (nom de guerre of Julio César Macías), commander in chief of the EGP from its founding in 1972 to 1976, responded: "Stoll lies. We never went up the mountains to look for the Ixils. They came down to the jungle looking for us, and demanding our help."[5] Stoll claims in "The Battle of Rigoberta":

> If you take the book (i.e., Menchú's book) at face value, as an eyewitness account, you will probably conclude that guerrilla warfare in Guatemala grew out of peasants' need to defend themselves from intolerable conditions.
>
> Because of the different story I heard from many peasants, this is what became the most important issue for me: Was the Guerrilla Army of the Poor (EGP) that Rigoberta joined, and whose version of events she gave us in 1982, an inevitable response by the poor to oppression? Should the conflict be understood primarily in social terms, as the inevitable outcome of centuries of oppression suffered by Guatemala's indigenous population? Or is it better explained on the political level, as the result of particular decisions made by particular groups including the U.S. government, the Guatemalan oligarchy, the Guatemalan army, and the opposition groups that decided to fight back with guerrilla warfare? (393)

This is a long, complex, and contradictory passage, so we should examine it carefully. Stoll claims, first, that it was because of Menchú's testimonial that white Americans believe that guerrilla warfare was necessary in her country and, second, that it was the EGP's version of what happened that Menchú reproduced in her 1982 *testimonio*. Because he reiterates these particulars more than once, adding a few pages later that "Rigoberta's story was a moral narrative that simplified the complexities of the Guatemalan

conflict in order to engage foreign sympathies" (399), we have to ask ourselves, are these assertions true? Regarding the first, I know that solidarity
committees in the United States during the 1980s did not understand it in
this way. I myself was one of the primary speakers touring the United States
in 1983, 1984, and 1985, giving lectures throughout the country under the
sponsorship of NISGUA (the Network in Solidarity with Guatemala) as well
as independently. Whether these were closed-door sessions or meetings open
to the public and the press, the simplistic political position Stoll describes
was not the one I espoused.[6] On the contrary, I offered an analysis that followed what I had already published by that date (articles to which I will
refer later), namely, that the crisis of the late 1970s in Guatemala was the
result of an accelerated process of modernization rather than the inevitable
outcome of centuries of oppression.[7]

Solidarity with Guatemala began when Noelle Thomas, a Guatemalan-
American, moved from her country to the United States in the early 1970s,
founded the first working groups on Guatemala in the Bay Area, and contributed to the volume edited by Susanne Jonas and David Tobis, *Guatemala*
(1974). This initiative was followed by the founding of the Guatemala News
and Information Bureau (GNIB) by José Gutierrez, Naomi Roht, Chris
Rosene, and Isabel Alegría, also in the Bay Area, in 1977. They began publishing *Report on Guatemala* (or *Guatemala!* as it was originally titled) in
1978. Other early members of the GNIB included Peggy Handler, Dede
Dotson, and Elissa Miller. GNIB's first public activity was a tour by Miguel
Angel Albizúrez focusing on the 1977 Guatemalan miners' strike, which will
be described later in this chapter. By 1981, three years before the publication
of Menchú's book in Spanish and four years before its publication in English, there was already a sufficient number of solidarity committees in the
United States to warrant the founding of NISGUA, in Washington, D.C., to
coordinate them and to create a lobbying group on Capitol Hill. Marcie
Mersky was hired as NISGUA's coordinator, and she played that role until
mid-1984. NISGUA sponsored Menchú's first national speaking tour in 1982,
after her book's contents had been recorded but before it was published.

In defense of his position, Stoll repeats in "The Battle of Rigoberta" the
same rhetorical ploy displayed in his book. He manipulates his prospective
reader into an either/or situation. Stoll asks whether we should understand
the situation in Guatemala socially or politically. This implies that Menchú,
the EGP, and the Unidad Revolucionaria Nacional Guatemalteca (URNG,

Guatemalan National Revolutionary Unit), which Stoll conflates—conveniently ignoring the endless polemics among leftist organizations within and outside of the URNG—offered a "social" analysis. In truth, the EGP did not advance a "sociological" explanation of the conflict prior to 1984.[8] Besides, political discourses are seldom monologic, especially in the case of heterogeneous leftist organizations. Indeed, every revolutionary organization cites different reasons to justify its existence, a fact that is more revealing about the nature of the imaginary of the organizations in question than about the conflict itself. Political explanations are ideological constructs based on singular understandings of an imagined community and illusory situations for which a multiplicity of meanings can obviously be offered. In this spirit, we could also ask, why should we give credence to a white American unfamiliar with the intimate or secret debates, conflicts, or dissidences within and between the revolutionary organizations of the time when he attempts to explain the organic implications of a political conflict among Guatemalans? Please do not think that I am plunging into racism in reverse here. There are many distinguished Americans who have spent their entire lives studying the country's political conflict. I do not see them in the same light as Stoll. What concerns me here, rather, are the consequences of Stoll's dwelling on this issue as if he were the ultimate arbitrator or authority on the subject, something that other non-Guatemalan experts have never done.[9]

It is crucial to keep in mind that Menchú's discourse did not come under attack because she was "Maya" or "Guatemalan," but because she was purported to be a "militant of the EGP," a revolutionary organization that, within the U.S. scheme of politics, was considered radical. In other words, the issue was not ethnicity or ethnic authenticity. Rather, it was that as she became "Westernized," she "chose" the "wrong" set of signs by which to insert herself within an acceptable U.S. protocol. That is, rather than embracing capitalism or the Republican Party, Menchú welcomed their "other." And because that other was the specter of the phantasms—"radical," "Marxist," "guerrilla," "revolutionary"—that conservatives abjured, her word became subject to intense scrutiny, the perfect candidate for "thought correction."

In "The Battle of Rigoberta," Stoll's fundamental argument against the EGP is not that they were wrong or evil, but that they took the war to Maya territory. He presents himself as showing that some Mayas were reluctant to join the guerrilla effort, that the guerrillas were often the first armed men to visit many Maya villages, and that guerrilla enlistment grew only as a response to military repression of those villages the guerrillas had visited. He also implies that all leftists somehow tried to keep this story from coming out:

> My books are controversial because they . . . challenge the assumption that the insurgency of the late 1970s and early 1980s was an inevitable Mayan reaction to oppression. That Mayans had very mixed feelings about the guerrillas is not a discovery made by myself. Although the EGP was stronger in Rigoberta's region . . . a string of ethnographers . . . have had doubts about the depth of its support, as have Yvon Le Bot (1995) and Carol Smith. (396)

In this passage Stoll introduces an endnote after his admission that he was not the one who discovered the Mayas' mixed feelings about the guerrillas. In that endnote he attributes some of his discovery to the chapters published by Víctor Montejo and Duncan Earle in *The Rigoberta Menchú Controversy*. This suggests, of course, that the information in those chapters was introduced after the publication of his book on Menchú and thus indirectly implies his own originality. He then wistfully laments that Mario Roberto Morales did not say more in his chapter, also in that volume, about his experiences in the Movimiento Revolucionario del Pueblo–Ixim, an organization at odds with the URNG. This desire to give Morales credit that does not belong to him might be a latent signal of Stoll's empathy with Morales's virulent dislike of the URNG.[10]

Yet in Stoll's bibliography on page 409 of *The Rigoberta Menchú Controversy*, the first works listed are my own, a book chapter published in Spanish beginning in 1985 and another published in English beginning in 1990.[11] And what do I state in those chapters? That Mayas were reluctant to join the guerrilla effort, that the guerrillas were often the first armed men to visit many Maya villages, and that guerrilla enlistment grew only after army repression began against those villages visited by the guerrillas. But those ideas are not even mine. I cite the previous sources in my endnotes to those chapters. Those ideas had been discussed in Guatemala since the early 1970s and had already been published by Ricardo Falla and Gustavo Porras in 1978 in *ECA* magazine. I merely quoted their arguments in my 1985 chapter, "Historia del Movimiento Indígena en Guatemala, 1970–1983," originally in Spanish and presented as a paper at a forum organized by FLACSO in San José, Costa Rica, in 1983 and published two years later in *Movimientos*

populares en America Central, edited by Rafael Menjívar and Daniel Camacho. Among the things that appear there are the following: "In the critical
self-evaluation [made in 1972], the different groups that survived the debacle suffered by the Rebel Armed Forces (FAR) [in the late 1960s] suggested
that one of the main causes of FAR's defeat had been its incapacity to mobilize indigenous people" (72, my translation).[12] This information, as I mentioned in a footnote to my chapter, came from Ricardo Ramírez's *Document
of March 1967*. Ramírez became commander in chief of the EGP under the
nom de guerre of Rolando Morán, and the document in question expressed
his explanation of FAR's original failure in the first half of the 1960s. It had
been published in 1967, nearly thirty years before Stoll made similar claims.
On the same page of my chapter, I quote Pedro Chamix's explanation of how
"this new concept of class struggle . . . within the Guatemalan left . . . was
the result, on the one hand, of the analysis of the failure of the revolutionary movement in [the 1960s] and, on the other, a consequence of the debate
about indigenous issues at the beginning of the 1970s" (72). This quote came
from an article in *Polémica,* a magazine that devoted its January–February
1982 issue to this topic. None of these sources are acknowledged by Stoll,
who reads Spanish, although he included my chapters in his bibliography.

Later in my 1985 chapter, I mentioned that the Maya movement began to
coalesce in the early 1970s as a result of the organizational efforts of Acción
Católica (Catholic Action) in the 1960s, the access that many Mayas then
attained to education, and the accelerated growth that the country underwent in the same decade, generating inflation and dislocating indigenous
peasants as they became "semi-proletarianized" (78). We may disagree with
the more Marxist tenor of the chapter nowadays (I myself do), but we cannot ignore the facts it presents.

In my 1985 chapter I also mentioned, when referring to the Ixil mayor of
Nebaj, Sebastián Guzmán, that the first time a group of Mayas were accused
of being "communists," in 1973, it was done by other Mayas (87), as the previously tightly knit Maya community was beginning to unravel in the wake
of the rapid development of the 1960s.[13] On page 96 I alluded to the fact
that violence in the Ixil country was initiated by the EGP when it executed
Luis Arenas, known as the "Tiger of Ixcán," on 7 July 1975, and that the
neighboring village of Ilom celebrated his death by playing marimbas for
two days straight.[14] On pages 97 and 98 I quoted Father Fidel Hernández of
the Sacred Heart order as saying that in February 1979, eighty-four leaders

from northern Quiché Ixil country had requested arms to protect their people from the army. He tried to calm them down, because not all Mayas identified with armed struggle at the time, and I added on page 99 that many were turning away from armed struggle and moving in the direction of ethnic-based organizations. I then listed the names of many of those that appeared in 1979 alone.

These statements were reformulated in the 1990 English version of my chapter, an abridged version from the Spanish published in *Guatemalan Indians and the State, 1540 to 1988*, edited by Carol Smith. In it I repeated aspects of the accelerated modernization of the 1960s and quoted a new Maya document written by the Ja C'amabal I'b collective and presented to the United Nations Subcommission on Ethnic Minorities in Geneva in August 1984 (232). The document makes it clear that the option for armed struggle chosen by a segment of the Maya population was the result of accelerated modernization and not of centuries of languishing in backward conditions. In this version I also clearly outlined where the roots of the confrontation lay:

> In late 1973, the Central American Common Market . . . was overwhelmed by a monetary crisis. . . . This undercut many of the development processes, thus closing off possibilities and expectations that had been generating since the early 1960s. The country once more began to polarize socially and politically. . . .
>
> As class differences within the (Maya) communities increased, the crisis of values became deeper and more pronounced. The traditional structure of authority was basically undermined. . . .
>
> Study groups, with topics such as peasant rights and the rights of all Guatemalan citizens, were formed (among Mayas). They studied the country's constitution in order to know what it said and to contrast what was written in reality. This, in turn, raised the issue of human rights and the discussions became more explicitly political. (240, 241)

In the English version I added information about the first political advances by Mayas in the 1970s, with the election of Tetzahuic Tohón as representative from the department of Sololá and Pedro Verona Cúmez from Chimaltenango (242), as proof of how Mayas were regaining control of local government from Ladinos in the 1970s. This information comes from Ricardo

Falla's 1978 article "El movimiento indígena," which appears in the bibliography of the book and had not been quoted in the 1985 version. Finally, I restated Porras's argument:

> As Gustavo Porras [1978] has already pointed out, we must note that the revolutionary crisis resulted from the modernization efforts initiated by the state. The state simultaneously fulfilled the role of agent for development and repressor of the population in order to keep the modernizing features introduced from bringing about changes in the power structure. Those attempts at modernization, nevertheless, generated expectations in the rural population and unsettled traditional order by generating rapid changes in society's class composition, especially among Indian cultivators and rural middle sectors. (255–56)

Porras's article is also in the bibliography, as are all other sources. Thus, when in "The Battle of Rigoberta" Stoll rhetorically asks whether the Guatemalan revolutionary crisis is better explained on the political level, as the result of decisions made by particular groups including the U.S. government, the Guatemalan oligarchy, the Guatemalan army, or opposition groups that decided to fight back with guerrilla warfare—purportedly because this is a more rational or enlightened conclusion than the ones offered by the Guatemalan left—he is on shaky ground. He is claiming as his own conclusions that were published decades earlier by Guatemalan academics, militants, and critics of the left from within the left itself. When he states, "If the EGP was to be believed, the Ixils were so oppressed that they had no choice but to join the insurgency" (393–94) or "The pre-EGP Ixils were not facing intense repression. Despite patronal backlashes, they were regaining control of local government from ladinos" (394), one can only conclude either that he is deliberately misinforming his readers by not acknowledging Guatemalan sources (present in his bibliography) or that he is referring to documents none of us knows. No EGP statement claims that the Ixils were oppressed. In fact, the EGP only once published an official article about the so-called ethnic question. It was written by Mario Payeras but published anonymously in the official magazine of the organization, *Compañero*, in 1982.[15] All other documents tangentially touching on these issues either address the consequences of accelerated modernity or explain in military terms the commencement of operations in the Ixcán rain forest that then climbed into the Ixil region. The intent was not to bring the war to the Maya villages, but it was easier to implant guerrilla columns where there was no great military presence. Payeras says this explicitly in *Days of the Jungle* (1980). In that text, the first famous *testimonio* out of Guatemala and the first to win the Casa de las Américas award, Payeras, a founding member of the EGP, its second in command, and a member of the Executive Commission of its National Directorate, traces the origins of the organization up to its entrance into the Ixcán jungle from Mexican territory on 19 January 1972. He talks explicitly of the early incursion into the Ixcán jungle and details the debate surrounding the need to enter villages with arms for political propaganda purposes.[16] Payeras also mentions the difficulty recruiting Mayas in the early stages of the organization's existence.[17] In the last pages he waxes poetic about the day when his guerrilla column will finally be able to operate in Ixil territory.

Thus we have a genealogy in which the proto-EGP, in the voice of Ramírez, began a critique of the revolutionary or indigenous paradigm in 1967. At the University of San Carlos in the early 1970s, this issue became a full-fledged academic debate in which major Guatemalan figures such as Carlos Guzmán Böckler, Mario Solórzano Foppa, and Severo Martínez participated. This dialogue led to a new problematization of indigenous issues among Guatemalan leftist intellectuals. The debates were published in the 1970s, some in book form.[18] The articles on indigenous mobilization as a result of modernization were published by Falla and Porras in *ECA* in 1978. That same year, Falla published *Quiché rebelde*, a book that evolved from his Ph.D. dissertation and dwells extensively on these issues. Falla defended his dissertation, directed by Richard N. Adams, in the Department of Anthropology of the University of Texas at Austin. Carlos Cabarrús published an equally important text, *La cosmovisión k'ekchí en proceso de cambio*, the following year.

The first massacre against a Maya community took place in May 1978 in Panzós, a town located not in Ixil, but in K'ekchí country, an area that was not organized by the EGP at the time. By 1979, there were spontaneous insurrectional conditions in the Maya highlands, leading to new massacres in the area. In early 1982, *Polémica* dedicated an entire issue to revisiting the issues of the revolutionary-indigenous paradigm. I quoted this material in my 1983 paper, published as a book chapter in Spanish in 1985 and later reworked, abridged, and published as a book chapter in English in 1990. New material appeared in the second half of the 1980s (as I will indicate later), including a journal titled *Opinión Política* and other books by Payeras. The 1990s also provided new texts analyzing the nature of political violence in Guatemala. Why does Stoll omit all of this evidence produced by Guatemalans while claiming that he has the authority to judge what is right or wrong in the country?

The main thing to note is that all these sources, antedating Stoll by decades, came from the ranks of the Guatemalan left in its various guises and tendencies. They were the first ones to raise the issue of the problematic indigenous incorporation into the revolution as a result of debates within the left itself.[19] Other U.S. academics never raised it because only Guatemalans involved in the intimate debates of the revolutionary left in the 1970s knew what had taken place, and no one was talking before the signing of the peace treaty (1996).[20]

In "The Battle of Rigoberta," tracing a brief genealogy of the revolutionary left, Stoll begins by claiming that violence was the end result of the U.S. overthrow of Guatemala's democratic government in 1954.[21] But afterward the dates he uses make it rather hard to establish a chronology of events. Granted, this is only a piece that he wrote to reply to his critics. Nonetheless, it aims to set the record straight. And yet he jumps from 1954 to 1979–82, when "the army began to lash back at the guerrillas by punishing nearby civilians" and "waves of Ixils joined the less homicidal EGP for protection" (394). He writes: "Only in the late 1970s did the guerrillas recruit large numbers of Mayas" (394). In the early 1980s, "the killing was at its peak" (396). In 1982, what mattered most was "orchestrating international pressure against the Guatemalan army to stop the killing" (396). All the dates, except 1954, refer exclusively to events in the Ixil and Quiché regions. Disassociated from other national events, they create an illusion of certainty. However, when we look at Guatemalan affairs in a broader sense, Stoll's dates become less categorical.

The response of both Guatemala's ruling elites and the United States to the events of 1954 was a fast-paced modernization. This has been amply documented by many sources that are available in both English and Spanish.[22] All sources agree that national and international elites promoted the development and diversification of Guatemala's economy in the 1960s. The creation of the Central American Common Market, together with the Alliance for Progress and other development programs, fostered the emergence of new crops for export and introduced new levels of technology and modernization. Indeed, the 1984 document by Ja C'amabal I'b states:

These processes contributed to major social and economic diversification in the Guatemalan countryside, processes with particular impact on Indian communities. In the highlands, textile industries began to appear, finding markets outside the local and regional environment, making incursions to the capital city and even in the international market. The growth in demand for artisan products stimulated production on a large scale and commercialization on a national and international scale.[23]

For Maya communities, this unprecedented growth brought about the construction of new highways and an increase in transportation services. It introduced mass communications and media to many of these communities for the first time:

> In the large villages and their surrounding fields, and in areas which began to be penetrated by highways, sectors of the campesino population began to learn to speak Spanish, breaking the barrier of monolingualism. They began to learn to read and write, accepting ideas and knowledge from beyond the borders of their language and community. People could buy radios and radio stations sprang up which spoke to them of their problems and linked them to a larger world.[24]

Thus, external processes acted on the internal economic, political, and religious issues confronting Maya communities. The tension and resolution of these issues changed the perspective and worldview of many Mayas. At the national level, however, the political situation was different. As Susanne Jonas states:

> The Counterrevolution entailed a redefinition of politics. The two political imperatives were the maintenance of a "favorable" (stable) climate for private investment and the elimination of popular organization and prevention of such mobilization in the future. . . .
>
> "Normal" democratic institutions were further distorted by the militarization of politics after 1954, not only during periods of overt military rule (1963–1966) but also as an integral feature of "civilian" governments. . . . During long periods of supposedly civilian rule (e.g., under Méndez) effective power remained in the hands of the military.[25]

In this rancid climate, the Guatemalan left, destroyed and massacred in the aftermath of the 1954 invasion, gradually reorganized in the late 1950s. This happened primarily through the impulse of a nationalist element within the army's young officers, who continued to harbor some of the developmental illusions left over from the pre-1954 period. They rebelled against the so-called liberation army conformed by foreign mercenaries in August 1956 and on 13 November 1960 attempted a coup to overthrow General Ydigoras Fuentes, who had lent the Helvetia plantation to Cuban dissidents for their use in training for their ill-fated Bay of Pigs landing. The attempted coup failed, but the surviving officers, hiding in the eastern region of the country, went on to found in 1961 the Rebel Armed Forces (FAR), the first guerrilla movement in the country. All of its commanders were former military officers, and most had trained in the United States prior to joining the nationalist movement.[26]

The United States, through the Alliance for Progress, offered military aid and training to Guatemalan governments in the course of the 1960s, thus enlarging and strengthening the counterinsurgency capacity of the army, which now began to operate primarily by forming death squads, "disappearing" political prisoners, and employing illegal means of power that alienated it from middle-of-the-road urban sectors. The weak guerrilla movement, divided because of disagreements between its political and military leaders, had been brutally destroyed by 1966. Among urban middle-of-the-road sectors, this continuous landscape of political instability and terror created a sense of living in a polarized society on the verge of a limit experience. Given the air of the 1960s, with a romantic yearning for third world revolution, admiration for Castro's Cuba, political chaos in the United States after the Kennedy assassination, and the Vietnam War and the events of 1968, it was not difficult to reach the subjective conditions that led many clear-headed individuals to conclude that the only solution to the country's problems was a revolutionary transformation.

By the 1970s, most elements of the new FAR were former Christian Democrats, the EGP had a Catholic contingent that included many priests and nuns, and members of the Organización del Pueblo en Armas (ORPA, Organization of People in Arms) were often labeled "social-democrats in arms." The main difference between the revolutionary organizations of the 1970s and those of the prior decade was that in the 1970s, determined not to allow political and military differences to surface, they centralized both commands under the same leadership. Also, they were no longer led by former army officers, but by seasoned cadres who had survived the debacle of the 1960s. Finally, they all agreed that their survival depended on their ability to recruit Mayas into their ranks. This was especially the case of the EGP and ORPA.

Nonetheless, the EGP, on which Stoll concentrates his attacks because of Menchú's later membership in it, was more concerned with implementing an orthodox *foco* strategy than in recruiting masses of Ixils or K'ichés. Mario Payeras makes this clear in his post-1984 publications. The organizing work among Mayas in the Quiché was actually done by Catholics. The original point of departure was a literacy campaign in 1972 that lasted three or four years. The vast majority of literacy workers had previously participated in the catechization experiences launched by the Christian organizations that grew out of Catholic Action. Many had studied in Santa Cruz del Quiché and had belonged to the Juventud de Acción Católica Rural Obrera (Catholic Action Rural Workers' Youth), the Asociación Pro Cultura Maya-Quiché (Association for Maya-Quiché Culture), the Asociación de Forjadores de Ideales Quichelenses (Association of the Forgers of Quiché Ideals), or the Pastoral Indígena, or they participated in the Seminarios Indígenas, a series of roundtables and discussion groups dealing with pressing ethnic issues.

The electoral fraud of 1974, which prevented General Ríos Montt, then a Christian Democratic candidate, from attaining the presidency, radicalized these organizations. The 1976 earthquake not only proved to the Christian organizations that had grown out of Catholic Action that the government was incapable of responding to local needs, but it also helped to empower them, as communities took the initiative and acted as *poderes populares,* local assemblies that negotiated directly for aid with international agencies.[27] Thus, as I stated in my 1990 book chapter:

> The earthquake relief efforts, sponsored by progressive Catholic groups and by urban labor unions . . . , brought Indians of different communities together with activist ladinos. At the same time, consciousness-raising and organizing efforts began to develop on the southern coast. Out of these, larger meetings of catechists, cooperativists, and members of some agrarian unions were held. Connections developed between Indians in the Chimaltenango and southern Quiché zones in the highlands, and rural workers on the southern

coast of the country, thus slowly weaving a relationship between Indians and poor ladinos. (248)

This "witches' brew" sparked revolutionary enthusiasm and led not only to the formation of the CUC (Committee for Peasant Unity), of which Menchú's father was a leader,[28] but also to CUC activism in the city itself. But even before this happened, a long miners' march from Huehuetenango in November 1977 took the country by storm, as I describe in my 1990 chapter:

> After nine days, they entered the capital accompanied by 150,000 people, including students, settlers, government employees, workers, and campesinos. It was undoubtedly the largest demonstration seen in the country since 1954. That great march, along with one by the workers of the Pantaleón sugar plantation located on the southern coast, which took place at the same time, created a growing feeling of euphoria in the mass organizations. (249)

The nascent CUC organization provided support and accompanied the miners for almost 275 kilometers of the way. Based on this success, they participated in public for the first time in the demonstration on 1 May 1978. It was the first time ever that Mayas demonstrated in the streets of Guatemala City, and even the EGP took notice. It was then that Commander Morán ordered Payeras to write an "indigenous line," and an internal debate began within the EGP's ranks that questioned for the first time the *foco* strategy. This strategy was soon supplanted by an accelerated incorporation of the masses into an irregular guerrilla force. Some members of the National Directorate tried to impose this radical strategic turn on Morán, acknowledging that Maya "masses" organized by Catholics could potentially become a "popular revolutionary army" infiltrated by the EGP.[29] However, the infiltration process went both ways. Radicalized Catholics were also infiltrating the EGP to such an extent that ultimately the so-called Augusto Cesar Sandino Front operating in the Chimaltenango area became almost exclusively a Catholic branch within the EGP, with a nun responsible for ideological education within it. (Payeras even complained that he was tired of having to argue about the existence of God with the priests and nuns in the organization.)[30] This happened when the newly elected government of General Lucas García was determined to show its mettle by bombarding the areas where the EGP was operating. Thus, as I wrote in my 1990 chapter: "In 1978, the state

initiated a counterinsurgency plan to strike at the popular, democratic movement. . . . Until late 1978, indigenous ethnic groups had favored mass organizations over armed struggle, but in early 1979, the army's active presence
began to be felt throughout the highlands, and this began to generate changes
in that judgment" (252).

In this context, people like Menchú's father began operating in paramilitary organizations, and the CUC implemented measures such as sabotage,
propaganda bombs, blockage of highways, and barricades. Vicente Menchú
on the eve of his death was not the dupe described by Stoll. Robert Carmack documents that he lived at La Estancia, near Santa Cruz del Quiché,
in either late 1978 or 1979, along with other CUC members who had fled
northern Quiché after repression became intolerable in that area of the
country. Carmack also describes the violence that shook southern Quiché
in the ensuing year, leading to the assassinations of the first Maya mayor of
the town, Avelino Zapeta, and of Baltasar Toj Medrano, director of Radio
Quiché.[31]

The quasi-spontaneous insurrection in the Maya highlands was out of
the hands of both the EGP and the URNG. Because they were unable to
control the uprising and to either arm or protect Maya protesters, the organizations left them exposed to the violence of the Guatemalan army in much
the same way as had been the case with Salvadoran indigenous groups in the
matanza of 1932. In the second half of 1981, the EGP's armed units decided
to withdraw to the Ixcán jungle, leaving Maya villages to their fate. This callous attitude led many Mayas to turn from sympathy for the EGP to intense
anger against it. They felt betrayed by the organization that had promised
to protect them. By 1983, some began to voluntarily surrender to the army
and enter the so-called Poles of Development. Others turned their energies
against the guerrillas. Payeras called for the EGP to issue a public apology to
the Maya people and for the EGP to rectify its strategy once again, but he
only earned a rebuke from commander in chief Morán. As a result, in late
January 1984 Payeras announced that he was abandoning the EGP. He was
followed by most mid-level cadres operating internationally at the time. Had
Menchú still been in Mexico, she would most likely have left the EGP as well,
given that all the members of her old unit did so. However, she had returned
to the interior of Guatemala in September 1983 to tour the communities
in resistance and was therefore shielded from the political infighting by
military cadres loyal to Morán. She broke instead with her then-boyfriend,

Domingo Hernández Ixcoy, another founder of CUC, who had led the operation that successfully occupied the Brazilian embassy in Guatemala City in 1982. Hernández Ixcoy joined Payeras's faction.

The dissidents organized themselves in a nonarmed revolutionary group known simply as "Contingente" until 1986, and as "Octubre Revolucionario" until its final dissolution in 1990. Directed by Payeras, Porras, and labor leader Miguel Angel Albizúrez, it immediately began a critique of the strategy of both the URNG and the EGP, accusing both of failing to conduct the war successfully due to a series of shortcomings, such as underestimating the military's capacity, overestimating their own military strength, believing their own propaganda about their successful conduct of the war, the corruption of leaders under duress, and the subsequent undermining of the militants' morale.

To better articulate this critique, the Contingente launched a journal, *Opinión Política*, published anonymously yet written for the most part by all three of its leaders.[32] Most of the criticism aimed primarily at the EGP was first published in this quarterly publication between 1985 and 1987.[33] Menchú eventually broke with the EGP in the early 1990s and set forth on her own independent path.

If we are to believe Stoll's bibliography in *The Rigoberta Menchú Controversy*, he was familiar with documents in Spanish published since the 1970s. Why, then, did he present his subject matter as he did in his chapter of that book? In his reductive reading he exploits Americans' traditional ignorance of Guatemalan affairs and sells a hoax to a nonspecialized audience. He implies that Menchú might still secretly be a member of the EGP. (This would imply that the EGP was still an underground organization by 1998, but it was not. It had become part of the URNG, a legal opposition party.) He also insinuates that the Guatemalan left still looks or thinks as it did in the early 1980s and that no Guatemalans had previously published a critique of the left or a serious analysis of the conditions that led to war between 1954 and the 1980s. Thus he can claim to have unmasked Menchú as an EGP member; exposed the falsehood of the EGP and, by extension, of the URNG and of guerrilla strategy in its broadest sense; explained to both Americans and Guatemalans (who in his portrayal never understood their own history) where the latter had gone wrong; and finally, and possibly most rewarding for him, proved wrong the United States' own intellectual left and their saccharine portrayal of Menchú as a *pobrecita* woman of color.

Unfortunately, in this scheme of things Stoll did not count on one thing: that just as neither Menchú nor the EGP could ever hide their past, he could not hide Guatemala's political history, the story of its revolutionary left, and the academic paper trail that documents both. Perhaps he also did not reckon that some of the people who had lived those events not as a distant or exotic adventure but as a life's ethical commitment (even when time proved to them that their choices had been wrong), and in the process lost loved ones, close friends, relatives, their own illusions, and their youth, would not take kindly to his callous portrayal of exotic bumbling leftists of color.

As I come to the end of this critique, I can agree with Stoll that Menchú's turning herself into "a composite Maya" (395), as he claims in "The Battle of Rigoberta," was indeed a problem, though not the "main" one, even while recognizing that Stoll was not the first to notice this. In February 1983, after the announcement that Menchú's *testimonio* had won the Casa de las Américas award, Megan Thomas, under whose direction I worked at the time, told me that Francisca Alvarez, another K'iché leader from the CUC, did not recognize herself in Menchú's *testimonio* because of her upbringing as a town Maya. (Alvarez was raised in Santa Cruz del Quiché and belonged to what was then euphemistically called the "Maya bourgeoisie.") [34] Once the split from the EGP was consummated in 1984, the creation of Ja C'amabal I'b was partly a response to this. After not recognizing themselves in Menchú's book, Alvarez and others—including Menchú's former boyfriend Domingo Hernández Ixcoy—saw the need to deepen their knowledge of heterogeneous Maya culture. Still, none felt the need to denounce Menchú, despite their disagreements at the time. Rather, they understood her narrative as a transitional subjective representation of identity made during a process of acquiring self-knowledge and empowerment.

To conclude, one could claim that the emergence of the subaltern subject as an "equal" of hegemonic subjects is always an ambivalent phenomenon accompanied by anxiety. In a reading such as the one exemplified by Stoll, we clearly see this refusal of the hegemonic world to hear the contextual and intertextual elements of the communicational exchange because it desires to negate the subaltern presence in its midst. As a result, Menchú's discursivity is never truly the heart of the matter. The interpretive shield built around her elocution shifts the meaning of her enunciation to a will to preserve the subaltern stereotype as "alien" or "foreign" so as to better remove its presence from the hegemonic comfort zone.

These terms frame Menchú's responses in such a way as to disqualify them. Hegemonic subjects know intuitively that all speech is a demand voiced against their interests. Thus what comes from the other will always be an appeal that threatens to erase their established order. In Lacanian terms, desire is a perpetual effect of symbolic articulation. It is essentially *menchú* eccentric and insatiable. That is why both the subaltern's need to have her grievances heard and the hegemon's need to have the subaltern "go away" = *Stoll* from his imaginary community and "leave him in peace" can never be fulfilled. Lacan claims that the issue becomes associated not with the subject who can satisfy it but with the one who causes the *malaise*. In this case, it is Menchú who ends up fetishized as the source of a *mal*.

The short genealogies traced here make it evident that we still need to revisit more Latin American historiography in contemporary analyses. One of the lessons learned is the need to include Latin American scholarship in North American research, an uncanny absence in most contemporary research to this day, especially in the social sciences. We also have to recognize that our own fields, including cultural studies understood here in its broadest sense, might also be to blame for the attempt to draw a new tabula rasa that ignores centuries of scholarship patiently elaborated in Spanish in Latin America itself. This attitude might not only have its own imperialist connotations, but it could also very well have contributed to a reductive reading of Latin American textuality that led to the simplistic interpretations manifested by some foes of Latin American positionalities.

6

Reading Truthfully: An American Reading of a Subaltern Text

Allow me to first bring a few issues of an apparently disparate nature to view. When the Rigoberta Menchú controversy first erupted at the end of 1998, I read it as one framed primarily for an uninformed American public, closely linked to the conservative drive to impeach President Bill Clinton. It was in that light that I understood the hysterical response of individuals such as David Horowitz and his Center for the Study of Popular Culture,[1] as well as David Stoll's self-promotion on conservative talk radio programs such as *TalkSpot*.[2] I was not really surprised by these responses given the extremist climate created by the U.S. culture wars. What shocked me was when, four years later, a close friend of mine, a Latin American scholar (the place of origin is not gratuitous), attempted to bring Menchú to a major U.S. university as commencement speaker. She ran into opposition from a highly respected American scholar whom I was about to propose as a possible presidential candidate for the Latin American Studies Association (LASA). He claimed that he had doubts about Menchú, both because of the well-documented claims that she had seriously distorted her life history for her own personal and political ends and because of her equivocal attitudes about guerrilla violence.

I could not believe that a scholar of this stature could have been swayed by the hysterical innuendo and hearsay of conservative radio talk shows or by Stoll's sloppy scholarship. There is no proof that Menchú had distorted her "life history," and at any rate, a *testimonio* is not a life history, as U.S. scholars know.[3] Menchú's *testimonio* was not produced to serve her personal ends. One could, at most, claim that there had been a distortion, but *not* for personal ends. It was for the "public good," namely, to benefit Menchú's "people," her ethnic, subalternized group, the Mayas. The scholar in question is no liar, no opportunist, no conservative, no fool, and, most likely, one who thinks of himself as my friend. We have usually agreed on issues. I have always admired his rectitude and honesty. The only explanation for his stance that I could come up with was that his reading of the controversy was somehow "different" from mine and from that of the majority of Guatemalans. Most likely it was different from that of a majority of Latinos and Latin Americans as well. But that did not invalidate it.

This is the problematic that I will be exploring in this chapter. I will analyze the different protocols of reading in both the United States and Latin America, as well as the political implications of Stoll's reading of Menchú, and then I will redefine her text along a more ethical delineation that suggests that it is based on the model of an exemplary life rather than on the more traditional definition of *testimonio*.

Two Different Types of Reading

Two entirely different elements, which could perhaps seem out of place in this chapter, have driven home for me the conclusion that there are, minimally, different and opposed forms of reading in the United States and Latin America.[4] Only days after learning of my colleague's stand, I traveled to Boston. On the airplane, reading two newspaper pieces, the Menchú issue came to mind. The first piece was in the travel section of the *New York Times*. The article in question was "On the Trail of the Maya in Belize," by Herbert Buchsbaum. I pored over it to distract myself, and besides, I always like to read everything about the Maya that I can get my hands on. It also reminded me of my own trip to Belize years before. What appalled me was the description of Actun Tunichil Muknal, the Cave of the Crystal Sepulcher, in an apparently innocent article about a gringo couple trekking in the interior of Belize. According to the writer, the name refers to "a chamber where the skeleton of a young woman . . . lies half-embedded in sparkling calcite" (10). Buchsbaum added:

> A leading theory holds that as a long drought swept the region in the ninth century, the Maya grew increasingly desperate, offering even greater sacrifices until finally they were giving up beating human hearts to an indifferent god. . . .

For the last, we climbed . . . to a separate chamber, the Crystal Sepulcher of the "Maya princess." . . . Her skeleton was shockingly intact, spread-eagle on the floor, her jaw agape and skull tilted as if she were looking up.

Her gaze stuck in my mind as we retraced our way back toward daylight. And as our SUV bounced and skidded out of the jungle, *I tried to reconcile the kind of people who plotted the course of the planets with those who had sacrificed a girl in her prime.* (12, my emphasis)

I was dismayed by the binary juxtaposition of sacrificing girls and plotting the course of the planets. To me this ending served to reassure the reader that the Mayas were indeed savages, fundamentally different from civilized Americans. It exoticized them, it othered them, and it ratified the primacy of Western values over that otherness. Do we, after all, say that we try to reconcile "the kind of people" who plotted the landing on the moon with those who sacrificed thousands of Vietnamese or Iraqi youth in their prime? Do we say that we try to reconcile "the kind of people" who produced the philosophy of the Enlightenment with those who chopped off the heads of thousands of their leading citizens? Why not be shocked instead, and describe with the same intensity, the state of skeletons of the 1980s massacres dug up by the United Nations forensic team from unmarked mass graves around Guatemala?

The clue to the uncanniness of American reading was offered to me by another article I perused on the same flight. The book review section of that same *New York Times* featured a biography of Andrei Sakharov by Richard Lourie. The review, written by Loren Graham, argued that the story of science in the former Soviet Union was "one of baffling paradoxes that challenge preconceptions and make us uncomfortable" (9). Never one to confuse "us" with me, as I am always fully aware of my own "alienness" within mainstream U.S. thinking, I kept reading. Reviewing the contradictions of Soviet scientists, Graham told us that Lourie's "revealing biography of Sakharov" (9) was to be commended because it showed "us" that Sakharov's own "scientific creativity and his later rise to political heroism were not simple. Throwing off Stalinism was extremely difficult for Sakharov, and like many of his colleagues he did his best scientific work while still in its thrall" (9). I wondered if the colleague I mentioned earlier would oppose offering a commencement invitation to Sakharov because he seriously distorted his scientific achievements by doing them in the thrall and at the service of

Stalinism and because he held equivocal attitudes about H-bomb violence
and its ultimate consequences.

It was reading that particular pair of articles that helped me understand
how Americans read. The book reviewer assumed that it would be difficult
for an average educated reader of this country (who else reads the *New York
Times* book review section?) to understand Sakharov's ideological or ethical "contradictions." Why would that be the case? In my understanding of
this culture, which is, I grant, a non-American understanding, it is because
many Americans, marked by a Puritan consciousness, tend to read morally,
as if all discursivity were an institutionally bound illocutionary act. Most
Latinos or Latin Americans, on the other hand, tend to read ideologically
or ethically.

By *morality* I mean something along the lines of what Rey Chow has
already pointed out in *Ethics after Idealism* (xxii, 192), following Ian Cham-
bers, namely, that morality is "the name of the law . . . , in which we are positioned, and apparently held in custody" (192). This coercive psychology
presupposes that the mind has an innate, coherent structure that resolves the
contradictions between nature and culture instead of seeing different forms
of consciousness, or identities, as historically produced. It authenticates
Americans as sovereign subjects of knowledge. Latin American readings, on
the other hand, tend to articulate differences, widening the spectrum of ethical possibility as they give voice to contradictory manifestations of subaltern
discourse.[5] This is because Latin Americans, for the most part, maintain a
dynamic tension between acceptance and refusal of Western-centric discourses in what is a mutually conflictive and transformative process of
accepting and refusing cultural artifacts emanating from the metropolitan
center. This causes hard problems of representation that often create a "syntax of disablement,"[6] with their singular grammar attempting to intervene
in the world, but ultimately they render the Latin American world more
satisfactorily complex in its heterogeneity. We can see that the American
way of reading, looked at in this way, intends to suppress differences. The
problem of representation becomes a problem of regulation, dominated by
a tone of serene conviction. The question of "truth" is often understood as
an issue outside of language. All that is needed is that language be brought
into it, pragmatically and rigorously. American readers tend to believe that
signifiers always point to signifieds and that reality resides in signifieds. Latin
American readers instinctively know that there are only signifiers, because

they have experienced too many signs ("democracy," "freedom," "subversive," etc.) that have social meanings contrary to those of most standard dictionaries. It should suffice to remember that the great Brazilian writer Machado de Assis appears as "black" on his birth certificate and as "white" on his death certificate, his fame having bleached him in social terms.

Étienne Balibar argues that the American type of reading practice can actually be racist, because it makes no allowance for cultural differentiations. In his understanding, this attitude affixes the discourse of individuals such as Menchú, coming from a differentiated cultural background, into a situation in which they have to be read from within Western moral paradigms that are not their own, thus "locking individuals and groups a priori into a genealogy, into a determination that is immutable and intangible in origin."[7]

Latin American reading tends to be ideological or ethical. By this I mean that it is along the lines of Levinas. It is a reading in which the encounter with the other allows that other to retain its integrity (something that does not happen in the moral reading of the United States, which intends to suppress the other). It is a dialogical reading in the sense that Latinos or Latin Americans raise questions about foreign (Western or U.S.) and domestic cultures to understand both in a creative way (knowing full well that we are not truly Westerners ourselves, even if many wish they were; rather, we are "hybrids," if not "mutants").[8] Because Latin Americans have always felt they were "not quite" Westerners (even if they also did not quite want to admit that they were not), they have always seen the West as the authoritative other, engaging it in an asymmetrical dialogue along the lines of Mary Louise Pratt's "contact zones."[9] Thus, when Latin Americans author a discourse, they have in mind what Pratt calls a "super-addressee" (126), that is, not just a particular person to whom they may be talking (as Menchú, say, talked to Elisabeth Burgos-Debray), but also a higher, a third, super-addressee whose understanding is presumed or hoped for either in some metaphysical distance or in some historical time (without its being some mystical or metaphysical being).[10] This type of understanding assumes various ideological expressions. It might happen because the ethical intention consists of contrasting different systems of thought (ideologies) so as to have the super-addressee ultimately validate one's own. It might also happen because Latin American subjects intuit that non-Western thought is precluded from the constitution of knowledge proper. Finally, it might also happen because in Latin America, thought usually originates as thought about others' thoughts (our thinking has as its point of departure Western systems of thought), behind which an authoritative recognition is always implicit. Thus, needing their own thoughts validated by hegemonic power, Latin Americans articulate their enunciations along ethical premises to "explain" their particular system of thought, their specific language system ("ideology"), as they seek authentication from the sources of power/knowledge that hegemonize their world. The third party is thus a constitutive aspect of the utterance, the very aspect from which the original discourse seeks responsive understanding.

The different forms of reading to which I allude in this introductory section produce different notions of truth, contradictory understandings of evidence, and qualitatively different discursive authorities, to name just the salient aspects of this protocol. In the case of American and Latin American readings of Menchú, we have a *différend* in the Lyotardian sense: "One side's legitimacy does not imply the other's lack of legitimacy. However, applying a single rule of judgment to both in order to settle their differend as though it were merely a litigation would wrong (at least) one of them (and both of them if neither side admits this rule)."[11] Lyotard's concept refers, of course, to a case of a conflict between at least two parties that cannot be resolved because there is lack of a rule or else of a judgment that may be applicable to both arguments. This is what exists in the Stoll-Menchú controversy and in the American–Latin American moral versus ideological or ethical reading of it.[12]

The Nature of the Debate in the United States and Its Other

Following the moral reading I delineated earlier ("the name of the law . . ."), in the United States the debate over Menchú's *testimonio* has centered on whether Menchú told the "truth" regarding details of her personal life. According to her critics, her "lies" discredit her testimony and reduce the moral authority of intellectuals who teach testimonial texts. This focus on verifiable facts conveniently ignores a discursive war tied to cold war politics, something I already mentioned in the first chapter of this section. It ignores the fact that the tasks undertaken by different people to transform their social environment depend on their ability to articulate their vision; the classic expression of this is politics. It also ignores the experience of being a subalternized, ethnic subject whose consciousness has been shaped in a totally different heterotopical space. As a result, in the first chapter of this part of the book I explored the problematics of "truth," the nature of the *testimonio* as a genre, and the relationship between political solidarity and subaltern narrative to question some of the premises on which Stoll's book is based.

It is evident that U.S. readers such as my colleague, besides wanting to separate politics from history, also believe that theory mirrors reality. Latin American readers instead take a relative position: theories provide, at best, partial perspectives on their objects, and all cognitive representations of the world are historically and linguistically mediated. Instead of expecting the coherence or causality of scientific pretensions anchored in Enlightenment rationality, Latin American readers favor fragmentation and indeterminacy because they understand that they (we) all are decentered and fragmented subjects. This is a "felt" experience for most Latin Americans.

There is no need to repeat my previous arguments here. Therefore, I will limit myself to teasing out some of the specific ways in which Stoll's defense of his book chapter "The Battle of Rigoberta"[13] continues to read Menchú within U.S.-centered moral protocols of reading rather than addressing the Guatemalan or Maya issues that the Nobel laureate herself raised in Burgos-Debray's book. By eliding her ethnic positionality, Stoll makes her fit an American stereotype. This attitude masks a perceived threat and subterranean tension that subjects of color present to the placid stability (and narcissistic tyranny) of American white society. Notwithstanding, it was this very factor that caused the controversy to be read in the United States as an "'internal' American ethnic phenomenon." What interests me is how Menchú has been constructed (and then slammed) as if she were a Native American, evidencing an essential transference of subaltern discourse into imperial discourse. On the one hand, this aspect of being read as if she were a "native" invites a healthy critique if it will unveil how, underneath the iconic idealism, a stereotype was constructed that enabled a Maya woman to become a synthetic representation of multiple identities in tension with each other. On the other hand, the controversy has become at least a possible means to historicize and reconstruct the Central American experience of modernity.[14]

In Guatemala there was no debate on the controversy that Stoll's book generated in the United States. Jorge Skinner-Klée, icon of the enlightened Guatemalan right (to be differentiated from the nonenlightened extreme right, primarily responsible for the genocidal policies of the 1980s), published an article in *Siglo XXI*, one of Guatemala's most important dailies, on Friday, 15 January 1999.[15] In it he stated that Stoll's book, "launched with a large publicity apparatus" (97), claimed to question Menchú's veracity. However, after reading it he perceived "a certain prejudice on Stoll's part concerning what Ms. Menchú did say." He proceeded to back Arturo Taracena, a former member of the Guerrilla Army of the Poor (EGP), whom he qualified as "a brilliant historian." He added that "it seems as if Dr. Arturo Taracena's judgment that Stoll is more of a journalist than an anthropologist is correct. His style of research is a journalistic one" (97). Skinner-Klée's position, coming from an icon of the right, was read authoritatively in Guatemala and was understood as signaling that Menchú was a national treasure and, as such, represented a source of patriotic pride and national unity worthy of defense. After his article came out, the debate was effectively closed. The issue was reopened only briefly in the spring of 2003, when Mario Roberto Morales used Stoll as a springboard to signal his ideological criticism of the Guatemalan left (thus offering a typical Latin American ideological reading) and to promote himself as a new ideological leader of an allegedly mestizo, left-of-center sector at odds with the Maya movement.

I argued in the previous chapter that Menchú survived the controversy just fine inside Guatemala, but she gained a negative public perception in the United States, and her image has been stripped of agency in this country. When the connections with Guatemalan political history are reestablished, however, a different reading of Menchú comes forth.

More needs to be said about this, of course, but I will get there in a roundabout way. Let us first look at what Stoll—whose discourse framed the debate in the United States—has said and how his claims run against accepted facts about Guatemala's recent history. As I stated in the previous chapter, he begins his defense of his book chapter, "The Battle of Rigoberta," by saying: "The story that [Menchú] told and Elisabeth Burgos turned into a book was instead an answer to the question: Why should *we* care? About another far-off conflict in which people *we* don't know are being killed for reasons *we* don't understand" (392, my emphasis). I have already problematized the nature of what that particular term "we," thrice repeated, represents. Suffice it to add here that although this might have been true in far-off France (far off, that is, from Guatemala), where the original interviews were recorded and where a mainstream audience might have been unfamiliar with Mayas or with what was happening in their country, this was not true in the United States in early 1982. Central America was sufficiently close that President Ronald Reagan could rhetorically argue that Sandinistas could march up to the U.S. border and invade the United States through Harlingen, Texas. Certainly this was a material impossibility, but it is evidence of the closeness and familiarity of the Central American issue to a broad American audience supportive of Reagan's policies. Is Stoll referring to France, then, or to the United States when he opens his chapter? Or is he being deliberately vague to avoid being pinned down? Indeed, immediately afterward he gives a backhand compliment to Menchú's book, stating that it provided an "immediacy and credibility" (392) through the first-person narrative. However, this fact worries him, because it makes the book "effective in spreading interest in Guatemala to wider circles" (392). Why should it worry him that interest in Guatemala is being spread? He never answers this question. But obviously what is implied in his writing is that he is worried that an interest in Guatemala's record of human rights violations will garner even more interest, as indeed happened from 1982 onward, until President Oscar Berger publicly apologized for some of those very human rights violations in 2004. Why should greater knowledge of these infamies worry Stoll unless he has a stake in keeping that information from being disseminated, and, if that is the case, what is his stake in doing so? This implicit question is never answered. He goes on to state that one cannot question "Rigoberta's story" unless one accuses her of "a hoax, fraud, or lie" (393). Notice Stoll's rhetorical strategy: he claims he is not doing this, yet he uses all three terms as a form of emphasis. Thus, indirectly and in a backhand way, he is indeed accusing Menchú of a hoax, fraud, or lie while at the same time hiding the hand that threw the stone. Of course he can claim that he never categorically or directly accused her, and he would be right. Instead he accuses the Guerrilla Army of the Poor (EGP), whose interest he claims Menchú served in her *testimonio*. Thus Menchú is further reduced; she is not even responsible for her own agency in perpetuating a hoax, fraud, or lie, but has simply been a useful tool, the manipulated puppet of the EGP, the true perpetrators of this hoax.

From that assertion Stoll goes on to claim that he feels obliged to point out gaps between "Rigoberta's story" and those of other Mayas, including her neighbors, "because of the enormous authority that so many readers have attributed to it" (393). Then he adds:

[margin note: inferring]

If you take this book at face value, as an eyewitness account, you will probably conclude that guerrilla warfare in Guatemala grew out of peasants' need
to defend themselves from intolerable conditions.

Because of the different story I heard from many peasants, this is what
became the most important issue for me: Was the Guerrilla Army of the Poor
(EGP) that Rigoberta joined, and whose version of events she gave us in 1982,
an inevitable response by the poor to oppression? (393)

We can safely conclude, based on this "moral" reading of Menchú's text,
that Stoll's stake lies in undermining not Menchú per se, but rather the
EGP's narrative. It is from this perspective that we should view his critique.
Paradoxically enough, his turn puts me on the spot as well. I made a sec-
ond career of critiquing the EGP after 1984, and yet here I am forced to bring
Stoll to task for doing the very same thing.

In the previous chapter I stated that Stoll's sources happen to be book
chapters of mine, in Spanish from 1985 and in English from 1990. So what we
have here is not a different set of sources (except for the fact that Stoll cleverly
tries to disguise his own), but rather a different set of interpretations. Stoll's
deliberate misreading of Guatemalan political history generated confusion
and, as a consequence, a moral reaction, in the United States alone. Many U.S.
social scientists have not been helpful in clarifying these matters to a confused
and uninformed public, primarily because they are more used to speaking to
a small coterie of colleagues and disciples, using highly professional jargon,
than in addressing the public at large as "public intellectuals." This vacuum is
filled in the United States by individuals like Stoll, trained as a journalist but
with an anthropology degree, more used to addressing a general audience
than highly trained professional experts. Latin Americans as a whole were not
confused, however. Neither were Europeans, whose more ideological reading incorporates historical knowledge as well. However, when he asks, in
his defense, "Why should we care?" (392), his use of "we" makes it clear that
his audience was not a global one: his aims were limited to sowing confusion in the United States. In this task, we have to recognize that he succeeded.

Pseudologies, Ethics, and Exemplary Lives

From a Latin American perspective, *testimonio* began as a means of creating primary sources for research to gain knowledge of Latin America's own

social formations in the 1970s. This process gradually evolved into an attempt to understand the social causality and subjective logic behind the break-down of civil society after the experience of political violence and increased authoritarianism. Ultimately, it also became part of efforts to support victims of social and political trauma as democratization and social reconstruction began. In the latter sense, it has also been a part of a broad process by which victims of dictatorship have attempted to reconstitute their memory and respond to the challenges raised both by democratization (decentralization, participation, etc.) and by globalization (a new way to insert themselves into the economy).

The discourses of victims of dictatorship offer insights into how segments of Latin American societies understand themselves, how they organize dis-cussions about themselves, how they stir deep contention. What needs em-phasis here is that *testimonios* were never considered an undisputed genre or embodiments of juridical "truth" south of the border. They were multiple discourses that represented a point of entry into the broader public discourse for disenfranchised subjects. With their entry into the public arena, they con-tributed to a broadening of the overall social exchange, previously limited to a small, hegemonic sector of what Angel Rama has called "the lettered city." Regretably, this dimension was not understood in the same way north of the border, and *testimonio* became mostly (though not exclusively) an instru-ment for a rearticulation of theoretical platforms on university campuses, in some instances for the sake of individual promotion and academic stardom.

We can see that Guatemalans (and many other Latin Americans) had a different understanding of the function of *testimonios* and "read" them dif-ferently. This happened more along the lines of what I pointed out in the first section of this chapter. In this context, let me return to the issue of different protocols of reading. The difference is that, whether they were sym-pathetic to *testimonios* or not, Latin Americans understood them as a first step on the part of *testimoniantes* to name an experience of loss, to attempt to express it in words. This meant trying to reign in the emotions and find the "right words" to name the lived nightmare. It also underscored the ulti-mate impossibility of doing so. Thus, *testimonios* always lead to equivocal perceptions of the self, even within the same cultures, while writing within preconceived notions of cultural meaning.

When subjects venture beyond their felt boundaries, dialogism becomes more like a high-wire act. They are trying to deal with "untouchable," deeply felt emotions and to translate them to the cold imprecision of the written word. We are dealing here with unpresentable raw feelings, with unresolvable lived experiences, mute witnesses of the "unnameable" (in a Beckettian sense). When disenfranchised subjects address this swelling of emotions, they are confronted by an uncontrollable eruption of passion that somehow has to be reigned in and kept under control to convey a sense of rationality, of sanity, to an interlocutor. In these circumstances, one cannot possibly be lying.[16] As Derrida says: "The question of the lie should also be a guiding thread for a reflection on the essence and the history of intentionality, the will, consciousness, self-presence, and so forth. . . . We must preserve a concept of the lie that has about it something unrefined, square, rigid . . . if we do not wish to dissolve it . . . in the torrential flux of undecidable half-tints that makes up our experience."[17] To this I could add, as well, the problematics of telling a "truth" that is actually a lie. This has happened to me. In March 1980, a well-known anthropologist who also happened to be a militant of the EGP told me that, beginning in the town of San Lucas twenty-six miles west of Guatemala City, the EGP had organized the entire population living on both sides of the Pan American Highway. I believed her and repeated her assertion on many occasions when giving public talks. Only years later did I find out that "organized" was a euphemism for small EGP columns now and then appearing in those villages and distributing propaganda before disappearing into the countryside. I am convinced that similar "lies" spoken as truths appear in Menchú's text.

I added the previous anecdote in the context of Derrida's reflection about what a lie really is. In this line of thought, we could equally claim that Stoll's "lies" (if we were to do a moral reading of his innuendoes and label them as such) have had the consequence that U.S. high schools, community colleges, and even universities have stopped teaching Menchú's text.[18] This does not mean, however, that a different Central American or Latino text has taken its place. It simply indicates that the U.S. mainstream has been led to a disidentification with Latinidad as a whole, uncannily represented by this Maya woman. Why bring this up at this point in the chapter? Because, beyond giving tacit disapproval to this consequence of the debate, I am also forced to ask: Why were Latinos identifying with Menchú? Was it because she was Maya or Guatemalan, a member of the EGP as Stoll would have it, or was she idealized in the sense defined by Chow, as an iconic representation of otherness that elided her own Central American specificity?[19]

I do think that it was the latter. Menchú was "read" as an iconic representation of "Latinness." By reconstituting her as a "native " subject of the
United States, we saw a gesture split between timelessness and history, where
post–cold war discourse in this country was searching for "authenticity"
amid the contradictions of its multicultural landscape at the same time that
Mayas were trying to become citizens of their Guatemalan nation by articulating a discourse along the lines of Menchú's emblematic text. Stoll tried
to close the American space by arguing that Menchú was not "authentic."
With his attitude he was, of course, depriving Menchú of her "felt" Mayaness, which is not the same thing as a "'lived experience' at the literal level,"
as Isobel Armstrong reminds us. Rather, it is a function of the way that "the
most intimate sense of the self is represented as subjectivity and context, as
subjectivity-in-community."[20]

The paradoxical situation of Menchú in the United States, where she was
actually more *spoken for* than actually speaking, points, perhaps idiosyn-
cratically, to the territorialized nature of the concept of identity as an imagined articulation, to its clear placement in a given space, regardless of the
positionality from which the subject can intervene in the rules of discourse.
Thus any understanding of the heterotopic subjectivity of an individual
such as the Nobel laureate has to refer to the interpretation of this multiple condition, given her apparent "locatedness in space."

From this affirmation could emerge a new way of rethinking subjectivity interspatially rather than placing it at the discursive site from which the
subject enunciates his or her own subjectivity. However, instead of leaning
in that direction, an analysis that would require much more space than the
limited one at our disposal, I return to the problematics of idealism raised
by Chow. As already mentioned, she pointed out that unless we invest the
same type of critical attention in the detail of texts representing otherness
that we do in canonical literary texts, we will never overcome the types of idealism that keep "native" texts basically illegible. Thus we are left with the issue
of "authenticity" versus its lack, the binary terms within which Stoll framed
his argument. Unfortunately, they are also the terms within which theorists
of subalternity framed their argument of *testimonio* versus literature.[21]

Now it is time to turn in a different direction. If Menchú was seen as
a sort of iconic trope of the Latino community, this was because she was
simultaneously read as a trope of "authenticity" (Maya leader genuinely
baptized by fire) and, at the same time and in a contradictory way, as a

trope of Western "success" (Nobel Prize winner honored by the French president, friend of the Queen of Spain, ally of the Swedish prime minister).
This attitude pointed in the direction of two different "felt" needs of the
Latino community: that of anchoring one's identity within a valued identitary horizon that spelled "roots" of some sort, the idealized Maya world
in this case; and a need to articulate the self-worth of the community and
gain recognition in a society where success matters above all else and where
the Latino subject is situated in asymmetrical relations of power.

These double codes are not the codes through which Menchú launched
her discursivity in Guatemala. The need to read her differentially, from
within localized codes articulating divergent horizons of meaning, led once
again to a *différend*-ic encounter in a Lyotardian sense: asymmetrical discourses, both of them "subaltern" yet different in their singular subalternity,
sailed past each other in the cold space of an unrecognizable and unnamed
identitarian horizon without ever meeting or establishing true dialogic relations. In this differentialized emphasis the Latino community, itself exotic
in hegemonic U.S. terms, in turn exoticized Menchú's signs just as much.
It assigned to them an iconic visibility that would not truly correspond to
Menchú if an alternative reading was to be done pointing in Maya directions. In the felt need of the community to constitute an imaginary "us" so
as to anchor its idea of Latinidad, Menchú became for Latinos, as much as
for Stoll's Anglo community, a phantasm of her very own Mayaness.

The community valued the tangential role that Menchú played within the
American horizon. She was perceived alternatively as associated with the solidarity efforts of the Guatemalan peoples' struggle, as a new sign, as a representative figure of alternative politics, as a new language that captured in her
image—reproduced to death on countless covers of academic books in this
country—the realities of grotesque injustice. Her presence on university
campuses or in communal spaces led members of the community to instinctively recognize in her the rich possibilities of a certain self-representation.
She was more like them than other political leaders they had known before.
She was a sort of imaginary identification who did not quite become symbolic, a sort of new Virgin of Guadalupe. Detecting this iconic adherence, academics talking about the need to rethink political strategies in a new context,
at the same time that old politics linked to so-called real socialism were exit-
ing the scene, emblematized her as a symbol of "newness." Menchú became
the image of this realignment, of this reconceptualization and redefinition

of the possibilities of change for the Latino community. At the same time, she still represented the old politics of Marxism and the cold war for a Guatemalan horizon. In this way she became a sort of simulacrum, a linguistic toy for academic posturing. Many profited from her image in the academic book market with the complicity of the most prestigious university presses. In this overall context, those who believed Menchú's utterances in a truly literal, Americanized moral sense represent the limits of idealism in identity politics.

However, my goal is not to do a spectacular turnaround and blame an abject sector of the wealthiest society in the world for trying to increase its own self-worth. Instead I believe that we have to reorient the challenge represented by the questioning of Menchú's veracity and take what she actually meant to say out of the false binary opposition of truth versus lies.

When we try to look "outside" of that binary, its dissolution takes us to a certain attitude of ethnicized subalternity within which we fall into the ethical space. It takes us to a relationship with the self. Menchú's feelings, motivations, and values suffer a transformation when we interpret them as a different sort of linguistic phenomenon. If we reintegrate them into the speaking act, into the enunciatory gesture that implies a place from which one speaks, this act transforms itself into an instant of engagement or else of taking a singular stand at an equally specific moment. One cannot articulate value without taking a position in relation to it. That is why Bakhtin defined the linguistic utterance, in his notes from the 1950s, as the minimum of that to which one can respond, with which one can agree or disagree.[22] As Hirschkop says regarding this matter, language does not "articulate values or principles from a neutral perspective" (35). The acceptance or rejection of values is not a matter for individual initiative. Rather, "its meanings are positions taken or refused, its forms opportunities for ethical relationships" (35). If language is therefore a substance of ethics, its limits are also the limits of our own ethical life. In this respect, Hirschkop quotes Bakhtin as saying, "Discourse was stronger than the person, he could not be responsible while in the power of discourse; he felt himself the herald of an alien truth, in the higher power of which he was caught" (36). Here the concept of style alludes to "the mutual interdependence of language and ethical life." Style denotes the moment in which language is charged with subjectivity. In this sense, the language that has Menchú as its source is "intersubjectivity incarnate," a language that leaves no possibilities of any ethical life to random factors. (And don't forget that this language is K'iché, which

Menchú more or less translates in her head to Spanish, which she speaks and [*language of Menchú*]
is then transcribed and edited by various individuals, translated to French,
and then translated to British English, to ultimately generate a debate about
her "words" in the United States.)[23]

At the same time, here the ethical element is located in the phantasmatic
aspect of the utterance, which in "History of the Lie: Proglomena," Derrida
associates sensu stricto with the fabulous in the sense of not belonging to
either truth or falseness, but to "an irreducible species of the simulacrum,
or even of simulation" (28). For Derrida, the phantasmatic elements of discourse are not true, but "neither are they errors or deceptions, false witnesses
or perjuries."

In this Derridean sense, Menchú's narrative is effectively a fabrication
that became a fable. But she did not tell a fable with the idea of fabulating
(lying, or inventing a greater self). Rather, as narrator she proceeded in a
way analogous to how Derrida describes Nietzsche's recounting the history
of "the true world" in *Twilight of the Idols*. She narrated a life as if a true history were possible in a context that was already a fabrication or a prefabri-
cation. She produced the idea of a true world that is actually a *coup de
théâtre*, in Derrida's words (29), where a possible lie is foreign to the problem of knowledge or truth. Derrida says:

> One can be mistaken, one can be in error without lying; one can communi-
> cate to another some false information without lying. If I believe what I say,
> even if it is false, even if I am wrong, and if I am not trying to mislead some-
> one by communicating this error, then I am not lying. One does not lie sim-
> ply by saying what is false, so long as one believes in good faith in the truth
> of what one believes or assents to in one's opinions. (31)

Derrida calls these narratives "pseudologies" (32), from the Greek *pseudos,*
which can mean deception as a result of poetic invention. It is in this way
("Fallendi cupiditas, voluntas fallendi,"[24] 35) that Derrida understands St.
Augustine, who claimed that there is no lie when one is convinced of being
on the right path, when there is no explicit will to deceive, an affirmation
we can easily attribute to Menchú in 1982 (the year when her *testimonio* was
recorded). Understood in the spirit of St. Augustine, the pseudology that
Menchú uttered (told in broken Spanish, not wrote) would be an ethical
model of an exemplary life, in the sense of both St. Augustine and Rousseau.

To Menchú, this model would not have been new in 1982. It was the type
of Christian ethics that she had been taught, as a Christian activist, by her
own father. As Phillip Berryman has argued, the ethical basis and legitimacy
of participating in movements aimed at taking political power in Central
America were anchored in "what should be," as opposed to "what now exists."[25] The revolutionary project justified the ethics of violence, as explained
by liberation theology. Berryman argues that Central Americans did not
write about it, that there is no major theological essay on this matter, and
that the subject was only a major preoccupation for people outside the
region, such as the concern manifested by the academic mentioned at the
beginning of this chapter. Berryman claims that this was because Central
Americans did not "choose" violence, but suffered it, to the point where
self-defense ultimately led to combat: "In other words, for people in the
middle of the violence of Central America . . . the question is entirely too
obvious to require any theoretical elaboration" (309). Berryman proceeds
to clarify what an ethics of violence would be. His explanation includes the
official teaching of the Catholic Church on violence, the pope's attitude
toward it during the 1960s, his response to Father Camilo Torres' espousal
of it at the Medellín Council (313), the Central American bishops' stance,
and Archbishop Romero's pronouncements on violence addressing the people's right to insurrection and legitimate defense (315). He then continues
to provide an ethical assessment of specific kinds of violence carried out by
the armed opposition groups (317–20).

However, even if no theoretical elaboration of this ethics was ever written by a Central American, Menchú's narrative frames ethical issues as well
as ethical instantiation as a tool of persuasion in political and ethical discourse. Her narrative is a performativity of an identity play with the purpose of constructing a subjective and intersubjective moral universe that
structures political choice. Her story gains rhetorical power from its narrative structure, because it is in fact articulating a theoretical elaboration as
storytelling in the process of creating an exemplary life, with a trace of utopian plot lines and literary devices that tell a story that integrates "is" and
"ought." It is this factor that makes her story compelling.

This would explain in a more comprehensive way why Menchú subsumed
the events her mother had witnessed, and others lived by her brothers and
close relatives, into her narrative. Not to "lie." Not because Mayas lack a

sense of self and think always as a "we," in communitarian terms, given their premodern status. It was because hers was not meant to be a representational narrative in a strict moral, literal sense. Her ethical performativity, which articulated a model of an exemplary life, is differentiated from the prevalent sense of a lie as an intentional act. It is a mistake to read Menchú's text as a *testimonio* in a narrow sense. It is even more limited to read it as an autobiography. It is neither one nor the other. It is a pseudology, the phantasmatic projection of a behavioral model that Menchú learned from her Christian teaching and outlined for herself as an ethnified subject. She was the oral author of a certain kind of heroism that she wanted to perform in her militant life. This is the tactical reading that her words implicitly solicit without repudiating any translatability. It happened also because she was forced to go beyond the parameters that constitute accepted knowledge, and she had to surpass them, to create not just a broader frame of reference, but also one of shifting boundaries. This way, she could fashion a tool of resistance without allowing anyone to ultimately possess her different form of subjectivity. Therefore, her boundaries constantly underwent mutation. She was instinctively aware of the instability of meaning and of the limitation of language to fully represent her complex being.

In this context, the key to an ethical existence is the disclosure of the self, the "entrance into community through speech," in the words of Hirschkop.[26] To make reality ethical, Menchú named the activity of its creation as social. Given her Christian background, Menchú (who, contrary to Stoll's simplistic argument that she represents the EGP's position and thus, implicitly, a Marxist-Leninist one, is truly a radicalized Catholic) conceived of a community of believers to ensure her ethical bearings. Her utterances were both a confession and a penance in one—an articulation of her failures and the construction of her own penance, the exemplary life that will ultimately lead to redemption. As Hirschkop reminds us, Scheler believed that memory can become an object of ethical action only when it has been externalized. Speaking defines who Menchú is. In *Toward a Philosophy of the Act* Bakhtin says that "when we become ethically and cognitively answerable for ourselves, we can rewrite life once and for all in the form of a fair copy" (54). Of course in this early quote the catch is the connecting particle "once and for all." Because self-determined change never ends, the process of answerability is continuous, the process of coming to terms with one's own life never stops, and "once and for all" remains only an ethical goal, much like the pot of gold at the end of the rainbow, never achieved because individuals continue to live actively.

Needless to say, here we are talking of ethics not in the traditional sense of a human essence, but rather in a more Foucauldian sense of "an ethic of whom we are said to be."[27] In other words, how we are constituted as the subjects of our experience by practices that are relative, contingent, and local. As Rajchman says, this implies the notions of choice and becoming.

Seeing the matter in this way, we break with the vulgar idealization of identity politics that traps a great many exponents of subaltern studies. Stuck in the Beverleyesque originary predicament, that is, the paradox of wanting to end racism by overemphasizing its most stereotyped aspects, these exponents mythify subaltern subjects as if they were totems, despoiling them of the contradictions that constitute their historical placement.[28] It is because of this that Chow has said that we have to attack the idealism found at the base of identity politics (xxi). In this way we return to a position of polysemic openness, to an enthusiastic resignation in the sense in which Chow sees Žižek's ethics as indicating the experience of an object through the failure of its adequate representation (53). When we put this kind of ethical reading into practice, we break with reductive simplifications. We also discover that in the volumes of material written about what Menchú or *testimonio* were supposedly about, few critics have really paid attention to what Menchú actually tried to say because what mattered to them was not what Menchú stood for, but their own critical stances.

Final Thoughts

We could very well conclude with the statement that the various positionings around the Menchú controversy imply not only different readings, but also a history of false identifications, parts of which can become meaningful in certain contexts. Precisely because pseudologies codify the contingencies of personal histories, they do not always point to an internal coherence.

To better understand how, in an age of globalization, subaltern discourses operate and break down traditional spatial symmetries, an ongoing analysis will have to emphasize both the nature of Guatemalan migration to the United States and how its growing presence creates a new understanding of Menchú within U.S. borders. In short, such an analysis will have to develop a reading that I merely outlined, but still needs to be elaborated more fully, one that could inform us of how migration also conditions North Americans' readings and of how this phenomenon has direct implications for North Americans' demographic composition and their own daily practices.

We could ultimately wonder whether Menchú's way of articulating an ethical subject, through the construction of an exemplary life to dominate and control the self, to display temperance, and to exercise and regulate a "style" of selfhood, has not itself been disciplined, controlled, and dominated, not just by her foes but, even more so, by her alleged allies: theoreticians of *testimonio*. Critics necessarily appropriate and disturb the text by which she is in turn determined and disturbed.

In the end, I wish that my U.S. colleague could understand at least that he misread Menchú. Unfortunately, pessimism leads me to think that this might not be possible. Even if he and I intimately recognize a certain rectitude, a certain mettle, a strong ethical behavior based on principle, we are still uncannily different. We stand for different principles. We defend opposing codes inserted within differentiated protocols, if only because my stand is that of eliminating the adjective *subaltern* from the phrase *subaltern subject* when speaking of Central Americans in the United States. This is not his reading of Menchú. I am afraid that this might prevent us from establishing a true understanding of each other's positions. Ultimately, for him Menchú will remain a "liar," if in a different sense than for Stoll. For me she will always be the artificer of an exemplary life, an ethical model for the future of Latin America and for Latinidad.

7

The Burning of the Spanish Embassy:
Máximo Cajal versus David Stoll

In his book *Rigoberta Menchú and the Story of All Poor Guatemalans*,
David Stoll presents, masked in allegedly objective language, a highly
biased, and incorrect, account of the tragic events that took place in
Guatemala City on 31 January 1980. On that date the military regime burned
the Spanish embassy to the ground. This event had far-reaching implications. First, it resulted in the deaths of thirty-six people in the conflagration and one more (tortured by paramilitary forces) later that same night.
Beyond that, it changed the political equation in Guatemala forever. Because
of this event, many Guatemalans, including well-known middle-class professionals and moderates, joined the revolutionary ranks in much the same
way that, impelled by 9/11, people in the United States engaged in a patriotic
outburst. The country entered a "state of armed internal conflict," a euphemism for civil war. Beyond Guatemalan borders, this barbaric episode also
contributed to the emergence, both in the United States and in Europe, of
strong committees in solidarity with the struggle of the Guatemalan people.
It disgraced the military in the eyes of the world. Spain broke off diplomatic
relations with Guatemala, and even the Reagan administration distanced
itself from the regime as a consequence of this savage act. As a final consequence, the daughter of one of those killed in the embassy, Vicente Menchú,
would two years later recount her experiences to Elisabeth Burgos-Debray,
and thus the future Nobel Peace Prize winner came to international public
attention for the first time.

Unlike the three previous chapters of this part of the book, this chapter will focus exclusively on this one particular event. In chapter 6 of *Rigoberta Menchú and the Story of All Poor Guatemalans*, titled "The Massacre at the Spanish Embassy," David Stoll puts forth the fallacious argument that, even as late as the writing of his book (that is, somewhere between 1995 and 1998), there was no consensus as to who had set the fire that burned down the embassy (71). The present chapter contends that this argument is untrue. Given the evidence to the contrary, I can only conclude that Stoll is deliberately falsifying information for ideological reasons when he states that the occupants of the embassy immolated themselves. By so doing, he hopes to discredit not only the Guatemalan left but also Vicente Menchú, thinking that perhaps this event began the rise of Rigoberta Menchú on the way to global recognition and to a Nobel Peace Prize. Stoll hopes that his innuendos about the role of Mr. Menchú and the left in this tragic incident will tarnish Ms. Menchú herself.

Let us begin by looking at what Stoll says when he details the events that took place inside the embassy. His narrative walks readers through the occurrences of the fateful day step by step; then, after presenting an ostensibly objective overview, it ends by arguing that the majority of the victims "seemed to have died of smoke inhalation" (75). This sentence is followed by a footnote in which the author cites as the source of his information "author's interview with municipal firefighter"—in the singular, meaning one individual—"July 5, 1996." Stoll performed this sole interview with the anonymous firefighter sixteen and a half years after the incident. What is more, he does not explain how he managed to locate this lone firefighter, nor does he give the firefighter's name so that other investigators might corroborate his information or provide additional details that would support the validity of this testimony over others. But even more telling is the statement at the end of the note, where Stoll asserts that "there were no autopsies because the bodies were in such bad condition" (292). At this point the question arises: If the thirty-six cadavers ("smoke-blackened corpses," 75) were in such bad condition that no autopsy could be performed, how did this lone firefighter, who was not a forensic doctor, know that the majority died from smoke inhalation rather than from their extensive burns? Was this an empirical deduction on his part? Is he a recognized expert in these matters? If so, why is this not stated in the footnote or elsewhere in the text? Finally, why does the researcher not explain these facts, given that he claims to hew to "objective data," purportedly in contrast to Menchú, who he claims is not objective because she represents the interests of a revolutionary organization rather than her own or those of the Maya people?

This is not the only inaccuracy in Stoll's text. He describes the occupation of the embassy in the following terms:

> The revolutionary movement *invariably memorializes* the occupation as a peaceful one. Certainly, the manner in which the protesters seized the embassy was nonviolent compared with how the police stormed it. But the embassy staff offered no resistance, so there was no reason for the occupiers to use force, and what followed *was hardly coercion-free*. The twenty-seven protesters were *armed with machetes, three or four revolvers, and Molotov cocktails*. Nor were they play-acting when they took hostages, who were *kept under close guard*. As confrontation loomed, the occupiers never gave their prisoners—including four Guatemalan women working for the embassy, and a fifth woman from Spain—the chance to flee to safety. Instead, the *hostages were herded along at gunpoint to be used as shields*. (79, emphases mine)

Next Stoll asserts that "the left accused the security forces of using an incendiary device such as napalm or white phosphorus to incinerate the victims" (79), in a tone meant to discredit or deny this information. The anthropologist adds that no proof was presented to corroborate the white phosphorus theory. Nor does he believe that any evidence shows that the police force had the explicit intention of burning the victims alive. He does mention the declarations of Elías Barahona, public relations and press secretary for the Guatemalan Interior Ministry, who affirmed on more than one occasion that he heard General Lucas give the order to Interior Minister Donaldo Alvarez Ruiz to burn the occupants inside (80). However, he discounts this source's credibility without stating why. We may assume that this is because Barahona later went on to join the ranks of the Guerrilla Army of the Poor (EGP), automatically delegitimizing himself in Stoll's eyes. The information provided by the press secretary is lumped together with all the other "leftist" arguments to which the author wishes to deny credibility.

Instead of analyzing the allegations of the source quoted, Stoll immediately makes a fascinating assertion: "Barahona corroborates the left's preferred version of events, but both are contradicted by the fire's sole survivor: Ambassador Máximo Cajal y López." Immediately thereafter, he cites a shortened version of the interview given by the Spanish ambassador to Radio

Nacional (Spain's National Radio) the day after the events. In it Cajal said that one of the peasants threw a Molotov cocktail. Stoll also cites a passage from the interview published the day after the event in *El País,* Spain's major daily. This information is more believable in his eyes. "Could Cajal be biased against the protesters?" he asks. "No—his sympathy for them was so evident that he was accused of staging the occupation" (81). He goes on to cite selected parts of the official report presented at the time by the Spanish Chancery (Spain's Department of State), then asserts:

> When I contacted ambassador Cajal fifteen years later, he confirmed seeing a masked occupier throw a bottle of gasoline and splash fuel. He also confirmed stamping out a match intended to light it—but this episode occurred well before the explosion and his escape through the door. The most important clarification he wished to make was that, not having eyes in the back of his head, he never saw the fire's actual source, therefore cannot say for sure that the protesters started it. (81)

Stoll augments this paragraph with extensive quotes from the ambassador. In note 21 he attributes these quotes to two telephone interviews carried out on 17 October 1995 and 18 January 1996 and to a letter dated 21 January 1996. We are not told whether the quotes come from the telephone conversations or the letter. Nor do we know whether the ambassador knew he was being recorded, in the case of information taken from the phone calls, or whether the ambassador spoke in English or Stoll translated statements recorded in Spanish, as would seem to be the case based on the syntax. On the whole, the notes are strikingly vague. For accusations as strong as those Stoll is making, these investigative lapses are revelatory. At best they could be qualified as sloppy scholarship. I believe, however, that they are part of a deliberate attempt to conceal the truth, as I will demonstrate further on.

In the middle of Stoll's chapter is the subheading "Who Started the Fire?" It introduces the most important section, for it is here that blame will be laid for the tragic events. The evidence comes from "two arson investigators in California" (82) to whom the anthropologist claims to have shown newspaper photos. He does not, however, provide names, dates, or any other information that would permit corroboration, as though this were not significant given the magnitude of his accusations and the writer's apparent anxiousness that they be taken seriously. This would seem to be just another instance of sloppy scholarship. But now comes the most interesting part. Stoll adds this: "Judging from appearances, they said, the relatively intact corpses and clothing suggested a fire of only medium intensity" (82). Had he not stated before, in note 7 on page 75, that "there were no autopsies because the bodies were in such bad condition"? So were the cadavers in bad condition because of an intense fire, or were they relatively intact because of a medium-intensity fire? If the latter was the case, why does Stoll not explain the failure to perform autopsies or at least question the firefighter who asserted the former, given that a medium-intensity fire would taint his claim that there could be no autopsies because of the intensity of the fire? One of these two claims must be incorrect.[1]

It is due to these key contradictions, which would barely be noticed by many readers who would not take the trouble to examine the notes or who are unfamiliar with the arcane issues surrounding the burning of the Spanish embassy in Guatemala, that the supposed evidence starts to fall apart and Stoll's claimed objectivity breaks down. Why does Stoll make it impossible for anyone to verify or disprove his account? We cannot check the methods of the California experts because we do not know their names or when and where they were interviewed and presented with the newspaper photo. We also cannot question them about the quality of the image they were shown. What does become clear is that, depending on what suits the author's argument, the cadavers were either burned beyond recognition in an intense fire or barely damaged in a medium-intensity fire.

The question is complicated by the evidence itself, a couple of newspaper photos, which, as a rule, are of poor resolution (and even fuzzier so many years after their publication) and printed with paper and ink of questionable quality, such as those used in Guatemalan papers (unless Stoll acquired the originals; we do not know this, either). Upon this dubious basis, two alleged experts whose names remain unknown—but whose reliability is established by their being "from California," a trope for trustworthiness due to the assumption that they are male, white, and North American— immediately establish that the substance used to burn down the embassy could not have been white phosphorus, but only gasoline. The alleged experts were never in Guatemala, they never examined the premises, nor did they test any of the residues. Nevertheless, their contention becomes the incontrovertible proof that forms the basis for the hypothetical argument that the occupants immolated themselves. On this evidence alone, Stoll clears the

government forces of any guilt and casts a shadow of suspicion on the occupiers, who are now presumed guilty of murdering the embassy's peaceful
employees and its honorable visitors, including a former vice president of
the republic and a former minister of foreign affairs, as well as the Spanish
consul. Or did Stoll track down the original photographs? If he did, why
does he not establish this fact or explain how he obtained them?

To justify his hypothesis, Stoll uses extrapolation. He takes the trustful
reader to the site of another occupation, that of the Brazilian embassy, taken
over in 1982. He quotes Domingo Hernández Ixcoy, leader of the occupiers
in this second case, as having declared publicly that if necessary they were
prepared to use the Molotov cocktails they had brought with them. Because
Hernández Ixcoy said this in 1982, Stoll assumes that the occupiers of the
Spanish embassy in Guatemala would have done likewise, by simple deduc-
tive analogy. He never mentions that the stakes were different in 1982, both
because of the escalation of the war itself and because of the precedent set
by the burning of the Spanish embassy in 1980. What does remain clear is
that Stoll's entire argument is based on assumptions. To reinforce them, he
also quotes from the "Plan de subida" (Uprising plan) supposedly found by
the police and at the time alleged to be the plan for entering the Spanish
embassy. This document stated the need to carry Molotov cocktails as weapons of self-defense. Significantly, Stoll makes no mention of the fact that
the "Plan de subida" was an invention of the Guatemalan military intelligence service and was later publicly acknowledged as such. Skipping this
crucial detail, he ends the section by commenting that "a frank account
from the left would be invaluable" (84) but will not be forthcoming, not
only because the embassy occupiers are all dead, but because the political
organizations were dismantled in the years that followed.

In his analysis Stoll also neglects to examine the nature of the Molotov
cocktail as an effective weapon of self-defense, restricting himself to not-
ing its presence in the embassy as culpatory proof that the occupiers were
armed. Nor does he discuss the fact that the people within the hierarchy of
the revolutionary organizations who were in charge of planning embassy
occupations are still alive, with the exception of Rolando Morán and Mario
Payeras. The members of the organizations that existed at the time of the
Spanish embassy bombing are now the leaders of the Unidad Revolucionaria Nacional Guatemalteca (URNG, Guatemalan National Revolutionary Unit), and they live in Guatemala City. An account of the plan could

certainly be put together by interviewing them. Even when Stoll has interviewed leftist leaders, such as Gustavo Porras (advisor and personal secretary to President Alvaro Arzú, 1996–2000), he does not quote them in the
chapter devoted to the events inside the embassy. Porras was part of the
urban leadership of the EGP in 1980 and was most likely involved in planning the occupation. Indeed, when President Arzú named him to his position, his past militancy was openly mentioned in the Guatemalan press and
Porras gave interviews on the matter. Would not an interview with him, a
key participant and one who had read all the reports on the subject sent to
the EGP central command, have been at least as valuable as one with a
municipal fireman or with California fire experts?

The absence of interviews such as this is not a simple omission or just an
academic mistake. That no one involved in the tragic episode is still alive is
patently false. Significantly, it is a claim that allows Stoll to impose his
vision of the facts, namely, the theory of self-immolation on the part of the
occupiers of the embassy. This strategy is particularly dangerous for an academic in this case, because there are so few people who know the chain of
command of the EGP, so he encounters little argument. It does not help
matters that the EGP archives, confiscated in Mexico City in mid-1981 by
agents of the Mexican Federal Police under the direction of Miguel Nassar
Haro (now in a Mexican jail, charged with innumerable human rights violations) in collaboration with the CIA, have still not been made public. Thus
Stoll ends this chapter by saying, "The massacre at the Spanish embassy
could have been a revolutionary suicide that included murdering hostages
and fellow protesters" (88). A statement like this feeds into the average American's fears of terrorism, now associated primarily with the Middle East.
The author's cover is the clause "could have been." But for the average reader,
it is the final phrases that sting the conscience: "revolutionary suicide" and
especially "murdering hostages and fellow protesters." Although such an
accusation is nothing more than another baseless insinuation, grammatically it bears the weight of the whole chapter. All the semantic content of
Stoll's aggregated reasoning resides in this one sentence. Thus, with one
stroke of the pen, he not only discredits the entirety of the Guatemalan left,
but calls into question the ethics and morals of the victims of the embassy
fire, including Vicente Menchú, and, by extension, his daughter.

From this initial discussion we can conclude that, although significant
contradictions appear in Stoll's version of the burning of the embassy, it is

possible for the casual reader to be won over to the position espoused by the anthropologist thanks to the lack of countervailing evidence. In particular, the extensive quotations from Ambassador Cajal given on pages 81–82 give credence to his theory, especially in light of Cajal's stubborn silence on the matter for nearly nineteen years.

Those comments would remain the ambassador's final word had he not published a book about the tragic occurrence in spring 2000 (eighteen months after Stoll's book appeared). Titled *¡Saber quién puso fuego allí! Masacre en la embajada de España* (Who can say who set the fire! Massacre in the Spanish embassy), the text had an enormous impact on the Iberian Peninsula. The first edition sold out, the second was widely read, and talks are under way with a well-known film director for a movie based on the book.

In the book Cajal y López puts forth a vision radically different from that favored by the North American scholar. *Saber* begins with the events that took place in the embassy, taken from the official report Ambassador Cajal himself presented to the Spanish minister of foreign affairs at the time, Marcelino Oreja. This account emphasizes the brutality of the Guatemalan Anti-Riot Squad and Detective Corps: "The police refused absolutely, in a brutal and intransigent manner, to accept a single one of [the occupiers'] conditions" and "They treated us, the hostages, exactly the same as they treated the occupiers" (35).[2] Likewise, Cajal unambiguously declares that when he emerged from the embassy, the police shoved him and tried to put him in a vehicle with the intent to kill him ("It seems there is a recording in which voices are heard saying 'Kill him, kill him,'" 38). He was rescued by Odette Arzú of the International Red Cross and, thanks to her efforts, taken to the Herrera Llerandi Hospital by ambulance.

Right after the official report in Cajal's book comes the account given by Mario Aguirre Godoy. He happened to be visiting the embassy that fateful day, along with the former vice president of the republic, Eduardo Cáceres Lehnhoff, and former chancellor Adolfo Molina Orantes. They had an interview with the ambassador at 11:00 a.m. Godoy's account differs in few particulars from that put forth by the ambassador to Chancellor Oreja. Also excerpted, in more extensive form, is the account of Elías Barahona, which originally appeared in a newspaper article published in Panama. In it Barahona recounts that Donaldo Alvarez Ruiz, the Guatemalan minister of the interior, gave the order to the third-ranking police chief, Colonel Arnoldo

Paniagua, to get everyone out of the embassy. When Paniagua discovered that Cáceres Lehnhof and Molina Orantes were among the hostages, he went back to Minister Alvarez Ruiz. The minister consulted President Lucas García, who replied, "No matter, they must be on the *guerrilleros'* side, get them all out" (64). The following day, Alvarez Ruiz met with Chancellor Castillo Valdez to devise an "official" version that would quell international protests. They decided to fabricate the story that the Spanish consul, Jaime Ruiz del Arbol, had called the authorities and asked them to intervene. The consul would be unable to deny it, as he was among the dead.

The next chapter of Cajal's book deals with the kidnapping and death of Gregorio Yuxá. It recounts what happened that same night, 31 January, in the Herrera Llerandi Hospital after the arrival of the ambassador and Yuxá, the sole Maya found alive in his embassy office, both suffering from third-degree burns. At around 1:00 a.m., the Spanish ambassador to El Salvador, Víctor Sánchez Mésas, who had traveled to Guatemala to check on the condition of Ambassador Cajal, received a visit from Chancellor Castillo Valdez. The chancellor acknowledged that he had tried to prevent the police from entering the embassy, but that President Lucas and Minister Alvarez Ruiz had made the decision to order a forced entry. Around 7:30 a.m. on the following day, the police guarding the hospital were suddenly withdrawn. The account then becomes almost like a horror movie: "Shortly thereafter twenty armed men in plain clothes, with kerchiefs over their faces, entered the hospital" (68). They herded the medical personnel into a room and kidnapped Gregorio Yuxá. Two of the kidnappers remained behind, guarding the ambassador's room, until about 9:00 a.m., when members of the national police force returned, gave friendly greetings to the kidnappers, and took over guarding the room. The book quotes, in addition, the tape recording of Yuxá's last words recounting what he lived through inside the embassy, including the sentence used as the book's title, which indicates that he had no knowledge that the occupiers had started the fire.

In Cajal's book, testimonies from various participants follow, such as that of Beatriz de Laiglesia, the ambassador's wife; Odette Arzú; and Frank Ortiz, U.S. ambassador to Guatemala. De Laiglesia recounts that she returned to the country the following day and went to see her husband in the hospital. There the decision was made to transfer him to the residence of the U.S. ambassador out of fear for his life, given the Guatemalan government's hostile attitude. Because the police had him practically blockaded in the hospital, it was necessary to mount an escape operation to remove him. His wife took him from the room in a wheelchair, stating that she was taking him to the X-ray laboratory to assuage the police and prevent them from following her. Once in the elevator, she went to the second basement level, where the ambassador of Venezuela, Jesús Elías, was waiting for her in the Venezuelan embassy vehicle. They placed Cajal inside and drove off, but they were followed by a security vehicle. The Venezuelan ambassador reprimanded those in the second vehicle, reminding them that the embassy vehicle was Venezuelan territory. The car managed to enter the U.S. embassy without incident. That night, security forces sprayed the residence of the U.S. ambassador with machine-gun fire. This serious occurrence is never mentioned by Stoll, but it is confirmed by the testimony of the U.S. ambassador, Frank Ortiz, on page 116 of Cajal's book. De Laiglesia recounts the episode as follows:

There we were, watching television [in the embassy residence, in the company of Ambassador Ortiz], when we heard noises outside, which I couldn't identify right away. Frank threw himself on the floor, began crawling around turning out the lights, and told me not to move, that they were gunshots. He left the room, still on the floor in the dark, to see what was going on. The telephone in the guard kiosk didn't answer, and we feared the worst. He returned; the marine [manning the kiosk] was alive, but from the floor he could not reach the telephone on the wall. They had in fact machine-gunned the embassy. (84)

Odette Arzú's testimony is also fascinating, because she recognized the voice of Germán Chupina, the police chief, saying by radio to the second in command of the Judicial Police, who was standing next to her, "I don't want anyone to get out alive" (103). Therefore, when the ambassador emerged from the embassy "with burns all over," the second-ranking Judicial Police chief ordered, "Kill him" (103). At that point Arzú threw herself on top of Cajal's body and began screaming that he was the Spanish ambassador and they could not kill him:

In the midst of all this the military and national police put us in a police van. I said to myself, They're going to shoot us in here, María Odette! A lieutenant in the bus said to me:
—Quiet! Shut up! Now we're going to take you where you belong.

Then I opened the windows and started yelling:

—I am María Odette Arzú Castillo, mother of six children. You can't take me anywhere, stop, let us out! (104)

Arzú raised such an uproar that finally, through the intervention of Dr. Augusto Bauer Arzú, her cousin, who had been called to serve as intermediary between the occupiers and the government, she managed to secure their release. It was then that arrangements were made to transfer the ambassador to Herrera Llerandi Hospital, the best in Guatemala.

Finally, the testimony of the U.S. ambassador, Frank Ortiz, expresses his surprise at the ruthless violation of protocol on the part of the Guatemalan government, which refused to listen even to Ortiz himself, and accused him of "complicity" with the "communist" Cajal. In Ortiz's words, "My Embassy and I received our share of vituperation as well" (116).

There follows in Cajal's book a series of chapters describing the actions of Spain's government toward that of Guatemala, the trip Ambassador Cajal made with Consul Ruiz del Arbol to the Quiché in January 1980, his return to Spain and convalescence there after the burning of the embassy, the smear campaign unleashed against him by the Guatemalan government in an attempt to blame him for the conflagration (he was accused of being a "communist" and of having arranged the occupation with "subversives" during his trip to the Quiché), and his later diplomatic activity as he tried to recall and reconstruct the events. In this last section Cajal quotes an article published by Elías Barahona on 29 March 1987, reprinted in the Sunday supplement of Guatemala's *El Gráfico* and never cited by Stoll:

> As a front-row witness present in the office of Minister Donaldo Alvarez Ruiz, I personally observed when he received the order to attack the Embassy from General Romeo Lucas García, and later how Alvarez Ruiz transmitted it to the Police Chief, Germán Chupina, and the Chief carried it out through Colonel Paniagua.
>
> Shortly thereafter, Chancellor Rafael Castillo Valdez and a journalist, Carlos Toledo Vielman, arrived at the office of Minister Alvarez Ruiz in order to follow the sequence of the next moments by radio, step by step, as Minister Alvarez Ruiz's secretary, Señorita Patricia Mencos, can also attest. Castillo Valdez was trying to evade the telephone calls from Spain, from [Foreign Affairs Minister] Marcelino Oreja.

While human beings were being burned alive, we were eating chicken sand-
wiches, and Alvarez Ruiz even made a joke about "having a drink and some
barbecued hors d'oeuvres." Moreover, he asked his secretary to refuse to put
through the constant phone calls coming from Ambassador Cajal. (311–12)

Far-right Guatemalan pundit Jorge Palmieri, who admits to being the
mouthpiece for Guatemalan military intelligence as regards this case (331),
replied to Barahona by saying that, for a thorough examination of all the
facts, it had to be taken into consideration that the Spanish ambassador
had interfered in the internal affairs of Guatemala. But he did not deny the
credibility of Barahona's assertions. On the contrary, he said that because
of them "it would be worthwhile to have a deeper investigation into what
happened" (313). Nonetheless, Stoll never mentions this public debate that
had taken place in Guatemalan newspapers more than ten years before his
book was published. This debate began to change even the right wing's view
of the events, possibly as a result of the country's return to a democratic
regime. In the last part of his book, Cajal mentions that on 25 March 1996
Guatemalan Chancellor Eduardo Stein (now vice president of Guatemala),
a member of the Arzú government, publicly lamented in Madrid the burning of the embassy and with tears in his eyes begged forgiveness from the
Spanish people for the events of 31 January 1980. The following day, in a
press conference, his exact words were these: "In a failure to comply with
the fundamental principle of respecting the sovereignty of diplomatic mis-
sions among friendly nations, the Embassy of Spain was attacked by force,
with the resulting fire and loss of human life which we all know" (333). The
Guatemalan government's official acknowledgment of responsibility for the
burning of the embassy is not mentioned in Stoll's book either, even though
Stein's declarations were made two and a half years before the anthropologist's work was published.

Cajal concludes his book with a summary of the account of the massacre
at the Spanish embassy given in *Guatemala: Nunca más* (Guatemala: Never
again), a report by the Recovery of Historic Memory project (Recuperación
de la Memoria Histórica, REMHI) of the Archbishopric of Guatemala, and
in *Guatemala, memoria del silencio* (Guatemala, memory of silence), issued
by the official Historical Clarification Commission under the auspices of
the United Nations.

In this debate about what happened when the Spanish embassy was burned, the two main points are the Guatemalan government's guilt in attacking the Spanish embassy, an act that violated the sovereignty of the Spanish state, and the question of who started the fire that cost so many lives. This is why, in his very first chapter, titled "Lo sucedido en la emba-jada de España" (What happened in the Spanish embassy), Cajal recounts in a first-person narrative the events he experienced starting at 11:00 on the morning of 31 January 1980. The ambassador emphasizes that, contrary to Stoll's insinuations, the occupation was carried out "in a peaceful manner" (28). The occupiers' chief demand was that the Spanish government trans-mit to the government of Guatemala the need to exhume the cadavers of a group of people who had been kidnapped by the army in the Uspantán region and had then been tortured, killed, and passed off as guerrilla fighters (28). The embassy occupiers wished to prove that the dead were not fighters but their friends, *campesinos* who had been kidnapped months earlier.

As to the key element of the debate, the foundational argument of Stoll's ethical-moral position, the question of who set the fire, Cajal is clear. The evidence gathered not only from the witnesses but also from the type of burns the victims suffered (the fact that they were burned only from the waist up, among other things, which, according to the California experts quoted anonymously by Stoll, indicated burning by gasoline), makes it plain that what burned them was white phosphorus. This could not have come from the Molotov cocktails brought by the occupiers. There is testimony regarding the presence of a member of the security forces, a "fat policeman," who went up the steps to the embassy with a "strange device hanging from his belt" (37) that looked like a fumigation apparatus and was similar to an Israeli-built launcher for paralyzing gas. Although the ambassador cannot personally confirm that this device started the fire, that conclusion can be drawn from various testimonies. Likewise, Cajal clarifies his own statements cited by Stoll and used in chapter 6 of the latter's book to prove his hypoth-esis. Cajal says:

> One important specification must be made here. In my first statements— including on the tape I made while still in the U.S. residence—I asserted that the explosion had been caused by a "Molotov cocktail" thrown by one of the occupiers. I said this not because I saw one of them throw it, but as a logical deduction, given that they were carrying several of them and had repeatedly threatened to throw them if the police entered (if they were going to die, it

did not matter which way). But thinking back on those moments, and in light of indications in several people's statements, there is the possibility that it was the police who threw some similar product (phosphorus?). Or that both things happened at once. There was one moment when I was holding in my hand, to prevent the police from pushing it through the shattered door, a red container that I thought was a smoke grenade. These suspicions caused me to ask that samples of the burned remains of my office be brought to Madrid for analysis. (36–37)

In addition, in note 6 of the same chapter Ambassador Cajal asserts:

On February 17, 1980, the magazine *Cambio 16* published a color photograph showing a police agent carrying a strange apparatus. The "Report of the Recovery of Historic Memory, *Guatemala: Nunca Más*" presented by Monsignor Gerardi on 24.4.1998 says about this:

At 15:20 thick black smoke was seen coming from the Ambassador's office, followed by flames. Desperate cries were heard from the people trapped inside, but it was all over in three minutes. Several eyewitnesses, among them Jaime Fuentes of the Spanish working mission for collaborative technology, assure that they saw a short, fat policeman enter toward the stairway leading to the second floor, with a strange device hanging from his belt. The February 17, 1980 issue of *Cambio 16* shows a color photograph of this policeman carrying the device. It is a launcher for gas that paralyzes, irritates the skin and especially the eyes, and can be extremely harmful if used in large quantities and at close range. It appears to be of Israeli origin.

Technicians who were consulted . . . consider that the room, although small, had a sufficient air supply because the door had been broken down and the windowpanes were shattered. If gasoline had been the only element causing the fire, the combustion would have been much slower, inducing the massive, immediate exit of the people closed inside the room. The person who gathered and examined the samples indicated that the petrified posture of the corpses (some were sitting upright) and the fact that several of them did not have mortal burns (there is abundant photographic evidence of this) lead to the conclusion that it is not possible for gasoline from "Molotov cocktails" to have caused so many deaths. (36–37)

Cajal also points out that both his wife and Judge Pedro Bermejo observed that the occupiers had taken large quantities of food and clothing to the embassy kitchen, enough provisions for about ten days. This indicated that the occupiers intended "a long and peaceful occupation" (39). Moreover, Cajal is emphatic about the fact that the police refused to allow members of the International Red Cross or Doctor Bauer Arzú to enter the building. He adds that they never phoned a single member of the Guatemalan government "with any influence over what was happening there" (40), even though the ambassador had attempted to phone all the high government officials he could and was able to communicate freely with members of the Spanish government, in addition to having made a direct request to the police surrounding the embassy to send in negotiators. Likewise, the police blocked firefighters from entering: "The police allowed the cadavers or bodies in my office to be consumed, knowing full well that this was the desirable outcome for their interests" (40).

While Stoll maintains that no autopsies were performed on the dead because the cadavers were too badly damaged, as I have indicated previously, *Guatemala, memoria del silencio* reports the conclusion of the General Staff of the Spanish Army, issued on 30 April 1981:

> It is considered highly likely that an inert gas or something similar was used, which would produce immediate paralysis in the victim. . . . Due to the conditions of the premises, the rigid posture of the cadavers, their frontal position, and the fact that there was no lack of oxygen in the room where the tragedy took place, it does not seem possible to conclude that gasoline from a Molotov cocktail would have caused all the deaths. (172)[3]

The United Nations document also includes the testimony of a witness who saw the cadavers in the morgue. He states that they had been heaped in one corner on top of each other: "It must have been something very powerful, like a flamethrower. . . . Moreover, the majority were lying face up with their arms outspread" (172). Shortly thereafter the witness received a call from a doctor who told him he had participated in the autopsy and explained that this type of death, judging from the way the bodies had been burned and how they were lying, "is only produced by white phosphorus" (172–73). Another witness who helped to remove bodies from the embassy states that they were falling apart and that they had become stuck to one another (173). The conclusion reached in *Guatemala, memoria del silencio* is that after breaking down the door to the ambassador's office, the security forces used a flamethrower or an inert-gas launcher against everyone inside, hitting them from the waist up and projecting them backward against one another. The use of this instrument also ignited the Molotov cocktails that the occupiers had brought with them (172). Finally, the United Nations document certifies that no reports were made by or declarations taken from the police and that the few pages that make up the sole existing legal record are evidence of "the absolute unwillingness of the Judicial Branch and the Ministry of Public Affairs to investigate the facts, and to prosecute and punish the guilty parties" (177). It also cites violation of Articles 22, 27, and 29 of the Vienna Convention on Diplomatic Relations (179). The report's conclusions hold the regime of General Lucas García directly responsible for the burning of the Spanish embassy (180–81). Within these conclusions is this categorical statement: "The theory that the victims immolated themselves is entirely without foundation." The report was published only two months after Stoll's book came out.

The same facts outlined in the United Nations report have been noted by Gonzalo de Villa, a Jesuit priest who is currently the president of Rafael Landívar University in Guatemala. The priest's mother, Teresa Vásquez de Villa, was one of the embassy victims. An employee of a travel agency that organized trips to Spain, she had the misfortune to be at work obtaining visas for future travelers at the time the occupiers took over the embassy. I asked de Villa about the situation. His e-mail reply stated:

> To answer your question, I was not in Guatemala at the time. I came to the burial, but it was too late to see my mother's body. The person who identified her was my brother-in-law, who recognized her shoes and slacks. What I heard was that the fire did not reach ground level, and the bodies were much more severely burned in the torso than in the legs. . . . One more thing. I did go to the site where it happened on February 2 or 3, when it was still sealed off. I was surprised that there was telephone cord on the floor that had not been burned. This confirms the impression that the fire was caused more by a flammable gas than by a liquid substance which, due to gravity, would have burned first at the bottom and then spread upward.[4]

Although Chancellor Molina Orantes's son continued to claim that what happened in the embassy was a "Spanish plot" in his testimony to *elPeriódico de Guatemala,* published 31 January 2000 to commemorate the twentieth anniversary of the tragedy, he gave no opinion as to how the fire could have started.

From the foregoing, it would be possible to conclude that Stoll carried out a poor investigation, that he did not take the trouble to interview all those involved, or even that he was unaware of data pertinent to the case. After all, the United Nations report was issued two months after the publication of his book, and its contents had been secret prior to that time. Likewise, Ambassador Cajal's book was published a year and a half after Stoll's, and the statements of Molina Orantes's son appeared in the press nearly fifteen months later.

In July 2000, however, I interviewed Ambassador Cajal in Madrid. The diplomat said he had spent years planning his text, as a form of personal therapy, to resolve the trauma he had suffered from the burning of the embassy. Writing had become an exercise in the reconstruction of memory, for his burn injuries and subsequent trauma had caused him to forget nearly all the details of the incident. In this interview he asserted that in 1995 (that is, three years before Stoll's book was originally published), Stoll had sent him the controversial chapter containing his theory of the occupiers' self-immolation. The ambassador, in the process of reconstructing the events himself, was stunned by this highly peculiar interpretation and wrote to Stoll immediately, contradicting it.

What is interesting about the exchange between Cajal and Stoll is that Cajal claims to have given Stoll all the information he had at his disposal. Nonetheless, the U.S. academic ignored it. He preferred to present his controversial hypothesis of self-immolation, knowing that evidence to the contrary existed in Madrid. Why? The only theory I can offer is that he did so to discredit not only Vicente Menchú, but all the victims of the attack on the embassy, and thereby strike a blow at the Guatemalan left. According to Cajal, he received a copy of Stoll's book in the mail. He confirmed, with a heavy heart, that the author had not made use of the material he had given him. Stoll had known that Cajal's book was in production but chose to ignore its existence. Finally, when Cajal's book was published in Spain, the ambassador sent a copy to Stoll. To this day, he has not received any acknowledgment. Cajal says that he learned, via contacts in relation to a possible film on the subject, that Stoll had in fact received the book, but there has been no further communication between the two.

Several conclusions may be drawn from this discussion. The burning of the Spanish embassy was, without a doubt, the most immoral act, and the one most directly in violation of international law, of the many abuses committed by the dictatorial regime of General Lucas García.[5] In Guatemala, only those individuals close to the military government, relatives of victims Cáceres Lehnoff and Molina Orantes, and journalists known to have collaborated with military intelligence have defended tooth and nail the version of the embassy burning that the occupiers were guilty of setting the fire. Yet even they have distanced themselves somewhat from this theory since 1987, although they continue to maintain that Ambassador Cajal had ties to the guerrillas and the Guatemalan left. The burning of the embassy was of such enormous magnitude that it constituted a watershed, becoming the defining event in Guatemala's armed internal conflict.

In the United States, very little of this information was known prior to the controversy generated by Stoll. Menchú's text, however, had become practically required reading not only in universities and community colleges but in many high schools. Thus it is indeed curious that Stoll has chosen to present, in a book meant to question Menchú's credibility by accusing her of favoring the EGP line as part of a broader questioning of the revolutionary left, a version of the facts about the Spanish embassy incident that turns out to be itself highly prejudicial and clearly favors the official version put forth by Guatemalan military intelligence in 1980. The chapter of his book that outlines events in which Rigoberta Menchú did not participate (she had nothing to do with this event and was far away, in a school in Huehuetenango, at the time), and in which her father, Vicente, is barely mentioned, is central to Stoll's moral questioning of Menchú. He uses the alleged violence and self-immolation of EGP members in the Spanish embassy to impugn Menchú's discursive credibility. And yet, at the same time and in the same act, he deliberately excludes information that had been generously provided to him by Ambassador Cajal in 1995, three years before his book was published.

Stoll has tried to present himself as a moderate, a "centrist" intellectual, a former leftist sympathetic to the Central American left during the 1980s who disappeared from the conservative radio talk show circuit because right-wing critics disliked his insistence that Menchú was not a fraud. In this version of his self-presentation he, ethically and morally disturbed by the lies he discovered within the Central American left, became disenchanted

and turned his energies to denouncing them. This is why moderately conservative U.S. academics took some of his allegations seriously. His accusations had a devastating effect in high schools especially, where Menchú's
book is practically never taught anymore, as I indicated in the previous
chapter. In passing, the generalized suspicion that people of color falsify
their lives to gain an edge has gained new strength as a weapon in the attack
on multiculturalism in education.

Before Stoll's radio engagements petered out in 2000 as he claims, Stoll
carried out much of his promotional campaign on conservative radio sta-
tions that specialized in railing against former U.S. president Bill Clinton
at the peak of his impeachment proceedings. The author actively contributed
to the smear campaign against the moral validity of the Latin American left.[6]
Likewise, he attempted to discredit progressive academics in the United
States, whom he attacks explicitly in his book.

In the context of academic responsibility, what can we say when we examine the argument that is the crux of Stoll's case against Menchú, which
he built around the burning of the Spanish embassy? We see Stoll defending positions taken by Guatemalan military intelligence in 1980, which were
no longer being put forth publicly within the country by the time his controversial book came out. Furthermore, we see that his analysis of the facts
presents contradictions in the evidence he himself provides to defend supposedly objective positions, using baseless allegations by "California experts"
or "a Guatemala City firefighter" without giving their names. Finally, we
discover that Stoll wantonly ignored information given to him in advance
of his book's publication that contradicted his most outlandish theories.
This was, at best, most irresponsible scholarship; at worst, it was an abuse
of power and knowledge for the purpose of influencing U.S. politics by discrediting the left in a kind of early Swift Boat campaign.

PART III

Immigration, Diaspora, and Globalization

8

The Maya Movement

L et us begin our discussion of the Maya movement with a local issue. It could very well be a crime story. In reality, it is an event with clear political connotations. On 16 May 1998, at 7:00 p.m., two husky, armed men intimidated and threatened the life of Licenciado Ovidio Paz Bal, one of the attorneys for the Defensoría Maya (Maya Legal Defense Fund). This happened in the town of Sololá, in the department (province) of the same name. The victim had been traveling on a public bus coming from the capital. When he got out, he was followed by two strangers. The individuals told him: "Back off. If you don't let up we're going to put a bullet in your head, and that goes for Juan and Ricardo too." The lawyer ran to a shop for help. When they saw this, the strangers left the scene. The names referred to by the thugs were those of Juan León, national coordinator of the Defensoría Maya, and Ricardo Sulugui Juracán, regional coordinator of Defensoría Maya for Sololá. León had worked for decades to promote and defend indigenous peoples' rights, not only within Guatemala but also in the international arena, including the United Nations. Sulugui is a leader of the Maya Kaqchikel people who has worked tirelessly against both militarization and the eradication of civil patrols (PACs) for self-defense. When these events happened, he was one of the negotiators in Sololá for the establishment of a Maya university in the region on the grounds previously occupied by Military Zone 14.

In a conventional political analysis, we could say that these acts of intimidation were framed within a general policy of threats and extrajudicial executions carried out by paramilitary bands in Guatemala, which intensified after the assassination of Bishop Juan Gerardi on 26 April 1998. Monsignor Gerardi, coordinator of the Guatemalan Archbishop's Human Rights Office, was bludgeoned to death two days after he had presented the Recuperation of Historical Memory report, which documented torture, kidnappings, massacres, and other crimes against humanity committed largely by the Guatemalan army during the armed conflict of 1960–96.

Now let us turn to a different case. This one is decidedly less dramatic. Maya writer Luis Enrique Sam Colop published a comment in his weekly column regarding the well-known director of the Guatemala City daily newspaper *La Hora,* Oscar Clemente Marroquín: "What I wish to call to your attention today is that columnist Oscar Clemente Marroquín, in his justified criticism of Congressional President García Regás and in opposition to the immorality of other public officials, also adds: 'Although at bottom I must say that the fault lies not with the Indian but with those who side with him.'"[1] Occurrences of this nature—from direct death threats to manifestations of the unconscious racism that crops up in the thought processes of someone who is allegedly one of the most progressive journalists in the country—exemplify the difficulty of fitting theories of cultural analysis engendered in urban, cosmopolitan academic circles, where concepts such as "globalization" or "postmodernism" are common, to the concrete events that rule the daily realities of ethnic groups in distant localities labeled "marginal" or "peripheral."

This first chapter of the present section on immigration, diaspora, and globalization will explore how concrete events such as those just mentioned challenge not only the authenticity of the ethnic subject, on a daily basis, but also the capacity of theorists to place an ensemble of heterogeneous issues within the unifying context of globalization. This analysis will make it easier to understand the emotional and cultural baggage that many immigrants, both Maya and non-Maya, bring with them on their diasporic journeys to North America. The next two chapters will examine the specificity of Central Americans in the United States in relation to issues of identity, history, and politics. Prior to taking that second step, however, I want to emphasize in this first discussion that in a globalized world, not only does specificity still count, but it can also be a singular burden, a problematic weight that itself becomes globalized as a consequence of diasporic movements. I will show as well the ways in which globalization affects the unfolding of the ethnic subject's identity when cultural power is reorganized within

new decentralized, multidetermined sociopolitical relations.[2] Along the way
I will also explore how different alternatives produce contradictory gazes in
the space of alterity as well as in the mechanisms of production and distri-
bution of meaning.

Disputing the Authenticity of "What Is Maya" in a Global World

In a book published some years ago, José Joaquín Brünner defined globalization as an attempt to explain the encasing within a single capitalist system of markets and information networks extending "to the limits of the
planet."[3] He differentiated this economic process from postmodernism,
which he saw as an attempt to "express the cultural style corresponding to
this global reality" (12). If indeed the current features of Maya culture must,
by extension, fit within this decentered, portable culture, the product of
multiple fragmentations and convergences, it must be borne in mind that
Maya culture is not a product or an offshoot of globalization and postmodernism, though they both brought renewed attention to a Maya subjectivity that had remained invisible for far too long. The Maya movement
as such arose from the consequences of a brutal civil war in Central America. Mario Payeras sums up the situation as follows: "Beyond their implications in other aspects, the social struggles of the 1970s were decisive in
defining the ethnic problem, emphasizing Maya agency and testing in real
life any unfounded beliefs and superficial theorizing on the subject. After
what has happened, no one denies the depth of the conflict nor, in progressive sectors of society, the legitimacy of ethnic identity."[4] In light of this particular political circumstance, the Maya movement's entrance on the global
scene, generated primarily through the iconic role played by Rigoberta Menchú's book in the U.S. culture wars at the end of the 1980s, is a contradictory one. Two of its salient aspects—a militant revolutionary history and
the instrumentalization of Menchú as an iconic symbol of pluralist subalternity within the United States—frequently contradict each other.

   Yet this is not the whole story. Because of deeply entrenched racism, Guatemala and all of Central America have denied any representational space
to Maya culture. For that reason, Mayas have had to use the high profile
they acquired in the international arena to assert a representationality within
the nation of which they technically form a part in order to escape from
their subaltern, racialized position. To further this process, they established

not only pan-Maya ties outside of their national space, but also pan-ethnic ties on a continental scale and even, we could add, on a global level. (A clear example of this last step is a meeting organized by the Menchú Foundation that was attended by a politico-cultural movement of self-described "first peoples"—Inuits, Laps, etc.)

It is as a result of these contradictions between the representationality of "the Maya" in both global and local scenarios that a national debate has emerged inside Guatemala regarding Mayas' newly gained global visibility. This is because the nation-state is still perceived by hegemonic Ladinos in a traditionally "modern" way: one ethnic group, one nation, one state. As a consequence, "Ladino" commentators are on the defensive and have generated a negative critique of Maya aspirations and Maya agency. To reinforce Ladino hegemony, they have purveyed uneven and partial interpretations of the position they label "Mayista" that are at odds with what we now see in the global space.[5] Unlike traditional reactionary, anticommunist discourse on this subject, neo-Ladinists argue that, politically, they are located within self-proclaimed "progressive sectors" of society.[6] Feeling threatened by Maya representationality, they attempt, with an adroit use of postmodern rhetoric, to save the Ladino world from what they perceive as the destructive forces unleashed by Mayaness. According to them, their critique targets only those essentialist and fundamentalist aspects of "Mayista" discourse that they consider "anti-Ladino" (see Morales in this regard). However, they claim to have no disagreements with regional autonomies or with the regularization of Maya languages presently taking place in the country. They assert that they respect Maya culture and identity and even the "difference" between the two ethnic groups. But they also argue that democratization would be better served by celebrating those spaces where mutual differences find confluence (spaces of cultural *mestizaje,* hybridization, transculturation, etc.) than by "inventing" or magnifying the actual differences that do exist. As Morales explains: "It was . . . my intention to dismantle discourses by self-proclaimed 'Maya' intellectuals in order to situate the debate beyond essentialisms (strategic or otherwise), whether indigenous or Ladino, taking as a point of departure the constructed nature of ethnic and cultural identities and pointing to the possibilities of interethnic negotiation."[7] This concept is not in itself without merit or validity. To defend their arguments, however, Ladino critics ignore many lessons garnered from the debates surrounding multiculturalism. They claim that concepts developed in the United States should not be mechanically transposed to other "national" cultural spaces, given that those positions were formulated exclusively for the benefit of American minorities. This allows them to ignore the complexity and heterogeneity of Ladino ethnicity itself as they argue that current constructions of Maya identity in Guatemala are inauthentic because they are not wholly autonomous or identical to those of pre-Conquest Mayas, but rather reflect the influence of modern technology and globalization. The revolution in communications, however, means that Mayas, like all other cultural groups in the world today, have access to knowledge, resources, and political strategies available everywhere. They use these tools for their benefit and are affected by this process. It is in the light of these essentialized constructions by Ladinos of "authentic" Maya culture that the conservative nature of Ladino postmodern critiques of Maya identity politics emerges.

A study by the Facultad Latinoamericana de Ciencias Sociales (FLACSO, Latin American Faculty of Social Sciences), edited by Alberto Esquit Choy and Victor Gálvez Borrel, sums up this position as follows:

> From the *ladino* side, the debate is led by columnists Mario Alberto Carrera and Mario Roberto Morales. Some of the points they have raised: The Mayas as a people have been extinct since the year 500 A.D. and that to talk of Mayas today is to resuscitate a people that have been dead for a thousand years; the present indigenous of Guatemala (principally the K'iché's) are descendants of the Toltecs who settled in Mexico; the majority of present day indigenous are in fact mestizos. . . . Identity is a process of addition and not subtraction. . . . In Guatemala we are all Guatemalans and to argue the contrary is to play into the interests of the powerful; in the context of ethnic and Maya fundamentalism, *ladinos* could also feel discriminated against.[8]

The contradiction we find when it comes to Maya subjectivity is the one that has divided cultural theorists between those who see a particular understanding of globalization as the negation of the ethnic subject, as a sort of worldwide Americanization of identities, and those who defend the authenticity of the so-called peripheral subject by arguing that specificity is more important than ever in a globalized world. In fact, neo-Ladinists do not recommend a return to those times when the Maya population was subjected to racism, oppression, or exploitation. Rather, they articulate their positions as follows: "It is worthwhile, rather, to propose an inter-ethnic negotiation based on the admission of cultural *mestizaje* that is diglossic, hybrid, and heterogeneous on both sides, in order to move in the direction of an ethnic-cultural democratization. That is to say, the free and egalitarian exercise of diverse cultural traditions that belong to the cultural ensemble known as Guatemala."[9] However, the debate cannot be reduced to the fact that one faction of Mayas may favor certain "essentialist" elements to configure their identity (which does happen) while Ladinos paternalistically point out to them that they are in error because essentialisms do not exist. Rather than the fabrication and articulation of one position or another via splendid theoretical pyramids, the real problem is the daily violence that Mayas still face and the asymmetrical relations of power that have existed between Ladinos and Mayas for more than five hundred years. In light of this imbalance and of the war unleashed by its exacerbation—followed, in turn, by a ferocious ethnocidal campaign on the part of the Guatemalan army that killed nearly a quarter of a million indigenous people—Maya factions are justified at present in constituting their subjectivity in whatever fashion they wish, regardless of any possible disagreement with traces of essentialism that may creep into those constructs. To argue, as Morales does, that Mayas presently constitute an "atomized movement" seeking an "ethnocentric, antiladino autonomy that emerged from the fact that both left and right-wing contenders instrumentalized indigenous peoples in a war that those very same sectors never made their own despite massive incorporation into their ranks"[10] not only is politically dangerous (as both Morales and Stoll have discovered), but relies on gross generalities that deny Maya subjectivity all possibility of agency. Mayas are reduced to the racist stereotype of helpless subaltern victims, hapless subjects who can go nowhere without the prior consent of Ladinos, who, as Westerners, have a legitimate handle on postmodernism. As Rigoberta Menchú aptly puts it:

> For some I am still the Indian, the abusive woman, subversive woman, born in a humble cradle and lacking in knowledge. . . . There is so much envy because an indigenous woman has become a protagonist in small spaces of leadership in the country. . . . I must fear not only death but also the possibility of political harassment from sectors that will never be able to tolerate the prominence of an indigenous woman in politics. . . . New generations will have to be born, and the new generations will have a different mentality and a different way of coexisting in our country, so that indigenous and

non-indigenous can be manifest in history and play a role benefitting our society.[11]

Those who contravene Maya agency take the position that construction of identities within the "global village" is an impossibility.[12] They do recognize cultural hybridization, but deny the complex relationships that still exist between hegemonic and subaltern sectors at the symbolic level, even in an era when so-called peripheries have nearly the same access to symbolic goods as does the center.

Esquit Choy and Gálvez Borrel have noted that to analyze the contemporary Maya movement it is necessary to consider not only the qualitative changes that have taken place since the 1980s, placing them within the current paradigm of globalization, but also the diverse forms of cultural resistance that have appeared on the scene since the beginning of the colonial era,[13] without falling into Lyotardian games about the flux of history or seeing history itself as either irreversible or metadiscursive.

In the latter context one understands how for a broad sector of Mayas the fuse lit by the revolutionary war was merely a mechanism, at times an excuse, for the communities to organize themselves, gain agency, and directly confront the racist state. As early as fifteen years ago, the top Maya leader in the Unidad Revolucionaria Nacional Guatemalteca (URNG, Guatemalan National Revolutionary Unit), Pablo Ceto, was already talking about participating in a "conspiracy within the conspiracy."[14] For him the revolutionary struggle and Marxist ideology were nothing but vehicles, mere instruments to be employed in the defense of and struggle for Maya identity, independent of any other goals the revolutionary movement had in mind. As Demetrio Cojtí has confirmed, Ceto's position on this has not changed. If anything, he has tried to reconcile, on the one hand, the URNG and its self-described "popular Maya" base, grouped more or less within the Coordinadora de los Pueblos Mayas de Guatemala (COPMAGUA, Maya Peoples of Guatemala Coordinating Committee), and, on the other, the allegedly "fundamentalist" positions defended by self-described "cultural Mayas."[15]

Given the conditions of structural racism on which the Guatemalan state rests, it is impossible for the nation to be truly democratized without first destroying Ladino hegemony, supposedly the most Westernized sector within the country, although not necessarily the most globalized. As

Haroldo Shetemul, then director of *Crónica,* noted in an editorial he wrote, the United Nations itself made a similar point in a document titled "Guatemala: Contrasts in Human Development."[16]

Those who object to this conclusion form a binary opposition between democratization and destruction even while they are accusing the Maya movement of creating a suprahistorical binary opposition between Maya and Ladino.[17] This presupposes that those favoring the "destruction" of Ladino hegemony cannot possibly be in favor of "democratization." Nonetheless, even in the best of cases, this is a fallacy. As Marta Casaús Arzú points out:

> Due to the penetration and dispersion of racism throughout all spheres of civil society and the State in recent decades, it is necessary to seek new formulas for the interrelationship of both spheres. . . . This change can only come about with a reconsideration of the nature of the State and a reformulation of the nation. . . . It has become necessary to modify the constitution and current legislation, to substantially modify the educational system and the cultural values of the population. . . . In turn it would be necessary to try to modify the racist, exclusionary national imaginary for upcoming generations under other assumptions and by modifying schoolbooks, communications media, etc.
>
> But in our opinion the key lies in modifying the system of domination and in redefining the social space of the different actors on the basis of respect and recognition of Indigenous Peoples' identities and of their social and cultural rights, and also by respecting other social identities such as gender and class.[18]

Since 1996, all Maya positions without exception have favored a democratization that includes the Ladino sector.[19] They also speak of sharing power in a multinational and plurilingual nation[20]—or, rather, in a multiethnic and plurilingual nation, for those who would quibble about whether Maya groups are nations, a debate that is far from being settled. The linguistic signifier may change, but the notion to which it refers remains the same, namely, a nation in which Ladinos and Mayas coexist under a Maya government. Like it or not, this would mean the reconfiguration of Ladino hegemony. We must remember that the word *hegemony* implies that one group exercises power while tolerating and respecting the legitimate spaces of others by negotiating agreements more or less democratically with them. In Guatemala, however, Ladinos construe their present subjectivity on the basis of domination and not of hegemony. To their way of thinking, they have won the war, and therefore should continue to be the dominant group in the country. Nevertheless, within the framework of the 1996 peace accords, seriously undermined beginning when the Portillo administration came to power in 2001 and made concessions to international policies of a globalized nature that reach Guatemala through institutions such as the United Nations or the Organization of American States, they are willing to tolerate and respect Mayas' subaltern spaces. But local spaces occupied by Mayas have become impregnated with a strong sense of their own subjectivity as a result of the globalized spaces in which they operate. For this reason, in their conceptualization of a multinational and plurilingual nation, Mayas think that both ethnic groups, Mayas and Ladinos, should exercise an equal measure of power. This assertion alone would imply breaking or destroying not only Ladino domination, but also Ladino hegemony.

Neo-Ladinist critics duck the issue by asserting that there is no such thing as a "Maya culture" that is diametrically opposed to a Ladino one. They go so far as to claim that recognizing a separate Maya culture would be no more than a form of paternalistic solidarity or a legitimization of inauthentic cultural formations that serve a strictly strategic purpose. This position suppresses the common knowledge held by Ladinos and Mayas alike, that the latter are always recognized as an ethnic group and have been the victims of exploitation, prejudice, violence, and neglect solely on the basis of their ethnicity. At this point in the debate, the semantic question of whether the Mayas are "really" Mayas is spurious. The issue is not one of identity, but one of concrete social and political power. Garífunas are not Garífunas, either, under this same logic, for their identity as such is a construct elaborated by African slaves who escaped from St. Vincent in the eighteenth century. Nor are Miskitos anything more than products of a mingling of indigenous people with groups of African and English descent. Pursuing this line even further, we could easily explain that "Americans" are not Anglo-Saxons and Germans are not "Aryans." It would be a never-ending story. As we all know, ethnic groups are de facto constructs deployed politically as positioning mechanisms to rearticulate power. Because there is no metaphysical truth, or even an essentialized or metadiscursive one, any positionality, however artificial, can take on a sheen of an imaginary truth laden with symbolism when articulated within a social space where agency is exercised.

Maya Transformations and Mimicries in the Unfolding of a New Ethnic Subject

On 29 January 2002, various Maya organizations categorically rejected the Anti-Discrimination Law approved the day before by the Guatemalan Congress. They argued that, as it had finally been approved, this law was too general, referring to Mayas as if they were simply one among many groups on the Guatemalan social landscape. "[This law] typified discrimination as something generic, an issue that could affect anybody in an abstract sense, denying the existence of our peoples; those are the reasons we feel frustrated," explained Rosalina Tuyuc, head of the Guatemalan Confederation of Widows (CONAVIGUA), a Maya organization made up of thousands of women who lost their husbands during the civil war that ravaged the country during the 1980s.[21] In 1997, when she was in Congress, Tuyuc had been one of the three original promoters of this law, together with Manuela Alvarado and Marina Otzoy. Other Maya organizations complained that members of Congress did not consult with them or even consider their opinion, let alone incorporate their recommendations, according to Marta López, head of MOLOJ (the Political Association of Maya Women). "It [Congress] considers discrimination as a problem, not as a crime, added Francisco Calí, president of CITI (the International Indian Treaties Council). "It should be categorical that racism is a crime."[22]

Mayas have chosen ethnic affirmation because they lack political power within the traditional spaces in which they have lived. They recognize a plurality of cultural practices, strategies, and even political goals within the pan-Maya movement. Indeed, Mayas recognize four groups among them that have been present within their ranks from the end of the 1990s, each exhibiting different tendencies: (1) those self-described as "cultural Mayas," whom their opponents have accused of fundamentalism or even anti-Ladino racism, represented primarily by Kaqchikel intellectuals; (2) "popular Mayas," organized in structures monopolized by the URNG; (3) Mayas operating within regional grassroots political groups, represented mainly by the mayor of Quetzaltenango and the 2003 presidential candidate, Rigoberto K'emé Chay, and his group, Xel-Huh, in alliance with other regional grassroots entities; and (4) the "military Mayas," located on the right of the political spectrum and linked to the power structure built by the army in the highlands and to "ex-PACs."[23] The latter group formed the base of support developed by *comisionados militares* (army representatives within the community) during the war, of which PACs were the mainstay. The first three groups were coordinated informally, and not without contradictions, within the Consejo de Organizaciones Mayas de Guatemala (COMG, Council of Maya Organizations of Guatemala) to negotiate accords that represented pan-Maya interests.[24] This body, however, was not strictly organic, nor did it necessarily guarantee agreement among the various groups. Basic conflicts existed between cultural Mayas and popular Mayas given that the latter often prioritized the interests of the URNG party over ethnic interests. As a result, cultural Mayas frequently made tactical alliances with regional grassroots political groups to oppose popular Mayas. Nevertheless, in the COMG an attempt was made to negotiate among those with divergent positions and to create cohesive agreements that benefited the Maya people as a whole. Military Mayas constituted the backbone of General Ríos Montt's support. Still, contradictions surfaced. In the early part of 2003, their demands eluded his grasp and that of the Portillo administration (Portillo represented Ríos Montt's Guatemalan Republican Front Party; his presidency ended in January 2004).

During the period leading to the peace process in 1996, various institutions were created both inside and outside governmental structures that facilitated Maya agency. A Secretariat for the Maya Woman was created as a government position and occupied for the first time by a Christian Democrat Maya leader, Gloria Tujab, in 1986. In 1993 Alfredo Tay was appointed minister of education, the country's first Maya cabinet member.

From a grassroots perspective, the Maya movement also created its own organizations, as well as cultural reappropriations. Mayas began to study and bring back to the community the hieroglyphic writing of their ancestors as an expression of Maya revitalization. While the American Anthropological Association conference was being held in Chicago in 1990, some scholars, led by Jak'alteko Víctor Montejo, performed a religious ritual at the Newberry Library in Chicago, where the original manuscript of the *Popol Vuh* is housed, to "bring it back" to its original community (they did take a photocopy of the original with them).[25] Maya clothing also became a source of critical creativity and a means for mobilizing widows and Maya women in general around the problematic of their identity, transforming their dress into an issue of "being."[26] Finally, some Maya public intellectuals appeared on the scene for the first time, from academically trained intellectuals such as Demetrio Cojtí Cuxil to diplomatic figures such as Otilia

Lux de Cotí to "organic" intellectuals in the Gramscian sense, such as Rigoberta Menchú and Catalina Tuyuc. They all began community-building from their respective positions, with Cojtí Cuxil providing the blueprint for the politics of Maya rights. In 1990 Cotjtí Cuxil published clear territorial, political, and jurisdictional demands that articulated territorial rights for the Maya nation, including the following: control and use of natural resources, political autonomy, Maya representation in Congress, Maya participation in public planning, the appointment of public functionaries based on ethnicity, the preeminence of international law, a politics of bilingualism, the codification and implementation of Maya law, the reorientation of the cultural policies of the Guatemalan state, the abolition of military solutions to social and ethnic conflicts, and a reduction of the discrepancy in material development between the nations. Some of these items were incorporated into the peace agreement, albeit under different terms.

After Rigoberta Menchú won the Nobel Peace Prize in 1992, tilting the balance of power in the country, she pushed for and endorsed the United Nations proclamation of the Decade of Indigenous Peoples in 1994 and advocated congressional approval of the International Labor Organization's Convention 169 on indigenous rights. Menchú first created the Vicente Menchú Foundation in Mexico in 1993, then dissolved it to re-create it as the Rigoberta Menchú Tum Foundation in Guatemala in 1995. One of the first efforts of the foundation, in 1996, was to mobilize Mayas to vote. This was part of the process of local empowerment, allowing Mayas to gradually gain control of their own town halls. Indeed, the Xel-Huh coalition won the mayoral election in Quetzaltenango, helping Rigoberto K'emé Chay to become the first Maya mayor in Guatemala's second-largest city. K'emé Chay was the first Maya presidential candidate ever in the 2003 elections.

As a document of the Hemisphere Initiatives states, the Maya movement emerged as the one distinctive, rising social movement during the peace accords:

> Maya organizations in the ASC [Assembly of Civil Society] fought vigorously for the Accord on Indigenous Rights and Identity (AIDPI), and grew in strength and stature during the negotiations. Forming COPMAGUA, the largest umbrella group of Maya organizations, was considered a crucial step for Maya unity. The peace accords recognized COPMAGUA as an official counterpart

of the government in peace implementation. These developments made many feel that the time of the Maya had finally arrived.[27]

The peace accords of 1996 established bilingual education for the entire Maya population. However, problems emerged almost immediately and have continued. By 2006, the commissions created by AIDPI under the banner of the peace agreements were officially discharged, having achieved during their tenure only minor accomplishments that seldom translated into law. Alfonso Portillo (2001–4), elected in 2000, opted for a policy of greater visibility but less substance. He named Maya K'iché leader Otilia Lux de Cotí as minister of culture. On her own, she named Maya novelist Gaspar Pedro González as literature director of the ministry, with the objective of pushing bilingual editions. Portillo also named the well-known Maya K'iché intellectual Demetrio Cojtí as vice minister for education. Cojtí, in turn, ensured that the AIDPI Commission on Education Reform retained its seat on the National Consultative Commission on Education, turning its members into his advisors and allies. Cojtí used this support and his own position to quietly push for bilingual education while keeping himself clearly out of the spotlight. By the end of Portillo's term in January 2004, Maya educators were in charge of managing all bilingual education programs in the Ministry, despite the fact that both economical and political support were lacking. Cojtí, however, had also run into problems. Non-Maya teachers and their union opposed bilingual education because they regarded it as a threat to their status and hierarchy, and they claimed that the meager budget of the Ministry of Education had prioritized it. As a result, a two-month-long strike paralyzed public schools throughout the country during January and February 2003.

In ways similar to the quiet path pursued by Cojtí, other institutions have made significant gains for the Maya in the past few years. Since 2001 Maya organizations have seemed to be absent from the national scene. In part this is because international funding has dried up. But it is in part an element of a new strategy to quietly achieve concrete steps to further their goals, although this has created a certain sense of frustration among activists because there appear to be only partial, localized gains. These can be important, however. For example, the Land Commission successfully established the Fondo de Tierras, or Land Fund, which provides credit for land purchases and technical assistance to landless peasants.

Needless to say, the foregoing hardly implies that there are no problems within these organizations. Machismo is still prevalent within Maya leadership, but it is masked with an added layer of secretiveness to avoid showing a bad face to the public. There are also interethnic conflicts, such as the one still extant between the K'ichés and the Kaqchikels, the largest groups within the Guatemalan Maya family, still acting out a rivalry that originated before the Spanish Conquest.

Other problems are more specific. For example, the following: The joint committees created by the peace accords, designed to forge policies that would transform the Ladino composition of the state, finished their work in 1998. This meant that it was time to shape the bilingual education program, one of several key strategic instruments aimed at changing the nature of the nation. According to the peace accords, the implementation of this initiative was to be carried out by a commission composed equally of Mayas and Ladinos. The government, however, proposed only two Maya members out of a total of eighteen. The government's rationale was the classic argument that there were not enough Maya cadres qualified to participate in such a high-level commission. By making this decision, however, the government not only nullified the principle of ethnic political representation but also refused to admit its responsibility for not producing more Maya professionals. After a great deal of negotiating, supporters of Maya inclusion managed to enlarge the commission to a total of twenty-two members, of whom seven were Mayas.[28] This was the commission charged with the creation of the first bilingual education program in the entire history of Guatemala. The commission in question was operative until 2006, then dissolved by the Berger government.

There were also, at times, byzantine issues such as the debate between a linguistic group called Oxlajuuj Keej Maya 'Ajtz'iib', which operated autonomously within the Centro de Investigaciones Regionales Mesoamericanas (Mesoamerican Center for Regional Investigations), and the Academia Maya de la Lengua (Maya Language Academy). The former claimed that K'iché has a double vowel, while the academy insisted that this was not the case. The academy attempted to impose its view based on the fact that it was legally recognized by the current constitution as the national body dealing with Maya languages. The result of this singular dispute was that for a long time no texts in K'iché were published at the institutional level, publicly or privately, at a time when they were more important than ever for training cadres and broadening civil and political rights.

The problems Maya organizations have to shoulder are numerous. Here is another concrete example: According to Menchú, her foundation has had to take charge of groups of former combatants, or members of the Comunidades Populares en Resistencia (Popular Communities in Resistance), a support group for the former guerrillas, who from either ethical or moral compunction refused to surrender to United Nations organizations. Although they have renounced the use of arms, individuals belonging to these groups wandered unarmed all over the Guatemalan territory for about three years after the signing of the 1996 peace accords. "Just yesterday," said Menchú in August 1998 (personal communication), "we held a meeting because there are now 185 *compañeros* who have sought us out."

Political hope for Mayas resides not in placing candidates for national elections (although Rigoberto K'emé Chay did run for president in 2003), but rather in increasing the local power of civic committees and in the Mayas' ability to win grassroots support at the town level. On this score, there are more Maya mayors now than ever. Both the Menchú Foundation and "cultural Mayas" have been working closely with them. "Not all of them have an ethnic consciousness, and not all are honest," Menchú stated, "but it is politically important that they get elected."

If we understand the modern state as a bureaucratic mechanism of control backed by force, it becomes clear that current internationalization processes have to a large extent surpassed the Guatemalan state. Should Mayas one day come to wield executive or legislative power within the nation, they would control the state—or, rather, part of it. But this would not make the country a "Maya nation" in which Mayas would be able to "throw the Ladinos to the sea," the grotesque fear of diehard defenders of Ladinismo. No matter which group exercises political power at the national level, globalizing issues would weaken their effective control over "deterritorialized" factors such as the economy or communications, now beyond government control. This would "normalize" a Maya-run government.

Problems and More Problems

The elements put forth in the previous sections might be seen as merely a discussion of local cultures. What we are dealing with here, however, is the elusive relation between specific cultures and globalizing tendencies. If for Europe the publishing sector is the basis for cultural politics and for the United States the entertainment industry plays an analogous role, it may be said that the various expressions of ethnic cultures constitute this basis in a large part of what used to be called the "third world."[29] The painful consequences of the contradictions that arise within global cultures implicate very specific, concrete events and lives, such as those of Ovidio Paz Bal, Juan León, and Ricardo Sulugui Juracán, mentioned at the beginning of this chapter. We could include plenty more anecdotes of this kind, but I will limit myself to two. On 5 June 2002, Irma Alicia Velásquez Nimatuj, who had just returned with a Ph.D. in anthropology from the University of Texas at Austin, was not allowed to enter the Tarro Dorado restaurant because she was wearing Maya clothes. She is presently suing the restaurant. In January 2004, the Miguel Angel Asturias Literary Prize, Guatemala's most important, was awarded for the first time ever to a Maya writer, poet Humberto Ak'abal. He rejected it, citing a long list of racist acts and abuses that would have made him feel treasonous to his people had he accepted this "Ladino" award. Thus, from within this transformative subalternity arises a consistent discourse that is effectively constructing new relations of power/ knowledge within a decentered intercultural festival of globality. These expressions generate not homogenizing tendencies, but rather heterogeneous disjunctions, Lyotardian *différends*.

The real problem is not whether the present Maya leaders are capable of articulating concrete or coherent positions within this constant flux of the global and the local. It is rather that, because the discourses they do articulate and that circulate by means of global communications skip that hegemonic, Ladino national space that they are addressing, they seldom reach the interlocutors with whom they want to dialogue. Whereas these enunciations contribute to the founding of new truths on a broader scale, they are not heard within the existing networks monopolized inside Guatemala by Ladinos. This brings about the paradox that, although Mayas' discourses do contribute to the shaping of deterritorialized truths, they remain excluded from national communication and education systems. This is why the Ladino sector can qualify those discourses as "imported ideas." They reach Ladino networks from abroad, often through the writings in English of American scholars, even when they were originally enunciated inside the Guatemalan national space by Maya voices. Maya cadres transmitted that knowledge to American scholars who then published it as a product of their academic research. However, an idea acquires a ring of truth only when adopted as a discourse of power within globalizing networks of communication and circulation of meaning. We know that it is not enough to speak the truth. One must be "within the truth"—the dominant one—discursively speaking. Apart from Menchú, no Maya leader has managed to take this final step in the globalized world. Menchú herself has done so only partially inside the national space, and only after winning the Nobel Peace Prize.

These Maya leaders, representatives of a certain fluctuating marginality within the larger global marginality that encompasses the whole of Guatemala, articulate worthwhile discursive positions. The problem is not the Mayas' skill in articulating meaningful discourses; it is rather that hegemonic Ladinos do not take them seriously because they deconstruct the Ladino project of rearticulating their postwar subjectivity as a triumph of the Americanizing Western neoliberal model, not as the recognition of a peripheral interculturality "of color." Horrified at the prospect of seeing themselves placed within such confines, many Ladinos refuse to hear any Maya discourse, regardless of its merits.

To arrive at some sort of workable, egalitarian society, or even one with a minimum of justice, asymmetrical power relations must be broken down. This can be done only by supporting the subaltern subject.[30] For the first time, thanks to the circulation of discourses through various communication and technological networks, one can actually see Maya and Ladino cultural differences colliding and coexisting, like tectonic plates in the interior of this debilitated state named Guatemala. This plurality, rather than diminishing, continues to intensify in the twenty-first century even though the armed conflict that seemingly represented its highest level of tension officially ended in 1996. What has disappeared is a foundational discourse that could justify the existence of a Guatemalan state with a subaltern Maya population. Thus the war comes to an end. But, at the symbolic level, ethnic differences are more polarized than ever. The representation of both groups in the mass media reflects the generally perceived differences in their particular identities, which are reinterpreted once more as they fuse with other globalizing tendencies.[31]

Conclusions

In his book *Globalización cultural y posmodernidad,* Brünner refers to the culture of globalization as a reorganization in time and space. As distance and time are compressed, global cultures have a nearly immediate local impact, thus shattering, among other things, many of those differences that vertically inflected center or periphery relations during the modern age. In this new "architecture of networks" (134), in this new nonlinear concept of temporality, the Maya ethnic problem previously located exclusively in a local space, marginalized from all modern truth, acquires a semblance of contemporaneity in the ensemble of interdependent links developed in those deterritorialized spaces we could label "postnational cultures," after García Canclini. It is in this context that, in another recent text, Mabel Moraña speaks of the globalization of indigenous issues as well.[32]

   With these developments, the traditional representational scheme of things—with its characteristically modern slant—comes tumbling down. Here I am referring to the erroneous assumption that it is possible to have cultural models that hypothetically can be implemented solely within the United States but have no validity in alterity, in other spaces with allegedly different characteristics. In fact, just as there is now a hybrid, or heterogeneous, cultural identity on a global scale, there is also a hybridization of knowledge at the postnational (or deterritorialized) level, flowing in multiple directions in such a fashion that local knowledges (Maya knowledge, in this particular case) become part of the global, and the theoretical or political discursivity that operates within globality is likewise appropriated by local forces—by means of the Internet, among other mechanisms of the digital age used by Mayas in their various organizations. For example, I was present in Madrid at the inaugural event constituting the "Friendship Generation" of Saharaoui poets and writers on 9 July 2005. They mentioned that they had formulated many of their own positions and identitary issues as subaltern subjects of both Spain and Morocco by following the Maya struggle both on the Internet and through the analyses relayed to them by a professor of the Autonomous University of Madrid who had done fieldwork in Guatemala.

   Is it possible in this context to criticize contemporary Maya intellectuals for having recourse to theories allegedly formulated for different national spaces in the process of subversively mimicking the academic discourse of the center to transgress ideologies that consolidate racist domination? Is it justified in the name of an imagined "national purity" to prolong the subordination or oppression of Mayas until the day they can produce an absolutely original and thoroughly national cultural theory? Certainly such an attitude has no sound basis in a world ruled by the immediacy that is constantly modifying all power/knowledge relations. Globalization has in fact transformed, when it has not actually erased, center-periphery relations, despite the setbacks generated by 9/11, 3/11, and 7/7,[33] as well as the perception that formerly "peripheral" cultures had of themselves. Now, instead, these groups appropriate those mechanisms that allow them to subvert the notion of a cultural center or periphery.

The debate on this issue is far from over. The intention of this chapter has been to outline a few of the conundrums emerging within it, with the intention of avoiding unidirectional binarisms in so-called center-periphery relations. Otherwise we would be guilty of fetishizing and essentializing subaltern cultures. Whether we like it or not, things as allegedly local as the K'iché-Kaqchikel conflict, the narrow-mindedness of certain strains of Ladino thought in Guatemala, and the perils confronted by Maya lawyers receiving death threats on the outskirts of Sololá are presently being discussed, debated, and often even resolved in the global arena.

9

Central American–Americans? Latino and Latin American Subjectivities

When I was in Los Angeles in September of 1992 for the International Congress of the Latin American Studies Association (LASA), a group of Mayas invited me to the Feria de San Miguel. A *feria*, as everyone of Latin American origin knows, is the annual celebration (like a country fair) in honor of the patron saint that names a given town, and it has become traditional in Latin America, as well as in Spain, to commemorate it with three days of festivities. In the Guatemalan case, these include amusement games, a procession of the saint through the streets of the town, Maya games such as *palo volador* (flying pole), and street dancing by the various *cofradías*, or religious groups responsible for the saint's upkeep. These groups reenact traditional dances such as *moros y cristianos* (Christians and Moors), *el baile de la conquista* (the Dance of the Conquest), and *el baile del venado* (the Deer Dance). The dances and games generally take place in the town's main square, which is elaborately decorated and crowded with food and drink stands. The Feria de San Miguel, celebrated according to the Catholic calendar on 29 September, honors the patron saint of San Miguel Ixtatán, a town populated by K'anjobal Mayas in the western corner of Guatemala, in the department (province) of Huehuetenango, in the middle of the Cuchumatán Mountains.

So what were we doing celebrating the Feria de San Miguel at the LASA conference? The answer might or might not be obvious, but on that particular date I myself became fully aware of it for the first time: Los Angeles is the second-largest city of Guatemala and the second-largest Maya city, to which the K'anjobal Maya fled to escape the massacres in their country of origin. Today there are more K'anjobal Mayas in the United States than in Huehuetenango, so the Feria de San Miguel, their major yearly festivity, has also been displaced to California.

The *feria* itself was held in a huge gymnasium in southeast Los Angeles. Once inside, however, the illusion was complete: except for the obvious fact that there was a roof over our heads, we felt as if we were in the town square of San Miguel Ixtatán. The Mayas had reconstructed the four sides of the "square" out of cardboard, and they performed the dances and music in the middle, just as if they were in their native town. The food and drink tables were a little to the side of the square, where the side streets would have been located in the original town. Ninety percent of the celebrants were Maya. Scattered among the crowd were one or two African-Americans and a few Anglos, most of whom obviously had married Mayas and were now part of the family. The only giveaways that we were in Los Angeles, other than the roof, were the punk haircuts of the Maya teenagers and the PA announcements in Spanish, K'anjobal, and English. After we had downed a couple of *cuxas* (the local brew of the Guatemalan highlands), the illusion seemed like the real thing, complete with the crisp air of the Cuchumatanes—until, that is, the time came to walk back to the "rancho," when we suddenly realized that someone would have to drive us back to our hotel in their *troca*.

This anecdote is my way of introducing the focus of this chapter: the invisibility of Central American culture, itself complex and contradictory, as we saw in the previous chapter, to the great majority of U.S. citizens despite its overwhelming presence in the United States. I will also point out those linguistic slippages that denote a lost, a past, identity and point out the difficulties involved in articulating the terms of that culture in a new, postnational space, difficulties that inevitably generate identitary conflicts that facilitate the aforementioned invisibility.

The high numbers of Central Americans in the United States are an inevitable result of the wars fought in the 1980s, when about three to four million people fled from the nightmare of violence and massacres to the apparent safety of the United States. Despite this presence, however, they have been nearly invisible within the imaginary confines of what constitutes the multicultural landscape of the United States. When Latinos are mentioned in this country, most average Californians still think primarily of Chicanos, and people in other regions might think of Caribbean-Americans.[1] Unless their presence is felt in our own particular neighborhoods, we seldom link the word *Latino* with that singular and contradictory trope, "Central American–Americans," an anadiplosis that sounds more like a redundancy, a radically disfigured projection of what "Latin Americanness" is assumed to be. It is useful, however, to underline the fact that it is an identity that is not one, for it cannot be designated univocally as "Latino" or "Latin American," but is outside those signifiers from the very start. For members of this group, life is not just "on the hyphen," as Gustavo Pérez Firmat put it, but it is also on the murky margins, and life not even on the margins of the Anglo, North American, or South American center: it is life on the margins of those marginal hyphenated others (Cuban-Americans, Mexican-Americans). A Latino identity is often constructed through the abjection and erasure of the Central American–American. Members of this group are doubly marginalized and thereby invisibilized, to coin a neologism. For this population, already large and multiplying at a faster pace than most other so-called minorities within the United States, their invisible status, their nonrecognition, generates a sense of nonbelonging, of nonbeing, a cruel invisibility that was first imposed on them in their countries of origin and has carried over to these latitudes. Whether we like it or not, the categories "Latin American" or "Latino" and "Central American" or "Central American–American" are not similarly constructed as intelligible identities.

The lack of an identity politics for Central American–Americans is a fact, an artifact still lingering as one of the unresolved residues of the cold war. This is true even within the academy. My own experiences with Spanish departments at most U.S. universities have made it painfully evident that when they speak of "Latin American literature" they really mean Mexican and Southern Cone literature, with García Márquez and Vargas Llosa thrown in as garnish. Oppression works as a mechanism of regulation as well as by closing off the possibility of articulating a given identity. Being a "Central Americanist" is synonymous with being a nonentity in traditional departments, indeed in most departments, despite a growing number of Central American students eager to learn about the literary history of their native cultures. Even in my professional life I have often heard, "Yes, your work is wonderful, but there's really no market for Central America." A well-known "progressive" professor from the Southern Cone once even asked informally, "Is there really a Central American literature?" My task is therefore to call these gestures into question. After all, a denial of Central American literature questions identification of place of origin as a narrative practice, one in which the identity principle is emblematic of the very difficulties of storytelling itself. It is this condescending attitude that keeps Central American literature invisible, like its subjects, so that students are embarrassed to manifest an interest in it for fear of derisive laughter from their faculty and rejection slips from major university presses. And yet, despite this discouragement, graduate students continue to write about the gripping issues, and the confusing melancholia, of being of Central American origin, of trying to come to terms with their identitary issues.

The exclusion of Central America is not just a problem in "mainstream" or canonical studies of Latin American literatures; it is even the norm in studies of "marginal" literatures. Let me give you an example. In the late 1990s I was asked to give a talk at Harvard for a course on Latino cultures. The professor of the course told me that the text was titled *The Latino/a Condition: A Critical Reader,* and she invited me to suggest a reading for the students prior to my lecture. When leafing through the text, I discovered that it dealt with all possible variations of subjectivity, gender, and sexuality for a Mexican-American or Caribbean-American population, but Central American–Americans were significantly absent. I would once again be forced to construct an identity out of a void, to scribble notes about my culture on the margins of marginal texts. Bearers of improper origins, we insidiously want to speak about a region that is outside the purview of the present regime of power in Spanish academia.

Why is there such resistance to Central American, and Central American–American, culture? Part of the answer still lies in the aforementioned cold war politics of the 1980s. Some Central American refugees, notably those who fled from the Sandinista government, were welcomed with open arms into the United States, settling primarily in the greater Miami area and openly coexisting with anti-Castro Cubans. These "freedom fighters" had no problem becoming U.S. citizens, in contrast to the refugees from right-wing governments who crossed the border to "El Norte" without official consent and were viewed suspiciously by the Reagan administration and left to languish for years, under threat of deportation, in the Kafkaesque confines of the immigration system.

Politics is not the whole story, however. Race is also a factor. A large percentage of Guatemalan refugees are of indigenous descent, or are at least mixed-race Ladinos. These are the types of populations that were suppressed or eliminated through genocidal policies in many other Latin American countries and were killed or placed on reservations in the United States. "Indians" have traditionally been invisibilized in the Americas. They are the visible signs of a non-Western origin, of nonwhite roots, a phantasm many Latin Americans themselves dread and run away from in their effort to become "white," Western, and easily integrated into U.S. society.

This does not fully explain, however, why many Latin Americanists also keep Central America at the bottom of the academic pecking order. Some of them, of course—those who were not exiled from their homelands for political reasons, but simply took advantage of fellowships to study in the Unites States—do not share the experience of oppression and exile with Central Americans. After all, most of those intellectuals who did leave their countries for political reasons recognize and value the culture of Central American exiles. But what of the majority of Latin Americanists who ignore the center? Rey Chow has discerned a neo-Orientalist anxiety in the anthropological desire to retrieve and preserve the pure, authentic native.[2] Might we argue that some Latin Americans or Latinos in the United States have an analogous desire to retrieve and preserve a pure, authentic Latin American or essentialized Latino subject, an imaginary construct made in their own idealized images and one in which Central Americans never fit?

There is another important question that must be asked: Why do Central Americans seem to consent to their own disappearance in these latitudes? Before they fled their homes, before their villages were razed by vindictive local armies, Central American subjects were already invisible in the eyes of their own Western-looking elites, simply because they were, for the most part, peasants, indigenous peoples, or women. In the eyes of authoritarian dictatorships, they did not count as subjects, and certainly not as citizens. They were likened more to beasts of burden. Even if this is less true for Salvadorans, more vocal and assertive in their demands and confident enough to have rioted in the Adams-Morgan neighborhood of Washington, D.C., it is certainly true of Mayas and other indigenous peoples from the isthmus. They do not come from a tradition in which standing out or affirming one's individuality yields any dividends; on the contrary, like many academics, they take literally the saying that the person who moves will not come out in the picture. Collectively they have assumed their invisibilization, their nonbeing, since the Spanish Conquest, and quietly, very quietly, often seek to gain minor advances while making as few waves as possible. For many of them, this has become a survival tool.

Thus the basic irony is that we now have in the United States a Central American population that is largely disconnected emotionally from the source of its own identity and whose forced exile is built on anguish. It is a population traumatized by war, with families torn apart by the physical disappearances of their loved ones through violent, arbitrary acts of wanton bestiality, whose hideous deaths were often accompanied by torture and a visible display of their mutilated bodies along highways or in town squares. For this population, victims of forceful displacement for the most part, exile carries a potential for salvation in their new homeland. However, the trauma of the crossing has compounded the trauma of war. Given the imprint of oppression and discrimination, this population has developed an instinct to preserve itself by pretending to be what it is not. Its singularity is linked to the evil of the genocide in the land of origin, yet this group does not build on its victimization to create an identity in this country or to obtain any recognition or privileges. Rather, the suffering is an oppressive burden from which it desires to distance itself, a mourning that it would prefer to bring to a closure but cannot because it symbolizes virtually the only roots left. The community often seeks to transcend this horror of a mutilated past by pretending the horror never happened, pretending that the group is another people, seeing its suffering as a source of shame. Therefore, its fractured identity dissolves into nothingness, and Central American–Americans end up living not only between borders, but also between identities. Often in denial of their own being, in the cultural context of the United States, the experience of the polysemic words *exile, border,* and *diaspora* ring very different bells for them than they do for those who are part of a more individualized migration coming from different social strata or else from other latitudes.

As a result, their experience in this country has been primarily one of disenfranchisement. Their nonidentity negates the possibility of an identity politics and, as a result, the possibility of justice. Their diasporic presence is affirmed through a loosely built network of cultural codes, such as the *feria* outlined at the beginning of this chapter or the *sociedades culturales* (cultural associations) created in Chicago, Providence, and Washington, D.C., a clear symptom of their yearning for an "imagined community" that can potentially be "pan-Maya" or "pan–Central American," to name just two possibilities, as they melancholically express their "pervasive disavowal" of loss by becoming the Central Americans they never were, to paraphrase

Wendy Ann Lee's analysis of Asian-Americans.[3] Neither of these concepts existed back in the homeland, but they are gradually being built here from scraps and fragments of culture perceived as being from "down there," which, in Lee's sense once more, presuppose the historical foreclosure of the possibility of a relation, as well as an enfranchisement through the mailing of economic aid to families back home, to Central America, and an ethnic or racial foreclosure of the possibility of a relationship with the United States.

Descriptions such as this one risk homogenizing what is, in reality, a very heterogeneous community, a phenomenon indicated in the first chapter of this section. We must remember that the cultural displacement and identity politics that characterize Central Americans not only contrast with those of other Latino groups within the United States, but also differ greatly among themselves. After all, Salvadorans, often entrepreneurial and talkative, are at the opposite end of the spectrum from quiet, taciturn Guatemalans. Maya Guatemalans behave radically differently than do Ladino Guatemalans. Hondurans or Nicaraguans are another story altogether, somewhere between the personality extremes of Guatemalans and Salvadorans.

Yet even these assertions beget a whole new series of contradictions. The moment when we talk of Central American–Americans, general presuppositions immediately pop up that merit being thrown up in the air. Who exactly is included in the all-embracing phrase "the Central American subject"? People from Belize? Panama? Costa Rica? Are Garífunas Central Americans? What about Caribbean peoples? And who decides, anyway?

Whatever our definition is, we need to think about categories such as "Central American" as multiple and discontinuous, not as categories with "ontological integrity." We can all be Central Americans only to the degree that we accept a history of identifications generated by the isthmus's own "grand narrative" of a mythical geopolitical unity that has existed in this region since the time of the ancient Mayas two thousand years ago. This would include, of course, Chiapas, Tabasco, and all of the Yucatan Peninsula, throwing into question Mexico's own "grand narrative" of origin in turn.[4] Indeed we can always activate any part of this history of identifications, and it can always be invoked in new contexts, such as the present-day diaspora and exile. Precisely because each part is only one of many conflicting histories, it cannot point back to an internally coherent and total history of a people or a region.

Nowadays we speak of being in the age of globalization.[5] The Central American problematic offers an interesting vantage point from which to view the shifts in the concept of "nation" associated with it, because Guatemala, El Salvador, and Nicaragua are truly being formed as nations only now, at a time when the "nation" is often considered less as a separate entity than as a member of or participant in larger, transnational constructs.[6]

Here we have to consider Arjun Appadurai's suggestion that, when confronting these sudden transformations of identity, there is a new role for the imagination than existed in the past, when identities seemed to be more fixed in time and place. "The imagination," he writes, "is now central to all forms of agency, is itself a social act, and is the key component of the new global order."[7] That is because all the parameters with which we used to define ourselves have quickly become obsolete. Following Appadurai's understanding of the world, we cannot but conclude that the "new global cultural economy, a complex, overlapping, disjunctive order . . . cannot any longer be understood in terms of existing center-periphery models" (32).

If, as has been suggested, globalization has largely dissolved cultures, and also processes of cultural reproduction, to such a degree that there is no longer any remnant of what Pierre Bourdieu termed *habitus*—that "structuring structure" at the intersection of agency and determination—this new factor presupposes that subjects now have more of a conscious choice in representing themselves by inventing or imagining their own particular identity. This particular representation is often not only hybrid or fragmented due to its multiple sources or components, but also spatially dislocated, lacking all certainty as to its "roots." More often than not, this imagined representation confuses oral mythology with factual history. Thus the desire to define the myriad ethnic communities becomes unbearable for those who traditionally exercised ethnic hegemony in a given space, such as Anglo-Saxons in the United States or Ladinos in Guatemala, while the emerging ethnic subjects struggle to define, imagine, or reinvent their ethnicity so as to reach a state of "belongingness" in a space where most ethnic groups are not of local origin. This is the case for Central Americans in California when confronted with Mejicanos and Mexican-Americans, African-Americans, Asian-Americans, and other groups that share their space, and often their own plight.[8]

Even back in their locus of origin, these communities did not identify themselves as a group. They were not Central Americans or even pan-Mayas;

they had their own internal divisions based on region, religion, traditions, ethnic subgroups, and so on. The very modern concept of identifying a community as a whole is imposed upon them all at once as they enter the globalized arena of their new territory, and along with it the difficulty of their being a particular subject to others and themselves. What are they? Guatemalan-Americans, Salvadoran-Americans, Nicaraguan-Americans, or simply Central American–Americans? It is not just a game of entangled signifiers; these utterances point to different strategic functions and can be generative of hierarchical configurations. After all, the tropes "Hispanic" and "Latino," conflictive themselves, are only umbrellas under which Mexican-Americans, Cuban-Americans, Puerto Rican–Americans, and Dominican-Americans seek refuge from the racist storm of white, Christian fundamentalism, but without losing their singular, self-defining traits.[9] Barely literate and not quite modern for concrete historic reasons, Central Americans in the United States are still trying to resolve the "uncertainty" of otherness and coming to terms with their own particular subjectivities.

Still, we were talking of Central American subjects who, for the most part, lacked any tradition of actual will to power as individual subjects, where agency has been a conflictive issue that wrenches apart its original meaning. Therefore, in this globalized arena of the United States they are often more lost than other subjects that have already been socialized not only in modern but also postmodern traits. They have not organized themselves around a name, around identity politics, and thus remain invisible in the fractured landscape of multiculturalism.

The problem with these vast numbers of subjects flowing in and out of their own countries of origin through Mexico and the United States, like a gigantic human current that circles back and forth like the Humboldt current or recurs cyclically like El Niño, is not only that very little has been done so far to explain their subjectivity within this country, but also that there is very little consciousness of their existence in their countries of origin, where, culturally oblivious to globalizing tendencies, the leaders are still attempting to form an elitist nationalist consciousness that, for the most part, excludes this population that flows invisibly across the border, in and out.

Economically, of course, this population is far from invisible. Central American countries know that their largest source of foreign exchange, other than the drug trade, is the money sent home by the millions of expatriates living in the United States. This explains the campaign supported by all the presidents of the isthmus to ask President Bill Clinton, when he visited the region, not to repatriate illegal aliens, but to allow them to remain in the United States so that their illegally earned dollars—without which, by the way, the California economy would collapse—could help the rebuilding effort after Hurricane Mitch. This is also why, on his first trip to Washington as president of his country in May 2004, the first thing Guatemala's President Oscar Berger requested from President George W. Bush was that Guatemalan "illegals" be allowed to remain in the United States.

If we accept postmodern precepts, we have to remap identities and reconfigure knowledge in a local-regional way with full understanding that the boundaries for redefining a concrete experience are inevitably limited, partial, fluid. Central American cultural producers failed to fully reimagine their own identity or subjectivity during the crisis years of civil wars. As the region itself moves away from that context and drifts toward a postwar globalization, it has an urgent need to reinvent itself. However, when looking carefully at its cultural production, we immediately see the impossibility of coming to terms with its symbolic production without first considering its unique specificity and singularity, different from the experience of the rest of Latin America.

Globalization implies primarily a new economic order that, prior to 9/11, "naturalized" the assumption that national barriers no longer existed. From a cultural viewpoint, an apparent contradiction results when economic trends toward globalization clash with centrifugal forces moving toward micropolitics and the reconstruction of local subjectivities in Central America.

The decline of state sovereignty per se might not be political news in the region, but culturally it is a new way to redefine identity. This contrasts with tendencies dating from the region's independence from Spain, in which cultural policies attempted to forge national or continental identities as "imagined communities" by homogenizing differences within territorial and symbolic spaces, even if citizens' loyalty to public authority might have been forever in question. This cosmopolitanism sought to subsume all nations into one higher unity, with the aspiration to Western modernity serving as the carrot driving the cultural enterprise.

We have to place issues of globalization and Central American nationalism in this context. One of the main things not to forget in the midst of this debate is that the Eurocentric nature of modernity implied that a significant amount of racism was still being exercised by otherwise right-thinking Latin Americans and Latin Americanists as late as the revolutionary projects of the 1960s, in which the illusion of universalist Eurocentric progressive models (i.e., socialism) impaired ethnic groups—Mayas, Afro-Caribbeans, and others—from deploying power in the sense of using their particular knowledge to frame their own issues. This was also true of women, gays, and other subjects.

After the fracture of those revolutionary ideals, globalization has attempted to link those many disparate voices within the notion of a fluctuating identity. When people are forced to recast the meaning of their own lives, the concept of identity is transformed. Reality is symbolically codified in a new way. A different world is created, one that enables individual subjects to integrate themselves in more adequate ways into their own imaginary horizons. Identity thus appears as a construct exposed to permanent adjustments.

A concrete example of this is visible in Guatemala. Mayas have emerged in recent years as groups recasting their own subjectivities, accepting their differences with Ladinos—who historically kept them at the margins of power—on equal terms. This reappropriation of marginal power that asserts complex intersecting "peripheries" as the actual substance of experience would appear to poise them in the direction of "a vestigial past" rather than that of globalized present concerns. After all, the process of ethnic subject constitution implies a reformulation of a mythical origin, an idealized past, and a symbolic attempt to nurture pre-Conquest values.

At the same time, Mayas themselves have moved, by virtue of concrete everyday needs, toward questions of subject formation that account for both the relationship between globalization and seemingly localized ethnic issues. High technology and new economic links to the "globalized" world resulting from the Guatemalan peace agreement have enabled them to reimagine their own peripheral position within a different framework. One example is this: The Pop Bank, the first Maya bank, created by the Cooperación para el Desarrollo Rural de Occidente in the early 1990s, is only a "virtual bank." It does not have a physical presence in Guatemala. However, it exists on Wall Street, managing Maya investments via computerized systems operated directly from Totonicapán.[10] In the words of Martín-Barbero, understanding this imaginary is a task of anthropological scope, for what is at stake is not only the displacement of capital and technological innovations, but also a deep-seated transformation of the culture of the majorities.[11]

The example indicates not an either/or binary opposition between a peripheral identity and a cosmopolitan globalized community, but rather new terms of cultural engagement whereby representations of difference between the global and the local must not be hastily read as fixed traits. This oppositional difference is a complex, ongoing negotiation, as critics such as Homi Bhabha have pointed out.[12]

In this context, let us turn to the alleged beginning of Central American culture, as described in the *Popol Vuh:*

> This is the beginning of the ancient word, here in this place called Quiché. Here we shall inscribe, we shall implant the Ancient Word, the potential and source for everything in the citadel of Quiché . . . in the nation of Quiché people. . . .
>
> There is the original book and ancient writing, but he who reads and ponders it hides his face. It takes a long account and performance to complete.[13]

As already stated in the last chapter of the first part of this book, the *Popol Vuh* is also the beginning of Guatemala's problematics of identity, of the never-ending redrawing of its own subjectivity. It is the beginning of all its textual references. It is the foundational base for its major writer, its only canonic writer, Miguel Angel Asturias, and it also gives texture to the better-known testimonial about Rigoberta Menchú's life. In Guatemala, everything begins with the *Popol Vuh*, everything begins in the *Popol Vuh*, nothing has escaped the *Popol Vuh*. The problem is that this text is not itself a beginning, the point of departure of an established teleology. The *Popol Vuh* is a simulacrum.[14] It refers to a previously existing text, allegedly original, that it is no longer possible to see or obtain—and that it may never have been possible to read. It is a specific strategy for responding to conquest and colonization. It is not really the affirmation of a foundational identity, but rather the fragmentation of one, an identity suspended in mid-air, between a past already lost and a present that has not been assimilated or understood, hardly visualized. Rolena Adorno reproduces Denis Tedlock's explanation according to which the sixteenth-century *Popol Vuh* was not a literal translation from pre-Columbian glyphs. On the contrary, it was an acting out, a representation of a text in corporal form:

> If the authors of the alphabetic Popol Vuh had transposed the ancient Popol Vuh directly, on a glyph-by-glyph basis, they might have produced a text that

would have made little sense to anyone but a fully trained diviner and per-former. What they did instead was to quote what a reader of the ancient book would say when he gave a "long performance," telling the full story that lay behind the charts, pictures, and plot outlines of the ancient book.[15]

Because of the particularities of this form of translation, it is assumed that the virtual readers of the text are a live audience rather than "readers" in the literal sense. They are even invited to drink a toast to the hero. It is therefore only textuality. This means a copy, a purported interpretation, fusing the borders between writing, graphics, ethnicity, and performance art, in which the cultural inheritance is posed by a reference to "first peo-ples" who were not themselves truly first peoples either, but Toltec invaders from the north with whom the local population eventually identified. This emphasis on a false, or failed, essentialized identification, a fetishization of an alien invader identified as "authentic," destabilizes all binary systems of meaning. It questions an alleged "truth" to which no one has access. It is simply an emblematic trace. It points to a problematic, a symptom, rather than to the actual beginning of the history of a nation. As we know, a text not only hides from all attempts at interpretation, but it also hides its own games and strategies. The impossibility of decoding it implies always the risk that the text will become lost in a vacuum, lost in space, without any-body noticing its absence or missing its presence. This last attitude has always been the dominant trait in Central American textuality.

What is more, the *Popol Vuh* is a hybrid text. Written in K'iché with a Latin alphabet, it is purportedly the memory of a hieroglyphic "text." However, its only known version is a manuscript by a Spanish priest, Father Francisco Ximénez, who claims to have copied it from the original shown him by the K'iché Elders of Santo Tomás Chuilá as a reward for his generosity toward them. However, the same elders then seem to have "disappeared" that par-ticular text, for it has never surfaced again anywhere. The Ximénez version, full of translation mistakes, dates from 1720, but claims that the original from which it was copied was a sixteenth-century manuscript. Because no one ever saw that version after Father Ximénez (if he ever did, and did not invent the entire story), we are forced to take his word that it ever existed.

The *Popol Vuh* is a pebble in the Guatemalan shoe. It makes it difficult to establish a clear point of departure for the country's national identity. It shakes all ontological value that the nation attempts to give to itself. It indicates, if anything, that this imagined community is rooted in the memory of an indigenous discourse that points simultaneously toward lost grandeur and ethnic contamination for all descendants of Spaniards, or else for those who desperately want to see themselves as such. It indicates that identity politics have always been out of kilter in both time and space, but it also insinuates that racism is still haunting the dreams of non-Maya "Ladinos" whose nightmare, to this day, is that the Mayas will someday come down from the mountains and cut off their heads. The *Popul Vuh* has thus become especially charged with an effective and affective power.[16]

Within this framework we can study all the texts produced in the region as ceaseless attempts to redefine the self, to retrace the notions of ethnicity present in those symbolic spaces in almost the same way as drawing a palimpsest, reinventing subjectivity according to new possibilities. These efforts also indicate identity displacements that have important consequences. They transform cultural differences into a relationship that is not only ethnic, but also ethical. Because of this, they will always corrode any attempt to achieve consensual representation. Every effort is condemned to fail to gain the endorsement of some of those opposing sectors within the nation that reimagine themselves differently in their very own textual practices.

Ethnicity creates a singular way of territorializing the region and makes its presence felt in all texts dealing with it. As stated in the last chapter of the first part of this book, we can see the trace of the "Mongolian stain" in novels such as Tatiana Lobo's *Assault on Paradise,* written in an alleged "white" country such as Costa Rica. It even appears in Sergio Ramírez's *Margarita está linda la mar* (translated as *Margarita, How Beautiful the Sea*). When we rethink Central American discursivity in this fashion, we can see how every social group reinvents itself deliriously in baroque manners that clearly map out a diverse ethnic presence, consciously or not.[17] These texts call attention to the ethnic tension within Central America between official knowledge, institutional knowledge, and subaltern representation.

These texts are good examples of how identities always search for a foundation, enacting a mythologized identification to enter history. These identitorial foundations then become travel baggage for immigrants, to be mined as needed for a reconformation of social intelligibility when they become deterritorialized subjects mailing monetary remittances back to their country of origin. In the case that concerns us in this chapter, Central American discursivity generates what Gareth Williams calls "the migratory lines of

flight that animate the new transnational El Salvador and its hitherto un-
mapped topographies."[18] The same would be true of Guatemala or Honduras. As it becomes deterritorialized, Central American discursivity, already
a very particular hybrid, acquires new symbolic mediations and experien-
tial flows as it becomes the anchor of a diasporic culture. It not only deconstructs all metropolitan languages that feed into it, cannibalizing them and
regurgitating them in carnivalized fashion, but it does the same to exoge-
nous, liminal hybrid discourses from the continent's own submetropolitan
peripheries, such as Mexico or Argentina. All of these discourses are mimed
(and mined) in fantastic or capricious ways and recomposed as deferred,
infallible referents whose awkward signs point in alternative directions to
those of their original, abject source. It suffices to name as an example the
rococo codes employed by the Mara Salvatrucha gang[19] in Los Angeles,
known only to its members. Traces of a national imagery are present, but
the latter is always displaced by the never-ending impossibility of achieving
a representation that ultimately works as a genuine corrective to previous
visions that happen to be equally partial and that only create the illusion of
a historical continuity. It is in this context that Williams problematizes postnational subaltern agency by decoding part narratives about members of
the Mara 18 gang[20] who visualize a defense of their Los Angeles neighborhood as a corollary (but not a historical continuity) of the FMLN (Farabundo Martí National Liberation Front) struggle of their parents.[21] This
leads him to embrace Bourdieu's notion of *habitus*. What interests me about
Williams's reflection are its discursive implications, of the "permanence in
change" of language, because of its identitorial implications.

These provisional notions might help to understand a few difficult elements in the shaping of defining identities both in the countries of origin
and in the expatriate setting. The difference between a Central American
being and other Latino identities should become clearer as its culture surfaces in this landscape, making it easier for people to notice how it differs
from essentialized, homogenized notions of what Latino cultural production has appeared to be.

Now that many Central Americans are no longer "down there," but "up
here," the spatial metaphor corrodes traditional relationships of power as
well. In the following chapter I deal further with how the newly arrived
have to cope not only with the trauma of dead relatives or razed villages
and the angst of being confused with Mexicans, which deprives them of

their particular identity, but also with the familiar trauma of all immigrant groups: learning a new language and a new culture, coping with separation from loved ones, and enduring the resentment of a hostile population, in this case including the Latino population. What interests me more in this chapter is simply pointing out the linguistic slippages that denote a past, often idealized, identity that articulates those fissures of continuity or discontinuity that Williams explores in the example given by Mirna Solórzano. These elements have implications for the reconfiguration of Latino identities in the United States.

After all, when a person identifies with someone else, he or she creates an internal corporeal image of that person or, more precisely, who he or she wants that person to be and then identifies with that internalized and idealized image. A person models an identity not on a concrete other, but on the image of his or her image, on what he or she wants the other to be rather than what the other really is. This is, nevertheless, a violent gesture that usurps an identity belonging to the other. This process can draw attention to the psychic devastation inflicted by systematically negative portrayals of Mexicans or Mexican-Americans by others who mimic them, who internalize these stereotypes as a result of the negative effects of their dissemination, yet perceive them without problematization or critical distance. For Central Americans, these stereotypes are instruments of survival. Nevertheless, the will to pass as Mexicans in the Angeleno landscape denotes instability, an unreliable exercise of agency, and a difficulty in valuing historical identitary continuities.

The way in which Central Americans were forced to parody ethnic stereotypes of Mexicans not only prevented their emergence and recognition, but served to undermine their identity, and contributed to the discrediting of Mexicans and Mexican-Americans as well. We must remember that these stereotypes are simplifications because they are forms of representation that deny the play of difference among all those involved. Stereotypes fix differences. As Homi Bhabha asserts, "The subjects of the discourse are constructed within an apparatus of power which *contains,* in both senses of the word, an 'other' knowledge—a knowledge that is arrested and fetishistic and circulates through colonial discourse as that limited form of otherness that I have called the stereotype."[22] These acts of mimicry often prevent migrant groups from deploying power and challenging authority in a unified fashion. Their behavior is more anarchic and contradictory, often fragmented and self-destructive when not simply senseless. More often than not, this behavior leads to conflict among ethnic groups, as witnessed especially by the struggle between Central Americans or Latinos and Korean-Americans during the Rodney King riots in Los Angeles. These events, along with the violent prominence of the Mara Salvatrucha and the Mara 18, confirm these words of Williams: "Along the intefaces of the postnational there can be no original nor origin of political identity and no common place for difference."[23]

To conclude, then, it is increasingly clear that if Central Americans are to operate as knowledgeable subjects within the United States, they must remap their subjectivities on both sides of the "Great Divide," that muddy suture named the Río Grande. It is certainly no easy thing to live on the rhetorical redundancy of a trope, "Central American–American," that, while repeating one of its terms (American-American), signifies something different from that term (Central American) and, while serving as a qualifier for a new type of American, divides instead of being a unifier. To deploy this identity, our steps have to teeter on the edge of the abyss. Still, being a Central American–American is not just a parody of nomenclature. It is also a transformative agency that invites rejoicing, because one's own sense of self is finally taking shape, reawakening a certain uncanny type of faith that can manifest itself only after survival on both sides of the Great Divide has been guaranteed. The eventuality of being actual citizens on both sides of that divide is no longer a chimera, but a true possibility, however difficult the path might be.

10

American Central Americans: Invisibility and Representation in the Latino United States

*T*he *Tattooed Soldier,* the first novel written in English by a Guatemalan-American author, Hector Tobar, begins with the eviction of the main character, Antonio Bernal, from his apartment in downtown Los Angeles.[1] A funny element is introduced: Antonio cannot understand his Korean landowner, because in this city both of them "could spend days and weeks speaking only his native tongue" (3).

Antonio, once a middle-class government worker in his native land, is now homeless in Los Angeles. Seven years before, he had escaped the death squad that came for him but instead killed his wife, Elena, and young son, a boy of two. His despair and shame at having fled continue to haunt him. In MacArthur Park, not far from Antonio's apartment, Guillermo Longoria is playing chess. Longoria was a member of the Jaguar Battalion of the Guatemalan army, and it was he who killed Antonio's wife and son in Guatemala. *The Tattooed Soldier* is the story of these two tormented, defeated men and the intersection of their lives in Los Angeles. By chance, Antonio sees Longoria in MacArthur Park one day, and, as Longoria lifts his arms to move a chess piece, Antonio sees his tattoo and recognizes him: "For several seconds, the man's bare arm was suspended above the table. . . . The arm was raised just long enough for Antonio to make out the tattoo of a yellow animal" (77). Later, in the middle section of the book, which recounts Elena's obsession with learning the Maya language, the image of the jaguar is recast as "Balam," the ancient Maya symbol of a warrior. Having seen Longoria once again in an environment in which their relations of power are more symmetrical, Antonio is electrified by the possibility of avenging his loved ones. This chance encounter provides a means for the story to unfold and takes us back to a lived past in Guatemala. As a result, the drama begun in their homeland will be played out in Los Angeles during the riots of 1992.

The tattoo that gives the book its title is a mark, a sign left on a body. It leaves the character marked for life, scarred for life. In fact, Longoria and Antonio are both marked, marked in particular as Guatemalans; that is, although both characters live in Los Angeles and they are represented as "Latinos" by a Latino writing in English, their life is "unpresentable" in this topographical site of migration. It has no meaning outside of Guatemala. Longoria now works for El Pulgarcito Express, a courier service that specializes in sending money and goods to Central America. Despite his seeming incorporation into mainstream U.S. society, however, his difference is manifested in his "angry eyes" (25). As the text reminds us, "this was his practiced soldier's gaze, his *cara de matón*. . . . Anyone in Central America recognized this look. . . . Dead dictators and demagogues lived on in these cold brown eyes" (25–26). Seeing Longoria's eyes, scar, and demeanor takes Antonio back to Guatemala, and this memory is literally embedded in the heart of the story, in the middle section, which explains the relationship between Antonio and Elena in their country of origin prior to her murder and his subsequent escape to Los Angeles. Once the novel returns to the Angeleno landscape in the third part, neither Antonio nor Longoria has dreams of reimagining himself, of constructing a new subjectivity. The uncanny situation they lived in their home country has shaped their attitudes forever.

If my interest in the previous chapter was to open up the terms of my discussion on Central American immigration and diaspora by pointing out the linguistic slippages that denote a past, often idealized, identity that articulates those fissures of identitary continuity or discontinuity, the purpose of this chapter is to explore this Central American "impropriety," this inability to properly represent a stereotypical immigrant narration. Here I want to examine the different baggage that Central Americans bring to the United States as immigrants to explain why they remain "invisible" to the great majority of U.S. citizens despite their overwhelming presence in the country, particularly since the wars fought in the 1980s, when three to four million Central Americans fled from the nightmare of violence.[2] In this last chapter I would therefore like to create a theoretical space for those dispersed faces of "otherness" that do not fit within the validated limits of either

Latin Americanidad or the recognized marginality of the United States.[3] I will do so by naming locations and relations selected from Central American intellectual and political history, as well as their representations in literature and film, in order to articulate the diasporic[4] consciousness of this new identity paradigm, "Central American–American," an awkward linguistic oddity already introduced in the previous chapter, in relation to other U.S. Latino groups.[5]

As I have stated, it was the civil wars of the 1980s that created the model described by Nora Hamilton and Norma Stoltz Chinchilla, in which Central Americans "differ from many other immigrant groups . . . in that they are neither strictly economic migrants nor accepted as refugees, but have the characteristics of both."[6] This population entered the country primarily through California and Texas, then fanned out throughout the vast North American territory. Thus, although the bulk of Central Americans still live mainly in California and Texas, with Los Angeles and Houston the dominant urban areas where they are clustered, significant pockets of Central Americans are present and visible in such diverse cities as Miami, Chicago, Washington, D.C., New York, Providence, and Boston. They are also present in rural areas of the United States such as Kansas, Iowa, Illinois, and Nebraska.

Despite its numerical presence, the Central American population remains nearly invisible within the imaginary confines of what constitutes the multicultural landscape of the United States. As a recent example, when I originally wrote this chapter, as a paper for a conference, it was amid great media excitement regarding the Oscar chances of the film *A Beautiful Mind*. Lost in the speculation over whether Australian actor Russell Crowe, who played mathematician John Nash, would win back-to-back Oscars and whether Nash was gay or anti-Semitic was the fact that Nash's wife happened to be a Central American woman, Alicia Lardé. In the film there is no mention of her Salvadoran origin and nationality, nor is she played by a Latina actress. However commanding Jennifer Connelly's acting might be, she is no Latina. When Nash met Alicia Lardé in the late 1950s, she was herself a student of physics at M.I.T., no mean accomplishment for a Central American woman in those days. Lardé is the niece of Salarrué, one of El Salvador's most distinguished writers of the twentieth century, who was married to Zelie Lardé.[7] The only other recent Central American–American "celebrity" I can think of is Rosa López. Followers of sensationalist journalism might remember that she was O. J. Simpson's maid, whose testimony was decisive in his being declared not guilty. She was a Salvadoran woman, too.[8]

"U.S. Latino" is a complex category whose specificity has come to refer to a variety of groups living in this country—Caribbean, even Mexican— but we seldom link the category with that singular and contradictory trope "Central American–Americans," a radically disfigured projection of what "Latin Americanness" has been assumed to be.[9] Here I am troping, of course, in a fashion analogous to Frances Aparicio and Susana Chávez-Silverman's usage of "tropicalization."[10] Unlike them, however, I do not believe that the latter, marked by its Caribbeanness, should be extended to embrace all of Latin America. There is too much risk of homogenizing and grouping what is a very heterogeneous array of cultural experiences and effects. The Guatemalan, Salvadoran, or even Central American experience as a whole is independent and irreducible to large unities that seek to discipline its singularity. In this context, this experience works more like Doris Sommer's "rhetoric of particularism."[11] Like Sommer, I would see the very term *Central American–American* as a dissonance that is, in reality, a "performative contradiction" that opens up the possibility for recognition of this as-yet-unnamed segment of the U.S. population.[12] Besides, the clumsiness of the sound itself, "Central American–American," underlines the fact that it is an identity that is not one, for it cannot be univocally designated either as "Latino" or as "Latin American," but is outside those two signifiers from the very start. It is more like "life off the hyphen," as Juan Flores proclaimed in a sense different from the original assertion by Gustavo Pérez Firmat.[13] Central American–Americans are off the hyphen not because they already inhabit a world that is a montage of cultures, with a hybridity so advanced that it has already conformed a new subjectivity, but rather because they are on the murky margins not of the Anglo, North American, or South American center, but on the margins of those hyphenated others (Cuban-Americans, Mexican-Americans). They are a population that has not yet earned the hyphen to mark its recognition, its level of assimilation and integration, within the multicultural landscape of the United States.

To make matters more complicated, we cannot even speak of "Central America" without running the risk of a greater homogenization of national identities than is the case in the region. Central American migration to the United States includes, after all, a heterogeneous array of social groups, among which we can name anti-Sandinista Nicaraguans, small groups of

Hondurans and Costa Ricans, and indigenous, Afro-Caribbean, and "Ladino" (mestizo) sectors from each of these nations. This does not take into account Belizeans and Panamanians, who have a greater degree of integration with African-American and Afro-Caribbean U.S. populations. We cannot but recognize, as a result, the unevenness of representation that is present in this very chapter. To create even the possibility of recognition, I play with the category "Central American," but I primarily emphasize the experience of Guatemalans and Salvadorans, who comprise the largest Central American groups in the United States.

The last step constitutes an inevitable danger, of course. If we are tempted at times to run the risk of reifying the Central American identity, it is because the Latino identity is often constructed in areas of the United States, such as Los Angeles, through the abjection and erasure of the Central American–American, in much the same way in which Gayatri Chakravorty Spivak points out that the Latin American identity was often constructed in regions of Latin America itself, such as the Southern Cone, through the abjection and erasure of the Central American, indigenous, or African subject "within the larger theater of the establishment of meritocratic individualism."[14] We might recall that when Spivak criticizes Fernández Retamar's substitution of Caliban for Rodó's model of Ariel as the emblematic Latin American, she reminds us that both of these binary opposites are cast in function of Europe. They exclude "the civilizations of the Maya, the Aztecs, the Incas, or the smaller nations of what is now called Latin America" (117). She reminds us of Gordon Brotherston's "effective foreclosure of the native Americas in the debate over the question of Latin American identity" (118), and she uses this argument to confront the "ethnocentric and reverse-ethnocentric benevolent double bind" (118) that effectively denies natives their own "worldling."[15] Is the marginalization of Central Americans somehow linked to our indigenous ancestry, which is as plain as the nose on my face and my skin color? Or are we marginalized because, as Spivak notes, hegemonic subaltern groups, however oxymoronic that phrase may sound, run the risk of effacing other groups in their own quest for power, reducing others to "inaccessible blankness" when they "claim to *be* Caliban" as a mechanism of legitimization?

Of course, when we speak of indigenous groups in the Central American context we run into another conundrum. In Guatemala alone there are twenty-two different Maya groups, and their rivalries can be fierce. El

Salvador has Lencas and Pipiles, who are Nahuatl speakers and, by extension, not descendants of the Mayas; thus, Maya history does not apply to
them. Nicaragua has Miskitos and Ramas, who are not Maya either. Costa
Rica had the Chiriquí, Chorotega, and Chibcha, who were culturally closer
to the Incas and related to the Rama of Nicaragua. Panama has the Kuna of
San Blas. Although Mayas are clearly the largest indigenous population in
Central America (close to six million at present), are the most powerful economically, have come the closest to asserting their own rights, and have even
been dreaming of their own nation-state in recent years, their experience
is not shared by other groups. Thus, when speaking of Central American
indigenous groups, we also run the risk of homogenizing their identity.
Given the actual conditions and numbers of Mayas both in Central America and in the United States, I will limit my analysis to them, but I am aware
of the irony inherent in that limitation.

There is another connection between these exclusionary processes of
identity formation—the Latino and Latin American connection. As in the
superstring theory of the universe, which sees all matter as generated by the
vibrations of microscopically tiny loops of energy, we can see that in representational issues the identitary factors of mobile, deterritorialized trans-
nationals in polyglot communities are, willingly or not, connected to the
territorializing forces of colonialism. I would like to suggest that the superstring that glues the smallest quarks to the most gargantuan supernovas in
this case would be the articulation of body or power relations by the colonizing gaze and discourse throughout the history of the region, including
those of the neocolonial forces at work today. The self-image imposed on
colonized peoples by their conquerors articulates a new sense of disciplinary order and generates a new iconography that is reenacted in deterritorialized, transnational spaces and is performed as a representation of an *axis
mundi* that blurs the boundaries between old and new homelands and creates patterns of continuity with colonial structures of power by perpetuating
certain cultural values imposed through conquest. However, this happens
through the deployment of a new rhetoric, one that generates new protocols of power that are, unfortunately, uncannily similar to the old ones.

In pre-Hispanic times, the Maya and Teotihuaca, Toltec, and Mexica
worlds played roles in Central America analogous to those of Greece and
Rome in the classical European world. For close to a thousand years,
whether the capital in the central valley of Mexico was Teotihuacan, Tula,

or Tenochtitlan and whether the leading Maya cities of the Central American isthmus—which extends from the isthmus of Tehuantepec, on what is now the border between the states of Oaxaca and Chiapas in Southern Mexico, to the gulf of Darién in the area where the Panama Canal is now situated—was Kaminal Juyú, Copán, Tikal, or K'umarcaaj, the cultures of both geographical sites complemented each other, not just through commercial exchange and economic interdependency, but also by creating a hybrid cultural matrix expressed in a metaphorical grid upon which culture was written.[16]

On this grid and as part of this matrix, Mayas and the peoples of the central valley of Mexico developed conceptions of the self and the other. Symbolically and metaphorically, both groups saw each other as complementary, with an identity based on their local ethnic group, lineage, and relationship to their gods. Both groups associated themselves symbolically with the warrior, which they represented emblematically in the duality of the sun and the moon. By choosing the symbols of day and night, which followed each other in the cosmos in a sequential pattern, they articulated a complementary identity between groups of both areas, the central valley of Mexico and the isthmus. One group was the sun, the other the moon. This duality was represented competitively in a ball game in which sun warriors and moon warriors competed against each other in a ritualized reenactment of the supernatural struggle between the gods of heaven and those of the underworld. The logic of this articulation is complex and could be the subject of a much longer piece.[17]

The Spanish Conquest, however, broke the complementary pattern in which both groups of people saw themselves. Instead it articulated a new logic of conquest and colonialism that changed the balance between them from a horizontal to a vertical axis. According to Max Harris, in the third decade of the sixteenth century, Catholic Europe was nervous, for the territory it controlled was being eroded by the emergence of Protestantism as well as by the advance of the armies of Süleyman the Magnificent.[18] As a result, some Spanish Catholics believed that the only hope for survival of Catholicism was its implantation in the New World. Thus, when Cortés arrived in 1523, he was accompanied by twelve Franciscan missionaries who were seen in the same light as the twelve apostles:

They believed themselves called to establish a pure church among the Indians that would, in turn, restore God's blessing to a Catholic Europe presided over by the Holy Roman Emperor and king of Spain, Charles V. The Franciscan order in Spain believed that the conquest and conversion of the New World presaged a resurgence of Spanish power and the imminent triumph of Catholicism in the Old World. Spain, it was thought, would sail the converted Indian armies of the New World across the Atlantic and into the Mediterranean to join forces with the Catholic armies of Charles V in a successful last crusade against the Muslims and Jews of the Old World.[19]

In this context, the first achievement of the Conquest was the "miracle" on the hill of Tepeyac north of Mexico City in December 1531, when the Virgin Mary allegedly appeared to an Indian convert named Juan Diego.

The fact that the Mexica kingdom was chosen as the site of the new Catholic kingdom with the apparition of an indigenous Virgin, and that Tlaxcaltec warriors were used by Pedro de Alvarado in his conquest of the northern part of the Central American isthmus, radically altered the relations of power that had predominated during the previous thousand years. For the first time, the complementary roles of the central valley and the isthmus were broken, and the power of the first, now renamed the Viceroyalty of New Spain, was imposed on the latter, now the Kingdom (and later the "Capitanía General") of Goathemala. The Spaniards' intervention thus changed forms of identity in the region and set in motion a new dynamic of power.

Richard Trexler had already pointed out, in *Sex and Conquest,* that Spaniards often feminized their enemies in warfare, and they often raped both the men and the women they conquered (60–81). Bizarre though it may appear, this gesture was supposed to show Europeans that the conquered peoples were less civilized than their conquerors. Sigal adds that "the Spaniards feminized their enemies in order to assert social distances between themselves and the Other."[20] Gendered notions of power existed in pre-Hispanic times as well, but defeated warriors were never raped, and they always had the choice of regaining their masculinity through human sacrifice. The latter celebration, macabre perhaps to Western eyes, was perceived by indigenous peoples as a symbol of rebirth that enabled a community to move on from one era to another. In this system of knowledge, human sacrifice was not just an exercise to placate angry gods, as it has been popularly depicted; rather, it was a marker of time in which the sacrifice was a creative act of self-empowerment that ensured survival and growth for the

community (47). Defeated warriors who had emblematically lost their manhood in battle could regain it and be held as heroes if they consented to the
ceremonial sacrifice. This exemplary process also helped to preserve the
balance between both regions of the Mesoamerican world. Consequently,
the ritualization of the Flower Wars ("Guerras Floridas") was staged to preserve Mesoamerican dualism, as was the ball game, with its ongoing struggle between sun warriors and moon warriors.

Nevertheless, once the military conquest by the Spaniards took place,
there was no further possibility of gender redemption. The masculinity of
the defeated Maya warriors could no longer be saved through the ritual of
human sacrifice. Many other elements of the Mayas' world also changed at
that moment, including the conflict between the concept of the warrior and
that of the sinner,[21] the participation of Tlaxcaltec warriors recruited by
Alvarado in the conquest of the Mayas, the name of the Mexica city, and the
designation of that city as the capital of the Viceroyalty of New Spain and
also as the location of the chapel of Guadalupe. Thus a new discipline of
both order and power was established in which the inhabitants of the isthmus were no longer equals of the Mexicas, but inferior and subservient to
the people of the viceroyalty. Defeated Maya warriors were feminized without the possibility of regaining their masculinity. They also came to be seen
as irretrievably feminized in the eyes of the original inhabitants of the central valley of Mexico.[22]

In other words, colonization changed the perception that the survivors
of the Mexica world, themselves subalternized by the Spaniards, had of the
people of the isthmus. Then they were seen as defiled and deflowered peoples, which justified their placement in a social strata below their own. In
this new order, as Garrett W. Cook says, Spain became the Tulan of post-
Conquest mythology, Santiago became the morning star, and Jesus became
the trickster whose pursuit by enemies established the world order.[23] One
of the direct consequences of this placement of indigenous peoples of the
isthmus at the bottom of the regional hierarchy was the racialized saying
by poor mestizo peasants still heard all over Guatemala to this day: "Mejor
pobre que indio" (Better to be poor than to be an Indian). This phenomenon is also the basis of David Theo Goldberg's argument that "race is integral to the emergence, development, and transformations . . . of the modern
nation-state."[24] According to Goldberg, racial definition of modern states
emerged conceptually from the debates between Sepúlveda and Las Casas

in the 1550s, in which the nature of "indianness" was to define the role the conquered population would play in the colonial model just emerging at that moment.

Of course a good part of the explanation for the pecking order that left Central Americans with such lowly status was that, in European terms, Mexico was wealthier than the isthmus. Although enormous deposits of silver were found in the Mexican Sierra Madre, no precious metals ever surfaced in Central America. As a result, during the colonial period the isthmus was subservient to the Viceroyalty of New Spain: the captain general of the Kingdom of Goathemala had to pledge loyalty to the viceroy of New Spain, the Goathemalan Inquisition was dependent on Mexico City's inquisitorial authorities because Goathemalan bishops were subordinate to the archbishop of New Spain, and all trade from the region to Spain had to stop first at Vera Cruz and receive a certificate from the viceroy before it could cross the Atlantic toward Cadiz.

When independence from Spain was declared in 1821, the Mexican armies of Vicente Filísola immediately invaded Central America and annexed it to Augustín de Iturbide's short-lived empire. Accordingly, when he fell from power, on 1 July 1823, Central America once again declared its independence, this time from Mexico. In the process, however, the provinces of Chiapas, Tabasco, and Campeche, Maya-inhabited areas that had been ascribed to the Kingdom of Goathemala during colonial times, were lost to the new Republic of Mexico. Two hundred years of tense cohabitation during the period of independence have made Central America a cultural province of Mexico where mariachis are for hire, crowds have idolized Cantinflas, and tacos dominate the gastronomic scene at the same time that paranoia about Mexico's political intentions has served to authorize and legitimize dubious political regimes in the region and parties have been organized whenever the Mexican national soccer team has lost a game during the soccer World Cup. This ambiguity appears in the film *El Norte.* When the character Enrique is working illegally in a Los Angeles restaurant, a Mexican-American denounces him to the Immigration and Naturalization Service (INS), but another Mexican illegal saves him from arrest.[25]

In my narrative I do not pretend to reduce to these few lines the complex historical events that conformed a singular colonial grid during a period of three centuries. I also do not mean to imply that the relationship between Mexicans and Guatemalans has become permanently tainted or that it represents an essentialized binary opposition.[26] In other words, I do not want to be either reductionist or coercive. Rather, I limit myself to signaling certain contradictory aspects of the relationship between Mexico and Central America, which I attribute to the conquest and colonization of the region. This "attitude of colonization" spells out the ambiguous perceptions that both populations have of each other. By "attitude" I mean a mode of relating to contemporary reality in a Foucauldian sense, denoting a way of feeling and thinking, a way of acting and behaving that marks a relation of belonging and presents itself as an ethos.[27] When it comes to rearticulating a symbolic identity in a deterritorialized context, I am more interested in showing how certain factors stratified the past into regimes of socialization and how, by generating supporting psychological values, they installed a normalizing discourse of power that generates reactive resistance in the realm of action.

When we examine the situation of Central American immigrants to the United States today, we have to keep these indicators in mind to understand their present-day behavior vis-à-vis the Mexican population cohabiting with them. This gesture, combined with the truism that most Central Americans entered the United States fleeing a war that the U.S. government supported, has given this population a triple taint: they have been perceived by Americans as both "illegal," and "communist" and by themselves as of less value than Mexicans.[28] This triple jeopardy has made them hide their own identity all the more, as we can hear plainly in this statement by Marlon Morales, a Salvadoran born in 1974 who migrated to the United States when he was a year old, published in Katherine Cowy Kim and Serrano Alfonso's *izote vos:*

In 1983, the few Salvadorans I knew went to Union Avenue, so at Norwood I thought everyone must have been Mexican. But maybe they were lying about it too.

On my first day in Mr. Bax's fourth grade class, a little boy named Alex asked me where I was from. . . .

"Mmmm," I started. "Mmmm," I continued looking him in the eyes. I was going to say Mexico. I'm supposed to say Mexico, add "but born here" and leave it at that. My mom said I'm supposed to say this all the time, even at Union Avenue Elementary School. Anything Salvadoran like *pupusas, pacaya, flor de izote* and Spanish was left at home, never in public. . . .

Always say you're Mexican
Always speak *inglish en la calle*
They'll leave you alone.[29]

The mixture of all these elements has intensified the burden familiar to all immigrant groups.[30]

The Central Americans fleeing to the United States had to cope not only with the trauma of dead relatives or razed villages, but also with the angst of having to pass as Mexicans. Being confused with Mexicans sometimes worked to the Central Americans' advantage, enabling them to camouflage themselves as a mechanism of survival. Although this was positive from the point of view of safety and refuge from the INS, it also forced them to adopt an identity that was not truly their own, an identity with which they were somewhat familiar but that they did not master, which did not allow them to act as casually as they could have if they were simply being themselves. Typical scenes of this problematic appear in the film *El Norte.* In one of them, Enrique and and his sister Rosa jump into the back of a truck stopped on the side of the road in Chiapas while the driver fixes a flat tire. When the truck driver discovers them, they claim to be "from Oaxaca." Unfortunately, Enrique and Rosa have no notion of geography. They point to the south, to Guatemala, when in fact Oaxaca is to the north. In a different scene, when they get caught at the border, they continually repeat the word *chingada,* a performance that seeks to gain them recognition as Mexican subjects. This makes it evident that "acting Mexican" is just another counterperformance for Central Americans in the United States that, contradictorily coherent, ultimately becomes only a parody of ethnic stereotypes.

After all, when a person identifies with someone else, he or she creates an internal image of that person or, more precisely, who they want that person to be, and he or she identifies with that internalized and idealized image. An identity is modeled not on concrete others, but on the image of the person's image, in this case the image of stereotyped Mexicans that popular culture has projected onto Central America. Consequently, in "acting Mexican" Central Americans articulate what they want that "other" to be rather than what Mexicans, themselves heterogeneous, really are. In fact, it can be argued that they are performing what the new colonial power thinks the Mexican other is because, as in the case of Spain and the Mexicas, the United States sees Mexicans as "preferred undesirables," this time for political rather than economic reasons. This process can draw attention to the psychic devastation inflicted by systematically negative portrayals of Mexicans or Mexican-Americans as others who resemble and mimic them and then internalize these stereotypes without problematization or critical distance.

The way in which Central Americans in the United States are forced to parody ethnic stereotypes of Mexicans in a sort of "performative transvestism" not only prevents their own emergence and recognition, but also undermines the identity of both the performer and the performed.[31] It is a reiteration of the normative. We must remember that this stereotype is a simplification because it is a form of representation that denies the play of difference between all those involved. Stereotypes fix differences. These embodiments not only prevent Central American migrants from working out a catharsis that enables them to relieve the trauma of war, but they are also a symbolic defilement of Central Americans' own subjectivity to the degree that, in being careful not to articulate any form of protest against racism, sexism, or any other oppressive practice, they prevent themselves from deploying power and from challenging authority.[32] More often than not, they only accentuate the conflict among ethnic groups and keep alternative imaginings from appearing on the Latino landscape.

This is why, when we turn to a Central American–American novel such as Mario Bencastro's *Odyssey to the North,* we read that the Salvadoran protagonist Calixto is "stunned, terrified, and livid, unable to say a word about the tragedy" (2) when he is asked about the death of his working companion, who fell when his rope broke while they were washing windows on the eighth floor of an Adams-Morgan building in Washington, D.C. The triple description connotes three different emotions that Calixto feels: shock at the death of his companion, fear of the police because he is illegal, but also anger, a by-product of war trauma that still haunts his relations with authority. He fears the police not only because "they would blame him for the death and he would end up in jail, if not deported for being undocumented" (2), like any other illegal immigrant to the United States, but also because he was unjustly persecuted in his homeland:

> When several men arrived at the family's room looking for Calixto, Lina, his
> wife, was at her friend Hortensia's apartment, at the other end of the building.
> A neighbor came running to tell them.

"They're looking for Don Calixto to arrest him!"

"Arrest him for what?" asked Lina, in startled disbelief.

"They say he's an enemy of the government!". . .

"They're looking for you!" she said, her cry muffled by distress and exhaustion. "Someone reported you as an enemy of the government!"

"It can't be! I'm not involved in politics, you know that!"

"You have to get out of here and hide, before they find you!"

"But it must be a mistake!" insisted Calixto. "Or someone's slandering me. One or the other."

"It doesn't matter; you've been reported!"

"Yes, but . . ."

He could not finish what he was going to say because the shout of "Calixto, someone's looking for you!" frightened him to the point of stealing his words.

"Go!" his wife begged him. (10, 11)

The third instance of Calixto's dilemma is summarized in the words "Yes, but . . . ." These words describe his position as a Central American, and it will inform the third emotion, which silences him.[33] The third emotion translates itself into a self-imposed impotence. The difficulty in explaining Calixto's persecution stands in the way of his responding without embarrassment to anyone who positions him, or anyone else like him, in a Central American identity. In a symbolic transposition, the impossibility of articulating an explanation for victimhood becomes as problematic for war's victims just as the acknowledgment of being rape victims was for Maya warriors in the sixteenth century. Both events—the present war trauma and the vestigial memory of rape—are clear indicators of why the "odyssey" of Central America's immigrants to "the North" is not the same as the conflicts that most immigrants face with the law, a factor recognized by another character in Bencastro's novel:

"Maybe he's from Central America," said a woman, clutching her purse to her chest. "A lot of them live in this neighborhood. . . . You know, they come here fleeing the wars in their countries." (3)

Central American immigrants faced elimination in their own countries for posing a threat to a certain kind of national identity in which they remained unrecognized. They were without a true identity, to the degree that they were always disenfranchised as national subjects. They neither functioned as an integral part of the community nor were they a true adversary standing outside of it. People who fled Central American countries, indigenous or not, stood in opposition to the oligarchic dream of self-realization. Peasants of all forms were the inverse of what the oligarchy stood for. Seen by the oligarchic gaze as formless, unaesthetic people who by definition could not constitute a subject, they came to represent the process of national destabilization itself. They were neither Western nor foreign to the land. They were silenced and invisible from their very conformation as an "improper" social group, an unnameable, undefined other that remains "unrepresentable" in the oligarchic vision of what the West is supposed to mean.[34] Thus they constitute a population that was never fully defined even at home, never "home" at home, with a tradition of its own (Mayas would be an exception to this, of course). Thus, as a traumatized population in the third of those negative emotions, they are not trying to reimagine themselves in the United States or to necessarily invent a utopian dream of greater political freedom or rising economic expectations, even though these two elements are also present in the community. Primarily, Central Americans in the United States are trying to come to terms with how the stabilizing structures of their own countries of origin tried to protect themselves by labeling them as an unpresentable and thus disposable population, an attitude expressed as a limit experience in the massacres and genocide of the 1980s. This is an "originary terror" in the sense of Lyotard. Its repercussions are felt in the present silence of Central American–Americans and in their tendency to mimic what they perceive as their privileged others: Mexican-Americans.[35]

In the film *The Silence of Neto* (1994), directed by Guatemalan Luis Argueta, a New York City resident, the reaction of the young child Neto to the double trauma of the bombing of Guatemala City in June 1954 and the fight between his favorite uncle Ernesto and his father is fear. When Neto asks Ernesto, "Couldn't you just keep quiet?"[36] the ever-observant Ernesto, a worldly, cosmopolitan figure who has traveled all over the world and returned from Morocco to live the overthrow of president Arbenz with his family and will die four months later, replies: "That would be easiest, wouldn't it, Neto? But no. If you have something to say, you must say it. How like your mother you are. You're quiet, just like her . . . just like this whole country. Neto, silence like this isn't good. It's ingrained in us from the time we're born. But it's up to us to tear it out from inside ourselves. Not until then will we be able to breathe."[37] That is why Josefina Gutierrez, living in the Pico-Union district of Los Angeles, says, "It was just easier to say I was Chicana."[38] Or why Josefina Martínez Pimentel, who came to this country legally and has a B.A. from UCLA and an M.A. from Berkeley, writes: "My identity isn't about asserting the difference between me and my *mexicana* sisters. . . . It isn't about asserting to someone in *MECHA* (Movimiento Estudiantil Chicano de Aztlán) that Aztlán doesn't include *salvadoreños*. . . . It's about the situations that make you stronger and test your ability to survive."[39] Still, Martínez Pimentel is silent about what the last phrase means. She is silent about the war experience that traumatized her and her family, although she recognizes that it is the formative element of her identity. Given the imprint of "originary terror," she and other members of this population preserve themselves by pretending to be what they are not. They do not build on their victimization to create an identity in this country or to obtain any recognition or privileges. In a convoluted psychic process, they are trying to transcend it while pretending at the same time that it never happened. Accordingly, Central American–Americans end up in denial of their own being. This nonidentity negates the possibility for an identity politics.[40]

It is when we trace the heritage of genocide and the patterns it engenders that we can undermine the self-certainty of an essentialized Latino representation in which subaltern discourse seems to merge into imperial discourse, becoming a reductionistic, coercive force in its practical implications. Of course we know about the complex specificities, the commonalities, issues, and existing tension, including racial tension, among Latinos themselves. Empirical data collected by Sara Mahler show these elements appearing among Salvadorans and other Latino communities on Long Island.[41] I agree with Agustín Laó-Montes when he claims that Latinization is first and foremost a power process of social differentiation and cultural production and that differences within Latino communities arise "as expressions of a desire for a definition of self and an affirmative search for collective memory and community."[42] By keeping the Central American–American at the center of inquiry, we generate a rupture of the Latino trope that allows a critique to take place, precisely to avoid an essentialization of the notion of "Latino." Cecilia Menjívar has worked along similar lines in her own research (see her *Fragmented Ties: Salvadoran Immigrant Networks in America*).

In *Ethics after Idealism* Rey Chow takes another look at the issue of cultural otherness that has been central to all of her work. She argues that, at a time when cultural identity has become imbricated with the way we read our many "others," what we must examine critically is no longer identity politics per se, but the idealism, especially in the sense of idealizing otherness, that lies at the heart of identity politics. Recognizing the need for a critique of idealism allows Chow to constitute a required set of ethics for the postcolonial, postmodern age. In particular, she uses "ethics" to designate the act of making decisions—in her context, decisions of reading—that might not immediately conform to prevalent social mores of idealizing our others, but that, in spite of this, enable such others to emerge in their full complexity.

We could place the Rigoberta Menchú controversy within the framework delineated by Chow. The controversy has at least created an opportunity to historicize and reconstruct the Central American experience of modernity. The view from the diaspora should now challenge the various expressions of Latino essentialism and open up intellectual spaces for the active contestation of meanings with political and cultural implications for all ethnic and national representations originating in Latin America that are now present in the United States.

In this framework, we also have to contextualize postcolonial or subaltern criticism as a site for the enactment of the anxiety and wish fulfillment of critics in coming to terms with their own cultural and professional identities. Indeed something along these lines was already expressed years ago by Gareth Williams during the debates pertaining to the Latin American *testimonio* as a genre. Chow's criticism as understood here represents a development in the field of Chinese studies that has come to theorize, in both content and form, a subaltern position as an alternative to the nation-centered theory of Chinese literature and culture. In an analogous fashion, the respective positions of Central Americans should address the complex issues of identity constructions under the rubric of "Latino diaspora." This task has become even more complex now that we must also pay particular attention to the ideological, military, and cultural discourse in the United States regarding immigrants following the events of 9/11. We should attempt to bring to light not only the emancipatory potential, but also the ironies of diasporic discourses, if we are to truly critique the complexity of postcolonial self-positioning both within and against the dominant cultures.

Rey Chow stakes her ground "neither in the Chinese nor the Western but rather on a dialectic on which 'Chinese' and 'Western' is played."[43] Like her, I cannot assign Central America an "absolute difference" from either Mexico or from the West, but I would like to make an analogous move by describing my own position as neither Central American nor Mexican nor U.S.-based, but rather as grounded in the dialectic in which all three are played to the detriment of the Central American subject. In this respect, it seems to me that what is different about the Mexican-American and the Central American–American is their diasporic consciousness. Thus, this is the complex area that we will have to problematize in order to understand the particularities of the Central American–American in the United States.

To return to the detail with which I began this chapter, the soldier's tattoo is ultimately the imprint of "originary terror." It is the mark of the historical weight that anchors Central Americans in the representational ambivalence of nonidentity. In Latino cultural politics this tattoo serves as a reminder not only of the difficulty of healing in diasporic displacements but also of the fact that the notion of a homogeneous identity politics is only an ongoing fantasy.

Conclusion:
Forever Modern, Forever Marginal

I n an article published in 2004 in the *Radical History Review,* Néstor
García Canclini tells us about the difficulties of knowing what to do
about Latin America's past and future. García Canclini talks of "the
disbelief about what happened and about what will come"—wondering
whether this means that present-day Latin American subjects can trust only
the denseness of the present moment, because there is no longer time for
memory or for utopian thinking—and he uses a key phrase, "the strange-
ness of lost time."[1] This condition derives from the fact that a satisfactory
balance has not been struck between a past that we will not (or cannot) forget and a future of apocalyptic prophecies. This imbalance evokes both denial
and rejection among many contemporary artists and writers, a pessimism
echoed by today's young people. Central Americans are doubly caught in
this conundrum. The region of their birth is haunted not only by an inability to come to terms with the end of the nineteenth-century dream of a
reunified, stronger Central America (the present-day Central American par-
liament notwithstanding), but also by the rekindling of the region's worst
nightmares in televised images of the current Iraqi experience: military occupation, torture, dissolution of a national culture, fear. The sense of relief
generated by the signing of peace treaties has faded. So have the utopian
illusions of a functional nation, one that truly benefits its people. Indeed, if
many individuals of the generation that militated in various revolutionary
organizations in the late 1970s lived their militancy more like a carnival, it
was not only because they were young or naive but because the utopian
dream of a revolution was to generate, ultimately, not a socialized economy

but rather a state that would expand its people's possibilities for happiness and build a decent society. As Spain's President José Luis Rodríguez Zapatero stated when arguing in favor of gay marriage, "A decent society is one that does not humiliate its members."[2] For five hundred years, Central Americans had lived humiliated and yearned for an end to their humiliations. They almost touched that possibility in the 1980s, but now it seems to have faded like a chimera, a mirage. Nowadays people are caught between the unsatisfactory memories of a traumatic past of civil war and the apocalyptic possibility of a virtual dissolution of their respective nation-states, presently run less by truly representative governments or even the traditionally corrupt politicians than by gangs of thugs operating outside of traditional channels of power. These gangs are newly ingrained institutions such as the Mara Salvatrucha (a transnational gang originally formed in Los Angeles by Salvadoran immigrants), which operates in the cultural corridor extending south to north from Panama to California, with a true globalizing vision that has made it as emblematic of a regional power as TACA Airlines.[3] Former army officers also form part of the extrainstitutional nongovernmental power structure. Though they are no longer in direct control of political power, they are still very much in control of the nation's economy, often through their participation in and fomentation of illegal operations such as smuggling or the drug trade. Globalized corporations exploiting neoliberal hegemonization in the region also have a strong influence on the governments and economies of Central America, as the case of Wal-Mart in Honduras demonstrates. In 2004 the *Los Angeles Times* ran a series of articles on this subject, demonstrating how a single corporation was able to set workers' compensation for the nation at a very low level. When workers pressed for higher wages and benefits, Wal-Mart simply pulled out of Honduras, leaving the nation's economy in ruins. New immigrants to California from Central America, then, are fleeing different forms of oppression and mistreatment than did the previous generation, and their identities should be recognized in light of these differences.

The tension, haunting, and disillusionment are clear in the negative reaction in Central America and among Central Americans to three memoirs regarding the Sandinista experience written by Gioconda Belli, Ernesto Cardenal, and Sergio Ramírez.[4] Despite the fact that all three authors have broken away from the Sandinista Front (they define themselves as members of a renovated Sandinista movement), we can easily verify that not enough thoughtful or self-reflexive criticism appears in any of their memoirs about their past militant experiences or about the need to evaluate the failure of their revolutionary movement, the only one to actually reach power in the region. Rather, the remembered histories they elaborate are more senti-mental and nostalgic evocations of a lost youth and of lost power than they are historically significant reflections on the guerrilla period of 1960–90, about what went right, what went wrong, and what a renovated movement ought to do in the future.[5]

These issues and hauntings are not insignificant. Much of what I have done in my life, for example, was done not out of rational choice, but out of an instinctive sense of ethics. My decisions have shaped my life, scarred me emotionally, and created an archive of convictions and ethical presupposi-tions that I cannot discard when I sit down to elaborate a cultural critique such as this book. For me, cultural critiques are not just intellectual exercises or means to improve professional standing or economic gain. They are ways of justifying my own existence in the eyes of my compatriots by contribut-ing, from within that narrow space that is my domain—fiction writing and cultural critique—whatever knowledge I possibly can that might, now or in the future, improve the quality of their collective lives, in direct or indirect ways, consciously or not, through my own agency or not. My theorizations about culture are, in short, an extension of my political beliefs, which have always been articulated in the interest of improving Central American peo-ples' lives, even if only by making their plight visible to the outside world.

It was in this context that I participated with Jeremy Adelman, Albert Fishlow, and Charles R. Hale, in a debate about Latin America and global-ization published in *LASA Forum* in 1998[6] and later represented by Alberto Moreiras, in *The Exhaustion of Difference,* as emblematic of the exhaustion of "epistemological models bequeathed by modernity at the very moment in which modernity becomes a thing of the past" (76). Moreiras quotes me at length as arguing that subaltern responses to globalization (articulated in his book as "popular," a term that is correct in Spanish but a misnomer in English, where *popular* is understood more as fashionable than as antihege-monic) "are the signs of the deployment of a new hybrid community that indeed might signify the death of modern nationhood but also the hopeful redefinition of a new spatialization/displacement of disenfranchised minor-ities,"[7] where at least the illusion, if not the actual reality, of creatively con-figuring what we could call "new strategies of resistance" was possible.

Although the debate in question was allegedly about Latin America and globalization, my response was located within my unique Central American ethos and perspective. I specifically had in mind concrete events and actions enacted by Guatemalan Mayas during 1995–98 that, as I have outlined in the last part of this book, framed the December 1996 peace accord. Moreiras did not assert that I was wrong. But after claiming that the discourse of all four scholars participating in this debate—whose positions, he says, "are the parameters of Latin Americanist mainstream reflection" (17)—consisted of no more than informed opinions, and that because of this all four failed to "reset the terms that are critically needed for a stronger reading of the situations that prompt their exchange" (78), he goes on to conclude that our response was insufficient: "An epochal change in people's lives cannot be adequately understood through minor adjustments in long-established forms of Latin Americanist representation" (78).

In 1998, marginalized as I was from "mainstream" debates about *testimonio* and analogous issues, I felt that I was far from being an exponent of Latin Americanist mainstream reflection. Indeed, because I was a Central Americanist originating from within Central America itself, it seems almost absurd that I was considered in that light. I owed the brief appearance quoted by Moreiras to a bulletin conceived as a vehicle for conveying news about the Latin American Studies Association (LASA) to its members, with a small space reserved for informing them, in a proactive way, about new developments and problematics in the fields comprised by LASA. My invitation to participate was due to my professional relationship with LASA's then-president, Susan Eckstein. The accidental friendship between the two of us allowed me to slip past what we could abstractedly imagine were the guardians of Latin Americanist mainstream reflection, with the caveat that the latter, if they ever existed, would always have been U.S. scholars writing primarily in English, working in more or less conventional areas of the social sciences, preferably progressive liberals who could fit in any given Democratic administration in Washington, D.C., with expertise in a large South American country. None of those traits described me, not to speak of even more heterodox ones that would have disqualified me even more as a guardian of the established order, such as my being primarily a novelist, placing myself critically somewhere on the periphery of the subaltern studies group without truly belonging to it or ever having been asked to join, working primarily out of a "second-tier" university (San Francisco State at the time), and not being invited to participate in any of the cutting-edge anthologies framing Latin American cultural studies in the 1990s. I was a Ladino who defended Mayas and thereby incurred the wrath of fellow Ladino writers and scholars, a former sympathizer with guerrilla warfare who by then felt a greater affinity for the goals and strategies of the gay and lesbian movement without being gay. In sum, I embodied too many contradictions, too many marginal locations, to be acceptable as an icon of orthodoxy. Finally, I was proud of grasping not the "big picture" about Latin Americanism in the United States, but rather the "little picture" that many orthodox colleagues had missed. I was more a specific intellectual than a crusader for a universal representation of Latin America.[8] In short, Moreiras failed to take into account my subjectivity, my ethos, the source of my singular affections.

Moreiras argued that the four scholars in question, myself included, were simply being reactive to "what was happening" and that we responded with "minor adjustments" to epochal changes. It had never occurred to me that scholars did anything other than react to what was happening. In modernity, determining what had to be done (to paraphrase the famous Leninist phrase) was the role of avant-garde political parties or revolutionary organizations that tried to force the hand of history, creating the subjective conditions for radical change. In postmodernity, this role has corresponded to new political actors (ecologists, indigenous peoples, gays and lesbians, etc.) engaged in micropolitics and intellectuals who, not belonging to disadvantaged or subaltern groups, no longer speak for them, instead usurping their representation, but have facilitated their ability to speak for themselves, while representing no one. In neither case did scholars *anticipate* "what was happening" (although poets and visionaries might have done so). Scholars have opened up new parameters of knowledge by researching the activities of those individuals or groups responsible for generating changes, by examining critically, yet a posteriori, the full implications of their actions in daily life, in which intellectual analysis has been closely bound to a specific problematic. As Poster has claimed, there is no place of privilege where knowledge can act as a will coming from the outside to fabricate new social conditions.[9] Academics expose patterns they detect only after they have appeared in a given collectivity as symptoms of that given group's agency, and they can do so only from within the boundaries of their given institutions. Afterward all they can do is to negotiate differences with the specific disciplines to which respective scholars belong.[10] Whenever political actors who also happened to be intellectuals (Mariátegui, Guevara, Dalton, Ramírez, Payeras) have justified articulating radical social transformations or proclamations, they have done so while embodying dual identities. Yet they have spoken only as political actors, never simply because they were intellectuals or scholars (and these totalizing statements can be equally problematized from my perspective). Despite my past sympathy for revolutionary change in Central America, even in the early 1980s, before developing a critique of guerrilla activities, I would never have claimed that my scholarly work anticipated or precipitated radical social change, and I would have looked askance at anybody who did. As for the "minor adjustments," they might seem such when viewed from a macro perspective (even though some of the tendencies I pointed out at the time as emerging in Guatemala have since had a major impact on the politics and economics of Ecuador and Bolivia, just as they were already present in Chiapas when the debate in question was published), but they are anything but minor when viewed from an indigenous perspective or from any specific, localized, limited circumstances. If there was no general truth and no general politics, all I could do was speak from my singular experience, imbued with my identity and affections, characterized by my personal relation to my chosen or visualized audience, fully accepting my burden as a Central American who wanted his word taken seriously. I was not an impersonal, distant, or bureaucratized representative of the Latin Americanist establishment, but a participant, bearing witness to a specific situation, albeit in academic jargon, but without any pretension of a transcendental presence. What Moreiras failed to ask in his robust allegory was this: Under what conditions, given the epochal change, would it be fair to ask scholars to anticipate what was actually happening socially and politically and risk offering major, totalizing solutions? One cannot avoid the concrete problems of Latin Americanists simply by negating them, and one cannot criticize them from within a universalizing position without first problematizing the locus where the speakers position themselves. Subjectivity, identity, and location all matter.

By definition, intellectual inquiry has always been a dynamic process, privileging the study and the relative uniqueness associated with singular places. It has often been region- and place-specific, and it has usually allowed a deep place-anchored analysis while being at the same time relational, that is, examining connections between different places, dissimilar phenomena, and so on. Nowadays, globalization has created an intensification and a series of overlaps that call into question the nature of fields of knowledge. This has encouraged a rapid breakdown of distinct and stable areas, but it has not radically transformed the originary, detail-oriented nature of scholarship.

I have engaged with Moreiras's statements here not to polemicize in a narrow sense or to write back to the academic center from my own peripheral placement to make a statement of some kind. Rather, I have done it to underline the differences in our tasks and, by so doing, to concretize the premises of this very book. I do not claim to state universal truths or to reset the theoretical framework for an epochal change. I limit myself to uttering informed opinions, from the singular perspective of that unique and uncanny minuscule place in the world named Central America, about what has happened there. I do so because, paraphrasing Cioran, he who wishes to be more than he is will never be but what he is. Central America is the demon that inhabits me, possesses me. All of my writing, whether fictional or critical, can name only it.

Ultimately, this book is my attempt to reconfigure knowledge, thought, and critical subjectivities as a way to rethink the political impact of the present on the reimagined intellectual, on the academic subject, and on public spaces within our current circumstance of globalization from the particular perspective of an array of Central American voices, including my own. The debate that has been initiated here, far from being concluded, allows us to speak of the memory and trauma of the past decades as a way of explaining our present diasporic reality. It is a continuous process of attempting to create dialogues about the crisis that afflicts us in our present moment and displacements. The result does not offer easy, narrow, rigid, or essential answers. It offers, rather, a dialogic space in which to experiment with new points of view about our present situation, viewpoints that at the same time generate new questions concerning the postnational, postliberal, post-9/11, 3/11, and 7/7[11] problematics. This discussion may allow us to confirm our diagnoses of previously detected issues, but it might also lead to small, discontinuous steps in our search for viable solutions.

The approach of this book is evidence that, whether in the study of literature or of culture, the intellectual impact of a localized production cannot be reduced to a single, generalizing story that encompasses an entire continent. There are complex contemporary factors that affect the lives of books such as those produced by Central Americans. As a result, it should be impossible to argue for a characteristic temper to Latin American life as a whole, and hence a characteristic, normatizing reading and interpretation of its works. Central American culture evidences diversity within Latin America. In fact, it evidences diversity within Central America itself. Therefore, it is impossible to speak of unity when addressing the intellectual and social life of the period covered in this book. This book also highlights the importance of everyday practices in understanding textual interpretation. It is proof that we should not approach literary and cultural criticism centered on towering "great writers" or on facile notions of literary quality.

Through these inconclusive conclusions I seek to bring this book to a close while admitting that, despite the generic inability for subaltern voices to reach the rarefied air of U.S. academic circles, ordinary Central American citizens continue—through various cultural means that include what I label a "space of *afectividad* (sensitivity or affection)"—to sustain a "politics of difference" in a world where the new order of globalization threatens to further homogenize diversity in the name of economic progress, security, and stability. I believe it is this *afectividad* that will allow Central Americans to contest the global processes that threaten to obscure them and construct a positive space in which to rework their singular identities.

Notes

Introduction

1. The actual translation of *patria* to English is "fatherland." This implies a masculine-gendered notion, whereas *patria* implies a feminine one. *La patria* is a notion that has ideologically conceived of Spain as the "mother country" and the Hispanic American nations (those whose residents speak Spanish, as opposed to any other language), like all former colonies of Spain, as her "children." Therefore, I will keep the term *motherland* here, as opposed to the more correct reference in English, *fatherland.*

2. The guerrilla period extended from 1959, the year Castro first came to power in Cuba, to 1990, the year in which the Sandinistas were defeated electorally and the Soviet Union came to an end. Some scholars place its beginnings in Central America on 13 November 1960, the date of an attempted coup d'état that first launched guerrillas in the country, and its end in the signing of the Guatemalan peace treaty on 28 December 1996.

3. Highbrow literature would be what we know as the accepted canon of Latin American novels, poetry, essays, and theatrical production, codified in the 1960s by professors such as Enrique Anderson Imbert and Emir Ramírez Monegal, at Harvard and Yale, respectively.

4. Gayatri Chakravorty Spivak has called for a radical renovation of comparative literature and states, regarding cultural studies: "Can the 'native informant' ever become the subject of a 'cultural study' that does not resemble metropolitan-based work? If one asks this question, one sees that the destabilization offered by a merely metropolitan Cultural Studies must exclude much for its own convenience, for the cultural claims of the metropolitan migrant." See *Death of a Discipline,* 10.

5. Spivak, *Death of a Discipline,* 16.

6. I use *cosmopolitan centers* with hesitation. I prefer not to use *center* by itself because of the risk of repeating the center-periphery binary opposition with all it

entails. Nevertheless, I acknowledge that *cosmopolitan center* raises difficult conceptual issues as well. Its unspecified indeterminacy can be erratic, or simply reduced
by others to the old center-periphery binary. Nevertheless, I coincide with Walter
Mignolo's stance on cosmopolitanism. I see it within the scope of the modern or
colonial world, where cosmopolitan centers act as the constitutive side of marginality. For Mignolo's reference, see "The Many Faces of Cosmo-polis."

7. Spivak, *Death of a Discipline*, 19.

8. Ibid., 23.

9. Florencia Mallon argues that the word *interdisciplinary* has been badly mis-
understood. What most academics do in our time is transdisciplinary work. The
latter implies working on the same subject, but from separate scholarly approaches
that never intersect. Mallon likes to illustrate this with the metaphor of a sandbox.
All children are playing in the sandbox, but all are playing separately, each with his
or her own toy. Truly interdisciplinary play would imply not only that all children
were in the sandbox, but that they were all playing together, sharing their toys. See
"Interdisciplinarity as Border Crossing."

10. Followers of cultural studies, especially those working in newly created programs such as women's studies, queer studies, and so on, might be surprised to
know that as late as 2005, most Spanish departments in the United States still
reacted negatively against cultural studies. They claimed that the theory of cultural
studies was a passing fad and ignored the theoretical body of work produced by it.

11. See Sommer, *Foundational Fictions*.

12. In Flores's next book he theorizes this concept regarding cultural remittances from the United States back to Puerto Rico.

13. It is odd to write this because, as a Central American subject, I cannot fully
place myself in the position of a U.S. subject even if I am writing in English, in the
United States, and for a primarily U.S. academic audience.

14. Spivak has mentioned this as a crucial element for Derrida and also for herself. The latest reference regarding this matter, which is worked into various texts,
appears on p. 30 of *Death of a Discipline*.

15. This term is used by Spivak.

16. Benítez Rojo, *The Repeating Island*, 1.

17. Schele and Freidel, *A Forest of Kings*, 38.

18. This might be an initial attempt to theorize Central America as a region,
something yet to be done despite the political rhetoric lasting nearly two centuries.
In reality, very few regional discourses have emerged from within Latin America
itself, as Arturo Escobar has pointed out (personal communication, 23 July 2005).
When identity has been problematized, it has usually been from a nationalist point
of view, as a result of a need to affirm a particular communal identity as the anchor
of an individual one. Good intentions notwithstanding, Central American writers,
thinkers, and intellectuals seldom occupy themselves with anything other than
national issues. Could it be that regionalism is perceived only from outside of the
area itself? Could regionalism be, as George Yúdice wonders, a construction that

responds more to the parameters of disciplines and institutions located in the United States, from which they are generated? Who constructs regional discourses? These are issues that remain to be explored. Indeed, when reading my first step toward defining Central America as a region, Yúdice pointed out that my own Central America is a markedly Guatemalan one, with notes on El Salvador, Nicaragua, or Costa Rica added to my construction. Honduras, Panama, and Belize are basically absent, except for their territorial contiguity. Besides, to include the latter two countries also complicates what a singular Central America might be (personal communication, 26 July 2005).

19. Culler, *Literary Theory*, 284.

20. See Nussbaum, *Upheavals of Thought*. Here Nussbaum elaborates many of the notions I myself had begun to employ rather haphazardly when speaking of an *espacio afectivo* (affective space) in my LASA 2003 presentations.

21. As stated in the introduction, I only fleetingly embrace the concept of diaspora because of the problematics of its use in a Central American migratory context, given both the conflict of naming a categorical point of origin for the diasporic process (1980? Central Americans had been migrating before that date; significant communities have appeared in California since the 1930s) and the difficulty of defining a "diasporic people," given the heterogeneity of Central American social groups within each country, not to speak of the variety of countries involved here.

1. Revolutionary Endgame

1. See Robinson, *Transnational Conflicts*. Robinson argues that Central America is positioned as a site of a transnational process and that the rapid transition to globalization generated the political crises of the 1980s.

2. Traditionally, the "guerrilla period" in Central America is dated from the insurrection of young nationalist officers in Guatemala on 13 November 1960—which was conducive to the formation of the first guerrilla group in the region and to an epochal experience of conversion to guerrilla activity in general that disdained peaceful or electoral solutions to political polarization—to February 1990, when the electoral defeat of the Sandinistas precipitated peace agreements in both El Salvador and Guatemala and peaceful democratic transitions in all countries of the region.

3. George Yúdice argues, nevertheless, that music is closing this gap. His own research in the region has emphasized musical production.

4. Reguillo, "Latin America," 36. This essay is part of a forum published by *Radical History Review* in spring of 2004 in a special issue titled *Our Americas: Political and Cultural Imaginings,* edited by Sandhya Shukla and Heidi Tinsman. I borrow the phrase "cultural imaginings" from them.

5. Honduran poet Galel Cárdenas argued in the Central American press in 2004 that a literary boom was taking place in the region. See "¿Un *boom* de la literatura centroamericana?" by Marta Sandoval.

6. Ramírez was a member of the "Group of Twelve," a group of prestigious

individuals leading a broad opposition to Somoza's dictatorship in the late 1970s. After the Sandinista victory in 1979, he became first a member of the governing Revolutionary Council, later vice president under President Daniel Ortega's two governments (1981–90).

7. In analogous fashion, a campaign was launched in the mid-1990s to promote Ernesto Cardenal's candidacy for the Nobel Prize for literature, centering it on his nonpolitical, neomystical book of poems *Canto cósmico (Cosmic Canticle)*, published in 1993 and translated into English that same year. Its publication was celebrated by authors as dissimilar as Allen Ginsberg, Robert Bly, and Harold Pinter.

8. All translations in this chapter are mine unless otherwise indicated.

9. "Ramírez Amaya Cazador de Gorilas," 3.

10. Rodríguez, *Transatlantic Topographies*, 129.

11. Adding to their frustration were the broken promises of international aid, only partially implemented at best despite the fact that those developing United Nations (U.N.)–sponsored peace processes stated the need to redynamize the region economically.

12. For more on this mural, see David Carey's article "Overcoming Geographic and Linguistic Barriers to Foment Cross-Cultural Learning: Maya History in a Southern Maine Classroom."

13. Rigoberta Menchú is recognized as a "founding mother" of the region's postwar period and has accepted a position as the "good will ambassador" of Guatemala's Berger government (2004–8). The controversy that surrounded her in the United States at the end of 1998 has barely had an impact in the region. See part II of this book for further clarification.

14. Carey, *Our Elders Teach Us*, 252.

15. The original edition was published by Seix Barral, the editorial house then publishing the Latin American boom writers. The fact that *Cenizas de Izalco* became the first Central American novel to be edited by the prestigious Barcelona house at the peak of its fame was not insignificant for the writers who attempted to emulate its trajectory.

16. I recognize here the audacity of listing Roque Dalton as a narrator instead of a poet. Regardless of the fact that in his lifetime he was better known as a poet, Dalton has left us three works of prose that merit his inclusion in the list of outstanding narrators from this period: *Miguel Mármol* (1973), *Historias prohibidas del Pulgarcito* (1979), and especially *Pobrecito poeta que era yo . . .* (1976). As Rafael Lara-Martínez points out, Dalton worked on the latter novel for over a decade, and a manuscript of it dating to 1964 has been found by family members. For more on this, see Lara-Martínez's "Roque romántico."

17. The first novel to come out after *Cenizas de Izalco* (1966) with an innovative structure and style was Alfonso Chase's *Los juegos furtivos* (The furtive games, 1968). *Cuerpos* (Bodies) dates from 1972. Lizandro Chávez Alfaro published *Trágame tierra* in Mexico in 1969. Among Carmen Naranjo's works of the 1960s we can include *Misa a oscuras* (1967) and *Memorias de un hombre palabra* (1968). *Responso por el*

niño Juan Manuel, published in 1971, is in fact a product of the previous decade as well. Her best work remains, nevertheless, *Diario de una multitud* (1974).

18. Dalton was a good friend of Julio Cortázar, as was Alegría. They were both familiar with the structure of Julio Cortázar's *Rayuela,* which was published in 1963 and translated as *Hopscotch* in 1966. However, they were equally familiar with the formal innovation in the Central American area introduced by Asturias, beginning with the publication of his *Hombres de maíz* (1949, *Men of Maize,* 1995) and continued by lesser-known figures who played with form, such as the Costa Rican Yolanda Oreamuno. Chase, who also began as a poet, was familiar with the French *nouveau roman* and developed his own narrative techniques from it.

19. Menén Desleal gained fame with his innovative play *Luz negra* (Black light, 1965). His most important works include *Una cuerda de nylon y oro* (A cord of nylon and gold, 1964), *Hacer el amor en el refugio atómico* (Making love in the atomic bomb shelter, 1974), and *Revolución en el país que edificó un castillo de hadas* (Revolution in the country that built a fairy castle, 1977).

20. In the wake of Arbenz's overthrow, social progress, especially land reform, was reversed, thousands of peasants were assassinated or imprisoned, and progressive sectors of the middle class were driven to exile, initiating a period of radical political confrontation that ultimately led to Guatemala's long civil war (1960–96). This chaos projected itself in the region. El Salvador had back-to-back coups in 1961, followed by a series of repressive military governments. Nicaragua experienced its first armed attempt to overthrow Somoza in 1959, and anti-American riots broke out in Panama in 1964, starting a long process to recuperate the canal.

21. As late as 1954, U.S. social scientists such as Richard N. Adams dominated the space of Central American social sciences. By the 1960s, individuals such as Humberto Flores Alvarado, an anthropologist who emerged as an acerbic critic of Adams; sociologist Edelberto Torres Rivas, who participated on the dependency theory team of the Facultad Latinoamericana de Ciencias Sociales (FLACSO)–Chile; and economist Gert Rosenthal, who worked for the U.N., had begun to make their mark. By the 1970s, Central America had a high number of economists, sociologists, and anthropologists and had held its first major debate on indigenous issues, spearheaded by anthropologist Carlos Guzmán Böckler and historian Severo Martínez Peláez. FLACSO had also opened its general secretariat in Costa Rica, where Salvadoran economist Rafael Menjívar and Costa Rican sociologist Daniel Camacho left their imprint.

22. Asturias's adage implies that the writer speaks for subaltern subjects, for those who "have no voice." John Beverley has already done an insightful critique of writers adopting such a stand in *Against Literature* when criticizing Neruda's similar take in his *Canto General.* Dalton's statement can be found in the introduction to Otto René Castillo's complete works (Castillo, *Informe de una injusticia*).

23. Here I employ the phrase "the lettered city" in the sense of Angel Rama's original conception as well as in the one furthered by Jean Franco in *The Decline and Fall of the Lettered City.*

24. Avelar, *The Untimely Present*, 12.

25. See Jean Franco's chapter on the cold war and culture in *The Decline and Fall of the Lettered City*.

26. García Canclini, "Aesthetic Moments of Latin Americanism," 14.

27. The *matanza* was the assassination of between ten thousand and thirty thousand peasants in January 1932. This action, carried out by the Salvadoran army under the direction of General Maximiliano Hernández Martínez, was the response to a peasant insurrection. Among the dead was Farabundo Martí, a labor organizer whose name became emblematic of the leftist Farabundo Martí National Liberation Front (FMLN). Salvadoran historians consider the *matanza* the beginning of the long historical cycle that ended with the civil war of the 1980s.

28. The only significant female antecedent to Alegría was Costa Rican Yolanda Oreamuno (1916–56). However, residing in Mexico, she remained largely unknown in Central America itself until she was rediscovered by Sergio Ramírez in the 1970s.

29. Alegría and Flakoll, *Ashes of Izalco*, 9. All further references will be to this edition. Even though Flakoll translated the text, some of the salient touches that most clearly mark the differences between "linear" and "pictorial" style have been lost in translation. For example, in this paragraph the line "Qué rico estar descalza" has been translated as "I've taken off my sandals" instead of "How nice it feels to be barefoot." Thus, the active reflective emotional element on the part of the narrator disappears, and instead we have a passive descriptive act, closer to the "linear" than to the "pictorial." The loss is also ideological. The active phrase is an ideologeme in the sense that it denotes a choice to be barefoot, underlining a link between Carmen and the poor, barefoot people of El Salvador, because to wear shoes or to go barefoot is a fundamental divide between rich and poor in Central America. This was especially so during the *matanza:* after all, it was the perpetrator of the *matanza*, General Maximiliano Hernández Martínez, who predicated that the poor people should go barefoot in order to absorb the effluvia from the earth. Growing up in Santa Ana in the 1930s, Carmen had to know of and react to such information.

30. My study centers on the six Spanish-speaking countries of Central America: Guatemala, El Salvador, Honduras, Nicaragua, Costa Rica, and Panama. I look forward to future comparative endeavors on the relationship between Hispanophone Central America and its Anglophone regional counterpart, Belize. See also note 18 of the introduction.

31. Nussbaum, *Upheavals of Thought*, 130.

32. Avelar, *The Untimely Present*, 29.

33. Nussbaum, *Upheavals of Thought*, 39.

34. Saldaña-Portillo, *The Revolutionary Imagination in the Americas*, 18.

35. Regarding the impact of development on revolutionary discourse, see Saldaña-Portillo's *The Revolutionary Imagination in the Americas and the Age of Development*.

36. Rodríguez, *Women, Guerrillas, and Love*, xvii; Saldaña-Portillo, *The Revolutionary Imagination in the Americas*, 63.

37. Except for writers who were well off—Dalton, Alegría, Guardia, Naranjo, or

Belli come to mind because of their cosmopolitanism. Most others remained relatively provincial until the 1970s and, as a result, frequently exoticized and reified foreign cultures. This was also a source of shame, because, in those radical times, such an attitude was perceived as individualistic, bourgeois, or treasonous. The fact that those who remained fixed in their undesired Central American topography were envious of the ones able to travel back and forth is indicative of this veiled class struggle within the literary world. Those left at home could think of no better epithet for traveling writers than "bourgeois sellouts." In response, elite writers were often forced to engage in extreme left tactics—such as visiting Hanoi at the peak of the Vietnam War, Cuba in the 1960s, or China before Nixon visited it—to prove their credentials.

38. Chem Sham, "Complejidad narrativa y principio autobiográfico en *Pobrecito poeta que era yo . . . ,*" 173.

39. Avelar, *The Untimely Present,* 36.

40. Lara-Martínez, "Roque romántico," 190, 194.

41. Ibid., 189.

42. Ibid., 188.

43. All three authors produced major testimonials in the 1970s and 1980s: Dalton came out with *Miguel Mármol* (1973, translated as *Miguel Marmol,* 1987), Ramírez with *Hombre del Caribe* (A man from the Caribbean, 1977), and Alegría and Flakoll with *No me agarran viva* (1983, translated as *They Won't Take Me Alive,* 1987) and later *Somoza, la historia de un ajusticiamiento* (1993, translated as *Death of Somoza,* 1996).

44. See Saldaña-Portillo, "The Authorized Subjects of Revolution."

45. Their juncture is impregnated with a highly didactic element. This didactic element is one of the flaws in the text. However, it remains hidden underneath the lyricism of Itzá's voice.

46. Massumi, *Parables for the Virtual,* 49, 50.

47. See Robinson's *Transnational Conflicts.*

48. Franco sees a decline in the importance of literature after the end of the cold war. After the collapse of utopia, little that really matters can be framed in literature, because the market alone sets the standards for what is published (*Plotting Women,* 274). In Foucauldian terms, all of literature is now "out of the truth."

49. Rodríguez, *Transatlantic Topographies,* 5.

50. In my book *Ideología, literaturay sociedad* (Ideology, literature, and society, 1979), I explained how this process happened in a concrete case: in the type of imaginary horizon that writer Mario Monteforte Toledo framed in his novel *Entre la piedra y la cruz* (Between the stone and the cross, 1949), whose representation better corresponded to the public yearnings generated both by the Guatemalan revolution (1944) and by the ideas publicly defended by Guatemala's President Arévalo (1945–50).

51. Avelar, *The Untimely Present,* 21.

52. All quotes come from Belli's interview in *El País* during the launching of her novel. See Inxausti, "Gioconda Belli novela la tragedia de Juana la Loca."

53. Franco, *The Decline and Fall of the Lettered City,* 275.

54. Claudia Milian suggests that *El asco* could also be translated "Nausea," if only because she reads this work as a profoundly existentialist one that evokes a particular queasiness, a particular desire to simply vomit. This sickness is demonstrated through the form of the novel, which is a continuous monologue, without blank spaces in the text, to denote the gagging that will, invariably, take place. Nausea, she also likes to think, suggests a conversation with Sartre's novel of the same name. See Milian, "Fashioning United States Salvadoranness."

55. There are an important number of young Central American critics who began completing their Ph.D.s in the United States in the second half of the 1990s and inserting themselves into the American academy. Their youth has prevented them from making their mark as yet, either in U.S. cultural debates or in their countries of origin. Time will tell if they succeed in creating a Central American–American academic space.

2. Erotic Transgression and Recodification of Values in Asturias's *Mulata*

1. *Mulata de tal* was originally published in Spanish in 1963 in Buenos Aires, by Losada. The English edition was translated by Gregory Rabassa and published in New York by Seymour Lawrence/Delacorte Press in 1967. The English title is *Mulata,* with a single *t,* illustrating a continuum with the Spanish title and showing a rupture with black-and-white discourses on notions of the "tragic mulatto." The *mula* (mule) also references a recurring image of temptation and infertility in the text, associated with the character Celestino's penis, which can be seen through the open "barn door" of his trousers in the opening pages and becomes the agent of a wild ride at the end of the text. All quotes in English are from the 1967 edition.

2. Nana Hollín's image is also interesting as a transgression of the Cinderella story. *Nana* means mother in most Maya languages, and *hollín* is soot. Thus, this image of a "Soot Mother" would evoke an abject and elderly Cinderella of sorts: old, ugly, but with a fiercely insatiable sexuality. She never found her prince charming and her castle. Because her story never had a happy ending, the Soot Mother evokes the national saga: Guatemala's post-1954 history is anything but a Cinderella story.

3. Martin's quote is from his classic essay "*Mulata de tal:* The Novel as Animated Cartoon," originally published in the *Hispanic Review.* I am quoting here from the compilation in *Mulata de tal de Miguel Angel Asturias,* ed. Arias, p. 1053.

4. In English, Rene Prieto, Gerald Martin, Jill Robbins, Margaret McClear, and Susan Willis are the only ones to have dedicated essays or chapters of books to this novel. Their writings on it are compiled in *Mulata de tal de Miguel Angel Asturias,* ed. Arias.

5. Prieto was the first critic to point out the connection with Bataille in *Mulata.* Prieto's analysis, *Miguel Angel Asturias's Archeology of Return,* led me to an essay titled "Masochism and Fetishism: Georges Bataille's *Histoire de l'oeil*" by John Phillips. The reading of this essay inspired the points of view presented in this

chapter. However, I believe that the source of Asturias's knowledge of masochism was not Bataille, but Robert Desnos. This point is argued by Stephen Henighan when he compares Desnos's *La liberté ou l'amour* (1927) to Asturias's "La barba provisional." See Henighan, *Assuming the Light*, 106–21.

6. See the end of the previous note. Henighan even quotes Desnos's novel's final pages, where the character Corsaire and his mistress Louise Lame beat a class of schoolgirls for an entire night, arguing that, "by torturing the girls, they introduce them to love" (*Assuming the Light*, 114). He then proceeds to show how Asturias adapted this material to Guatemala's more squeamish attitude during the 1920s in "La barba provisional." Louise Lame can certainly be a reference for the Mulata's behavior.

7. This claim is already present in Prieto's reading, albeit in a slightly different form. He points out the symbiotic relationship that existed between Asturias and his mother and outlines the sexual conflicts deriving from this particular issue.

8. Elements of this kind are also evident in Prieto's work. In fairness to him, he does not limit himself to a political reading of *Mulata*. The novel deals more with issues such as anger, generated by the writer's loss of his family, his country, and his political ideals. As a result, it could well be read as an allegory of an emotional state of the author, of his complex psychic structure.

9. All personal references to Dr. Falicoff are documented in the "Historia del texto" (History of the text) section of the critical edition of *Mulata* in Spanish. See *Mulata de tal de Miguel Angel Asturias*, ed. Arias.

10. Asturias lived in Paris from 1924 to 1933. It was there that he conceived most of his magnum opus, including the beginnings of the ideas that later appeared in *Mulata*.

11. The question of Asturias's sexual orientation may never be answered. There is indirect evidence, such as the fact that Dr. Falicoff moved in with Asturias and his wife in Buenos Aires and even went with them to Europe when they moved there in 1963, staying with them for years and sharing their summer home in Majorca virtually until Asturias's death. Amos Segala, a sort of adopted son of Asturias presently directing the Archives of Twentieth Century Latin American Literature in Paris—an openly gay person who refers to Asturias as "the great love of my life"—has himself encouraged research in this direction. He has intimated what might have been taking place with Dr. Falicoff. Nonetheless, he has not provided any evidence of bisexuality on Asturias's part.

12. Deleuze, *Masochism*. In this chapter we agree with Deleuze's definition. We understand that masochism and sadism are not the same thing and are not two faces of the same coin.

13. Deleuze, *Masochism*, 106.

14. Williams, *Hard Core, Power, Pleasure, and the Frenzy of the Visible*.

15. Occasionally the narrative voices jump in the direction of other characters' perspectives, as is the case with Nana Hollín in the scene mentioned at the beginning of this chapter. However, this game played by the narrative voices throughout the text does not invalidate the employment of Yumí's viewpoint.

16. Deleuze, *Masochism*, 91, 20.

17. The dwarf Catalina is named Lili Puti (spelled *Lilli Puti* in the English translation). The obvious intertextual play with Swift's *Gulliver's Travels* underlines the political aspect of the text, one already present in the work of the English author.

18. The Spanish text reads as follows:

"Yumí se mordía. Convivir, sin poder chistar palabra, con su verdadera mujer, convertida en juguete, en diversión, en muñeca en manos de su otra mujer. Oír llamar a su Niniloj, Lili Puti. . . .

"Pero si sufría en su amor propio, otro mayor era su quebranto doblado de temores. El miedo a que la mulata, vándala por naturaleza y sin más ley que su capricho, se cansara de la enanita y sus vestidos y la estrellara por allí, la golpeara o, lo que hizo, la castigara."

Mulata de tal de Miguel Angel Asturias, ed. Arias, 61. All Spanish quotations are taken from this edition.

19. Transgression affirms the crossing of established limits. It dissolves the subject because he or she does not find finitude, where internal life becomes separated from external life. Rather, finitude is where the movement toward otherness begins to reconfirm that otherness is nothing but the repetition of oneself.

20. Butler, *Excitable Speech*, 1–2.

21. In the Spanish text, Asturias's excerpt reads: "¡Ardiloso! ¡Lépero! ¡Cochino! Jugar a vivo entre gente sencilla, llegada de campos y aldeas a gozar del bullicio de la feria, que no era feria, sino furia de bienestares tempestuosos" (5). It is obvious that my linguistic critique works much better with the original Spanish than with its flatter English version. *Mulata* was not one of Gregory Rabassa's best translations, despite his being recognized—and justifiably so—as the best translator from Spanish to English in the twentieth century.

22. The latter phrase echoes Jean Franco's analysis in *Plotting Women: Gender and Representation in Mexico.*

23. Here it is also worth considering the original Spanish: "¡Relamido! ¡Reliso! ¡Remañoso! ¡Resinvergüenza! ¡Hijuesesentamil! ¡Casado y, a juiciar por su bragueta parpadeante como mampara de fonda, en busca de una de esas que andando paren y dicen que son doncellas o, dicho a lo decente, que andan por pares y dicen que son docenas!" (5).

24. The excerpt reads in Spanish: "Y cada luna nueva, la enana cuidaba de llevar hierba fresca a la mulata. Alguna vez oyó sus risotadas de loca feliz. Hierba a la mulata y maíz amarillo, granudo, al Pájaro Enojón convertido en guardián de aquella cueva tapiada con un cachete de cerro. Sólo un pigmeo podía colarse por donde ella penetraba, igual que araña de caballo, totalmente deforme en sus movimientos. Se desprendía, por dentro, de peña en peña, sin que la mulata, a quien espiaba, se diera cuenta. Humo de mariguana, risa de mujer feliz y el eterno callar de la luna, llenaban la cavidad" (70).

25. The text follows in Spanish, "Gentío, y entre el gentío este zutano con su desmán de bragueta que abriendito se le cerraba y cerrandito se le entreabría, como

hecha con botones de hueso de muerto de risa y ojales de ácierrate sésamo. . . .
¡Ojalá te abras, ojalá te cierres!" (5).

26. Butler, *Gender Trouble*, 134.

27. The original Spanish reads: "La mulata era terrible. A él, con ser él, cuando estaba de mal humor, se le tiraba a la cara a sacarle los ojos. Y de noche, tendida a su lado, lloraba y le mordía tan duro que no pocas veces su gran boca de fiera soberbia embadurnábase de sangre, sangre que paladeaba y se tragaba, mientras le arañaba, táctil, plural, con los ojos blancos, sin pupilas, los senos llorosos de sudor" (49).

28. In Spanish, the Spider's full name is Araña Ensotanada (Cassocked Spider). In the English translation, he or she is simply designated as "the Spider," and we are told that he or she is dressed in a cassock.

29. In Bataille's *Oeuvres Complètes*.

30. See Phillips's "Masochism and Fetishism: George Bataille's *Histoire de l'oeil*."

31. The original Spanish title of the book reflects how the "mulata de tal" is spoken about in the text, whereas the English designation, "the certain Mulata," fails to grasp the double connotation of the Spanish phrase. In fact, I would suggest that an equivalent in English, like "mulata-such-and-such," points to the anonymity of the "Mulata's" being, her interiority as an empty signifier, and to the disposability—the "everywhereness"—of her fetishized location.

32. In the original Spanish, the excerpt reads: "No sé lo que es, pero no es hombre y tampoco es mujer. Para hombre le falta tantito tantote y para mujer le sobra tantote tantito. A que jamás la has visto por delante . . ." (60).

33. See Freud's "Fetishism."

34. Frappier-Mazur, *Writing the Orgy*, 80.

35. The Spanish text reads: "El padre hizo notar que se acercaba. Ruido de badajo el de sus piernas y sus pies, bajo la campana de la sotana" (239).

36. Asturias created this distinction consciously. He said in various interviews that not only had Christian gods come across the ocean with the Spaniards to compete with Maya gods; Christian devils competed with Maya devils as well.

37. I include the original excerpt in Spanish: "Catalina se acuclilló, panzona, despernancada, como si fuera a hacer su necesidad de aguas, y la hizo, de aguas de preñada por Tazol" (120).

38. Asturias wrote, in Spanish: "La Catalina sintió gases en el estómago, pero aunque por la encomienda que cargaba tenía el vientre como tambor, se lo golpeó con la palma de la mano. No eran gases. Notó que no eran gases. Y soltó lo que era. El vástago de Tazol que llevaba en la panza le hablaba por entre las nalgas, con la voz apretada, como si no pudiera expresarse bien entre aquellos enormes cachetes inseparables de tan gordos" (125).

39. Phillips, "Masochism and Fetishism," 78.

40. This scene also appears to be taken from Sade's black mass. It would have constituted a burlesque parody of the collective rites of a decadent society for Asturias as well as for Sade.

41. I use *abjection* here in the sense defined by Julia Kristeva, whose conceptualization was surprisingly anticipated in *Mulata*. See Kristeva's *Powers of Horror: An Essay on Abjection*.

42. In Spanish, the passage reads: ". . . bajo cuyas amplias capas negras orinaban sin ruido damas de alcurnia y doncellas con sonoridad de mimbres, en lagos de cerveza" (257).

43. In this regard, Jill Robbins tells us: "The urine, like confession, contains secrets vital to other people's self-interests, and the Bacinicarios (chamber-potters) are always being tempted to spill them, but spilling one secret implies spilling the whole chamberpot, as the episode with the 'Fiscal del Santo Oficio' illustrates." See Robbins's "The Abject Poetics of Asturias and Buñuel."

44. In the original Spanish, the passage reads: ". . . con el pretexto de presentarle la bacinilla, [trata] de despojarlo de sus atributos varoniles" (260).

45. Deleuze, *Masochism*, 88.

46. *Hombres de maíz* tried to portray a consensual nationalist identity. One of its objectives was to find in the realm of the imaginary a common ground on which to forge a national-popular unity that fused Maya and Ladino cultures for the benefit of the democratic Ladino state. Asturias designed his text as a symbolic instrument that could help President Juan José Arévalo consolidate his political vision and enable his party to continue its hold on power. His "cosmic race" (as Mexican Secretary of Education José Vasconcelos named this experiment in the 1920s) was to be created first by his writing.

47. In the original Spanish, "¡Los hombres verdaderos, los hechos de maíz, dejan de existir realmente y se vuelven seres ficticios, cuando no viven para la comunidad y por eso deben ser suprimidos. ¡Por eso aniquilé con mis Gigantes Mayores, y aniquilaré mientras no se enmienden todos aquellos que olvidando, contradiciendo o negando su condición de granos de maíz, partes de una mazorca, se tornan egocentristas, egoístas, individualistas . . . hasta convertirse en entes solitarios, en maniquíes sin sentido!" (213).

48. See Suleiman's "Transgression and the Avant-Garde: Bataille's *Histoire de l'oeil*." The remark in question appears on p. 316.

49. See Derrida's "De l'économie restreinte à l'économie générale."

50. Suleiman, "Transgression and the Avant-Garde," 316.

51. Paradoxically, in the name of preserving "Catholic values," the Catholic hierarchy wanted a return to the model of the old, oligarchic state, which excluded all hybridizing possibilities.

52. In this context it is important to remember that the body of President Arbenz was itself "violated." After the CIA-sponsored invasion, Arbenz sought asylum in the Mexican embassy. Before being authorized to leave the country for exile, he was forced to be publicly strip-searched at the airport. It was alleged that he was hiding "state secrets" under his clothes. The pictures of a naked President Arbenz were printed on the front pages of all Guatemalan newspapers and in many more

periodicals around the world. The rape of his presidential body, coupled with the rape of the country as a whole, come together in Asturias's imaginary.

53. The original Spanish reads: "Amanecía en el cerro de los jabalíes. Sol empapado en añil, tierra empapada en azul. Peñascales recubiertos de líquenes azulverdosos, en los que los colmillazos de los Salvajos dibujaban signos caprichosos. ¿Sería su forma de escribir? ¿Guardarían en aquellos trazos hechos a punta de colmillo, su historia?" (91).

54. Prieto, *Miguel Angel Asturias's Archeology of Return*, 233, 213.

55. Ibid., 172.

56. This idea was first stated by Roberto Rivera, who tells how Foucault was pre-invented by Guatemalan Juan José Arévalo and also how the seventeenth-century Mexican nun Sor Juana Inés de la Cruz reinvented Platonism all by herself.

57. This, in principle, is the plot of Bataille's *Histoire de l'oeil* (1928, translated as *Story of the Eye*, 1987). It is also the plot of Asturias's *Hombres de maíz*. Gerald Martin has already pointed out, in the critical edition of the latter, the relationship between its plot and the conflict experienced by Asturias around his simultaneous loss of his mother and divorce from his first wife.

58. Suleiman made the original claim that Bataille was not rediscovered until the mid-1960s. I base my assertions on French transgression in this chapter on her article "Transgression and the Avant-Garde."

59. This is due to the context in which the modernist-progressive project represented by Arévalo and Arbenz in Guatemala collapsed in 1954, in much the same way that President Allende's fall in Chile (1973) generated similar traits in Chile's literary production of the 1980s.

60. Prieto says: "As was typical of Asturias, the blueprint for *Mulata* was not without precedent. In this instance, he turns for inspiration to a curious philosophical and metaphysical treatise in the guise of a play: Jose Vasconcelos's little known and today seldom read *Prometeo vencedor* (1920)" (*Miguel Angel Asturias's Archeology of Return*, 166–67).

3. Identity or Literariness

1. Understood in the sense developed by Foucault in his genealogical texts.

2. The definitive English edition is that of Dennis Tedlock.

3. Myth has it that the Mongolian origin of indigenous peoples of the Americas can be detected by a Mongolian spot that all indigenous children have at birth, which disappears after a few weeks. This "spot" was a source of racist scorn and abjection, but it became fashionable after the late 1960s for those in progressive circles to claim that they had been born with a Mongolian spot.

4. Monterroso, *Los buscadores de oro*, 11, 12, my translation. All translations in this chapter are mine unless otherwise indicated.

5. In the original Spanish: "Centroamérica, como bien pudiera haber dicho Eduardo Torres, ha sido siempre vencida, tanto por los elementos como por las naves enemigas . . . pero es mi deber señalar una vez más que a lo largo de los siglos no

ha sido sólo plátano lo que producimos. Recordaré que nuestros ancestros mayas, refinados astrónomos y matemáticos que inventaron el cero antes que otras grandes civilizaciones, tuvieron su propia cosmogonía en lo que hoy conocemos con el nombre de *Popol Vuh*, el libro nacional de los quichés, mitológico, poético y misterioso." The mention of Eduardo Torres is an allusion to the main character of Monterroso's novel *Lo demás es silencio* (The rest is silence, 1978); Torres is a goofy provincial man of letters. Indeed, the novel has as a subtitle "La vida y la obra de Eduardo Torres" (The life and the work of Eduardo Torres). The quote is taken from the Centro Virtual Cervantes Web site, http://cvc.cervantes.es/actcult/monterroso/cronologia/1973_2003.htm.

6. Biggs, "An Open and Shut Case."

7. Avelar, *The Untimely Present*, 25.

8. Ibid., 26.

9. Sarmiento, *Facundo: Civilization and Barbarism*.

10. Martin claims this in "Asturias, *Mulata de tal* y el 'realismo mítico' (en Tierrapaulita no amanece)," published in the critical edition of *Mulata de tal*. In his chapter he is quoting from Monegal's article "Los dos Asturias," published in *Revista Iberoamericana* in 1969, the same year he published his book *Narradores de esta América*.

11. Cornejo Polar, "*Mestizaje* and Hybridity," 761.

12. Taken from Cornejo's chapter "Indigenismo and Heterogeneous Literatures," in *The Latin American Cultural Studies Reader*, quote on 114.

13. Henighan, *Assuming the Light*, 198.

14. See Molloy, "Latin America in the U.S. Imaginary," 189–90, in *Ideologies of Hispanism*.

15. Brotherston, *Book of the Fourth World*, 215.

16. Ibid., 216.

17. Rodríguez, *Transatlantic Topographies*, 81.

18. The historical federation grouped the five members of the Capitanía General of Guatemala under Spanish rule (Guatemala, El Salvador, Honduras, Nicaragua, and Costa Rica) and constituted the United Provinces of Central America from 1821 until its dissolution in 1841.

19. "Mesoamérica" is the name given to the region extending from the southeastern part of present-day Mexico to northern Central America, where the most important pre-Hispanic civilizations flowered. It stretches from the territory of the ancient Olmecs, in present-day Veracruz and Tabasco, to the lands occupied by the Mayas in the Yucatan Peninsula, Chiapas, Guatemala, Belize, and Honduras. This region includes the territories of the Mixtec-Zapotec culture in present-day Oaxaca and those of the Totonac culture north of Veracruz.

20. Relations between the highlands and the lowlands of Guatemala and the central valley of Mexico date back at least to A.D. 350–400, when a Teotihuacano presence has been documented at both Kaminaljuyú (present-day Guatemala City) and Tikal.

21. Brotherston, *Book of the Fourth World,* 237.

22. All quotes from this book in this chapter are my translations from the original 1990 edition published by UCA in San Salvador.

23. *Gacela Cartesiana* in the original. In Spanish, *gacela* simultaneously has two meanings, that of "shy female" and that of "gazelle," the African animal of the same name. The original nickname in Spanish thus evokes an oxymoron: an "African" (i.e., a trope for "exotic" or "savage," yet timid) rationalist individual.

24. In this sense, the novel evokes Foucault's description of *Herkunft* (descent) in "Nietzsche, Genealogy, History" (in *Power/Knowledge*).

25. "Netza" is short for Nezahaulcóyotl, the poet-king of Texcoco (d. 1472). It serves as an affectionate nickname for the artist in exile, but also ties Roberto to an elite indigenous identity, that of poet-king.

26. Without question, Belizean and Maya literature are even more invisible. The former is written in English or in a pidginized English mixed with Garifuna, the latter in various Maya languages.

27. *Mayab* would normally translate as "Maya homeland." *Ukush Mayab* is a Maya-K'iché phrase meaning "essence." It conflates the notions of the Maya region, people, culture, and history (both oral and written) within a single concept, thus superseding the simpler translation "homeland." Traditionally, *Mayab* also refers to the territory covered by the classical Maya kingdoms (A.D. 200–600).

28. The novel won the Premio Centroamericano de Novela in 1976. All quotes from this book in this chapter are my translations from the original 1977 edition published by EDUCA in San José, Costa Rica.

29. Criollos are pure descendants of Spaniards, born in Central America. Though *criollo* is often translated to English as "creole," it does not mean the same thing as the latter, which is usually understood in the United States in its Caribbean definition of either a descendant of the British or French or a person of mixed ancestry with African blood.

30. Besides connoting as semantic meaning a person of indigenous origin, in Mexico and Central America the word *Indio* is the strongest epithet that can be uttered against another individual, not unlike various ethnically centered epithets in the United States, such as *spic, kike, nigger,* etc.

31. *El último juego* is the first of two Central American novels to represent the real-life occupation of Chema Castillo's house in Managua, Nicaragua, by members of the Sandinista Front. The event took place in December 1974, and the U.S. ambassador to Nicaragua was held as one of the prisoners. The other novel representing this tantalizing experience is Belli's *La mujer habitada.*

32. Romanticized as a symbol of Panamanian patriotism, the name Urraca, interestingly enough, recalls that of Queen Urraca, Spanish queen of Castile and León (1109–26), daughter and successor of Alfonso VI. Guardia is aware of this. Thus, although the Urraca Command named itself after an indigenous chieftain to stress its "otherness," its symbolic indigenous nationalism, in reality the name is a hybrid trope that also implies femininity and thus signals the impossibility of seeking a

masculinist essentialized identity. *Urraca* is also Spanish for the magpie jay, an astute, picaresque thief of a bird according to Aesop's fables. This offers one more meaning to the commando's name and, by extension, to the indigenous and Castilian leaders.

33. I could even mention my own *Jaguar en llamas* (1989) in this respect.

34. Born in San Juan del Obispo, Sacatepequez, de Lión was disappeared by the Guatemalan army on 15 May 1984 as his country's repression began to wane. All quotes from this book in this chapter are my translations from the 1996 edition published by Artemis Edinter in Guatemala City.

35. This is expressed in the following untranslatable passage: "Mejor abrir y cerrar los ojos, mejor abrir y cerrá los ojos, mejor abrí y cerrar los ojos, mejor abrí y cerrá los ojos, mejor abril y cesá los ojos, mejor abril nací y aserrar los ojos, mejor abrilocho nací abril locho nací abril locho . . ." (85). This passage, as well as the use of abjection and feces in Sadean fashion, clearly evoke Asturias's *Mulata*.

36. In the original Spanish this reads:
"Y Estaba solo.
"Entonces, para consolarse, buscó a su otro. . . . Buscó el espejo que era otra de las únicas cosas que le había dejado la Concha. Quería que siquiera el otro lo acompañara. Se paró frente al pilar, pero con miedo, sin mirarse todavía, sólo asomando la cara poco a poco. Cuando creyó que ya estaba todo él del otro lado, entonces atravezó los ojos para saludarlo, para que lo saludaran, para que le dijeran que no tuviera pena, que estaba El con El acompañándolo."

37. In the original Spanish: "Cuando Pascual regresó al pueblo traía, además de los años que lo habían llevado de niño a hombre, una cara como si ya fuera de otra parte . . . traía en la boca palabras raras, desconocidas como de hombre que ha aprendido otros idiomas; traía en los pies zapatos en lugar de caites; traía en la cabeza sombrero de vicuña en lugar de la gracia del sombrero de petate y en el cuerpo ropa distinta de la que se usaba en la aldea. Ya no era de aquí."

38. In the original Spanish: ". . . así como podría desnudar un ladino a su mujer la noche del casamiento."

39. All English quotes from this book in this chapter are from this translation. All Spanish quotes are from the original 1992 edition.

40. See Shea's article "Los universos indoamericanos."

41. See Contreras's article "¿Pero existe la nación guatemalteca?"

42. Saldaña-Portillo, "The Authorized Subjects of Revolution," 152.

43. Ibid.

44. Goldberg, *The Racial State*, 90.

45. Lienhard, *"La Noche de los Mayas."*

46. In the Spanish version there is a passage that was deleted from the English translation, making this act more prescient, if heavier from a narrative point of view. It reads: "Tenderás estos brazos . . . para socorrer a los débiles y ayudarlos a incorporarse en sus condiciones de humanos; usarás tus pies para marcar las huellas de

los caminos que conduzcan a la paz y a la libertad del hombre de las cadenas del egoísmo" (29).

47. Dussel, *Etica de la liberación*, 421.

48. In Spanish: "Metodológicamente, se presenta el trabajo en tres momentos históricos: período prehispánico, período colonial y período contemporáneo."

49. In Spanish: "*Kotz'ib*' abarca las distintas maneras de expresar el pensamiento mediante signos, símbolos, colores, tejidos y líneas. La literatura maya como producto cultural de una sociedad, que tiene un particular punto de vista filosófico sobre el mundo y la vida, no siempre debe ser sometida al análisis bajo los cánones de la cultura occidental. Pues los ojos y los sentimientos de sus autores, se enmarcan dentro de esa cosmovisión que les permite la cultura."

50. This is the Spanish title; the original is in Jak'alteko. All Spanish translations of the work are from the 1998 Spanish edition. The English translations are my own, from the Spanish, with the page numbers of the Spanish edition given.

51. Montejo miraculously survived an army massacre in the early 1980s, as he narrates in *Testimony: Death of a Guatemalan Village* (1987). He fled to Chiapas, from which he succeeded in entering the United States. He completed his university education in the United States, becoming a professor at the University of California at Davis before returning to Guatemala in a cabinet position in 2004.

52. Víctor Montejo, personal communication, 1995.

53. In Spanish it reads: "Yo digo que es padre, porque tiene una estatura descomunal. Su cabello es rubio, sus ojos son verdes o azules; y ahora que viene caminando bajo el sol parece que la sangre se le fuera a reventar debajo de su piel de ratón tierno."

54. In Spanish: "—Muy bien Mister, dijo Xuxh Antil. —Usted debe también aprender a decir los nombres de sus amigos en idioma Popb'al Ti'. Llámeme siempre 'Antil,' en vez de 'Andrés.' A mí me gusta mucho ese nombre, aunque así se llama también una clase de ranas que durante la estación lluviosa se trepan a los árboles a cantar."

55. In the Spanish version: "—Don Lamun dice que su nombre en nuestra lengua se pronuncia como *T'ut'*. Mr. Puttison se paró de su asiento inconforme y gritó: — Oh, por favor, no me busquen otro nombre. Mi nombre es Dud. —Sí, míster, pero la D no existe en nuestra lengua. Lo más parecido es *T'ut'*, pero es otra cosa. Todos se rieron. —¿Qué es *T'ut'* entonces? Xhuxh Antil se adelantó a explicar, con una sonrisa picaresca. —*T'ut'* es el ruido que produce el aire al soltar un pedo disimulado."

56. In Spanish: "Los antepasados la escogieron para esconder sus tesoros de los ambiciosos conquistadores."

57. In Spanish: "los objetos sagrados de sus antepasados."

58. See Cojtí Cuxil's chapter in Edward Fischer and R. McKenna Brown's *Maya Cultural Activism in Guatemala*.

59. See England's chapter in Fischer and McKenna Brown, *Maya Cultural Activism in Guatemala*, 178.

60. Rappaport, "Alternative Knowledge Producers in Indigenous Latin America."

4. Authoring Ethnicized Subjects

1. This question, in fact, is the title of Gayatri Spivak's "Can the Subaltern Speak?"

2. *Me llamo Rigoberta Menchú y asi me nació la conciencia* was originally written in Spanish by Elisabeth Burgos-Debray from interviews with Menchú conducted in Paris in January 1982. *Menchú* spoke basic Spanish, translating in her head from her native K'iché-Maya. After winning the Casa de las Américas *testimonio* award in 1983, the book was translated into English by Ann Wright and published in 1984.

3. Born in the tiny village of Chimel in the Western Guatemalan highlands, Menchú is a Maya-K'iché woman, a member of one of twenty-three Maya groups living in this Central American country the size of Tennessee. Born in extreme poverty, Menchú tells us that she started working at the age of eight. Two of her siblings died from malnutrition and pesticides. In Guatemala, indigenous peoples have suffered discrimination since the Spanish Conquest in the sixteenth century in much the same way that blacks have in South Africa. Menchú's father, Vicente, fought as a progressive Catholic leader against the government, which had helped Ladinos to take away the Mayas' land by force.

4. Now that the U.S. government has released Central Intelligence Agency documents regarding the U.S. role in replacing democratic governments with repressive military dictatorships and supporting genocidal campaigns in Central America, and the U.S. president (Bill Clinton) has apologized for that role to the Central American people, we may rightly feel confused about the rhetoric used to justify that intervention: "freedom fighters," "contras," "Marxist guerrillas," "government forces." These expressions varied throughout the 1980s according to the ideological orientation of the Central American government in question; thus the freedom fighters were not called "guerrillas," even though they used guerrilla tactics, because they were trying to topple the Sandinista government. Guerrillas were always Marxist, so much so that the two words almost always appear together—"Marxist guerrillas." Even the word *guerrilla,* pronounced "gorilla" by most newscasters and politicians, conjured up images of dark primitives launching a bestial battle against enlightened Westerners in the jungles "down there," the implied trope of "South of the Border" being itself synonymous with barbarism.

5. Stoll, *Rigoberta Menchú,* xii–xiii. All quotes from Stoll in this chapter refer to this book.

6. Gugelberger, *The Real Thing,* 1.

7. Beverley, *Against Literature,* 82.

8. Bhabha, *The Location of Culture,* 23. The complete quote appears toward the end of this chapter. See note 20.

9. On 31 January 1980, a group of CUC peasants (including Menchú's father, Vicente) and university students occupied the Spanish embassy in Guatemala City. They demanded an international press conference to denounce the government's atrocities against Maya villages in the Quiché region. The Spanish government immediately acquiesced. However, the Guatemalan government refused and ordered the

army to storm the embassy. In the ensuing attack, all occupiers, including Vicente Menchú, were burned to death, alongside visitors and embassy personnel. The only survivors were the ambassador, who jumped from the embassy's roof, and a Maya peasant, who had third-degree burns. He was kidnapped from the hospital by security forces and murdered that same night. Spain broke diplomatic relations with Guatemala as a result of this incident. See chapter 7 of this book for a more detailed analysis of this crucial incident.

10. Menchú Tum, Megan Thomas, and Elizabeth Alvarez, personal communication, Mexico City, 1983.

11. This is a chapter of *The Rigoberta Menchú Controversy.*

12. Moreiras, "Pastiche Identity and Allegory of Allegory," 225.

13. I am referring here to their chapters "The Primacy of Larger Truths: Rigoberta Menchú and the Tradition of Native Testimony in Guatemala" (by Lutz and Lovell) and "Truth, Human Rights and Representation: The Case of Rigoberta Menchú" (by Montejo) in *The Rigoberta Menchú Controversy.*

14. As a non-Maya opposition militant, I witnessed this and discussed it with fellow militants in the early 1980s.

15. Sommer, "Rigoberta's Secrets," 34.

16. Moreiras, "Pastiche Identity and Allegory of Allegory," 205.

17. Ibid., 204.

18. Thus, when Stoll complains, "Still, the chronology of how Chimel becomes a militant village is perplexing. . . . This is not the first point where *I, Rigoberta Menchú* becomes confusing" (92), we may well ask, is this a critique of Rigoberta Menchú's Maya style of narration, of her poor Spanish, of her alleged EGP puppeteers for not being clearer about the chronology they imposed on her, or of Elisabeth Burgos-Debray's editing talents? Or could he simply be arguing that a "genuine" Maya subject could not think in such a fashion?

19. The hurried composition and oral nature of Menchú's text and her status as an exile created even more ambiguities, silences, and absences. They precluded the verification of any of the facts she narrated, so that the interplay of fiction and history in memory becomes a central issue in Menchú's text. For more theoretical clarification on this issue, see Elzbieta Sklodowska's "La forma testimonial y la novelística de Miguel Barnet."

20. The "Elisabeth" to whom Stoll refers is Elisabeth Burgos-Debray, the official compiler of Menchú's book, who appears as "author" in the first editions in both English and Spanish. Subsequently, under pressure from Menchú, she voluntarily withdrew her name as author, but has retained the copyright and the title of "official compiler" of the text. The latter role has also been questioned by both Menchú and Arturo Taracena. Stoll interviews Burgos-Debray in his book, using this "testimony" of Menchú's interviewer to bolster his own argument that Menchú was complicitous with the guerrilla movement. Menchú and Taracena have contested this claim in interviews published in Guatemala and circulated worldwide on the Internet in 1999.

21. Bhabha, *The Location of Culture*, 11. The original Bhabha quote was pointed out to me by Marina Pérez de Mendiola. She used it in one of her articles before I did, and we discussed my usage of it after the original publication of my article. Due to an editorial error, reference to her was omitted in the original publication of my article.

5. After the Controversy

1. As I have stated elsewhere, "Guatemala," more than a trope, is a chronotrope signaling a will to belong.

2. For a defense of this argument, see the previous chapter of this book, "Authoring Ethnicized Subjects."

3. In short, Stoll ratifies a monological rhetoric of exclusion, a protocol that makes all dialogism impossible. It undermines the articulation of any subjective position that does not recognize itself within the essentialized framework of a central white American male gaze.

4. Here we can tentatively assume that, displeased with the indifferent reception this book received from scholars and readers, he dressed up the premises expressed in it by targeting Menchú's testimonial, knowing full well that it would be an attention-getting device certain to guarantee a large audience. Contrary to his purported goals, the ulterior debate centered on the veracity of Menchú's words themselves.

5. César Montes, personal communication, La Jolla, California, 22 November 2001. Jill Robbins, Regina Marchi, and Ignacio Ochoa were present during this exchange.

6. It could be argued that other speakers invited to solidarity committee meetings in the United States gave more simplistic explanations than I did. Nonetheless, this would evidence only that the international line of the URNG (Guatemalan National Revolutionary Unit) was contradictory at best, certainly inconsistent, and that the ability to explain the position of its member organizations was left in the hands of heterogeneous speakers with varied backgrounds, educational levels, understandings of the situation, and so on. Ultimately, this would prove that Guatemalan speakers did not mimic a fixed revolutionary explanation. Rather, they interpreted what was happening in their country from their own subjective experience as well as from their ability to interpret the U.S. audience's needs.

7. Evidence of these presentations survives in the form of press clippings from those seemingly remote tours and the transcript of a long interview published by Jonathan Fried in 1983. See his *Guatemala in Rebellion: Unfinished History.*

8. My disillusionment with the EGP led to my joining members or sympathizers who publicly broke with that organization at the end of January 1984. I am less familiar with the EGP's explanations of their own trajectory after 1984, because the EGP slowly imploded and sank into irrelevance. Nonetheless, this should not alter this discussion. Menchú is accused of reproducing the EGP's position in January 1982, when the material for her book was originally taped. At the time, I was familiar

with the EGP's literary production and happened to be in the home of Arturo Tara-
cena, Menchú's host in Paris, while Menchú was recording her tapes for Elisabeth
Burgos-Debray. Taracena's spouse at the time, Sophie Feral, and mine, Pantxika
Cazaux, were also present at this time, as was Juan Mendoza. We all knew that
Menchú's interview was Taracena's personal initiative, not an official gesture on the
part of the EGP.

9. In this light, Stoll's attitude becomes possible only if one falls back on the
traditional premises of Eurocentric discourse, where "Maya" or "Guatemala" are
but exotic tropes to denote the limits of textual knowledge, the marginality of marginality, those dark voids at the outer edge of rationality where jingoism matters
more than careful research.

10. Stoll says: "In the same vein, I wish Mario Roberto Morales had shared with
us his memoir of how he came to be a member of MRP-Ixim, the dissident guerrilla group that was repressed by the URNG as well as the army (Morales 1998). As
a militant from the 1960s to the 1980s . . . Morales understands how Guevarist youth
gave the Guatemalan right more excuses for escalating repression" (407). Although
it is public knowledge that acts of banditry took place in the 1960s (this was established by a couple of articles published in 1980 and 1981 by José Luis Morales—
pseudonym of Miguel Angel Sandoval, one of the EGP's founders—in *Cuicuilco*,
the journal of the National School of Anthropology and History of Mexico), this
activity hardly justifies the Guatemalan army's actions during the same period.

11. "Historia del Movimiento Indígena en Guatemala, 1970–1983" (1985) and
"Shifts in Indian Identity: Guatemala's Violent Transition to Modernity" (1990).

12. All translations in this chapter are mine unless otherwise indicated.

13. In the mid-1990s Stoll telephoned me at home to inquire about this. I stated
that the piece "Sebastián Guzmán, principal de principales" that circulated anonymously in the early 1980s was written by Father Javier Gurriarán of the Sacred Heart
order. Stoll had suspected that it had been written by Mario Payeras, given that it
fit his scheme of an overreaching EGP conspiracy. He was disappointed that this
was not the case. I did not tell him on that occasion that Marcie Mersky had confirmed to me that Father Gurriarán told her he had written the article in question.

14. Beatriz Manz documents that the army went into the region shortly afterward to combat the EGP, killing Rosa Aguayo, a schoolteacher who was a member
of a Christian youth group. Manz, "The Transformation of La Esperanza," 77.

15. "Los pueblos indígenas y la revolución guatemalteca." Payeras himself offered
this information after his break with the EGP in 1984. Two other important articles on
the "ethnic question" were also published by EGP militants polemicizing with their
directorate. They are an unpublished article that circulated in mimeo form, Manuela
Ocampo de la Paz's "Etnia y clase en la revolución guatemalteca" (1981), and Aura
Marina Arreola's "Guatemala: Contrainsurgencia y guerra de exterminio" (1982).

16. Although César Montes later broke with the EGP and had serious differences
with Payeras, he agrees with this version of events.

17. Stoll does mention Payeras, but only in a quote attributed to Carol Smith,

whom he is refuting: "Both [Mario] Payeras [of the EGP] and Gaspar Ilóm ... have discussed how difficult it was to enlist Maya" (397). Recognition of Payeras's contributions, however, is nowhere to be found in Stoll's work. Despite his increasing criticism of the EGP's overall strategy, even Payeras's later books, *El trueno en la ciudad* (1987) and *Los fusiles de octubre* (1991), are not present in Stoll's bibliography.

18. Severo Martínez's *La patria del criollo* and Carlos Guzmán Böckler and Jean-Loup Hebert's *Guatemala, una interpretación histórico-social*.

19. Stoll does mention that other American anthropologists, John Watanabe, Shelton Davis, and Carol Smith, documented that the EGP's implantation in the Huehuetenango region had been weak at best (396). Nonetheless, none of them extrapolated their data to the entire national territory; they confined their conclusions to the small areas they had researched in depth.

20. In the late 1960s, Richard N. Adams was the last U.S. academic to offer a political analysis of Guatemalans inside Guatemala itself. Despite his friendship with the secretary general of the Guatemalan Communist Party and the protection of Jesuit Ricardo Falla, his own academic disciple and a future sympathizer with the EGP, he nearly paid for his daring with his life.

21. "On the national level, the guerrilla movement was a seemingly inevitable response to the 1954 CIA intervention" (394).

22. Edelberto Torres Rivas, among others, began a series of brilliant analyses of the period with the publication of *Interpretación del desarrollo social centroamericano* in 1971, as did Susanne Jonas on the American side when she published *Guatemala* in 1974 with David Tobin. Important contributions have been made by many others, including Beatriz Manz, Jennifer Schirmer, Piero Gleijeses, Mario Solórzano Martínez, Víctor Gálvez, Gabriel Aguilera Peralta, and Carlos Figueroa Ibarra, among many names I could cite.

23. Ja C'amabal I'b, "La primera gran confrontación," 6, quoted in my 1990 chapter, 232.

24. Ja C'amabal I'b, "La primera gran confrontación," 7, quoted in my 1990 chapter, 232.

25. Jonas and Tobias, *Guatemala*, 59, 61.

26. This was documented in the United States by Richard Gott's *Guerrilla Movements in Latin America* (1970). When the Central America crisis became fashionable in the 1980s, most academic commentators rehashed this material.

27. Arias, "Shifts in Indian Identity," 243.

28. Stoll throws even Vicente Menchú's membership in CUC into question in his book. Prior to this controversy, however, in his book *El trueno en la ciudad* Payeras had already attested to Vicente Menchú's role as one of the CUC's leaders who led the protests from Quiché to Guatemala City—"los dirigentes Gaspar Viví y Vicente Menchú, catequistas, cabezas de las parcialidades ..." (49)—prior to describing the burning of the Spanish embassy.

29. Payeras, personal communication, Mexico City, 1986.

30. Ibid., 1985.

31. Carmack, "The Story of Santa Cruz Quiché," 52.

32. Later Payeras reissued his anonymous articles critiquing the EGP's military strategy under his own name in a book titled *Los fusiles de octubre.*

33. By the time *Opinión Política* ceased publication, practically all that needed to be criticized about both the EGP and the URNG had been improved, and the members of the Contingente had already paid the price for doing so: they were branded as traitors, accused of bourgeois deviations, and in some cases even kept from visiting their own children in Cuba.

34. In 1985 Alvarez lived in my house in Mexico City (the same house where Rigoberta Menchú lived in 1983, Rancho El Encanto No. 29, Villa Coapa), and she confirmed this.

6. Reading Truthfully

1. The Center for the Study of Popular Culture, based in Los Angeles, paid for advertisements in campus newspapers at Brandeis, Columbia, Harvard, and Yale Universities and at the Universities of Illinois at Urbana-Champaign and of North Carolina at Chapel Hill. They called Menchú a "Marxist terrorist" who has been "exposed as an intellectual hoax" and added: "This fraud was originally perpetrated and is still defended by your professors and by the Nobel Prize Committee." They invited students to denounce their professors and to boycott their classes.

2. The program I recall was advertised on *The John Carlson Show* as claiming that "Rigoberta Menchu is a Fraud" and added that "author David Stoll guests on talkspot.com." The ad ended with "*Rigoberta Menchu and the Story of All Poor Gua-temalans* right now!!! Hear how Bill Clinton isn't the only fake, phony, fraud out there." The links between impeachment and Menchú's alleged lies were also established on similar radio programs.

3. The *testimonio* as a genre has been debated nearly to death. For brief references to this debate, it will suffice to read *The Real Thing* by Georg Gugelberger, published in 1996, two years prior to Stoll's *Rigoberta Menchú and the Story of All Poor Guatemalans,* and the summary in chapter 4 of this book. For the position of John Beverley, see his new compilation of all of his articles, *Testimonio: On the Politics of Truth* (2004).

4. The generalization "two" is, of course, implicitly dangerous. It could very well be said that there are as many readings as there are readers. At the risk of falling into an undesirable form of reductionism, I will claim here that by "form of reading" I mean a certain way of understanding and processing metaphoricity, rhetorical devices, and the overall comprehension of signifiers in general, as a "productive matrix" (Bhabha, *The Location of Culture,* 23) that circumscribes the social understanding of a given text within the familiar context of one's own cultural referents.

5. This was indicated by French professor Noël Salomon in the 1970s in both "La crítica del sistema colonial de la Nueva España en *El Periquillo Sarmiento*" and *Realidad, ideología y literatura en el Facundo de D. F. Sarmiento.*

6. Scarry, *Resisting Representation*, 8.

7. Balibar and Wallerstein, *Race, Nation, Class*, 21–22.

8. In the metaphorical sense created by the *X-Men* series.

9. Described in Pratt's *Imperial Eyes*. The contact zone is the space of colonial encounters where colonizers and colonized come into contact and establish ongoing relations in asymmetrical conditions of power. However, it is an area where the intelligibility of the world of conquest, domination, and resistance is possible.

10. In Guatemala we have a popular saying that names this particular act: "Decírselo a Pedro para que lo oiga Juan" ("Telling Pedro so Juan can hear it"). In that light, we can be sure that Menchú was talking to an international European audience with the idea that Guatemala's Ladinos would hear what she said, as indeed they did. This is another angle of Menchú's discourse that Stoll misses.

11. Lyotard, *The Differend*, xi.

12. Best and Kellner's understanding of Lyotard's *différend* is that, although one must judge without universal categories (something hard for Americans to do), one "should seek the differences and listen for the silences" that point toward *différends*. Then one should encourage the mute voices to speak "the principles or positions that oppose the majority discourses." One can then accept a plurality of reasons rather than one unitary reason in this way. By framing this concept in Kantian terms, Lyotard establishes an unspoken tension between modern and postmodern discourses, akin to what happens to American and Latin American readings of Menchú. See Best and Kellner, *Postmodern Theory*, quotes on 169.

13. Published in *The Rigoberta Menchú Controversy*.

14. This critique is further complicated by the reassessment of the notion of "Central Americanness." The view from the diaspora should challenge the various expressions of Latino essentialism and open up intellectual spaces for the active contestation of meanings with political and cultural implications for all ethnic and national representations originating in Latin America now present in the United States.

15. See Skinner-Klée's chapter in *The Rigoberta Menchú Controversy*.

16. It is unnecessary to reproduce here all the written psychoanalytical material on the Holocaust experience, which deals amply with this matter. From a more cultural approach, Žižek has also dealt with this problematic, as Chow reminds us. See Chow, *Ethics after Idealism*.

17. Derrida, "History of the Lie," 35.

18. In a letter to the *LASA Forum*, Stoll claimed that he had checked with Verso, publishers of *I, Rigoberta Menchú*. According to them, the number of sales had not been significantly reduced. However, I know for a fact that the University of California at Santa Cruz came close to banning the book; it was spared only by the energized efforts of Professor Susanne Jonas. I was also asked to speak at high schools in the Bay Area, where the children of colleagues of mine at San Francisco State University claimed that the book had been pulled after the controversy. Even at my own teaching institution, the University of Redlands, I had to justify both granting Ms. Menchú an honorary doctorate and teaching the text in an introductory course.

I also know that a former member of the LASA Executive Council prevented Ms. Menchú from receiving an honorary doctorate at the University of Notre Dame based on Stoll's arguments.

19. In *Ethics after Idealism*, Chow takes another look at the issue of cultural otherness. She argues that at a time when cultural identity has become imbricated with the way we read our many "others," what must be examined critically is no longer identity politics per se, but the idealism, especially in the sense of idealizing otherness, that lies at the heart of identity politics. Recognizing the need for a critique of idealism allows Chow to constitute a required set of ethics for the postcolonial age. In particular, she uses "ethics" to designate the act of making decisions—in her context, decisions of reading—that may not immediately conform with prevalent social mores of idealizing our others, but that, in spite of this, enable such others to emerge in their full complexity.

20. Armstrong, *The Radical Aesthetic*, 221–22.

21. John Beverley's *Against Literature* is emblematic of this type of reductionism. I admit that it is somewhat unfair to critique Beverley's position solely on the basis of this book, given that he reframes his arguments in a more sophisticated fashion in *Subalternity and Representation*, where he expresses the academy's difficulty in representing subaltern discourse, and by LASA 2004 he was publicly renouncing his 1995 position. However, his previous book has, for good or ill, had a decisive effect not only in interpretations of *testimonio* as a whole, but in interpretations of Menchú in particular. Nowadays it is easier to trace his evolution in defining the genre in his book *Testimonio: On the Politics of Truth* (2004).

22. See Hirschkop's meditation about the relation between language and ethics in the introduction to *Mikhail Bakhtin: An Aesthetic for Democracy*.

23. Read Arturo Taracena's account of the editing process in "Arturo Taracena Breaks His Silence."

24. This may be translated "To deceive desire is to deceive the will."

25. Berryman, *The Religious Roots of Rebellion*, 281. Berryman was a pastoral worker in Central America during the years when liberation theology took shape (1965–73). Later he was the Central American representative of the American Friends Service Committee (1976–80) until death threats in Guatemala forced him to return to the United States in 1980.

26. Hirschkop, *Mikhail Bakhtin*, 166.

27. Rajchman, "Ethics after Foucault," 166.

28. This idea is fully developed by Chow in "Ethics after Idealism."

7. The Burning of the Spanish Embassy

1. More will be said later about the condition of the bodies and possible causes of death.

2. Cajal's book has not yet been translated to English. All quotes from the book that appear in this chapter have been translated by Elizabeth Bell.

3. The page numbers given here are from Cajal, who quotes the document.

4. De Villa's e-mail, originally written in Spanish, was translated by Elizabeth Bell.

5. In April 2004 Spanish Judge Baltazar Garzón announced that he was traveling to Guatemala to depose General Lucas García because he had been accused of crimes against humanity and that the Spanish Court was open to prosecuting top Guatemalan military officers for the burning of the Spanish embassy and for related human rights violations. Lucas García, by then residing in Venezuela with a Venezuelan wife, was indicted in Spain, but the Venezuelan government refused to extradite him. He died there of natural causes in May 2006.

6. It was an unusual time to wage a battle against the *guerrillerista* left. This segment of the left had stopped being a factor after the Sandinista electoral defeat in February 1990, and even old Guatemalan and Salvadoran leftists were in government at the time. Latin America's "democratic" left, represented by new figures such as Hugo Chávez of Venezuela, Luis Ignacio da Silva Lula of Brazil, and Néstor Kirchner of Argentina, had not yet made their appearance when Stoll's book was published in 1998. Thus the only logical explanation for his action was that the book was aimed at an internal liberal-conservative divide within the United States itself, given the iconic role that Menchú's text played in the multiculturalism debate, or that its writing can be seen as a broader attempt to discredit whatever moral credibility the Latin American left still had left. The only other possible conclusion would be that Stoll rode the impeachment coattails for profit motives.

8. The Maya Movement

1. Sam Colop, "Ucha'xik: Del racismo subyacente," 13. All translations in this chapter are mine unless otherwise indicated. Here Sam Colop is saying that Clemente Marroquín reveals his underlying assumption that all Indians are savages when he says that it is not the fault of Indians if allegedly civilized public officials are acting "like Indians" (i.e., "like savages").

2. I closely follow Nestor García Canclini's analysis of "oblique powers" in *Culturas híbridas* (Hybrid cultures).

3. Brünner, *Globalización cultural y posmodernidad* (Cultural globalization and postmodernism), 11.

4. Payeras, *Los pueblos indígenas y la revolución guatemalteca*, 132.

5. A "Ladino" is the non-Maya mestizo subject. Aspiring to Westernness, this subject denies his or her own Maya origins, underlines his or her European ascendancy, or both.

6. Typical of this position is a paper by Mario Roberto Morales, "La articulación de las diferencias: El discurso literario y político en el debate interétnico en Guatemala," as well as his subsequent book, *Leyendas de Guatemala: Edición Crítica*. His newspaper columns in Guatemala's *Siglo XXI* emphasized this topic throughout 1997 and 1998.

7. Morales, "La articulación de las diferencias," 2.

8. Esquit Choy and Gálvez Borrel, *The Mayan Movement Today*, 44.

9. Morales, "La articulación de las diferencias," 3.

10. Ibid., 4.

11. Menchú, *Rigoberta: La nieta de los mayas*, 177–78.

12. Brünner, *Globalización cultural y posmodernidad*, 179.

13. Esquit Choy and Gálvez Borrel, *The Mayan Movement Today*, 85.

14. Pablo Ceto, personal communication, August 1983.

15. Demetrio Cojtí, personal communication, 18 August 1998.

16. Shetemul, "La esquina del Director," 2.

17. Morales, "La articulación de las diferencias," 4.

18. Casaús Arzú, *La metamorfosis del racismo en Guatemala*, 144.

19. See all writings by Demetrio Cojtí concerning this matter, especially *Ri Maya Moloj pa Iximuleu: El movimiento maya (en Guatemala)*.

20. Concerning this matter we can see, as one example among many, an editorial published in *Guatemala Hoy* on Tuesday, 8 September 1998: "'All the proposals and political initiatives of Maya organizations concerning the constitutional reforms presently being discussed in Congress, do not question relations among Guatemalans, but, rather, complement them,' affirmed the Defensoría Maya, when it ratified its will to contribute to the advancement of the Peace Process. 'In this historical moment,' their spokesperson argued, 'we have to avoid that certain political sectors take advantage of our proposals to create chaos by defending constitutional reforms that are not contemplated in the Peace Agreements,' said the representative of Defensoría. The organization 'regretted that some political parties do not take seriously their proposals for constitutional reform, and that certain government sectors demand that the Maya people renounce their own aspirations, accusing them of putting the peace process at risk.'" The article may be found at http://xelajuj.tripod.com/guatenews.htm (last accessed 12 December 2006).

21. Tuyuc, quoted by Olga López and Martín Rodríguez P. in an article in *Prensa Libre* titled "Indígenas rechazan ley: Consideran que norma es general y deja de lado identidad cultural" (Indigenous peoples reject law: They consider it generic, leaving cultural identity by the wayside).

22. Ibid.

23. Haroldo Shetemul, personal communication, 13 August 1998. This information was corroborated by Demetrio Cojtí in his personal communication of 18 August 1998. "Ex-PACs" are former "civil patrol" members. Civil patrols were counterinsurgency organizations created by the army at the peak of the armed conflict (1983–84).

24. The COMG was created on 20 June 1990 to coordinate Maya institutions. It integrated fifteen member organizations, both nongovernmental and academic. The COMG was also part of the Coordinadora de Organizaciones y Naciones Indígenas del Continente (Association of Indigenous Organizations and Nations of the Continent). See the book by Santiago Bastos and Manuela Camús, *Quebrando el silencio: Organizaciones del pueblo maya y sus demandas, 1986–1992*.

25. For a brief explanation of the *Popol Vuh,* see chapter 3 of this book.

26. Fischer and McKenna Brown, *Maya Cultural Activism in Guatemala,* 154.

27. Spence et al., "Who Governs?" 21.

28. There are other Mayas working in the commission. They are there as government workers, however, and they represent the government rather than Maya organizations.

29. See both "El 140 Encuentro de Editores termina con un homenaje a Pérez González," in *El País,* Saturday, 18 July 1998, p. 24, and "19 Nations See U.S. as a Threat to Their Cultures," in the *New York Times,* Wednesday, 1 July 1998, p. B1.

30. The position defended by Ladino intellectuals argues that to share hegemony, an interethnic negotiation has to take place. They understand this as a pact in which both sides negotiate under conditions of absolute equality. This is a fallacy to start with. Mayas cannot have "conditions of absolute equality" in an asymmetrical relation of power tinged with racism. As a first step to break this asymmetry, Mayas are constructing their subjectivity and gaining agency by employing many of the very symbolic elements that Ladinos disqualify.

31. Ladino strategy has consisted of cornering Maya leaders by negating the importance of Maya subjectivity on the basis that their discursivity is essentialist, fundamentalist, anti-Ladino, and guilty of reverse racism. To stop the hegemonic reversal of ethnic relations, "Ladinoists" have attempted to categorize all Maya leaders as essentialist without nuances of any kind so as to build a following among Ladino sectors that is, de facto, racist.

32. Moraña, *Indigenismo hacia el fin del milenio* (Indigenous issues at the end of the millennium).

33. These refer to three significant dates in the war on terrorism: 9/11 to 11 September 2001, the date of the attack on the World Trade Center in New York; 3/11 to 11 March 2004, the date of the attack on Madrid's Atocha station, and 7/7 to 7 July 2005, the date of the attack on the London Underground system.

9. Central American–Americans?

1. It was because of this that José Antonio Mazzotti organized a conference titled "What about the Other Latinos?" at Harvard University in April 2002.

2. Chow, *Writing Diaspora,* 12.

3. Lee, "Passing as Korean American," 285.

4. For a more historical approach to Central America–Mexico relations, see "American Central Americans: Invisibility and Representation in the Latino United States," chapter 10 in this book.

5. *Globalization* is a term that has made its way into contemporary culture to describe a variety of issues. On the cultural front, it refers to a tendency to homogenize culture all over the world, replacing local specificity with mass culture. In the economic realm, we assume it means the integration of markets and the increasing flows of capital, information, commodities, and people across national boundaries

and between continents. In politics it is often invoked to explain the decreasing power of the nation-state while more decisions are being made on the basis of transnational flows of capital. Current globalization tendencies have had an effect on the experience of race, gender, nationality, and class on a variety of different levels.

6. This development leaves traditional professors who focus on "national" literatures feeling somewhat unsettled about the nature of their discipline and where its boundaries might lie. Hence their defensiveness, witnessed at times when they want to hire an expert in, say, Mexican literature or Colombian literature, at a time when such notions are obsolete.

7. Appadurai, *Modernity at Large*, 31.

8. Similarly, terms that might be taken for granted in the United States, such as "majority" and "minority," only confuse these matters further, for they are new concepts for Central Americans that refer to social concepts such as "consensus" that did not exist in their own recent political experience.

9. Concerning this debate, see the opening of Juan Flores's chapter, "The Latino Imaginary: Dimensions of Community and Identity," in Frances R. Aparicio's and Susana Chávez Silverman's *Tropicalizations: Transcultural Representations of Latinidad.*

10. Another example is this: The Menchú Foundation is fund-raising in the United States and has offices in Mexico and New York as well as a presence in Europe by virtue of Menchú's global exposure as a human rights advocate. In a similar context, Mayas' control of the mayor's office in Quezaltenango, Guatemala's second city, has enabled them to sign and implement cooperation agreements with sister cities in Europe and Asia. Finally, the children of Maya academics in the United States speak English and a Maya language while sporting "punk" haircuts and taking marimba lessons.

11. Martín-Barbero, "Desencantos de la socialidad y reencantamientos de la identidad."

12. See Bhabha, *The Location of Culture.* These new terms of cultural engagement are the signs of the deployment of a new hybrid community. They are also the hopeful redefinition of a new spatialization or displacement of disenfranchised minorities with at least the prospect of new strategies of resistance to dynamize their subaltern subjectivities within a heterogeneous whole where new ways of making transnational connections already exist. We bring to mind Bhabha's assertion, in *Nation and Narration,* that nations are "narrative" constructions that arise from the "hybrid" interaction of contending cultural constituencies. In *The Location of Culture* he extends his explanation of the "liminal" or "interstitial" category that occupies a space "between" competing cultural traditions, historical periods, and critical methodologies. Bhabha examines the "ambivalence of colonial rule" and seeks to find the "location of culture" in the marginal, "haunting," "unhomely" spaces between dominant social formations.

13. Tedlock (trans.), *Popol Vuh*, 71–72.

14. We understand this concept in Baudrillard's sense, without forgetting that

the author himself warned us about iconoclasts who destroyed images of God because they knew of his nonexistence. In other words, we understand it by problematizing this signifier and placing ourselves inside its own instability so as not to be
reduced in a simplistic way to the notion of a cheap, ordinary imitation.

15. Tedlock, quoted by Adorno in "Cultures in Contact," 32–33.

16. The bulk of discursive elements that explain the particular identity of Central America as a whole—but especially those of Guatemala, whose linguistic traces
are tangled in a very intimate manner with Maya culture—can be found in this
first hybrid multicultural and heteroglossic text. It is the first post-Conquest expression of an entire set of discursive practices that creates an alternative subjectivity
to the one employed by most outsiders to the region: that of the Latin American
"mestizo" or mixed Indian-Spanish subject.

17. Usually this is done by deploying a hybrid, convoluted syntax that often leads
traditional critics to dismiss it as "baroque literature" without weighing its cultural
implications.

18. Williams, *The Other Side of the Popular*, 199.

19. The Mara Salvatrucha is a Los Angeles–based gang formed in the 1980s that
is involved in various criminal activities from Panama to the United States. The
gang's name is commonly abbreviated MS-13 (*mara* is Central American Spanish
for "gang"; *salvatrucha* means something like "wily Salvadoran; the number thirteen
is a reference to the thirteenth parallel, the location of El Salvador), and its members are mostly Salvadorans or Salvadoran-Americans. The first large population
of El Salvadoran refugees settled in the Rampart area of Los Angeles. This influx of
immigrants looking for low-cost housing and employment was not readily welcomed by the members of the Mexican-American population who were already
residing in that area. The area was already plagued with gangs and crime. For self-
defense purposes, the Mara Salvatrucha was founded in this area, expanding along
migratory routes. With arrests and deportations to Central America, the gang was
able to expand in its country of origin and easily monopolize crime in the Central
American region. The Mara Salvatrucha has factions in all cities of the United
States and is unique in that it retains its ties to its Salvadoran counterparts. Gang
members have tattoos on their bodies and faces and wear blue and white colors
taken from the Salvadoran flag. According to the FBI, their membership totals over
fifty thousand in the United States alone, and their criminal activities include drug
smuggling and sales; gun running; human trafficking, including near-monopoly
control of bringing illegals to the United States from Central America; committing
theft, arson, and assassination for hire; and strong-arming the locals.

20. The Mara 18 gang was also born in Los Angeles in the 1980s, on Eighteenth
Street. The name Mara 18 can be translated as "Eighteenth Street Gang." Most members of the Mara 18 are Hondurans or Honduran-Americans. However, because
there are smaller numbers of Hondurans than Salvadorans in the United States,
this gang incorporates many more Mexican-Americans and Guatemalan-Americans
than does the MS-13. Its members compete for territory and activities with members

of the Mara Salvatrucha. They are known for human smuggling, prostitution, and extortion and are known by tattoos of roman numerals or the names of the gangs on their bodies. Their bodily markings are symbols of a powerful wordless identification system among themselves as gang members. They claim that they are not as "savage" as members of the MS-13, but they constantly engage in turf wars with the Salvatruchas in Central America as well as in U.S. cities.

21. Williams, *The Other Side of the Popular*, 203.

22. Bhabha, *The Location of Culture*, 78, emphasis in original.

23. Williams, *The Other Side of the Popular*, 211.

10. American Central Americans

1. Some critics have noted that Francisco Goldman's *The Long Night of White Chickens* (1992) is the first Central American Latino text. However, Goldman's identity is that of a binational writer: Goldman was the son of an American living in Guatemala, who acquired his knowledge of the country while attending an American school there for some years. Others have pointed to Carlos René García Escobar's *La llama del retorno* (1987). However, this novel, though it deals with Los Angeles immigrant life, was written in Spanish for a Guatemalan audience by a writer who spent only a short period in California, and the book has never been translated into English. In this sense, Tobar's novel fits the mold of being a true Latino novel: it was written in English by the son of an immigrant Guatemalan couple who was raised in the United States within an immigrant Latino community, and it narrates some of the activities of this same community in the United States.

2. In the previous chapter, "Central American–Americans?" I stated that we need to think of the definition of categories such as "Central American" as multiple and discontinuous, not as having "ontological integrity." We can all be Central Americans only to the degree that we accept a history of identifications generated by the isthmus's "grand narrative" of a mythical geopolitical unity that has existed since the time of the ancient Mayas two thousand years ago. We can always activate any part of this history of identifications, and it can be invoked in new contexts, such as that of the present-day diaspora and exile.

3. Subjectivity is, after all, a transgressive position that reconfigures traditional understandings of the self, the nation, and citizenhood. In this respect, the textual in-betweenness enacts a space of resistance that critiques a normativity conceived within the parameters of ethnic sameness.

4. As Barkan and Shelton argue in *Borders, Exiles, Diasporas*, the concept of "diaspora" is an explanatory paradigm that creates a "nonnormative" community in which "the restoration of a collective sense of identity and historical agency in the home country may well be mediated through the diaspora" (5). Thus, diasporic identity provides only aleatory responses that are discontinuous and open-ended while intertwining the margins and the center.

5. It must be noted, as some critics have observed, that Mexican-American

authors such as Helena María Viramontes and Demetria Martínez, who was involved in the Sanctuary Movement to harbor Salvadoran war refugees in the 1980s, have also explored these identity issues about invisibility, silence, and representation among Central Americans. Moreover, their texts also deal with the relational identities between Salvadorans and Mexican-Americans within the United States.

6. Hamilton and Stoltz Chinchilla, *Seeking Community in a Global City*, 2.

7. A similar point was made in the *Los Angeles Times* in an article titled "Why the Whitewashing of Alicia Nash?" by Lisa Navarrete. In it Navarrete argues: "We could have witnessed the portrayal of a true rarity—a three-dimensional Latina role model—by a well-known, critically acclaimed actress. Even better, this could have provided a career-making opportunity to a Latina actress. . . . At the very least, [director Ron] Howard and [writer Akiva] Goldsman owe the Latino community an explanation."

8. Since I published this chapter as an article in *Explicación de textos literarios*, Claudia Milian has pointed out to me that supermodel Christy Turlington is also of Salvadoran origin, though her father was an American, a pilot for Pan Am. Milian herself has published a chapter on this matter, "Fashioning United States Salvadoranness: Unveiling the Faces of Christy Turlington and Rosa López," published in *The Latin American Fashion Reader*, edited by Regina A. Root.

9. See the previous chapter, "Central American–Americans?"

10. In Aparicio and Chávez-Silverman, *Tropicalizations: Transcultural Representations of Latinidad*.

11. See Sommer, *Proceed with Caution*.

12. Jorge Tetzagüic, a Guatemalan immigrant who works with Latino urban gangs, argues that young Central Americans do not necessarily think of themselves as such. They mainly articulate their point by saying that "they don't feel comfortable with Mexicans, they don't feel comfortable with South Americans, but they feel comfortable in the company and complicity of other Central Americans, even though they themselves have not thought of a Central American identity." Jorge Tetzagüic, personal communication, Cambridge, Massachusetts, 6 April 2002. The statistical category "other Central Americans" displayed by Michael Jones-Correa in the graphs he employs in his paper "Swimming in the Latino Sea: The 'Other' Latinos and Politics" might also point to a small segment of the Central American population in the United States that chooses not to identify itself by national origin (Guatemalan-American or Salvadoran-American, for example). A few individuals, such as poet Maya Chinchilla, have also expressed themselves publicly about feeling more "Central American–American" than "Guatemalan-American."

13. See Flores's "Life off the Hyphen: Latino Literature and Nuyorican Traditions" (2001), a response to Pérez-Firmat's *Life on the Hyphen: The Cuban-American Way* (1994).

14. Spivak, *A Critique of Postcolonial Reason*, 119.

15. For me this is emblematic of the situation that I myself have lived, though I have not suffered the fate of many of my compatriots, who have experienced this

multiple marginalization in a more dramatic, tortured, or tragic fashion. We are natives, too, as Spivak reminds Benita Parry when she criticizes her for not letting the subaltern speak. "We talk like Defoe's Friday, only much better" (Spivak, *A Critique of Postcolonial Reason,* 190).

16. Pete Sigal comments on this in *From Moon Goddesses to Virgins.* See especially p. 41 for an analogous analysis of this matter.

17. These images have been developed further in my novel *Jaguar en llamas* (1989).

18. See Harris, *Aztecs, Moors, and Christians,* especially the section headed "The Conquest of Rhodes (Mexico City, 1539)," beginning on p. 123.

19. Harris, *Aztecs, Moors, and Christians,* 123.

20. Sigal, *From Moon Goddesses to Virgins,* 44.

21. Ibid., 61.

22. This theme is the focus of my analysis of the character Kukulkán in Asturias's *Leyendas de Guatemala* (Legends of Guatemala) in "El nacimiento del neo-indigenismo: Quetzalcoatl Resimbolizado." The symbolic feminization of Maya warriors might also explain why in modern times the greatest insult in the region, beyond the much-belabored *hijo de la chingada,* is *hueco,* a euphemism for "gay." In the Iberian world a "hueco" is not the "top" male, the male who penetrates another male, but the "bottom" or penetrated one.

23. Cook, *Renewing the Maya World,* 23.

24. Goldberg, *The Racial State,* 4.

25. I simply note the phenomenon here. Elsewhere one might problematize both the nature of this filmic representation and the negative effect these scenes had on Mexican-American viewers during the 1980s.

26. Indeed it was the experience of most Guatemalan exiles in Mexico during the twentieth century that they were welcomed with open arms in that country, offered jobs, given residence papers, and provided all sorts of solidarity, both human and political. I myself benefited from this in the 1980s.

27. I am referring here to Foucault's description of modernity in "What is Enlightenment?"

28. Guatemalan immigrants José Mercedes Sotz, René Funes, and Byron Titus spoke openly to me of their ambivalence in relating to Mexican immigrants. Personal communication, Cambridge, Massachusetts, 6 April 2002.

29. Morales, quoted in Cowy Kim and Alfonso, *izote vos,* 66.

30. I am referring here to things that have traditionally been a burden, such as learning a new language and culture, separating from loved ones, and enduring the resentment of a hostile population, which in this particular case includes Latinos from other national groups who have arrived earlier.

31. I prefer the term *performative transvestism,* which underlines the performative aspect of identity as delineated by Judith Butler's work, rather than similar terms, like *cultural transvestism,* which has been used by young critics like Jossiana Arroyo in presentations such as "Carnaval, masculinidad y máscaras de la identidad en Cuba

y Brasil: El travestismo cultural de Fernando Ortiz," to contextualize some Cuban, Brazilian, and Latino writers.

32. Here it might be useful to remember the distinction that Slavoj Žižek makes in speaking of imaginary identification as an imagined resemblance to an image that can be seen and symbolic identification as an imagined resemblance to the way we think we look to others, thus appearing in a certain way, likable or contemptible, to ourselves. See Žižek, *Gaze and Voice as Love Objects*. Rey Chow has already commented on this in *Ethics after Idealism*, 41–42.

33. Guatemalan immigrants José Mercedes Sotz and René Funes spoke openly with me of this fear, which prevents the community from organizing itself in the United States. Personal communication, Cambridge, Mass., 6 April 2002.

34. These reflections closely follow Brandt's analysis of the Jews in the Nazi regime in her article "Sharing the Unsharable." There is an obvious similarity between the Holocaust experience and the Central American genocides in both 1932 and the 1980s.

35. It is in this context that Hamilton and Stoltz Chinchilla find in their sociological research that "children and young people were totally desensitized to violence" (*Seeking Community in a Global City*, 52). They also note that Central Americans came to the United States under similar traumatic circumstances as the population of Southeast Asia, but although the latter had legal status and were entitled to U.S. economic assistance, Central Americans were not recognized as refugees by the U.S. government and rarely obtained political asylum. As a result, their fear of deportation became an obsession that enhanced the trauma of the "originary terror." That is why Hamilton and Stoltz Chinchilla conclude by saying: "Salvadorans and Guatemalans could not be welcomed as refugees or entitled to asylum. Their undocumented status shaped their experiences and limited their options in coping with the psychological and emotional scars they brought with them" (53).

36. In the original Spanish: "¿Por qué no mejor se queda callado?"

37. In the original Spanish: "Eso sería lo más fácil, ¿verdad Neto? Pero no. Cuando hay que hablar, hay que hablar. Cómo te parecés a tu mamá. Tan callado como ella. . . . Tan callado como todo este país. Neto, ese silencio no es bueno. Nos lo metieron adentro desde que nacemos, pero hay que luchar hasta sacarlo por completo. Entonces podremos respirar."

38. Gutierrez, quoted in Cowy Kim and Alfonso, *izote vos*, 28.

39. Martínez Pimentel, quoted in Cowy Kim and Alfonso, *izote vos*, 59.

40. As I have indicated in the previous chapter, "Central American–Americans?," descriptions also run the risk of homogenizing what is in reality a very heterogeneous community. We must remember that the cultural displacement and identity politics that characterize Central Americans not only contrast with those of other Latino groups within the United States, but also differ greatly among them.

41. See Mahler's book *American Dreaming*. Her study focuses on a group of Salvadoran immigrants who settled on Long Island. Mahler critically examines academic theories about immigrant behavior and communities to argue that marginalization fosters antagonism within ethnic groups while undermining ethnic solidarity.

42. Laó-Montes, introduction to *Mambo Montage: The Latinization of New York*, 17, 18.

43. Chow, *Women and Chinese Modernity*, xvii.

Conclusion

1. García Canclini, "Aesthetic Moments of Latin Americanism."

2. *El País*, Friday, 1 July 2005, 31. In the original Spanish: "Porque una sociedad decente es aquella que no humilla a sus miembros." All translations in this chapter are mine unless otherwise indicated.

3. Originally a Salvadoran airline with capital from Pan American, TACA (Transportes Aéreos Centro Americanos, or Central American Air Transport) bought all other Central American national airlines in the wake of neoliberal globalization in the early 1990s. It is now a truly Central American airline, with headquarters in San Salvador.

4. Belli's *The Country under My Skin: A Memory of Love and War*, Cardenal's *Vida perdida* (Lost life), and Ramírez's *Adios muchachos: Una memoria de la revolución sandinista* (Goodbye my friends: A memoir of the Sandinista revolution).

5. The other problem, pointed out by García Canclini, is an aesthetic one. We are at a moment in which criticism distrusts, or even ignores, aesthetics. Nevertheless, those revelations that form the basis of artistic creation continue to be there. To my way of thinking, what matters about aesthetics, to follow the example of Berger, is to determine who is playing the power/knowledge relations. In other words, the problem does not lie with aesthetics itself. Rather, it lies with whether the captured instant represented aesthetically is the result of someone's agency-imbued initiative or a reified symbolic object generated purely for consumer purposes. Allergic to the consumer market, critical thought has turned antiaesthetic in the last twenty-five years or so. It is necessary to rethink aesthetics from a new critical stance that is capable of explaining the roles that both affection and emotions play in contemporary culture.

6. My contribution is titled "Latin America and Globalization: Response to Jeremy Adelman's Paper."

7. Arias, "Latin America and Globalization." 13; quoted in Moreiras, *The Exhaustion of Difference*, 77.

8. Foucault problematizes the crusader for universality in "Truth and Power." Mark Poster develops this in "Sartre's Concept of the Intellectual," in his *Critical Theory and Poststructuralism: In Search of a Context*. See especially pp. 36–38.

9. Poster, "Sartre's Concept of the Intellectual," 48.

10. In a very random way, as I wrote the previous line, I thought of an array of books in which this very thing happened, across the spectrum of academic disciplines. Without favoring any, among those that popped into my mind were William I. Robinson's *Transnational Conflicts: Central America, Social Change, and Globalization;* June C. Nash's *Mayan Visions: The Quest for Autonomy in an Age of Globalization;*

María Josefina Saldaña-Portillo's *The Revolutionary Imagination in the Americas and the Age of Development;* Diane M. Nelson's *A Finger in the Wound: Body Politics in Quincentennial Guatemala;* and George Yúdice's *The Expediency of Culture.*

11. These refer to three significant dates in the war on terrorism: 11 September 2001, the date of the attack on the World Trade Center in New York; 11 March 2004, the date of the attack on Madrid's Atocha station; and 7 July 2005, the date of the attack on the London Underground system.

Bibliography

Adelman, Jeremy. "Latin America and Globalization." *LASA Forum* 29, no. 1 (1998): 10–12.

Adorno, Rolena. "Cultures in Contact: Mesoamerica, the Andes, and the European Written Tradition." In *The Cambridge History of Latin American Literature*, vol. 1, *Discovery to Modernism,* ed. Roberto González Echevarría and Enrique Pupo-Walker. Cambridge, England: Cambridge University Press, 1996, 33–57.

Alegría, Claribel, and Darwin Flakoll. *Ashes of Izalco.* Willimantic, Conn.: Curbstone, 1989.

———. *Cenizas de Izalco.* Barcelona: Seix Barral, 1966.

———. *Death of Somoza.* Willimantic, Conn.: Curbstone, 1996.

———. *No me agarran viva: La mujer salvadoreña en lucha.* Mexico City: ERA, 1983.

———. *Somoza, la historia de un ajusticiamiento.* Managua: Editorial el Gato Negro/Latino Editores, 1993.

———. *They Won't Take Me Alive: Salvadorean Women in Struggle for National Liberation.* London: The Women's Press. 1987.

Aparicio, Frances R., and Susana Chávez-Silverman, eds. *Tropicalizations: Transcultural Representations of Latinidad.* Hanover, N.H.: Dartmouth University Press, 1997.

Appadurai, Arjun. *Modernity at Large: Cultural Dimensions of Globalization.* Minneapolis: University of Minnesota Press, 1996.

Arguedas, José María. *Todas las sangres.* Buenos Aires: Losada, 1968.

Arias, Arturo. "Historia del Movimiento Indígena en Guatemala, 1970–1983." In *Movimientos populares en America Central,* ed. Rafael Menjívar and Daniel Camacho. San José, Costa Rica: Ediciones FLACSO, 1985.

———. "After the Rigoberta Menchú Controversy: Lessons Learned about the Nature of Subalternity and the Specifics of the Indigenous Subject." *MLN* 117, no. 2 (2002): 481–505.

————. "Authoring Ethnicized Subjects: Rigoberta Menchú and the Performative Production of the Subaltern Self." *PMLA* 116, no. 1 (2001): 75–88.

————. "Central American-Americans? Re-mapping Latino/Latin American Subjectivities on Both Sides of the Great Divide." *Explicación de Textos Literarios* 28, nos. 1–2 (1999–2000).

————. "Forum on Anthropology in Public: Consciousness, Violence, and the Politics of Memory in Guatemala. Comments to Charles R. Hale." *Current Anthropology* 38, no. 5 (1997).

————. *Gestos ceremoniales: narrativa centroamericana, 1960–1990.* Guatemala City: Artemis-Edinter, 1998.

————. *La identidad de la palabra: narrativa guatemalteca a la luz del siglo veinte.* Guatemala City: Artemis-Edinter, 1998.

————. *Ideología, literatura y sociedad durante la revolución guatemalteca, 1944–1954.* Havana: Casa de las Américas, 1979.

————. *Jaguar en llamas.* Guatemala City: Editorial Cultura, 1989.

————. "Latin America and Globalization: Response to Jeremy Adelman's Paper." *LASA Forum* 29, no. 1 (1998): 12–15.

————. "El nacimiento del neo-indigenismo: Quetzalcoatl resimbolizado." In *Leyendas de Guatemala: Edición Crítica,* ed. Mario Roberto Morales. Madrid: Archivos, 2000.

————. "La psique interior de los guatemaltecos, las cuestiones del biculturalismo." *Mesoamérica* 34 (1997).

————. "Shifts in Indian Identity: Guatemala's Violent Transition to Modernity." In *Guatemalan Indians and the State, 1540 to 1988,* ed. Carol Smith. Austin: University of Texas Press, 1990.

————, ed. *Mulata de tal de Miguel Angel Asturias: Edición crítica.* Madrid: Archivos, 2001.

————. *The Rigoberta Menchú Controversy.* Minneapolis: University of Minnesota Press, 2001.

Arias, Arturo, and Gilberto Arriaza. "Claiming Collective Memory: Mayan Languages and Civil Rights." *Social Justice* 25, no. 3 (1998): 70–79.

Armijo, Roberto. *El asma de Leviatán.* San Salvador: UCA, 1990.

Armstrong, Isobel. *The Radical Aesthetic.* Oxford, UK: Blackwell, 2000.

Arreola, Aura Marina. "Guatemala: Contrainsurgencia y guerra de exterminio." *ENIAL* (1982): 19–23.

Arroyo, Jossiana. "Carnaval, masculinidad y máscaras de la identidad en Cuba y Brasil: El travestismo cultural de Fernando Ortiz." Presentation at Cuban Counterpoints: The Fernando Ortiz Symposium on Cuban Culture and History, 22 March 2000, The Graduate Center, City University of New York.

Asturias, Miguel Angel. *Hombres de maíz.* Buenos Aires: Losada, 1949.

————. *Hombres de maíz: Edición crítica.* Coord. Gerald Martin. Madrid: Archivos, 1992.

————. *Leyendas de Guatemala.* Madrid: Oriente, 1930.

————. *Men of Maize.* Trans. Gerald Martin. Pittsburgh: University of Pittsburgh Press, 1995.

————. *The Mirror of Lida Sal: Tales Based on Mayan Myths and Guatemalan Legends.* Trans. Gilbert Alter-Gilbert. Pittsburgh: Latin American Literary Review Press, 1997.

————. *Mulata.* Trans. Gregory Rabassa. New York: Seymour Lawrence/Delacorte Press, 1967.

————. *Mulata de tal.* Buenos Aires: Losada, 1963.

————. *Mulata de tal de Miguel Angel Asturias: Edición crítica.* Ed. Arturo Arias. Madrid: Archivos, 2001.

Avelar, Idelber. *The Untimely Present: Postdictatorial Latin American Fiction and the Task of Mourning.* Durham, N.C.: Duke University Press, 1999.

Bakhtin, M. M. *The Dialogic Imagination.* Ed. Michael Holquist. Trans. Caryl Emerson and Michael Holquist. Austin: University of Texas Press, 1981.

————. *Speech Genres and Other Late Essays.* Trans. Vern W. McGee. Ed. Caryl Emerson and Michael Holquist. Austin: University of Texas Press, 1986.

————. *Toward a Philosophy of the Act.* Trans. Vadim Liapunov. Austin: University of Texas Press, 1993.

Balibar, Etienne, and Wallerstein, Immanuel. *Race, Nation, Class: Ambiguous Identities.* Trans. Chris Turner. New York: Verso, 1991.

Barkan, Elazar, and Marie-Denise Shelton, eds. *Borders, Exiles, Diasporas.* Stanford, Calif.: Stanford University Press, 1998.

Bastos, Santiago, and Manuela Camús. *Quebrando el silencio: Organizaciones del pueblo maya y sus demandas, 1986–1992.* Guatemala City: FLACSO, 1996.

Bataille, Georges. *Oeuvres complètes,* vol. 1. Paris: Gallimard, 1970.

————. *Story of the Eye.* Trans. Joachim Neugroschel. San Francisco: City Lights, 1987.

Belli, Gioconda. *The Country under My Skin: A Memory of Love and War.* Trans. Kristina Cordero. New York: Knopf, 2002.

————. *The Inhabited Woman.* Trans. Kathleen March. Willimantic, Conn.: Curbstone, 1994.

————. *La mujer habitada.* Managua: Editorial Vanguardia, 1988.

————. *El pergamino de la seducción.* Barcelona: Seix Barral, 2005.

————. *Sofía de los presagios.* Managua: Editorial Vanguardia, 1990.

Bencastro, Mario. *Odyssey to the North.* Trans. Susan Giersbach Rascon. Houston: Arte Publico Press, 1998.

Benítez Rojo, Antonio. *The Repeating Island: The Caribbean and the Postmodern Perspective.* Trans. James E. Maraniss. Durham, N.C.: Duke University Press, 1996.

Berryman, Phillip. *The Religious Roots of Rebellion: Christians in Central American Revolutions.* Maryknoll, N.Y.: Orbis Books, 1984.

Best, Steven, and Douglas Kellner. *Postmodern Theory: Critical Interrogations.* New York: Guilford, 1991.

Beverley, John. *Against Literature.* Minneapolis: University of Minnesota Press, 1993.

————. *Subalternity and Representation: Arguments in Cultural Theory.* Durham N.C.: Duke University Press, 1999.

————. *Testimonio: On the Politics of Truth.* Minneapolis: University of Minnesota Press, 2004.

Bhabha, Homi. *The Location of Culture.* London: Routledge, 1994.

————. *Nation and Narration.* London: Routledge, 1990.

Biggs, Melissa. "An Open and Shut Case: Mexico's National Museum of Anthropology." http://www.planeta.com/planeta/00/0010mexicomuseum.html.

Blandón, Erick. *Vuelo de cuervos.* Managua: Vanguardia, 1997.

Bourdieu, Pierre. *The Field of Cultural Production: Essays on Art and Literature.* New York: Columbia University Press, 1994.

Brandt, Joan. "Sharing the Unsharable: Jabès, Deconstruction, and the Thought of the 'Jews.'" In *Borders, Exiles, Diasporas,* ed. Elazar Barkan and Marie-Denise Shelton. Stanford, Calif.: Stanford University Press, 1998.

Brotherston, Gordon. *Book of the Fourth World: Reading the Native Americas through Their Literature.* Cambridge, England: Cambridge University Press, 1992.

Brünner, José Joaquín. *Globalización cultural y posmodernidad.* Santiago: Fondo de Cultura Económica, 1998.

Buchsbaum, Herbert. "On the Trail of the Maya in Belize." *New York Times,* 7 April 2002, Travel Section, 10–12.

Burgos-Debray, Elisabeth. *I, Rigoberta Menchú: An Indian Woman in Guatemala.* London: Verso, 1984.

————. *Me llamo Rigoberta Menchú y así me nació la conciencia.* Havana: Casa de las Américas, 1983.

Butler, Judith. *Excitable Speech: A Politics of the Performative.* New York: Routledge, 1997.

————. *Gender Trouble.* New York: Routledge, 1990.

Cabarrús, Carlos. *La cosmovisión k'ekchí en proceso de cambio.* San Salvador: UCA, 1979.

Cajal, Máximo. *¡Saber quién puso fuego ahí! Masacre en la embajada de España.* Madrid: Siddartha Mehta, 2000.

Cardenal, Ernesto. *Canto cósmico.* Managua: Nueva Nicaragua, 1989.

————. *El estrecho dudoso.* San José, Costa Rica: EDUCA, 1971.

————. *Vida perdida.* Barcelona: Seix Barral, 1999.

Carey, David, Jr. *Our Elders Teach Us: Maya-Kaqchikel Historical Perspectives: Xkib'ij Kan Qate' Qatata'.* Tuscaloosa: University of Alabama Press, 2002.

————. "Overcoming Geographic and Linguistic Barriers to Foment Cross-Cultural Learning: Maya History in a Southern Maine Classroom." http://research.usm .maine.edu/articles/article_10.stm. Last accessed 8 December 2006.

Carías, Marcos. *Función con mobiles y tentetiesos.* Tegucigalpa: Guaymuras, 1980.

Carmack, Robert. "The Story of Santa Cruz Quiché." In *Harvest of Violence: The Maya Indians and the Guatemalan Crisis,* ed. Robert M. Carmack. Norman: University of Oklahoma Press, 1988, 39–69.

Carmack, Robert, and Francisco Morales Santos, eds. *Nuevas perspectivas sobre el Popol Vuh*. Guatemala City: Piedra Santa, 1983.

Casaús Arzú, Marta. *Guatemala: Linaje y racismo*. San José, Costa Rica: FLACSO, 1995.

———. *La metamorfosis del racismo en Guatemala*. Guatemala City: Cholsamaj, 1998.

Castellanos Moya, Horacio. *El asco*. San Salvador: Arcoiris, 1997

———. *Donde no estén ustedes*. Mexico City: Tusquets, 2003.

Castillo, Otto René, ed. *Informe de una injusticia*. San José, Costa Rica: EDUCA, 1975.

Chakrabarty, Dipesh. *Provincializing Europe: Postcolonial Thought and Historical Difference*. Princeton, N.J.: Princeton University Press, 2000.

Chamix, Pedro. "La importancia revolucionaria de conocer los movimientos indígenas." *Polémica* 3 (January–February 1982): 47–57.

Chase, Alfonso. *Cuerpos*. San José: Editorial Costa Rica, 1972.

———. *Los juegos furtivos*. San José: Editorial Costa Rica, 1968.

Chávez Alfaro, Lizandro. *Trágame tierra*. Mexico City: Editorial Dióógenes, 1969.

Chem Sham, Jorge. "Complejidad narrativa y principio autobiográfico en *Pobrecito poeta que era yo . . . .*" In *Otros Roques: La poética múltiple de Roque Dalton*, ed. Rafael Lara-Martínez and Dennis L. Seager. New Orleans: University Press of the South, 1999, 167–81.

Chow, Rey. *Ethics after Idealism: Theory—Culture—Ethnicity—Reading*. Bloomington: Indiana University Press, 1998.

———. *Women and Chinese Modernity: The Politics of Reading between West and East*. Minneapolis: University of Minnesota Press, 1991.

———. *Writing Diaspora: Tactics of Intervention in Contemporary Cultural Studies (Arts and Politics of the Everyday)*. Bloomington: Indiana University Press, 1993.

Cojtí Cuxil, Demetrio. "The Politics of Maya Revindication." In *Maya Cultural Activism in Guatemala*, ed. Edward F. Fischer, and R. McKenna Brown. Austin: University of Texas Press, 1996, 19–50.

———. *Ri Maya Moloj pa Iximuleu: El movimiento maya (en Guatemala)*. Guatemala City: IWGIA-Cholsamaj, 1997.

Contreras, Ana Yolanda. "¿Pero existe la nación guatemalteca? Nociones y perspectivas sobre la identidad y la nación a través de la novelística indígena de Gaspar Pedro González." *Diáspora* 14 (2004): 48–55.

Cook, Garrett W. *Renewing the Maya World: Expressive Culture in a Highland Town*. Austin: University of Texas Press, 2000.

Cornejo Polar, Antonio. *Escribir en el aire: Ensayo sobre la heterogeneidad socio-cultural en las literaturas andinas*. Lima: CELACP-Latinoamericana Editores, 2003.

———. "Indigenismo and Heterogeneous Literatures: Their Double Sociocultural Statute." In *The Latin American Cultural Studies Reader*, ed. Ana del Sarto, Alicia Ríos, and Abril Trigo. Durham, N.C.: Duke University Press, 2004, 100–115.

———. "*Mestizaje* and Hybridity: The Risks of Metaphors—Notes." In *The Latin*

American Cultural Studies Reader, ed. Ana del Sarto, Alicia Ríos, and Abril Trigo. Durham, N.C.: Duke University Press, 2004, 760–64.

Cortázar, Julio. *Hopscotch.* Trans. Gregory Rabassa. New York: Pantheon, 1966.

———. *Rayuela.* Buenos Aires: Sudamericana, 1963.

Cortés, Carlos. *Cruz de Olvido.* Mexico City: Alfaguara, 1999.

Cowy Kim, Katherine, and Serrano F. Alfonso, eds. *izote vos: A Collection of Salvadoran American Writing and Visual Art.* San Francisco: Pacific News Service, 2000.

Culler, Jonathan. *Literary Theory: A Very Short Introduction.* Oxford: Oxford University Press, 2000.

Dalton, Roque. *Historias prohibidas del Pulgarcito.* Mexico City: Siglo Veintiuno, 1980.

———. *Miguel Mármol: Los sucesos de 1932 en El Salvador.* San José, Costa Rica: EDUCA, 1973.

———. *Miguel Marmol: A Testimony.* Trans. Kathleen Ross and Richard Schaaf. Willimantic, Conn.: Curbstone, 1987.

———. "Otto René Castillo: Su ejemplo y nuestra responsabilidad." In *Informe de una injusticia,* ed. Otto René Castillo. San José, Costa Rica: EDUCA, 1975.

———. *Pobrecito poeta que era yo . . . .* San José, Costa Rica: EDUCA, 1976.

De Certeau, Michel. *The Practice of Everyday Life.* Trans. Steven Rendall. Berkeley: University of California Press, 1984.

Deleuze, Gilles. *Masochism.* Trans. Jean McNeil. New York: Zone Books, 1991.

Derrida, Jacques. "De l'économie restreinte à l'économie générale." In *L'écriture et la différence.* Paris: Seuil, 1967.

———. *Dissemination.* Trans. Barbara Johnson. Chicago: University of Chicago Press, 1981.

———. "History of the Lie: Proglomena." In *Without Alibi,* trans. Peggy Kamuf. Stanford, Calif.: Stanford University Press, 2002, 28–70.

———. *Writing and Difference.* Trans. Alan Bass. Chicago: University of Chicago Press, 1978.

Dussel, Enrique. *Etica de la liberación en la edad de la globalización y de la exclusión.* Madrid: Trotta, 1998.

Earle, Duncan. "Menchú Tales and Maya Social Landscapes: The Silencing of Words and Worlds." In *The Rigoberta Menchú Controversy,* ed. Arturo Arias. Minneapolis: University of Minnesota Press, 2001.

Echeverría, Maurice. *Labios.* Guatemala City: Magna Terra, 2003.

England, Nora. *Autonomía de los idiomas Mayas: Historia e identidad. Rukutamil, Ramaq'il, Rutzijob'al; Ri Mayab Amaq'.* Guatemala City: Cholsamaj, 1992.

———. "Doing Mayan Linguistics in Guatemala." *Language* 68, no. 1 (1992): 24–31.

———. "The Role of Language Standardization in Revitalization." *In Maya Cultural Activism in Guatemala,* ed. Edward F. Fischer and R. McKenna Brown. Austin: University of Texas Press, 1996.

Escudos, Jacinta. *A-B-sudario.* Guatemala City: Alfaguara, 2003.

Esquit Choy, Alberto, and Víctor Gálvez Borrel. *The Mayan Movement Today: Issues of Indigenous Culture and Development in Guatemala.* Guatemala City: FLACSO, 1997.

Falla, Ricardo. "El movimiento indígena." *ECA* 353 (1978): 438–61.

———. *Quiché Rebelde.* Guatemala City: Editorial Universitaria, 1978.

Ferman, Claudia, ed. *The Postmodern in Latin and Latino American Cultural Narratives.* New York: Garland, 1996.

Fink, Leon. *The Maya of Morgantown: Work and Community in the Nuevo New South.* Chapel Hill: University of North Carolina Press, 2003.

Fischer, Edward F., and McKenna Brown, R. *Maya Cultural Activism in Guatemala.* Austin: University of Texas Press, 1996.

Flores, Juan. "The Latino Imaginary: Dimensions of Community and Identity." In *Tropicalizations: Transcultural Representations of Latinidad,* ed. Frances R. Aparicio and Susana Chávez Silverman. Hanover, N.H.: Dartmouth University Press, 1997.

———. "Life off the Hyphen: Latino Literature and Nuyorican Traditions." In *Mambo Montage: The Latinization of New York,* ed. Agustín Laó-Montes and Arlene Dávila. New York: Columbia University Press, 2001.

Flores, Ronald. *The señores of Xibláblá.* Guatemala City: Palo de Hormigo, 2003.

Foucault, Michel. *Power/Knowledge: Selected Interviews and Other Writings, 1972–1977.* Ed. and trans. Colin Gordon. New York: Pantheon, 1980.

———. "Preface to Transgression." In *Language, Countermemory, Practice,* ed. Donald F. Bouchard. Ithaca, N.Y.: Cornell University Press, 1977, 29–52.

———. "What Is Enlightenment?" In *Power/Knowledge: Selected Interviews and Other Writings, 1972–1977.* Ed. and trans. Colin Gordon. New York: Pantheon, 1980.

Franco, Jean. *The Decline and Fall of the Lettered City: Latin America in the Cold War.* Cambridge, Mass.: Harvard University Press, 2002.

———. *Plotting Women: Gender and Representation in Mexico.* New York: Columbia University Press, 1991.

Frappier-Mazur, Lucienne. *Writing the Orgy: Power and Parody in Sade.* Trans. Gilian C. Gill. Philadelphia: University of Pennsylvania Press, 1996.

Freud, Sigmund. "Fetishism." In *On Sexuality,* vol. 7. London: Pelican Freud Library, 1977.

Fried, Jonathan L., et. al., eds. *Guatemala in Rebellion: Unfinished History.* New York: Grove, 1983.

Galich, Franz. *Managua Salsa City ¡Devórame otra vez!* Managua: Anamá, 2001.

García Canclini, Néstor. "Aesthetic Moments of Latin Americanism." In "Our Americas: Political and Cultural Imaginings," ed. Sandhya Shukla and Heidi Tinsman. Special issue, *Radical History Review* 89 (Spring 2004): 13–24.

———. *Culturas híbridas: Estrategias para entrar y salir de la modernidad.* Mexico City: Grijalbo, 1990.

García Márquez, Gabriel. "Ramírez Amaya cazador de gorilas." In *Sobre la libertad, el dicator y sus perros fieles,* ed. Arnoldo Ramírez Amaya. Mexico City: Siglo XXI, 1976.

Geertz, Clifford. *Works and Lives: The Anthropologist as Author.* Stanford, Calif.: Stanford University Press, 1988.

Goldberg, David Theo. *The Racial State.* Oxford: Blackwell, 2002.

González, Gaspar Pedro. *Kotz'ib': Nuestra literatura maya.* Rancho Palos Verdes, Calif.: Fundación Yax Te', 1997.

———. *A Mayan Life.* Rancho Palos Verdes, Calif.: Yax Te' Foundation, 1995.

———. *La otra cara.* Guatemala City: CEDIGUAT, 1992.

Gott, Richard. *Guerrilla Movements in Latin America.* London: Nelson, 1970.

Graham, Loren. "From the H-Bomb to Human Rights." *New York Times,* 7 April 2002, Book Review Section, 1.

Guardia, Gloria. *El último juego.* San José, Costa Rica: EDUCA, 1977.

Gugelberger, Georg M., ed. *The Real Thing: Testimonial Discourse and Latin America.* Durham, N.C.: Duke University Press, 1996.

Guzmán Böckler, Carlos, and Jean-Loup Hebert. *Guatemala, una interpretación histórico-social.* Mexico City: Siglo XXI, 1970.

Halfon, Eduardo. *El angel literario.* Barcelona: Anagrama, 2004.

———. *Esto no es una pipa, Saturno.* Guatemala City: Alfaguara, 2003.

Hamilton, Nora, and Norma Stoltz Chinchilla. *Seeking Community in a Global City: Guatemalans and Salvadorans in Los Angeles.* Philadelphia: Temple University Press, 2001.

Hardt, Michael, and Antonio Negri. *Empire.* Cambridge, Mass.: Harvard University Press, 2001.

Harris, Max. *Aztecs, Moors, and Christians: Festivals of Reconquest in Mexico and Spain.* Austin: University of Texas Press, 2000.

Henighan, Stephen. *Assuming the Light: The Parisian Literary Apprenticeship of Miguel Angel Asturias.* Oxford: Legenda, 1999.

Hirschkop, Ken. *Mikhail Bakhtin: An Aesthetic for Democracy.* Oxford, England: Oxford University Press, 1999.

Holquist, Michael. *Dialogism: Bakhtin and His World.* London: Routledge, 1990.

Inxausti, Aurora. "Gioconda Belli novela la tragedia de Juana la Loca en *El pergamino de la seducción.*" *El País* (Madrid), 3 May 2005, Culture Section. http://www.elpais.es/articuloCompleto.html?d_date=20050503&xref=20050503elpepicul_3&type=Tes&anchor=elpporcul. Last accessed 3 May 2005.

Ja C'amabal I'b. "La primera gran confrontación: El movimiento campesino indígena del altiplano guatemalteco." Geneva: United Nations Subcommission on Ethnic Minorities, August 1984.

Jonas, Susanne, and David Tobis. *Guatemala.* New York: NACLA, 1974.

Jones-Correa, Michael. "Swimming in the Latino Sea: The 'Other' Latinos and Politics." Paper presented at the conference What about the Other Latinos? Central and South Americans in the United States, 5 April 2002, David Rockefeller Center for Latin American Studies, Harvard University.

Klor de Alva, Jorge, Gary H. Gossen, Miguel León-Portilla, and Manuel Gutiérrez

Estévez, eds. *De palabra y obra en el nuevo mundo,* vol. 4: *Tramas de la identidad.* Madrid: Siglo XXI, 1995.

Kristeva, Julia. *Powers of Horror: An Essay on Abjection.* Trans. Leon S. Roudiez. New York: Columbia University Press, 1982.

Laó-Montes, Agustín. Introduction to *Mambo Montage: The Latinization of New York,* ed. Agustín Laó-Montes and Arlene Dávila. New York: Columbia University Press, 2001.

Lara-Martínez, Rafael. "Roque romántico." In *Otros Roques: La poética múltiple de Roque Dalton,* ed. Rafael Lara-Martínez and Dennis L. Seager. New Orleans: University Press of the South, 1999.

Lara-Martínez, Rafael, and Dennis L. Seager. *Otros Roques: La poética múltiple de Roque Dalton.* New Orleans: University Press of the South, 1999.

Lee, Wendy Ann. "Passing as Korean-American." In *Relocating Postcolonialism,* ed. David Theo Goldberg and Ato Quayson. London: Blackwell, 2002.

Levinas, Emmanuel. *Totality and Infinity and Ethics and Infinity: Conversations with Philippe Nemo.* Trans. Richard A. Cohen. Pittsburgh: Duquesne University Press, 1985.

Liano, Dante. *El misterio de San Andrés.* Mexico City: Praxis, 1996.

Lienhard, Martin. "*La Noche de los Mayas:* Indigenous Mesoamericans in Cinema and Literature, 1917–1943." *Journal of Latin American Cultural Studies* 13, no. 1 (March 2004): 35–62.

———. *La voz y su huella: Escritura y conflicto étnico-social en América Latina (1492– 1988).* Havana: Casa de las Américas, 1990.

Lión, Luis de. *El tiempo principia en Xibalbá.* Guatemala City: Serviprensa, 1985.

———. *El tiempo principia en Xibalbá.* Guatemala City: Artemis Edinter, 1996.

Lobo, Tatiana. *Asalto al Paraíso.* San José: EU de Costa Rica, 1992.

———. *Assault on Paradise.* Trans. Asa Zatz: Willimantic, Conn.: Curbstone, 1998.

López, Olga, and Martín Rodríguez P. "Indígenas rechazan ley: Consideran que norma es general y deja de lado identidad cultural." *Prensa Libre,* 30 January 2002. http://www.prensalibre.com/pl/2002/enero/30/index.html. Last accessed 12 December 2006.

Loucky, James, and Marilyn M. Moors, eds. *The Maya Diaspora: Guatemalan Roots, New American Lives.* Philadelphia: Temple University Press, 2000.

Lovell, George, and Christopher Lutz. "The Primacy of Larger Truths: Rigoberta Menchú and the Tradition of Native Testimony in Guatemala." In *The Rigoberta Menchú Controversy,* ed. Arturo Arias. Minneapolis: University of Minnesota Press, 2001.

Lux de Cotí, Otilia, Christian Tomuschat, and Alfredo Balsells Tojo, eds. *Guatemala, memoria del silencio: Informe de la comisión para el esclarecimiento histórico* [CEH]. 12 vols. Guatemala City: CEH, 1999.

Lyotard, Jean-François. *The Differend: Phrases in Dispute.* Trans. Wlad Godzich. Minneapolis: University of Minnesota Press, 1988.

————. *Heidegger and "The Jews."* Trans. Andreas Michel and Mark Roberts. Minneapolis: University of Minnesota Press, 1990.

Magner, Denise K. "Through Ads, Conservative Group Attacks Professors Who Defend Controversial Book." *Chronicle of Higher Education,* 5 March 1999. http://chronicle.com/weekly/v45/i27/27a01002.htm. Last accessed 12 December 2006.

Mahler, Sara J. *America Dreaming.* Princeton, N.J.: Princeton University Press, 1995.

Mallon, Florencia. "Interdisciplinarity as Border Crossing." *LASA Forum* 36, no. 3 (Fall 2005).

Manz, Beatriz. "The Transformation of La Esperanza, an Ixcán Village." In *Harvest of Violence: The Maya Indians and the Guatemalan Crisis,* ed. Robert M. Carmack. Norman: University of Oklahoma Press, 1988, 70–89.

Martin, Gerald. "Asturias, *Mulata de tal* y el 'realismo mítico' (en Tierrapaulita no amanece)." In *Mulata de tal de Miguel Angel Asturias: Edición crítica,* ed. Arturo Arias. Madrid: Archivos, 2001, 979–86.

————. "*Mulata de tal:* The Novel as Animated Cartoon." *Hispanic Review* 41 (1973): 397–415; rpt. in *Mulata de tal de Miguel Angel Asturias: Edición crítica,* ed. Arturo Arias. Madrid: Archivos, 2001, 1042–55.

Martín-Barbero, Jesús. "Desencantos de la socialidad y reencantamientos de la identidad." *Anàlisi* 29 (2002): 45–62.

Martínez, Demetria. *Mother Tongue.* New York: Random House, 1996.

Martínez, Severo. *La patria del criollo.* San José, Costa Rica: EDUCA, 1973.

Massumi, Brian. *Parables for the Virtual: Movement, Affect, Sensation.* Durham, N.C.: Duke University Press, 2002.

Menchú, Rigoberta. *Crossing Borders.* London: Verso, 1998.

Menchú, Rigoberta, with the collaboration of Dante Liano and Gianni Minà. *Rigoberta: La nieta de los mayas.* Madrid: El País/Aguilar, 1998.

Menén Desleal, Alvaro. *Una cuerda de nylon y oro.* San Salvador: Dirección General de Publicaciones, 1964.

————. *Hacer el amor en el refugio atómico.* San José, Costa Rica: EDUCA, 1974.

————. *Luz negra.* Quezaltenango, Guatemala: Colección Juegos Florales, 1965.

————. *Revolución en el país que edificó un castillo de hadas.* San José, Costa Rica: EDUCA, 1977.

Menjívar, Cecilia. *Fragmented Ties: Salvadoran Immigrant Networks in America.* Berkeley: University of California Press, 2000.

Menjívar, Rafael, and Camacho Daniel, eds. *Movimientos populares en America Central.* San José, Costa Rica: Ediciones FLACSO, 1985.

Menjívar Ochoa, Rafael. *Historia del traidor de nunca jamás.* San José, Costa Rica: EDUCA, 1985.

Mignolo, Walter D. *The Darker Side of the Renaissance: Literacy, Territoriality, and Colonization.* Ann Arbor: University of Michigan Press, 1995.

————. *Local Histories/Global Designs: Coloniality, Subaltern Knowledges, and Border Thinking.* Princeton, N.J.: Princeton University Press, 2000.

———. "The Many Faces of Cosmo-polis: Border Thinking and Critical Cosmopolitanism." In *Cosmopolitanism,* ed. Carol A. Breckenridge, Sheldon Pollock, Homi K. Bhabha, and Dipesh Chakrabarty. Durham, N.C.: Duke University Press, 2002, 157–87.

Milian, Claudia. "Fashioning United States Salvadoranness: Unveiling the Faces of Christy Turlington and Rosa López." In *The Latin American Fashion Reader,* ed. Regina A. Root. Oxford, UK: Berg, 2005, 263–79.

Molloy, Sylvia. "Latin America in the U.S. Imaginary: Postcolonialism, Translation, and the Magic Realist Imperative." In *Ideologies of Hispanism,* ed. Mabel Moraña. Nashville: Vanderbilt University Press, 2005, 189–200.

Monegal, Emir Rodríguez. "Los dos Asturias." *Revista Iberoamericana* 67 (1969): 13–20.

Monteforte Toledo, Mario. *Entre la piedra y la cruz.* Guatemala City: El Libro de Guatemala, 1949.

Montejo, Víctor. *Las aventuras de Mr. Puttison entre los mayas.* Rancho Palos Verdes, Calif.: Fundación Yax Te', 1998.

———. "Pan-Mayanismo: La pluriformidad de la cultura maya y el proceso de autorrepresentación de los mayas." *Mesoamérica* 18, no. 33 (1997): 93–123.

———. *Q'Anil: El Hombre Rayo. Komam Q'Anil; Ya'K'Uh Winaj.* Rancho Palos Verdes, Calif.: Fundación Yax Te', 1999.

———. *Testimony: Death of a Guatemalan Village.* Trans. Victor Perera. Willimantic, Conn.: Curbstone, 1987.

———. "Truth, Human Rights and Representation: The Case of Rigoberta Menchú." In *The Rigoberta Menchú Controversy,* ed. Arturo Arias. Minneapolis: University of Minnesota Press, 2001.

Monterroso, Agusto. *The Black Sheep and Other Fables.* Trans. Thomas Bewick. Garden City, N.J.: Doubleday, 1971.

———. *Los buscadores de oro.* Mexico City: Alfaguara, 1994.

———. *Lo demás es silencio.* Mexico City: Joaquín Mortiz, 1978.

———. *Movimiento perpetuo.* Mexico City: Joaquín Mortiz, 1972.

———. *La oveja negra y demás fábulas.* Mexico City: Joaquín Mortiz, 1969.

Morales, Mario Roberto. "La articulación de las diferencias: El discurso literario y político en el debate interétnico en Guatemala." Presentation at El Simposio Internacional, New Perspectives in/on Latin America: The Challenge of Cultural Studies, 21 March 1998, Department of Spanish, University of Pittsburgh.

———, ed. *Leyendas de Guatemala: Edición crítica.* Madrid: Archivos, 2000.

Moraña, Mabel, ed. *Indigenismo hacia el fin del milenio: Homenaje a Antonio Cornejo Polar.* Pittsburgh: Instituto Internacional de Literatura Iberoamericana, 1998.

Moreiras, Alberto. *The Exhaustion of Difference: The Politics of Latin American Cultural Studies.* Durham, N.C.: Duke University Press, 2001.

———. "Pastiche Identity and Allegory of Allegory." In *Latin American Identity and Constructions of Difference,* ed. Amaryll Chanady. Minneapolis: University of Minnesota Press, 1994, 204–38.

Naranjo, Carmen. *Diario de una multitud.* San José, Costa Rica: EDUCA, 1974.

————. *Memorias de un hombre palabra*. San José: Editorial Costa Rica, 1968.

————. *Misa a oscuras*. San José: Editorial Costa Rica, 1967.

————. *Responso por el niño Juan Manuel*. San José, Costa Rica: EDUCA, 1971.

Nash, June C. *Mayan Visions: The Quest for Autonomy in an Age of Globalization*. New York: Routledge, 2001.

Navarrete, Lisa. "Why the Whitewashing of Alicia Nash?" *Los Angeles Times*, Calendar Section, Monday, 1 April 2002, F3.

Nelson, Diane M. *A Finger in the Wound: Body Politics in Quincentennial Guatemala*. Berkeley: University of California Press, 1999.

Nussbaum, Martha. *Upheavals of Thought: The Intelligence of Emotions*. Cambridge, England: Cambridge University Press, 2001.

Ocampo de la Paz, Manuela. "Etnia y clase en la revolución guatemalteca." Mexico City, 1981. Mimeo.

Oficina de Derechos Humanos del Arzobispado de Guatemala. *Guatemala nunca más: Proyecto Interdiocesano de Recuperación de la Memoria Histórica* [REMHI]. 4 vols. Guatemala City: REMHI, 1998.

Payeras, Mario. *Days of the Jungle: The Testimony of a Guatemalan Guerillero, 1972–1976*. Trans. Noelle Thomas. New York: Monthly Review Press, 1983.

————. *Los días de la selva*. Havana: Casa de las Américas, 1980.

————. *Los fusiles de octubre*. Mexico City: Juan Pablos, 1991.

————. *Los pueblos indígenas y la revolución guatemalteca: Ensayos étnicos, 1982–1992*. Guatemala City: Magna Terra, 1997.

————. *El trueno en la ciudad*. Mexico City: Juan Pablos, 1987.

Perez Firmat, Gustavo. *Life on the Hyphen: The Cuban-American Way*. Austin: University of Texas Press, 1994.

Phillips, John. "Masochism and Fetishism: Georges Bataille's *Histoire de l'oeil*." In *Forbidden Fictions*. London: Pluto Press, 1999, 60–85.

Porras, Gustavo. "Guatemala: La profundización de las relaciones capitalistas." *ECA* 353 (1978): 374–406.

Poster, Mark. *Critical Theory and Poststructuralism: In Search of a Context*. Ithaca, N.Y.: Cornell University Press, 1989.

————. "Sartre's Concept of the Intellectual." In *Critical Theory and Poststructuralism: In Search of a Context*. Ithaca, N.Y.: Cornell University Press, 1989.

Pratt, Mary Louise. *Imperial Eyes: Travel Writing and Transculturation*. London: Routledge, 1992.

Prieto, René. *Miguel Angel Asturias's Archeology of Return*. Cambridge, England: Cambridge University Press, 1993.

"pueblos indígenas y la revolución guatemalteca, Los." *Compañero* 5. (1982): 17–26.

Rajchman, John. "Ethics after Foucault." *Social Text* 13, no. 14 (Winter–Spring 1986): 165–83.

Ramírez, Ricardo. "Documento de marzo de 1967." Guatemala City. Mimeo.

Ramírez, Sergio. *Adios muchachos: Una memoria de la revolución sandinista*. Madrid: Aguilar, 1999.

———. *Hombre del Caribe*. San José, Costa Rica: EDUCA, 1977.

———. *Margarita, está linda la mar*. Madrid: Alfaguara, 1998.

———. *Margarita, How Beautiful the Sea*. Trans. Michael T. Miller. Willimantic, Conn.: Curbstone, 2005.

———. *Mil y una muertes*. Mexico City: Alfaguara, 2004.

———. *Sombras nada más*. Mexico City: Alfaguara, 2002.

———. *¿Te dio miedo la sangre?* Caracas: Monte Avila, 1977.

———. *To Bury Our Fathers*. Trans. Nick Caistor. London: Readers International, 1985.

Rappaport, Joanne. "Alternative Knowledge Producers in Indigenous Latin America." *LASA Forum* 26, no. 1 (Spring 2005): 11–13.

Recinos, Adrián, trans. *Popol Vuh: Las antiguas historias del Quiché*. Mexico City: Fondo de Cultura Económica, 1952.

Reguillo, Rossana. "Latin America: A Study in Three Movements." In "Our Americas: Political and Cultural Imaginings," ed. Sandhya Shukla and Heidi Tinsman. Special issue, *Radical History Review* 89 (Spring 2004), 36–48.

REMHI. *Guatemala: Nunca más. Informe proyecto interdiocesano de recuperación de la memoria histórica*. Guatemala City: ODHAG, Oficina de Derechos Humanos del Arzobispado de Guatemala, 1998.

Rey Rosa, Rodrigo. *Cárcel de arboles*. Guatemala City: Fundación Guatemalteca Para las Letras, 1991.

———. *El Salvador de buques*. Guatemala City: Vista, 1993.

Robbins, Jill. "The Abject Poetics of Asturias and Buñuel: *Mulata de Tal* and *L'Âge d'Or*." In *Mulata de tal de Miguel Angel Asturias: Edición crítica*, ed. Arturo Arias. Madrid: Archivos, 2001, 987–1002.

Robinson, William I. *Transnational Conflicts: Central America, Social Change, and Globalization*. London: Verso, 2003.

Rodríguez, Ileana. *Transatlantic Topographies: Islands, Highlands, Jungles*. Minneapolis: University of Minnesota Press, 2004.

———. *Women, Guerrillas, and Love: Understanding War in Central America*. Minneapolis: University of Minnesota Press, 1996.

Rossi, Anacristina. *Limón Blues*. San José, Costa Rica: Alfaguara, 2002.

Said, Edward. *Orientalism*. New York: Pantheon, 1978.

Saldaña-Portillo, María Josefina. "The Authorized Subjects of Revolution: Ernesto 'Che' Guevara and Mario Payeras." Part II, chapter 3, of *The Revolutionary Imagination in the Americas and the Age of Development*. Durham, N.C.: Duke University Press, 2003.

———. *The Revolutionary Imagination in the Americas and the Age of Development*. Durham, N.C.: Duke University Press, 2003.

Salomon, Noël. "La crítica del sistema colonial de la Nueva España en *El Periquillo Sarmiento*." In *Historia y crítica de la literatura hispanoamericana*. Vol. 1, *Epoca colonial*, ed. Cedomil Goic. Barcelona: Crítica/Grijalbo, 1988, 421–26.

———. *Realidad, ideología y literatura en el Facundo de D.F. Sarmiento*. Buenos Aires: Rodolpi, 1984.

Sam Colop, Luis Enrique. "Ucha' xik: Del racismo subyacente." *Prensa Libre*, 12 August 1998, 13.

Sandoval, Marta. "¿Un *boom* de la literatura centroamericana?" *El Periódico de Guatemala*, 3 May 2004, 24.

Santiago, Silviano. "Crítica cultural, crítica literária: Desafíos do fim de século." *Revista Iberoamericana* 176–77 (1996): 363–77.

Sarmiento, Domingo Faustino. *Facundo: Civilization and Barbarism*. Trans. Kathleen Ross. Berkeley: University of California Press, 2004.

Scarry, Elaine. *Resisting Representation*. Oxford: Oxford University Press, 1994.

Schele, Linda, and David Freidel. *A Forest of Kings: The Untold Story of the Ancient Maya*. New York: William Morrow, 1990.

"Sebastián Guzmán, principal de principales." Guatemala City, 1988. Mimeo.

Shea, Maureen E. "Los universos indoamericanos en *Todas las sangres* de José María Arguedas y *La otra cara* de Gaspar Pedro González." In *Literatura indígena de América: Primer Congreso*. Guatemala City: B'eyb'al, 1999, 184–94.

Shetemul, Haroldo. "La esquina del Director: La multietnicidad guatemalteca." *Crónica* 533 (3–9 July 1998): 2.

Sigal, Pete. *From Moon Goddesses to Virgins: The Colonization of Yucatecan Maya Sexual Desire*. Austin: University of Texas Press, 2000.

Skinner-Klée, Jorge. "About David Stoll's Book *Rigoberta Menchú and the Story of All Poor Guatemalans*." In *The Rigoberta Menchú Controversy*, ed. Arturo Arias. Minneapolis: University of Minnesota Press, 2001, 97–98.

Sklodowska, Elzbieta. "La forma testimonial y la novelística de Miguel Barnet." *Revista/Review Interamericana* 12, no. 3 (1982): 375–84.

———. "The Poetics of Remembering, the Politics of Forgetting: Rereading *I, Rigoberta Menchú*." In *The Rigoberta Menchú Controversy*, ed. Arturo Arias. Minneapolis: University of Minnesota Press, 2001, 251–69.

Smith, Carol, ed. *Guatemalan Indians and the State, 1540 to 1988*. Austin: University of Texas Press, 1990.

Sommer, Doris. *Foundational Fictions: The National Romances of Latin America*. Berkeley: University of California Press, 1991.

———. "No Secrets: Rigoberta's Guarded Truth." *Women's Studies* 20 (1991): 51–72.

———. *Proceed with Caution, When Engaged by Minority Writing in the Americas*. Cambridge, Mass.: Harvard University Press, 1999.

———. "Rigoberta's Secrets." *Latin American Perspectives* 18, no. 3 (1991): 32–50.

Spence, Jack, Rachel Sieder, Megan Thomas, and George Vickers. "Who Governs? Guatemala Five Years after the Peace Accords." *Hemisphere Initiatives* 3. Cambridge, Mass.: January 2002.

Spivak, Gayatri Chakravorty. "Can the Subaltern Speak?" In *Marxism and the Interpretation of Culture*, ed. Carry Nelson and Larry Grosberg. Urbana: University of Illinois Press, 1988, 271–313.

———. *A Critique of Postcolonial Reason: Toward a History of the Vanishing Present*. Cambridge, Mass.: Harvard University Press, 1999.

————. *Death of a Discipline*. New York: Columbia University Press, 2003.

Stoll, David. "The Battle of Rigoberta." In *The Rigoberta Menchú Controversy*, ed. Arturo Arias. Minneapolis: University of Minnesota Press, 2001, 392–410.

————. *Between Two Armies in the Ixil Towns of Guatemala*. New York: Columbia University Press, 1993.

————. "The Massacre at the Spanish Embassy." In *Rigoberta Menchú and the Story of All Poor Guatemalans*. Boulder, Colo.: Westview, 1998.

————. *Rigoberta Menchú and the Story of All Poor Guatemalans*. Boulder, Colo.: Westview, 1998.

Suleiman, Susan Rubin. "Transgression and the Avant-Garde: Bataille's *Histoire de l'oeil*." In *On Bataille: Critical Essays*, ed. Leslie Anne Boldt-Irons. Albany, N.Y.: State University Press, 1995.

Taracena, Arturo. "Arturo Taracena Breaks His Silence." Interview by Luis Aceituno, *el Periódico de Guatemala*, 3 January 1999, 24.

Tedlock, Dennis, trans. *Popol Vuh: The Definitive Edition of the Mayan Book of the Dawn of Life and the Glories of Gods and Kings*. New York: Touchstone, 1985.

Tobar, Hector. *The Tattooed Soldier*. New York: Penguin USA, 2000.

Torres Rivas, Edelberto. *History and Society in Central America*. Trans. Douglass Sullivan-Gonzalez. Austin: University of Texas Press, 1993.

————. *Interpretación del desarollo social centroamericano: Procesos y estructuras de una sociedad dependiente*. San José, Costa Rica: EDUCA, 1977.

Trexler, Richard. *Sex and Conquest: Gendered Violence, Political Order, and the European Conquest of the Americas*. Ithaca, N.Y.: Cornell University Press, 1995.

United Nations Comisión Para el Esclarecimiento Histórico [CEH]. *Guatemala, memoria del silencio*. Vol. 6, *Casos Ilustrativos*, annex 1. Guatemala City: Informe de la CEH, 1999.

Viramontes, Helena María. *The Moths and Other Stories*. Houston: Arte Publico, 1995.

Warren, Kay B. *Indigenous Movements and Their Critics: Pan-Maya Activism in Guatemala*. Princeton, N.J.: Princeton University Press, 1998.

Williams, Gareth. "The Fantasies of Cultural Exchange in Latin American Subaltern Studies." In *The Real Thing: Testimonial Discourse and Latin America*, ed. Georg M. Gugelberger. Durham, N.C.: Duke University Press, 1996, 225–53.

————. *The Other Side of the Popular: Neoliberalism and Subalternity in Latin America*. Raleigh-Durham, N.C.: Duke University Press, 2002.

Williams, Linda. *Hard Core, Power, Pleasure, and the Frenzy of the Visible*. Berkeley: University of California Press, 1989.

Young, Robert. *Colonial Desire: Hybridity in Theory, Culture, and Race*. London: Routledge, 1995.

Yúdice, George. *The Expediency of Culture*. Durham, N.C.: Duke University Press, 2003.

Zardetto, Carol. *Con pasión absoluta*. Guatemala City: F & G, 2005.

Zavala, Magda. *Desconciertos en un jardín tropical*. San José, Costa Rica: Guayacán, 1998.

Zavala, Magda, and Seidy Araya. *Literaturas indígenas de Centroamérica.* Heredia, Costa Rica: EUNA 2002.

Zimmerman, Marc. *Literature and Resistance in Guatemala: Textual Modes and Cultural Politics from "El Señor Presidente" to Rigoberta Menchú.* Vol. 2, *Testimonio and Cultural Politics in the Years of Cerezo and Serrano Elías.* Athens: Ohio University Center for International Studies, 1995.

Žižek, Slavoj. *Gaze and Voice as Love Objects.* Durham, N.C.: Duke University Press, 1996.

Index

Arturo Arias is director of Latin American studies at the University of Redlands in California. He is the author or editor of several books, including *The Rigoberta Menchú Controversy* (Minnesota, 2001).